The 102nd
Ambulance Company
in World War I

The 102nd Ambulance Company in World War I

"Bridgeport's Own" Serves the Yankee Division, 1917–1919

Andrew W. German

McFarland & Company, Inc., Publishers
Jefferson, North Carolina

Frontispiece: Sergeant Leslie R. "Bob" Barlow, the true historian of the 102nd Ambulance Company. In this 1919 image, he shows off his YD shoulder patch and his three service chevrons, indicating 18 months in the zone of advance. He submitted this photograph with his Connecticut Soldiers' Questionnaire in 1920 (courtesy Connecticut State Archives).

LIBRARY OF CONGRESS CATALOGUING-IN-PUBLICATION DATA

Names: German, Andrew W., 1950– author.
Title: The 102nd ambulance company in World War I : "Bridgeport's Own" serves the Yankee Division, 1917–1919 / Andrew W. German.
Description: Jefferson, North Carolina : McFarland & Company, Inc., Publishers, 2023. | Includes bibliographical references and index.
Identifiers: LCCN 2023034649 | ISBN 9781476689517 (paperback : acid free paper) ♾
ISBN 9781476649320 (ebook)
Subjects: LCSH: United States. Army. Ambulance Company, 102nd. | World War, 1914–1918—Regimental histories—United States. | United States. Army. Division, 26th. | World War, 1914–1918—Medical care—France. | Barlow, Leslie R., 1886–1940—Diaries.
Classification: LCC D570.355 102nd G47 2023 | DDC 940.4/753—dc23/eng/20230728
LC record available at https://lccn.loc.gov/2023034649

BRITISH LIBRARY CATALOGUING DATA ARE AVAILABLE

ISBN (print) 978-1-4766-8951-7
ISBN (ebook) 978-1-4766-4932-0

Front cover image: Orderly Charles D. "Dud" Mills (left) and Corporal Ray E. "Pinaud" Pomeroy pose in a Ford ambulance at Ansauville, April 1918. A 33-year-old clerk, Mills was one of the Company's first enlistees and had been trained at Fort Oglethorpe before being assigned as orderly. Pomeroy was a 22-year-old car salesman when he enlisted a few days after Mills and had also been trained at Fort Oglethorpe. He would be gassed at Seicheprey on April 20. Mills received a head wound while riding as orderly with Tod Gillett of SSU 647 on June 19, when a shell struck the ambulance and killed Gillett. Mills would be cited for bravery in attending to Gillett and the other wounded soldier. Notice the gas-mask bags and helmet hanging on the side lamp. Photo by Merritt Learned, 102nd Infantry (courtesy Connecticut State Archives).

Printed in the United States of America

McFarland & Company, Inc., Publishers
Box 611, Jefferson, North Carolina 28640
www.mcfarlandpub.com

To Sergeant Leslie R. "Dick" Barlow (1886–1946),
the true narrator of this story, who lived,
recorded, and preserved it.

Table of Contents

Preface

As a teenager in the 1960s, I developed an interest in World War I aviation. The romance of the early fliers, who told such exciting stories of their exploits, was sure to catch the attention of one intrigued by history. And as my father had turned 18 just before the Armistice, it didn't feel like an impossibly distant past.

Fifty years later, with a more adult interest in the war on its hundredth anniversary, I visited some of its fields in France and saw the remaining scars on the landscape that convey a sense of the violence of that conflict. Here, the teenage enthusiasm for the adventures in the air was offset by a clearer comprehension of the physical and emotional ordeals of the soldiers who fought in the trenches and across the fields. Considering the terrible losses, I began to focus on the "sanitary" efforts to sustain the health and tend the wounds of those brave men, especially the ambulance companies and field hospitals that served them in the field. I may have been influenced by the fact that my father had been trained by the pioneering neurosurgeon Harvey Cushing, who refined his surgical artistry in the wartime hospitals in France.

Back home in Connecticut, the 26th Yankee Division World War I Living History Group introduced me to so much of the material culture pertaining to an ambulance company, and Alan Michael Crane's reproduction Ford Model T ambulance was especially inspiring. Then I began to search for sources on New England's Yankee Division ambulance companies and information to assist in the interpretation of the ambulance.

One can find plenty of diaries and photographic studies of the American Field Service and U.S. Ambulance Service drivers who volunteered to drive for the French. However, except for a few works published soon after the war, there are very few studies of ambulance companies that served in the American Expeditionary Forces. I came across Sergeant Leslie R. Barlow's small 1919 book, *Letters to the Bridgeport Comfort Club*, and that engaging serial account of the 102nd Ambulance Company led to Barlow's unpublished typescript diary of the Company, which he had typed up and deposited in the Bridgeport Public Library and the Connecticut State Archives in the 1920s. Raised in Bridgeport, this company was part of New England's 26th Division—popularly the Yankee Division—the first full division to arrive in France, and it served on five different fronts, accumulating more time under combat conditions than almost any other American ambulance company. The company's significance, the degree of detail in Barlow's diary, plus the local connections, suggested it as an ideal source for a new book on ambulance company duty. Letters and accounts from several other members of the company add to the details and give us a window into the men's interests and emotions. The story has extra significance because some of the men participated in the experiments to determine the origins of the debilitating "trench fever," and others operated the division's distinctive Thresh-Foden steam disinfesting machines that "cooked the cooties" (lice) out of the soldiers' uniforms.

Many people have directly and indirectly contributed to this work. I thank Alan Michael Crane, Chris Douglass, Don Eaton, Tom Jordan, Tom Sommer, and the rest of the 26th YD World War I Living History Group. Christopher J. Daley and other members of the online AEF Sanitary Troops 1917–1918 group shared discussions on the details of field medicine. Christine Pittsley, of the Connecticut State Library, assisted in the location of research material and images, and shared her knowledge and enthusiasm for the McIntyre sisters' Salvation Army group that supplied the 26th Division with doughnuts. The staff of the Connecticut State Library and Connecticut State Archives were all very helpful, and they had the great forethought to digitize Sergeant Barlow's diary and valuable portions of the 26th Division photostat records deposited there, including the sanitary train history written by one of the Company's men. The staff of the Bridgeport History Center were generous in providing access to the files and microfilm collection there. Michael Shay, modern historian of the Yankee Division and author of the valuable 103rd Field Hospital history, *A Grateful Heart*, offered encouragement. Peter Wever generously shared his knowledge and enthusiasm for the material culture and processes of the American Expeditionary Forces hospitals.

I was eager to include as many images of the men and their work as possible. Fortunately, the U.S. Signal Corps captured the 102nd Ambulance Company in both still and moving images in several locations. The Signal Corps images published here were obtained through the National Archives and Records Administration. Dave Brendel kindly shared images of his grandfather, Charles W. "Pop" Brendel, in the service, and Franck Besch (Le petit musée du Doughboy) made available period photographs of members of the Company. For other images in the book, I am grateful to Christine Pittsley of the Connecticut State Library; Elizabeth VanTuyl of the Bridgeport History Center; Director of Exhibitions and Registrar Stacie Petersen of the National World War I Museum and Memorial in Kansas City; Bob Cullum, representative for the Family of Leslie R. Jones held by the Boston Public Library; and the staff of the Imperial War Museum in London.

My wife, Amy, whose grandfather also went "over there," was greatly supportive, and always nodded her assent whenever I said, "I'm working on my book."

In the end, I found that these military noncombatants, roaming the battlefields with their litters and careening down the shell-pocked roads to deliver their ambulance loads of wounded to the field hospitals, were nearly as brave and daring as the aviators above them, and I am happy to help the 102nd Ambulance Company, "Bridgeport's Own," tell its story.

1

Developing an Ambulance Service

When he looked back on the history of military medicine from the perspective of 1910, Captain Louis Duncan exclaimed, "the history of the sanitary service of armies is unfortunately a short one."[1] Research into the fragmentary evidence from as early as the Trojan War suggests little more than individual efforts to assist one's comrades. By the time Roman legions ranged across Gaul around 18 A.D., they were supported by skilled practitioners of Roman medicine who treated the sick and wounded in their well-organized military camps. They did not, however, have a system to tend the wounded on the field of battle or retrieve them in an organized way.[2] By the late 500s the successors to the Imperial Roman Army in the Byzantine Empire had refined the process and added a mounted contingent to carry the wounded from the battle line to the surgeon, the riders being paid for each man they delivered.[3]

But it would take nearly 1,000 years for military medicine to return to Roman standards. In Florence in the mid–1200s, the idea of an organized delivery service for the sick materialized as the Compagnia della Misericordia, or "Company of Mercy," which was organized by the porters' guild to collect the city's ill and deliver them to the hospital. This concept of dedicated carriers of the infirm would later be adopted by European armies.[4] The wheeled military ambulance appeared in Spain during the 1470s, during the battles to drive the Moors out of the Iberian Peninsula after the unification of Spain under Queen Isabella and King Ferdinand. These were large wagons that visited the field after a battle and collected the Spanish wounded.[5]

Gustavus Adolphus began to provide surgeons for his regiments during the Thirty Years War in the 1630s, and the other European nations also allocated similar self-styled barber surgeons to their military units. Their medicines were an array of potions, and treatment was an attempt to balance the four bodily humors, a concept of medicine that would last until the discovery of the germ theory in the middle of the 1800s.[6]

The French first established field hospitals, or hospitals ambulantes, around 1640. Some were stationary, located in towns behind the army, but some mobile Jesuit units followed more closely and offered daily support. By 1747, French regulations called for three classes of military hospitals, roughly equivalent to the field, evacuation, and base hospitals of later wars.[7]

During the Napoleonic Wars, French surgeon Dominique-Jean Larrey proposed a "flying ambulance"—ambulance volante—system in which lightweight wagons would follow closely behind the line of battle, collecting the wounded soon after they fell and conveying them to the ambulance hospital for prompt treatment. Part of Larrey's inspiration was the recognition that amputation—a very common result for wounds imparted by large-caliber lead projectiles—was most successful if performed during the few hours after wounding, when shock dulled the pain. During Napoleon's 1796 Italian Campaign, Larrey established his system, with one ambulance volante for each 10,000 men. These units were commanded by a surgeon and had 340 men divided into three divisions. Each division had eight, two-wheel, two-horse wagons, accommodating two patients, for use in flat terrain, and four heavier, four-wheel, four-horse wagons, carrying four patients, for use in hilly conditions. Fitted with springs, these ambulance wagons provided quick and fairly painless evacuation from the battlefield. This system was successful enough that it was adopted by Napoleon's Imperial Guard and was used during the Egyptian Campaign in 1799.[8]

Napoleon's French army also refined the retrieval of individual wounded soldiers. Surgeon Pierre François Percy developed another form of mobile hospital wagon with eight surgeons and 120 orderlies to attend to as many as 1,200 wounded. During France's invasion of Spain in 1808, Percy organized a unit of litter- or stretcher-bearers (brancardiers), each of whom carried a lance that, along with that of his partner, could be laced together to form a litter. By the 1850s, the combination of dedicated litter-bearers and ambulances or evacuation wagons would be adopted by most other European armies.[9]

Captain Louis C. Duncan drew this simplified version of Dominique-Jean Larrey's two-wheel, spring-suspended, two-horse ambulance wagon, ca. 1796. The driver would ride the near horse, and Duncan opened the side flaps to illustrate the position of the wounded soldier. Duncan derived his drawing from an engraving in Larrey's 1812–17 *Mémoires de chirurgie/militaire, et campagnes*. (Louis C. Duncan, *The Medical Department of the United States Army in the Civil War* [Washington, D.C.: n.p., ca 1910]), 108).

The U.S. Army was small and widely dispersed, so it did not progress much beyond regimental surgeons, even during the Mexican-American War in 1846. However, as it expanded in the 1850s and studied the advances made by European armies, the Army established a medical board in 1859 and began to consider ambulance design. The board ordered tests of two- and four-wheel ambulances in the West, but research was incomplete when the Civil War broke out in 1861.[10]

At the beginning of the war, Regular and volunteer regiments still relied on their individual surgeons, without organized ambulance or field hospital units. In the western theater, field hospitals and regimental ambulances were first organized at the brigade (four-regiment) level in February 1862.[11] In the eastern theater, surgeon Jonathan Letterman first organized an ambulance corps on the corps (three-brigade) level for the Army of the Potomac in the summer of 1862, and this organization would be adopted in the west the next year. Although the Quartermaster Department normally supervised the army's vehicles, the corps medical directors had overall command of these ambulance trains. By 1864 the medical officers had developed close coordination between ambulances and field hospitals, providing rapid evacuation and good primary care for the wounded. At the Battle of the Wilderness in May 1864, for example, the field hospitals were only about a mile and a half behind the battle line, and the army's more than 600 ambulances evacuated over 8,000 wounded men from regimental aid stations to the field hospitals during the two-day battle.[12]

During the Civil War, the Union army relied on the four-wheeled, four-horse Tripler ambulance, which had accommodations for four reclining patients. The four-wheel, two-horse Wheeling ambulance was also used near the front, carrying two reclining patients plus four seated, or up to 12 seated passengers. Both models had springs to cushion the body in rough terrain, but the ride was far from smooth, sometimes requiring a wounded man to "hold on with both hands" to keep from being thrown off the litter. Because of its light weight and economical construction, the Wheeling model remained in army use through the 1870s.[13] It would be replaced in 1881 by the large, heavy McDermott ambulance, and a refined model would be adopted in 1892.[14]

The design of military litters or stretchers was refined by several nations through the 1870s, '80s, and '90s in the interests of fast evacuation of the wounded. In the United States, the eight-foot Halstead litter designed during the Civil War continued in service until a new design was accepted by the War Department in 1895. The new pattern, with seven-and-a-half-foot bars and a six-foot canvas bed twenty-two inches wide, had stirrup-shaped iron legs and hinged braces, making it easy to fold, and at 24 pounds, it was easy enough to carry. It would remain in military and civilian use for decades.[15]

As a result of public outrage over the heavy casualties during the 1859 war between the Italian states and Austria, European nations called for a convention at Geneva, Switzerland, in 1864 to consider more humane treatment of the wounded and displaced in war. The United States sent representatives to observe. As ratified by most of the European nations, the Geneva Convention called for an international relief organization with regional units under the name Red Cross (derived from the design of the Swiss flag but reversing the colors to a red cross on a white field). The Red Cross would be recognized as a neutral, unarmed organization that was exempt from military attack. Anyone operating under the red cross flag or wearing a red cross armband (brassard) would be recognized as a neutral noncombatant.[16]

As part of the U.S. Army's modernization efforts, military medicine received a new professional emphasis. The U.S. Army Hospital Corps, established in 1887, created specialized, trained medical troops rather than assigning untrained personnel from line units.[17] However, not until after 1900 did the Army fully develop its field hospital and ambulance company system and issue training manuals for its "sanitary" troops.[18]

Connecticut had redesignated its pre–Civil War militia units as the Connecticut National Guard in July 1865.[19] Between 1880 and 1913, the state would build 18 armories in the principal cities and large towns to provide meeting, training, and storage facilities for the different National Guard units. And in 1881 the legislature approved the purchase of an 88-acre tract at Niantic in southeastern Connecticut as a site for annual training. This flat, open peninsula near the mouth of the Niantic River, not far from the railroad station, was well suited for the annual summer encampments, training exercises, and maneuvers of the Guard's infantry, cavalry, and artillery units, and eventually the practical training of its sanitary ambulance and field hospital companies.[20]

After the mobilization for the Spanish-American War in 1898 demonstrated the weaknesses in the individual states' National Guard or militia units, the Efficiency in Militia Act, or Dick Act, passed by Congress in 1903, reorganized state militias into a uniform National Guard equipped and trained in line with the Regular Army. Weekend or evening drills were required, as was a summer training encampment, paid for with federal funds. The War Department would also pay for the attendance of National Guard officers for training at U.S. Army schools. The act authorized the president to call up the National Guard for national defense, or to suppress rebellions, but for no longer than nine months and only within the borders of the United States. The Militia Act of 1908 would remove the restrictions on length of service or overseas duty.

At the same time the Army, like the U.S. Navy, was updating its equipment and its uniforms. By 1909 the standard dress was a high-collar service coat or blouse with four patch pockets, reinforced breeches, sturdy shoes, and canvas leggings. The uniform color had been changed from blue to olive drab, and soldiers received both a cotton summer uniform and a wool winter uniform. In 1911, the army campaign hat was redesigned with a wide brim and "Montana" peak.

After the Civil War, urban hospitals were increasingly served by horse-drawn ambulances similar to the wartime military ones. The first self-powered ambulance, which was driven by an electric motor, appeared on the streets of Chicago in 1899, followed the next year by a similar vehicle in New York. By 1905, gasoline-powered ambulances had been introduced in New York, and just ten years later the last of the city's horse-drawn ambulances was retired.[21] The Army had experimented with a motorized ambulance in 1905 and authorized a few for hospital use in 1912, but the expense and unreliability in off-road situations prevented the general adoption of powered ambulances.[22]

In 1909, the year after the Ford Motor Company introduced its Model T automobile, the War Department refined its 1898 model of four-wheel ambulance. Designed to be drawn by two horses or mules in regular service, or four in the field, it had a covered bed seven and a half feet long and four feet wide. The ambulance could accommodate four patients on litters, with two on the floor and two suspended on hangers and straps above. A folding bench on either side accommodated eight passengers if no one was on a litter. Up front, the wagoner or driver managed the horses and the orderly kept an eye on the patients.[23]

The army was also revising its regulations for ambulance companies. Based on the Field Service Regulations of 1910, ambulance companies were to contain a captain, two lieutenants, seven sergeants and corporals, and 36 privates, for a total of three officers and 43 enlisted men. But four years later the number had been increased to 56 in peacetime, with a captain, a lieutenant, nine sergeants and corporals, a cook, a horseshoer, a saddler, a farrier, 15 wagoners (drivers), and 26 privates. They operated 12 ambulances plus a support wagon and pack animals, and they managed about 60 horses or mules. The privates not assigned as orderlies on the ambulances served as litter bearers. For wartime service, the army projected that an ambulance company would expand to 84 men, with the addition of three lieutenants and 25 men, and would require more than 80 animals.[24]

In the years after the Spanish-American War, in accord with U.S. Army revisions, Connecticut expanded the medical or sanitary side of its National Guard and established an ambulance company and a field hospital. Medical officers were required to be trained physicians, and a new generation of young doctors obtained commissions as citizen soldiers. One was Dr. Frederic J. Adams of Bridgeport. Born in Saline, Michigan, in December 1868, he was the son of a Congregational minister who served various churches. The family lived in New Hartford, Connecticut, when Frederic graduated from high school in 1885. After two years at the Robbins School, he followed his brother to New York University, graduating in 1891 and completing his medical degree there in 1895. While his brother went to Syria as a medical educator, Frederic married and served internships at several hospitals, including Bellevue. He then moved to Bridgeport and opened a practice specializing in gynecology. But he was also interested in military medicine, and he joined the National Guard as a lieutenant and assistant surgeon of the medical corps in February 1904. By 1911 he had been promoted to major and would serve as chief surgeon of the Connecticut National Guard.[25]

Another Bridgeport doctor would also become active in the National Guard. Frank W. Stevens was born in Vineland, New Jersey, in March 1873. He entered the Yale School of Medicine in 1896, obtaining his M.D. in 1900. After interning at Bridgeport Hospital in 1901–02 he settled in the city and served as a pathologist at the hospital, 1905–07. He went into practice as a gynecologist in 1906 and served as chair of the hospital's medical staff in 1915. He married in 1907 and had three children, but that did not deter his professional connections as medical examiner for the Northwestern Mutual Life Insurance Company, beginning in 1912, president of the Bridgeport Board of Health in 1915, and membership in the Bridgeport and Fairfield County Medical Associations. Nor did his professional and family obligations stand in the way of the National Guard. In 1905 he enlisted as a private in the National Guard hospital corps. Two years later he was commissioned as a lieutenant in the 3rd Infantry, and he rose to captain in the medical corps in 1912.[26]

Otto G. Wiedman was born in Philadelphia in 1884 and graduated from the University of Pennsylvania School of Medicine in 1905. After residencies at the New York Neurological Institute and Boston Psychopathic Hospital he settled in Hartford and went into private practice. Interested in the sanitary side of National Guard Service, he passed the medical examining board in March 1911 and was assigned to the new ambulance company as lieutenant. That October he was promoted to captain of the company.[27]

Dr. Wiedman's Hartford colleague in psychiatry, Dr. Paul G. Waterman, passed the examining board in April 1911.[28] Born in Westfield, Massachusetts, in 1877, Waterman graduated from Williams College in 1894. He then attended Cornell University Medical School in New York City, receiving his M.D. in 1902. He spent three years at Bellevue Hospital and two years studying in Europe before settling in Hartford in 1909. Specializing in nervous and mental diseases, Waterman shifted from neurologist to psychiatrist at Hartford Hospital and became very active in the Hartford Medical Society and Connecticut Society for Mental Hygiene. Beginning in 1915, he promoted the psychiatric needs of children through his work at the Newington Home for Crippled Children. Waterman would serve as a medical officer with the National Guard infantry until a reassignment to ambulance duty in 1917.[29]

As Connecticut's units further integrated into the National Guard, three of the medical officers attended a "joint encampment, maneuver and field instruction" at the U.S. Army Maneuver Camp near San Antonio, Texas, in April and May of 1911.[30] That summer, Connecticut's new field hospital and ambulance company each spent five days at Camp Baldwin in Niantic. The ambulance company then comprised two officers and 23 men, and it shared the camp with a signal corps company and one troop of the National Guard cavalry.[31]

In the fall, Dr. William T. Owens joined the National Guard and was assigned as a lieutenant in the ambulance company. Born in 1875, Owens grew up in Ohio and attended the University of Buffalo, where he joined the New York National Guard as a private in the Hospital Corps. He obtained his M.D. at the University of Vermont in 1899 and came to Hartford in 1902, where he established a general medical practice.[32]

By 1912 the Ambulance Company had recruited up to 36 men and was being organized to "conform to Army Regulations."[33] Rather than its stationary summer encampment at Niantic, in 1912 the company would take part in a war exercise in southwestern Connecticut. Lieutenant George C. Marshall of the U.S. Army had devised a large-scale field operation with 2,300 Regular Army troops and 15,000 National Guardsmen from Maine, Vermont, Massachusetts, Connecticut, New York, and New Jersey, simulating an infantry invasion toward New York City. Four ambulance companies would support the armies, the Connecticut company and one other being part of the assaulting Red Army. Under Captain Wiedman's command, the company's two officers and 30 men took the train from Hartford to Seymour on August 10 to find their place with the infantry. In this first combined operation, the company would benefit greatly from the "most thorough, painstaking and efficient" instruction provided by Captain G. L. McKinney of the U.S. Army Medical Corps.[34]

On August 12, the Company drove its wagons and ambulances across the hilly country with the support vehicles to a camp beside the Housatonic River. The next day the Company broke camp at 7:30 and moved up and across the river to set up a dressing station 1,500 yards behind the firing line. Six ambulances with litter squads moved forward on two roads to gather the "wounded," collecting 42 men who were designated as casualties. The litter bearers got them to the ambulances, which made several trips to the dressing station, while 29 walking wounded were conducted back by a noncommissioned officer. At the dressing station the officers dressed the "wounds" while the attendants offered food to revive the men. The ambulances completed their duties by carrying 13 of the "critical cases" a mile further to the field hospital.[35]

On August 17, the war game continued with an attack through Newtown. The Ambulance Company broke camp at 7:00 and moved forward behind the infantry. At 10:15 the Company received orders to set up a dressing station. Arriving at the appointed location at 10:25, they had the station set up within 20 minutes. This day the ambulances evacuated 43 men from the infantry aid station to the dressing station. The Company then packed up the dressing station and marched on five miles to Hawleyville. The next day they loaded their ambulances, horses, and equipment on the train and returned to Hartford with a new perspective on handling horse-drawn ambulances, coordinating with infantry and field hospital units, and operating on a military schedule.

Major M.E. Maus remarked that this exercise was the "first time in history that the Medical Corps of the Militia (National Guard) has received practical instruction in the treatment of men on the line of battle."[36] The National Guard brigade commander was very pleased, reporting: "the work of the Medical Corps, both Regular and National Guard, was very satisfactorily performed. The sanitary rules prescribed in F.S.R. were strictly observed and the health of the command was excellent throughout the entire period. The almost total absence of sore feet was remarkable."[37]

But Captain Wiedman was not completely satisfied. He had found that the six ambulances were not sufficient to serve both the frontline evacuation needs and the trips to the field hospital. He reported that "two more ambulances would be an absolute necessity in active service." And he recommended recruiting the Company up to the prescribed number of 54 and including a blacksmith, a farrier, and a saddler to keep the horses shod and the equipment repaired.[38]

The week in the field gave Wiedman and the commander of the field hospital a bit of practical preparation when addressing an order to "submit a course for instruction."[39] The resulting General Orders 45, issued on September 27, 1912, outlined a standard army course of instruction. One evening a week at the armory they would gather on the drill floor to practice the school of the soldier, the school of the detachment, and the litter drill, all specified in the ambulance company manual. They would attend lectures and individual instruction on personal and camp hygiene, service in the field, first aid, the contents and use of the Hospital Corps pouch, bandaging, anatomy, the medicines and medical implements used in ambulance dressing stations, nursing, military courtesy, and the specific Connecticut National Guard regulations pertaining to enlisted sanitary troops. The instructors had a ready textbook in the form of Colonel Charles F. Mason's *Complete Handbook for the Sanitary Troops of the U.S. Army and Navy and National Guard and Naval Militia*, which was revised in 1909 and again in 1916 to represent the latest practices. In June they would attend outdoor instruction in the early evening, in preparation for their July week in Niantic.[40]

In July 1913, the Ambulance Company brought two officers and 39 men to Niantic.[41] A recent recruit, John A. Holzheimer of Staten Island, New York, was working as a typewriter assembler at the Underwood plant in Hartford. That November, as recruiting continued, Charles W. Brendel of Rockville, Connecticut, enlisted in the Company. The son of German immigrants, Brendel was a 19-year-old hardware salesman.

In 1914, the Company received a new lieutenant. Dr. Robert M. Yergason of Hartford had attended Trinity College before transferring to the College of Physicians and Surgeons at Columbia University, receiving his M.D. in 1909. After further study, he returned to Hartford as an orthopedic surgeon. He enlisted in the Connecticut National Guard in January 1914, and after passing the medical examination he received a commission as a lieutenant in April and was assigned to the Ambulance Company.[42]

For its 1914 field experience, the ambulance company had three officers and 37 men at Niantic for a week in the middle of July. The year before, regulations for federal pay for National Guard troops were changed to require 60 days of service, including 14 hour-and-a-half instruction sessions. In 1914, all but one of the ambulance men were fully qualified.[43]

Two weeks before the ambulance men reported to Niantic, the assassination of the archduke of the Austro-Hungarian Empire led to a month of bluff and bluster between Germany and Austria-Hungary on one side and the allied nations of

The 1st Connecticut Ambulance Company was photographed during its week of summer training at Niantic in July 1914. In this detail from a "yard-long" photograph by the Thompson Photo Company, the officers are mounted, and the litter bearers and the wagoners (ambulance drivers) in their horse-drawn ambulances face each other across the picket line. Three of the men—Charles W. Brendel, William F. Foley, and John A. Holzheimer—would serve in the 102nd Ambulance Company. This photograph belonged to one of them, Sergeant Charles W. Brendel, whose grandson donated it to the National World War I Museum (courtesy National World War I Museum and Memorial, Kansas City, Missouri, USA, 2016.115.7).

England, France, and Russia on the other. In defense of their client states, Germany declared war on Russia on August 1; France mobilized in support of Russia the next day; Germany invaded Belgium and declared war on France on August 3; and Britain declared war on Germany, in support of France, on August 4. The German advance rolled into France, threatening Paris by the middle of August. But the French Army and British Expeditionary Force counterattacked, and in September the two sides settled into trench warfare from Flanders in Belgium down through eastern France past Verdun to Alsace.

In support of its hard-pressed divisions, the French Army began the war with two units of motorized ambulances, with 20 ambulances in each section.[44] While the United States was maintaining its neutrality, many Americans went to war in support of France, especially adventurous college students. In March 1915 the first group of American volunteer ambulance drivers was sent to a quiet sector in the Vosges Mountains and proved their worth. As a result, the American Field Service organized Sections Sanitaire États Unis (SSUs), each equipped with 20 ambulances and several support trucks, all driven by American volunteers. Ten of these units would serve before the U.S. entered the war in April 1917.[45] At least one Bridgeport, Connecticut, man, Howard Manion, set off to join them in February 1917.[46]

The ambulances they drove were a Field Service invention. Rather than the large, heavy vehicles used by the British and French as ambulances, the Field Service chose a lighter, more efficient and agile model. Though offered both American commercial ambulances and vehicles by several manufacturers, they settled on the Ford Model T chassis, which was readily available and very maneuverable and reliable. But Henry Ford did not make the decision easy. "Here let it be said that in doing so [choosing Ford] we received no favor or assistance from their manufacturer, who with his peculiar ideas of philanthropy, was averse to giving any assistance to war activities, even to the relief of suffering entailed by war," wrote the American Field Service historian. "From him we could obtain not even the favor of wholesale rates in the purchase of cars and parts, for every Ford car and for every Ford part imported from America."[47]

Through donations from many wealthy and influential families, the American Field Service purchased about 1,200 Ford Model T chassis, which were boxed up and shipped to France. At the AFS facilities in the Paris neighborhood of Billancourt, in a loop of the Seine opposite the Eiffel Tower, the ambulance bodies were built to AFS specifications and installed. To accommodate the seven-and-a-half-foot French litters, the body extended well aft of the rear axle. But by reinforcing and raising the rear spring they produced a very smooth ride for the wounded. The body was carefully sized to accommodate two men on litters side-by-side on the deck and one suspended above, or five seated on folding benches, in a space only about half the size of a heavy four-litter ambulance. The earliest AFS ambulances had canvas covers, but the service soon settled on a mahogany body. After they encountered longer litters in the field, the service altered the ambulance design by cutting slots in the front wall and tailgate, with canvas sleeves to protect the protruding litter handles at the back.[48] These ambulances proved the worth of the design during the early weeks of the Battle of Verdun in 1916, when they could dart in and out of the regulated convoys to and from the battlefield, even racing across fields to get the wounded back to the hospitals and return quickly to the front.[49]

Some changes came to the Connecticut Ambulance Company for the 1915 season. After three years in command, and having accomplished much organizational work, Captain Wiedman was replaced by his lieutenant, William T. Owens, in October 1914.[50] And several new men joined in the spring. Born in Avigliana, Italy, in about 1894, Rocco D. Francolini had emigrated sometime before he enlisted in March 1915. Christopher Cody had been born in New Brunswick, New Jersey, and was a 20-year-old resident of Hartford when he joined the Company in April 1915. George Cormier of East Longmeadow, Massachusetts, was about 18 when he joined the next month. That summer, the Ambulance Company and field hospital spent a week at a camp of instruction at the Army's new ambulance corps training center at Tobyhanna in northeastern Pennsylvania.[51]

These improvements in the Connecticut National Guard Ambulance Company took place as the Army Medical Department was further refining its equipment. At the end of 1913 an effort began to improve the way sanitary troops carried bandages and emergency dressings in the field. Since the 1890s, sanitary troops had carried these supplies in a large pouch worn over the shoulder. On their belt they carried a bolo knife for shaping splints and other wood-cutting duties. But in field conditions the pouch was awkward to carry, supplies might be damaged, and the bolo knife was ill-suited to sanitary uses. The review of this equipment resulted in an equipment belt inspired by the web ammunition belt designed for the U.S. Army in 1910. The company established by Major Anson Mills in the 1870s to weave cotton web belts for the Army had produced a sequence of belts to suit the changing ammunition needs of the Army since 1880. The 1910 belt had pockets for clips of ammunition for the small-caliber, high-velocity firearms adopted by the Army in 1903.

The review board worked with the Mills company to develop a belt with pockets that fit existing dressing packets and the other items then carried in the shoulder pouch. And the board replaced the bolo knife with a more practical hatchet. The new design had ten pockets, containing, from the left, a tourniquet, safety pins, and roll of zinc-oxide adhesive tape in the first pocket; two boxes (a dozen) of iodine disinfectant swabs in the second pocket; two packages of sublimated (disinfectant) gauze bandages in the third pocket; two individual dressing packets of compresses, bandages, and safety pins in pockets four through eight; six packets of compressed gauze bandages in pocket nine; and a small flask of aromatic spirits of ammonia, a stimulant for fainting, and a paper of common pins in the tenth pocket. Suspended from the belt by hangers were the hatchet in its holder, a personal dressing packet in a pouch for the wearer of the belt, the issue canteen and cup in a pouch with an extension to hang below the belt pockets, and a pouch containing a small scissors and forceps, a pencil, and a booklet of diagnosis tags to be attached to the wounded to track their treatment. The belt was first produced in 1915 and after adoption was described in the 1916 Medical Department manual. However, it is not clear that its distribution had reached the National Guard ambulance or field hospital units by 1916, though it would be issued throughout the Army's sanitary units in 1917.[52]

While the United States was watching developments in the war in France, another war was simmering on the southern border. Since the overthrow of Mexican president Porfirio Díaz in 1910, revolutionary armies had been contesting for rule. Francisco "Pancho" Villa led one of the principal armies, and the United States considered backing him, but he was defeated late in 1915 and the U.S. backed the victor, Venustiano Carranza, instead. Incensed at the U.S., Villa demonstrated near the border and in March 1916 crossed into New Mexico to attack an army outpost at Columbus. At President Woodrow Wilson's order, General Frederick Funston of the Army's Southern Department sent General John J. Pershing with 4,800 Regular Army troops, including one ambulance company and one field hospital, across the border in pursuit of Villa. To avoid a full confrontation with Mexico, President Wilson and Secretary of War Newton D. Baker initially opposed sending a force to hold the border. However, following Villa's Glenn Springs raid into Texas on May 6, Wilson relented and three days later called up the 4,000 available National Guard troops from Arizona, New Mexico, and Texas. With a 1,700-mile border to guard, this force was completely insufficient.[53]

On June 3, 1916, Congress passed the National Defense Act, which expanded the size of the National Guard. In order to increase the Guard's efficiency, the term of service was set at six years, with the first three in an active unit and the second three in a reserve unit. The number of paid drill days required of members was increased from 24 to 48, and the annual summer training was increased from five days to fifteen. The act also authorized emergency deployment of the National Guard with the Regular Army outside the borders of the U.S., if required.[54]

On June 16, Mexican general Jacinto Treviño warned that he would attack General Pershing's still-advancing force if it moved in any direction but north.[55] Fearing that threat was a prelude to war, President Wilson called up the full National Guard on June 18 for duty on the border.[56] In response to the president's summoning of the National Guard, the Connecticut units mobilized on June 20.[57]

In June 1916, the 1st Connecticut Ambulance Company, commanded by Captain William Owens, now approached full strength, with five officers and 85 enlisted men. That number included some very recent recruits. Robert E. Kuhn of Hartford was just 17 when he enlisted in May 1916. John A. Holzheimer had been discharged in the fall of 1915 but reenlisted on June 20 and would serve as a sergeant. Canadian-born James S. Garvin was 21 when he joined two days later, along with 18-year-old Fred E. Pinney of Bloomfield, Connecticut. The next day they were joined by Walter L. Scott of Hartford, 21. These last men barely had time to draw uniforms before the company was ordered to form at the Hartford railroad station with all its equipment on June 24 for the trip to Niantic.[58]

Wilson's order called 156,000 men into federal service, with more than 110,00 assigned to posts on the Mexican border. Connecticut furnished 3,300 men, or 71 percent of its estimated war strength. Its ambulance company was one of 22 National Guard ambulance companies then in existence.[59]

The Ambulance Company spent several days at Niantic organizing its equipment and loading it on a train. On June 27, the men boarded the train and it departed for Nogales, Arizona, situated south of Tucson, in the middle of Arizona's border with Mexico.[60] Riding in the coaches, with three men for each two seats, the Connecticut National Guard troops made their way west and south, arriving in Nogales on July 4 after a seven-day trip of 2,9126 miles, the longest of any of the initial National Guard contingents. They arrived just three days after the first National Guard troops took position on the border.[61]

Many of the men developed nose bleeds from the hot, dry dust and 125-degree heat. Camping outside Nogales, the Ambulance Company quickly established its round of visits to each camp after sick call to make deliveries to the field hospital. Already one infantry battalion had been exposed to smallpox, but fortunately it did not spread through the force. The Connecticut National Guard first camped in gullies near Nogales, which were prone to flooding during downpours and intense heat otherwise. Soon the force relocated to a plateau a mile north of town. Under the supervision of the 12th U.S. Infantry, the Connecticut soldiers performed routine drills until the middle of August. Later in August, one section of the Ambulance Company probably accompanied the 1st Connecticut Infantry on a 68-mile march northeast to Fort Huachuca, headquarters of the 10th U.S. Cavalry "Buffalo Soldiers." The other section would have accompanied the 2nd Connecticut Infantry when it set out for Fort Huachuca about September 1. During their two weeks at the fort, the Ambulance Company got some field experience during war games between the infantry regiments. The Guard then marched back to Nogales, having gained considerably in fitness. They had marched about 10 miles a day on the way to Fort Huachuca but were able to make 15 miles or more each day coming back.[62]

Private Charles W. Brendel, who joined the 1st Connecticut Ambulance Company in 1913, does a handstand in the Company's camp at Nogales, Arizona, during its time on the Mexican border in the summer of 1916 (courtesy Dave Brendel).

With most of the National Guard mustered on the border, U.S. Army inspectors had a chance to survey the fitness of these troops. None of the sanitary units was considered fully fit for field service. However, most were judged to be only a few months shy of proficiency, and the overall record of health among the troops, and particularly the infrequency of typhoid, reflected very highly on the proficiency of medical officers in maintaining sanitary conditions.[63]

The deployment to the border, and General Pershing's 400-mile pursuit of Pancho Villa into Mexico, tested the Army's transportation system. In March 1916 the U.S. Army had only 105 trucks, just 16 of which were in the Southern Department near the border.[64] It would soon purchase another 588 cargo trucks and support vehicles for use there.[65]

While the National Guard ambulance companies were all equipped with the standard horse-drawn ambulances, the Army also experimented with a few ambulances based on the General Motors ¾-ton truck. The General Motors vehicles proved to be the most reliable of the different trucks used to supply the Army in the roadless, high-altitude conditions of northern Mexico. And both trucks and motorized ambulances were clearly more efficient and economical than the vehicles drawn by horses or mules, which required tons of forage and ready supplies of water. The Army would soon convene a board to design new models of trucks and ambulances for military use.[66]

To settle the standoff on the border, a Mexican-American commission was proposed at the end of July and finally began to meet in September.[67] Although Pershing's Regular Army force remained in Mexico, much of the National Guard was relieved from duty on the border in October.

On October 14 the Connecticut Ambulance Company loaded up its equipment and boarded the train for its return to Connecticut. Back in Hartford on October 21, the men of the Company were escorted to the State Armory by the First Company, Governor's Foot Guard. Then the city of Hartford hosted a parade with the Ambulance Company, cavalry, and signal corps troops on October 27.[68] The next day, the Ambulance Company was mustered out of federal service.[69]

Regular Army officers who assessed the performance of the National Guard troops were critical of their preparation, but especially of their disposition, feeling they were too accustomed to the ease of civilian life and not up to the daily requirements of active military service. They feared that many, if not most, of the men who went to the border would vanish from National Guard units thereafter. So it was with Connecticut Ambulance Company Number 1, which ceased to exist when it demobilized.[70]

2

Forming the 102nd Ambulance Company

March–September 1917

For two and a half years the United States had watched across the Atlantic as the war in Europe blazed. Divided between support for Great Britain and support for Germany, and hoping to avoid being drawn into the fight, the nation had absorbed several affronts, especially the sinking of the transatlantic liner *Lusitania* in May of 1915, with the loss of 128 Americans among the 1,198 dead. When Germany then responded by calling off the unrestricted submarine warfare that sank her, the U.S. sat back but built up its military preparedness, resulting in the combined operations on the Mexican border.

Since the return and demobilization of the Connecticut National Guard in October, the Mexican-American commission had finally come to a resolution on the border in December. General John J. Pershing would lead his Regular Army troops back from Mexico on February 5, 1917, and the remaining National Guard troops were finally relieved of their watch on the border.[1]

But in January, the U.S. learned that German foreign secretary Arthur Zimmermann had telegraphed the acting Mexican administration, urging Mexico to escalate the situation with the U.S. to keep it from intervening in Europe. In return, Germany promised that after it won the war in Europe, it would return Texas, New Mexico, and Arizona, which had been part of the U.S. for 70 years since the treaties concluding the Mexican-American War. When President Woodrow Wilson released the text of the Zimmermann telegram on February 28, the nation became more inclined to join the war.[2]

The situation had already intensified on January 31, when Germany announced that it was removing restrictions on its U-boats in an effort to cut off the British Isles from their provisions and defeat the British Army before America could decide to join the Allies in France. On February 1, American transatlantic shipping again faced the threat of torpedo attack from the depths.

President Wilson announced he had cut diplomatic ties with Germany on February 3, and it appeared to be only a matter of time before the U.S. would go to war. The National Guard was clearly destined to be part of the effort, and Connecticut needed to reorganize its Guard after the border experience. Since 1911 the Ambulance Company had been located in Hartford, but once it was mustered out of federal service in October, most of its members decided they had fulfilled their service. When efforts in Hartford to recruit the Company up to strength failed, National Guard officers turned to the Guard's chief surgeon, Major Frederic Adams of Bridgeport. He challenged his adopted city to create the state's Ambulance Company.[3]

Located between the long-established towns of Fairfield and Stratford on the Connecticut shore, Bridgeport was a little farming community on the Pequonnock River until residents built a drawbridge over the river and it was incorporated as the borough of Bridgeport in 1800. By 1836 it was a city. For 100 years its port was home to a busy oyster industry, but its location on the mainline of the New York, New Haven & Hartford Railroad helped its growth as an industrial center. Known as the "Park City" for its two large public parks designed by Frederick Law Olmsted, and having several elegant, prosperous neighborhoods from the mid-nineteenth-century days of Phineas T. (P. T.) Barnum, by 1917 it was largely defined by the brick factories that had begun to appear along the railroad after the Civil War.

P. T. Barnum had adopted Bridgeport as home during his early success as a showman and businessman. In the 1850s he invested heavily to develop the east side of the city and lured the Jerome Clock Company to the site, but when the company failed, he lost much of his fortune. Always resilient, Barnum recovered and went into politics; he served in the legislature and was elected Bridgeport's mayor in 1875. Among his greatest contributions to the city was the establishment of Bridgeport Hospital. During his administration, the legislature approved the incorporation of the hospital, and Barnum was named president of the board of trustees. The hospital was built on Mill Hill, overlooking East Bridgeport, and opened in 1884. It would attract talented young doctors to the busy city.[4]

Barnum's other innovation in the 1870s was P.T. Barnum's Grand Traveling Museum, Menagerie, Caravan & Hippodrome of 1870. In 1881 Barnum merged his traveling show with that of James Bailey, eventually billing their traveling circus as the "Greatest Show on Earth." Barnum died in Bridgeport in 1891, but his show lived on and maintained a seasonal home in the city.[5]

To the west of downtown, the Howe Machine Factory was established in 1856 to produce Elias Howe's patented sewing machines, but in 1887 the factory was taken over by the American Graphophone Company. The company built the phonograph players for wax-cylinder audio recordings for the Columbia Phonograph Company. In about 1902, the industry shifted to the more durable new flat-disc records. To produce these records as well as the players, the company built a new six-story building on its 11-acre complex. A few years later, in 1908, the company acknowledged its relationship to Columbia and changed its name to Columbia Graphophone. By 1917 it employed 6,000 people, including 1,500 women. They produced both an array of graphophones, with large external horns, and graphonolas, with the audio horn within the cabinet, and almost 400,000 records a day.[6]

The Howe Machine Factory was joined in the production of sewing machines by the Wheeler and Wilson Manufacturing Company, which moved to the Jerome Clock Company factory on the expanding east side of town in 1856. By the 1870s it was producing almost 128,000 sewing machines a year, and in the 1880s the plant covered seven acres. In 1905 the Singer Sewing Machine Company purchased the plant and eventually doubled it in size.[7]

The Bullard Machine Tool Company was established by Edward P. Bullard in 1879 to produce lathes. By 1916 the company occupied a full block along the railroad in downtown Bridgeport. Gearing up for wartime production and encouraged by a lifetime employment offer from the company, the Bullard workforce of 1,200 built turret lathes for sequential metal cutting in the manufacture of interchangeable parts.[8]

Along the shore, the Lake Torpedo Boat Company was established by Simon Lake in 1912 to build navy submarines for several foreign navies as well as the U.S. Navy. Eight of them would go into production in 1918. At the same site, the Lake Aeroplane Motor Boat Company built flying-boat motors.[9]

Nearby on the shore, the Locomobile Company had expanded a former bicycle plant to produce the highly regarded Locomobile car. Locomobile had shifted from steam-powered to gasoline-engine-powered vehicles about 1902 and was known for its high quality and high price. Locomobile's own advertising called it "easily the best built car in America." After 1910 it had introduced the Riker truck, which was highly regarded for its power and durability by the British Army. Unlike Ford, which had adopted the assembly line to produce each Model T in just 93 minutes—and half a million in 1916 alone—Locomobile produced only four perfectly built vehicles a day. Where a Model T could be had for $345, a Locomobile would run from $3,000 to $10,000.[10]

On the east side, the Union Metallic Cartridge Company had established an ammunition factory in 1867. It had recently built its landmark 190-foot-tall shot tower when it merged with the Remington Arms Company in 1912. In 1915, Remington added an 80-acre rifle plant, with a million square feet spread across four floors. By 1917 the ammunition factory employed 11,000 while the rifle plant employed 9,000. Remington also constructed more than 600 houses in the "Remington City" neighborhood to accommodate its workers. By 1917 it was the largest manufacturer of arms and ammunition among the Allies, shipping huge quantities of munitions, including a million and a half rifles for the Russian Army, and it contributed to Bridgeport's self-styled nickname "the Essen of America," an allusion to the German city that housed the Krupp Works, Germany's largest arms producer.[11]

Other major companies scattered around the city included the Warner Brothers corset factory, the nation's largest manufacturer of "healthy" cloth corsets and the newly patented brassiere; the American Tube and Stamping Company, which produced iron and steel products; and the Crane Company, which produced brass valves for plumbing and industry. The Whiting Manufacturing Company, silversmiths, had moved from New York to Bridgeport in 1910 and employed from 400 to 500 people in the design and production of decorative silverware and trophies. The wages earned at all these factories could be spent at the five-story Meigs & Company department store on Main Street, or nearby at Howland's department store. And Bridgeport residents could stay informed of local and world news through four newspapers, most prominently the morning *Bridgeport Post* and the evening *Bridgeport Telegram*.[12]

In 1904, the New Haven Railroad had begun to acquire and consolidate the electric street railways that developed in the late 1890s across Connecticut. By the time the railroad was charged with holding a monopoly on rail transportation in the state in 1914, it controlled almost every streetcar route under the name of the Consolidated Railway Company. Antitrust issues aside, Bridgeport residents were mostly happy that they could hop on a streetcar to go uptown or downtown, along the shore as far west as Stamford, inland up the Naugatuck River Valley, or east to New Haven and beyond.

With all this industrial development, Bridgeport's population grew from 71,000 in 1900 to 102,000 in 1910, and to nearly 140,000 by 1917. With 10 percent of Connecticut's population, Bridgeport then stood second only to New Haven. And with more than 12,800 men eligible for military duty, it would be ready grounds for enlisting an ambulance company.[13]

A fixture in the city's medical community for more than 15 years, Dr. Frederic Adams was also a Free Mason and a member of several other fraternal orders, he was a golfer, and he enjoyed musical performances. With all these professional and social connections, he was well positioned to entice or prod his colleagues to take positions as officers in the proposed ambulance company. And he had at least 150 potential candidates among Bridgeport's medical doctors.[14]

Even as Major Adams began his recruiting, the news of unrestricted U-boat warfare, diplomatic scheming, and shortages of consumer goods alarmed coastal Bridgeport. "CITY NEEDLESSLY NEAR TO PANIC, RAIDS GROCERIES; LIMITS SET" ran the headline of the *Bridgeport Post* on February 21, and "ZIMMERMAN [sic] IS CONNECTED WITH THREAT PLOTS OF TEUTONS IN U.S.," it warned on March 8. National Guard troops were assigned to guard railroad and highway bridges, machine gun crews were set up on the roof of the Remington Arms plant to repel saboteurs, and guards were posted at the armory. "LOCAL MILITIAMEN PREPARE FOR WAR," announced the *Bridgeport Telegram*, and recruiting went on at the armory, "both day and night," for infantry, naval militia, coast artillery, and a proposed air militia unit, as well as the ambulance company.[15]

The National Guard armory stood on Main Street in the center of the city. The wide, two-story brick-and-stone building, with steep slate roof, was built in 1885 in a Romanesque Revival style design by Robert W. Hill, a prominent Connecticut architect who designed five of the state's armories in the 1880s.[16] In front, the building had offices, meeting rooms, and storage areas for arms and equipment. Behind was a very large indoor drill room for physical training and practicing maneuvers. But the military did step aside for the annual auto show held at the armory in mid–February.[17]

For captain of the proposed ambulance company, the most qualified local physician was 44-year-old Frank W. Stevens, Adams's colleague as a gynecologist and National Guard medical officer. Stevens had been a captain in the Connecticut National Guard Medical Corps since 1912, and he had served on the Mexican border in 1916.[18]

One other local physician was already a National Guard lieutenant. John T.H. Powers, 29, was born in New Glasgow, Nova Scotia, and immigrated in 1909. He

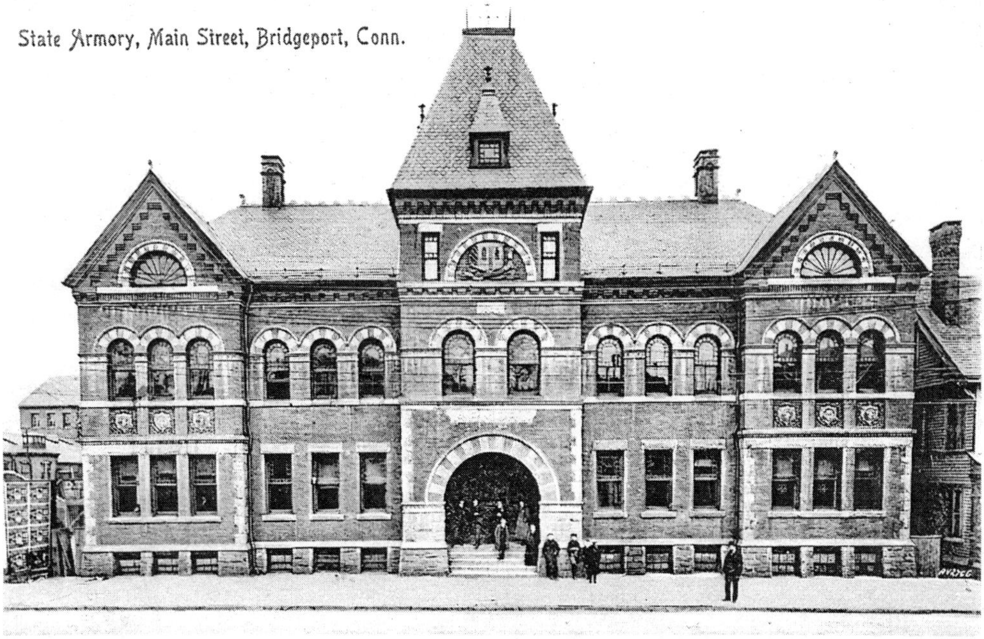

The Bridgeport Armory, ca. 1909. Built on Main Street in 1885, this elaborate building and its large drill hall served the local National Guard infantry, artillery, and naval units. The Ambulance Company was recruited at the Armory and began to drill here in March 1917. Postcard by H.H. Jackson, Bridgeport, ca. 1907 (author's collection).

received his M.D. from the College of Physicians and Surgeons in Baltimore in 1910 and came to Bridgeport, where he married a surgical nurse trained at Bridgeport Hospital and went into private practice as a physician and surgeon. Since the fall, Dr. Powers had joined the National Guard Medical Corps and would be transferred to the new ambulance company as its senior lieutenant.[19]

Two interested doctors had no military background. Thirty-six-year-old Charles H. Sprague was born in Greenwich, New York, and grew up in New Hampshire. He obtained his M.D. degree at Columbia in 1904, then came to work at the Bridgeport Hospital before going into private practice in the city. Adams nominated him to the War Department and received approval for his commissioning on February 8.[20]

Thirty-year-old Daniel H. Lawler had only recently joined Bridgeport's medical community. Born at Windsor Locks, Connecticut, he had attended the University of Maryland and received his medical degree in 1912. He interned at St. Francis Hospital in Hartford before becoming resident house surgeon at Children's Hospital in Washington, D.C., for two years. He then joined his brother in Bridgeport and opened his practice there. Major Adams nominated him to the War Department in early March and he accepted a commission even though he was engaged to marry Eva Wright of Baltimore. They would take their vows on June 16, 1917.[21]

Recruiting started slowly in snowy February and March. When Major Adams held a recruiting night at the armory on March 7, only three men turned out. So far he had just 30 potential recruits and two officers, and needed another three officers and at least 21 men.[22] The mid–May recruit Leslie R. Barlow suggested, "only men in good physical condition and of good standing in the community were accepted."[23]

Urged on by the Connecticut adjutant general, Major Adams held a meeting at the armory on March 12 "for the purpose of furthering plans for the campaign for recruiting." Adams assured that "a large attendance is expected and those who are desirous of enrolling can obtain all necessary information at the gathering."[24] The first three men signed up on March 14. Charles Dudley Mills, 33, who had been married for ten years, was a clerk for the Adams Express Company, while Harry A. Worley, 23, originally of New York City, was a rifle-barrel-driller at the Remington Arms Company, and Max H. Landman (originally Mordechai Yitzhak b Zishe), 22, a gold-plater at the Columbia Graphophone Company with National Guard experience, was transplanted from Brooklyn. Gerald Northrop, 19, and another man enlisted the next day, then one or two each day for the rest of the month. They included clerk Charles H. Cockerton, 24, and Granville M. Wilcox, 22, who worked at Remington Arms. John Elliano, 18, was an immigrant from Italy who operated an automatic screw machine at the Columbia Graphophone Company. Arthur Lieberum, 36, son of German immigrants, worked in the family undertaker business and was married with children. Frederick Johnson, 22, was a New York native who worked at Bridgeport's principal department store, Meigs & Company. Harry Monahan, 20, was an assistant to a lathe operator at the Singer Sewing Machine factory. Adrian Slootmaker, 18, had come to Bridgeport from Grand Rapids, Michigan, and was working in the advertising department of the Bridgeport Post Publishing Company. By the end of the month 17 men made up the 1st Connecticut Ambulance Company.[25]

The likelihood of war seemed even greater by the first of April. Six men enlisted on the second, including 18-year-old streetcar conductor Anthony Diorio, the American-born son of an immigrant Italian tailor. Another thirteen stepped up on the third. By the time President Wilson made his declaration of war on April 6, the Ambulance Company numbered 42 enrolled men. The new men included Hugh Lawler, 24, who worked in one of the city's corset factories, and Missouri-born Albert Honeck, 44, who had spent six years as an Army Quartermaster Department blacksmith in Oklahoma. He was the oldest man to enlist, but his skill would be welcome in a horse-drawn ambulance company. Lewis Hough, 22, had come from New Haven and Joseph Wellwood, 19, had come from Bridgewater to work at the Remington Arms plant. George F. Oppenheimer, 23, was born in Paramaribo, Surinam, and was working as a nurse at the Locomobile factory. And two more employees of the Meigs department store, William Cumming, 22, and William Cowie, 19, also joined before the declaration of war. Employers had been expected to provide paid, or at least unpenalized, leave for their National Guard employees. Now some firms, in the spirit of patriotism, were encouraging employees to enlist.[26]

By the end of April the Company had 51 men, and another 37 would join in May. Remington added machinist Ralph Hull, 21, on May 2, and Locomobile contributed machinist Edwin Hough, 44, and clerk William McElroy, 37. The Columbia Graphophone Company gave up two clerks, New Zealand-born David Jarvis, 23, and Ralph

Carleton, 27. Earle Radikin, 23, a native of Pawtucket, Rhode Island, was working as a sales clerk at Howland's department store, while Albert Wright, 18, was a drug store clerk. James Peck, 24, had come over from Newtown, Connecticut, and was working as a clerk for the Bridgeport Manufacturers' Association. He enlisted on the sixteenth, and the next day his farmer friend from home, Jesse L. James, signed up, followed on the eighteenth by their Newtown friend George Herbert Beers, 23, the only son of a dairy farmer. Leslie R. "Dick" Barlow, 30, the third of seven children of a Watertown, Connecticut, house painter, enlisted on the twenty-third. He had seven years of National Guard experience in Waterbury and Bridgeport and was working as a toolmaker and inspector at the Union Metallic Cartridge Company. His pals at the company would send him off with an inscribed wristwatch. Several practical metalworkers joined, including Albert Noren, 25, a gear specialist at the Bullard Machine Tool Company; Polish-born Stanley Shipkowski, 23, a machinist at the Farnum Company; and George Dubee, 22, a machinist at Burns & Bassick, the world's largest manufacturers of furniture casters, as well as furniture and automobile hardware. Clayton Bell of New York, 22, was assistant superintendent of the Eastern Malleable Iron Company's Bridgeport foundry, and English-born Frank Wall, 23, was a silversmith at the Whiting Manufacturing Company. Howard Davis, 22, had been studying for the ministry at Wesleyan but was working as an inspector at Remington Arms when he enlisted on May 28. On the last day of the month the Ambulance Company acquired a professional driver, Leland Gilbert, 22, who drove a jitney, or informal taxi, around town.[27]

President Wilson wished to raise an army of a million men, but by mid–May only 73,000 had volunteered. Secretary of War Baker proposed a draft, as had been used in the Civil War, and Wilson agreed. On May 18, Congress passed the Selective Service Act, and the next day newspapers across the country announced that all men between the ages of 21 and 30 who had not enlisted must register on June 5 and would be subject to a draft for military service. Twenty-six men enlisted in the Ambulance Company between May 19 and June 5. Enlistments tapered down to 16 in June and 7 in July, but by the end of that month the Company could field 110 enlisted men. Some of the men were enticed by Corporal Gerald Northrop, who managed the recruiting tent on the City Hall Green and the recruiting desk at Hindle's Drug Store.[28] Reflecting Bridgeport's increasing immigrant population, while 28 of the men were born in Bridgeport, 20 others had been born outside the United States, including Canada, England and Ireland, Russia, Poland, Belgium, Italy, Turkey, Surinam, and even New Zealand.

Sometime after he registered for the draft on June 5, Dr. William T. Nagle, 25, would obtain his commission and join the Company. A native of Southington, Connecticut, he had received his M.D. at the Medico-Chirugical College of Philadelphia in 1914. In 1917 he was in general practice in Fairfield. He would become the Company's junior lieutenant.[29]

The armory became the evening destination for an increasing number of young men. As Leslie Barlow recalled, "the Company was drilled two or three evenings each week at the State Armory in Bridgeport and old style horse drawn Ambulances were used for instruction purposes."[30] Earle Radikin would later remember the armory, "with its lights, its laughing men, its polished floor, its game room and reading room—everything which could make for the comfort of the embryo soldier."[31] Besides learning to assemble the harnesses and load and unload litters, the recruits received lectures in basic first aid and practiced drilling in close order and with the litters.[32] Writing with a bit of humor, Barlow would recall, "sergeants were drilling us as they read it from the book, some of us had uniforms and some didn't, those that did automatically becoming fixtures abut town."[33]

They also learned that an ambulance company had two separate functions. The obvious one of transporting patients in the company's twelve ambulances would occupy one officer, two sergeants, a cook, and 28 privates, of whom 13 were drivers and 12 were orderlies to accompany the drivers. The larger portion of the company would serve according to the original definition of the word ambulance, as a moving hospital. In this case the "hospital" would be a dressing station to stabilize the wounded, who were collected and brought to the dressing station by the company's litter bearers before being taken to field hospitals in the ambulances. The dressing station and its litter bearers included four officers, seven sergeants, a cook, and 40 privates. While the drivers, or wagoners, and their orderlies needed some experience with handling litters, their duties were very different from the litter bearers, who might be required to assess and stabilize wounds even before carrying patients on their litters.[34]

The National Guard was training with horse-drawn ambulances, but the War Department had already decided to modernize the sanitary service with motorized ambulances. After Pershing's experience with the General Motors trucks south of the border, the department had worked with the company to design an ambulance based on its Model 16 ¾-ton truck chassis. Its size made it less maneuverable than the American Field Service Ford conversion, but its sturdiness and capacity made the Model 16 the standard U.S. Army vehicle for both trucks and ambulances. After signing the contract on April 25 to produce the Model 16 chassis for $1,117, General Motors would construct more than 13,300 of the Model 16, approximately 3,000 of which were the Model 16AA ambulances. The company's plant could build as many as 50 of these ambulances a day.[35]

About 150 miles west of Bridgeport, a training camp for ambulance troops opened at the Allentown, Pennsylvania, Fairgrounds on June 1. This facility, called Camp Crane, was devoted to training volunteers for the U.S. Army Ambulance Service. However, the National Guard ambulance companies would not be trained there. In April, the French marshal Joseph Joffre and former French prime minister Rene Viviani had come to the U.S. and obtained agreement that the U.S. would supply 100 volunteer ambulance companies, each with 45 men and 20 Ford ambulances—a total of 2,000 ambulances and 4,500 men—to the French army.[36] Therefore, the US Army Ambulance Service was intended to carry on the work of the American Field Service in providing ambulance support for the French Army, not the American Expeditionary Forces (AEF). Many of these men were college students seeking a noncombat role during the war, and many of their ambulance sections were formed around specific college contingents.[37]

Because the French wished to continue with the Ford ambulance design of the

American Field Service, examples were brought to the U.S. for study. For American manufacture, the Field Service specifications and materials were changed slightly. The French Fords had mahogany board bodies. Produced for $475 per vehicle, the U.S. version used quarter-inch composition board (pressed fiber material) for the body, and yellow-pine floorboards with open seams to allow blood to drain. Channels on the floor accommodated the iron shoes of the litters, ensuring that they would be secure. And unlike the French Fords, the U.S. version had the engine exhaust line run close under the body to heat the wounded in the rear compartment. The Field Service was skeptical of some of these changes, but by October 15, the War Department would ship 2,350 U.S. Ford ambulances to France.[38]

Not far from the American Field Service depot in the Paris neighborhood of Billancourt is the Neuilly-sur-Seine neighborhood. There, the American Hospital of Paris had set up a facility at the Lycée Pasteur at the beginning of the war. Called the Ambulance de l'Hôpital Américain, or American Ambulance Hospital, the four-story building occupied an entire city block. Donations from wealthy Americans supported its operation, and beginning in 1915, rotating teams from American medical schools provided surgical and rehabilitation care. American Field Service ambulances delivered the wounded to it. By the end of 1916 the American Hospital was treating 1,600 men a day. The American Hospital model would inspire the U.S. base hospitals that the Ambulance Company would often serve in the coming months, and a few of the Company would find themselves recuperating at the American Hospital.[39]

For army ambulance training, Fort Oglethorpe, Georgia, became the location for National Guard units organized in the east. In north Georgia, Congress had established the Chickamauga National Military Park in 1895 on the site of the 1863 Civil War Battle of Chickamauga. By legislation in 1896, the U.S. Army was given access to the nation's military parks for training purposes, and Chickamauga was used for several months in 1898 to house troops during the Spanish-American War. In 1902 a new military post named Fort Oglethorpe was established next to the battlefield. After the declaration of war, it became one of the Army's principal training camps, again spilling onto the Chickamauga Battlefield.

Around the middle of June, the Connecticut Ambulance Company received orders to send a small contingent of officers and enlisted men to Fort Oglethorpe for two months of training that they would later share with the entire company. The contingent marched to the station around June 18, only to learn that their tickets had not arrived. After "a good deal of kidding from relatives and friends," on June 25, Lieutenant Charles H. Sprague, sergeants Charles H. Cockerton and Arthur B. Lieberum, and privates William P. Adams, John A. Forsyth, Charles D. Mills, Vernon M. Peck, Ray E. Pomeroy, and Granville M. Wilcox marched from the armory to the Bridgeport railroad station and boarded a train for Georgia.[40] Lieutenant Daniel H. Lawler was on his honeymoon in Baltimore and would join the group in Georgia, leaving his wife with her parents in Baltimore for the duration of the war.

Next to Fort Oglethorpe, Camp Greenleaf was just being completed on the northern portion of the Chickamauga Battlefield, with new barracks, mess halls,

The group assigned to training at Fort Oglethorpe, Georgia, stands ready for travel at the Bridgeport railroad station on June 25, 1917. From left to right, they are: Lieutenant Charles H. Sprague, Sergeant Arthur B. Lieberum, Sergeant Charles H. Cockerton, Private Granville M. Wilcox, Private William P. Adams, Private Ray E. Pomeroy, Private John A. Forsyth, Private Vernon M. Peck, and Private Charles D. Mills. They have their blankets rolled in their shelter tent halves over their shoulders, and several clutch a box lunch (courtesy the Bridgeport History Center, Bridgeport Public Library, BHC-PHC 00002.000039).

lavatories, and a drill ground. The contingent joined National Guard representatives from the East Coast states. Regular Army Medical Corps officers provided instruction. The lieutenants joined a contingent of 450 officers. Lieutenant James B. Griffin of the Florida Field Hospital commanded the enlisted battalion, which totaled 286 men and was organized into six ambulance companies for training.[41]

Enlisted men were formed into groups for instruction that included basic military routines and drill, as well as specialized training for either field hospital or ambulance company men. As the system evolved, ambulance company men were to receive 120 hours of field work, including calisthenics and drill on foot; drill in marching, fighting, and setting up camp; drill in setting up tents; and stretcher and ambulance drill. They also received 45 hours of instruction in their expected field duties, from military discipline and sanitation to basic physiology, bandaging, and first aid.[42]

In their free time, the men set up baseball teams and engaged in boxing matches. The commemorative book for the camp session added that "a fly-swatting contest between the four companies lasted one week, at the end of which there was hardly a fly in camp. Company No. 3 carried the day, taking a vacation at the expense of Company No. 4 which did extra fatigue duty for a day."[43]

General Frederick Funston, who had commanded the Army's Southern Department during General John J. Pershing's incursion into Mexico, was the expected candidate to lead America's forces toward war, but he died of a heart attack in February

1917. General Pershing, an 1886 graduate of West Point, a veteran of the Indian Wars, the Spanish-American War, and the Philippine-American War, had been promoted to general in 1905 and had commanded the force on the Mexican border from April 1914 until February 1917. A month after the declaration of war, President Wilson appointed Pershing as commander of the American Expeditionary Forces (AEF) on May 10. But the plan for those forces was not yet clear, even when Pershing departed for France on May 28. While they encouraged the arrival of America troops, Great Britain and France favored the scattered deployment of American soldiers in British and French units to reinforce their war efforts, and some in Congress favored mobilizing at home but not venturing overseas. President Wilson, Secretary of War Baker, and General Pershing chose to send an American army to operate independently in France, but they felt it would take time—perhaps a year—to train and transport the AEF to France.

American war plans called for the use of self-sufficient "square" divisions of approximately 27,000 men. Each division fielded four infantry regiments divided into two brigades, supported by three machine gun battalions and four artillery regiments. The fighting force was supported by a regiment of engineers, ammunition, supply, and transportation trains, and a sanitary train of four ambulance companies and four field hospitals.

On paper, the armed force that would become the AEF included 20 Regular Army divisions, of which only 8 would be filled; 17 National Guard divisions; and a National Army of drafted men filling 18 divisions. The National Guard divisions, numbered 26 through 42, were organized in late July, mostly based on geography, east to west. The 26th Division would contain New England National Guard units, the 27th Division would have New York units, the 28th Division would represent Pennsylvania, and so on. The last one, the 42nd Division, authorized on August 1, was designed to include men from 26 states and, under the name Rainbow Division, was planned symbolically to be the first entire U.S. division sent to France after a summer of organization and training on Long Island, New York. It was presumed that the 26th Division would be organized in the summer and sent south for a winter of training at Camp Greene in Charlotte, North Carolina, before crossing to France in the spring of 1918.

While the nine men at Fort Oglethorpe immersed themselves in ambulance company details in Georgia, the 100 men back home continued their basic drills at the Bridgeport Armory through July. The New England National Guard received orders on July 18 to form the 26th Division. The units were federalized on July 25 and ordered to their training grounds.[44] Leslie Barlow recalled: "our orders came that we should report at the Armory, ready to move at a minute's notice. Well, we were there, suit cases, hand bags, and all everyone excited, but we had a chance to cool off for we did not leave for three days."[45]

Then the orders came for July 28. The company was proud to be known as "Bridgeport's Own," and also as the first unit to leave Bridgeport for the war.[46] Barlow noted on July 28, "the Company paraded from the armory down the Main Street of Bridgeport and entrained for camp. Sandwiches and coffee were issued on the train and we arrived at Camp Niantic, near New London, Connecticut, in the afternoon and were ordered to pitch tents. We had no supper and found about 1,000 troops were already in this camp."[47]

This was one of the smaller training camps for the New England National Guard units. While the engineers and division headquarters were in Boston, the Rhode Island ambulance company was at its training camp, and the Connecticut infantry was at its camp near New Haven, the division's largest training camps were at Framingham and Westfield, Massachusetts. In Niantic, the ambulance company joined the Connecticut cavalry (soon to be converted to a machine gun battalion), the field hospital, the signal corps, and the Separate Infantry Company. Each unit had its own company street, lined by its tents. Barlow noted, "Eight men are assigned to each tent, some snore but others cough all night."[48]

On July 29, Barlow recorded a slow transition to military life. "Was a fine day and there were many visitors in camp and not much work was done. No cots have been issued as yet. There are two soldiers sick but neither serious. The 1st Separate (Colored) Company of New Haven are two streets below us and the Signal Corp are just east of us."[49]

In the segregated National Guard, Connecticut did enlist black soldiers but put them in a separate company, most but not all of whom were from New Haven. This company had been left at home during the mobilization on the Mexican border. It was the only infantry company at Niantic so it would train itself. At the beginning of September, it would be sent off to join similar National Guard companies from Massachusetts, Maryland, the District of Columbia, and Ohio, plus drafted men from Michigan and Wisconsin, to form the 372nd Infantry. Arriving in France in April 1918, it would serve in the French 157th "Red Hand" Division on the line from May 31 until November 11. The regiment would return to the U.S. in February 1919.[50]

July 30 continued more like a day at a summer camp than at a military one. Barlow recorded: "Fine day. Food is very good. Plenty of shower baths. Good swimming over back of the grove, where Long Island Sound backs up into a cove."[51]

On August 1, after some hiking the evening before, Barlow noted the beginning of training: "First aid lectures. Still hot. No clothing or mess kits have been issued yet and will not be until officers find out what men are to be rejected."[52] The next day they had group swimming instruction in the late afternoon, and a green lantern, the symbol of the medical tent, was hung on the 1st sergeant's tent.[53] On the third, the men were mustered into the Regular Army during a heavy rain, and the next day they received military shoes and canvas leggings.[54]

Whether in Niantic, Rhode Island, or Massachusetts, the introduction to military service for the ambulance and field hospital troops was similar. As Earle Radikin, who wrote the history of the sanitary train, remembered, "it was 'fours right' and 'carry litters' and kitchen police and fatigue—there were lectures on first aid and lectures on the care of the horse; but there were always Sundays—and glorious camp-and-home Sundays they were! We worked hard and played harder: war was wonderful."[55]

Fronting the railroad and the shore of Niantic Bay, the village of Niantic was a farming, fishing, granite-quarrying, and depot community. And as long as the National Guard had been camping on its field along the Niantic River behind the

In 1881, Connecticut purchased 88 acres at Niantic, near the railroad in southeastern Connecticut, to serve as its National Guard training camp. Before the war, units would spend a week each summer there. In 1917, the Ambulance Company and other organizations occupied it for two months, from late July to late September. Each of the units had its own company street and made the transition to military life, with the Ambulance Company refining its duties on the job. Postcard by L. Solomon, New London, ca. 1917 (author's collection).

village, Niantic had been a summer resort community. Small summer colonies had been established alongside the local beaches and the Niantic River, and a hotel stood in the center of the village. By the summer of 1917, even with war declared, Niantic had a holiday feel. "Town people are very friendly and gave a dance this evening in honor of soldiers in this camp," recorded Barlow on August 4. Four days later he noted, "we are but one half mile from Niantic and many attended the Lawn Party in the Main Street this evening."[56]

In previous years the National Guard units had only spent five days each at Niantic. In 1917, with so many men there for so long before heading to war, the summer community embraced the soldiers more than ever, visiting the camp to watch the drills during the day and welcoming them downtown in the evening, where young women were happy to socialize with them. "Troops sure do enjoy the Social Center at Niantic," wrote Barlow on August 22.[57]

The Young Men's Christian Association (Y.M.C.A.), founded in England in 1844, became a very popular institution in the United States and served the military at war, beginning with the Civil War in 1861. Starting in 1917, it deployed more than 50,000 paid and volunteer staff to offer food, recreation, and spiritual and personal assistance to the U.S. Army and Navy. The Y.M.C.A. would set up canteens at most training camps and bases in the U.S., and it would follow the troops overseas. In the camp at Niantic, the Y.M.C.A. had set up a "canteen" tent. On August 5, Barlow recorded: "Crowds here today to look over camp and troops, all seem well to-do. Y.M.C.A. had [moving] pictures at Camp this evening. Plenty of home made food in camp."[58]

The Y.M.C.A. was known for its generosity to young men and soldiers in need. At Niantic, "canteen checks were issued and entitle one to two dollars credit per month at the canteen."[59] But it also offered educational and musical events. On August 13, "there was a lecture on the Spanish War at the Y.M.C.A. canteen," and a month later, "the Chicago Grand Opera Singers at the canteen were enjoyed more than the four and five mile hikes that we now have each day."[60]

Sporting events between the different units also began. On August 14, "A corporal from the Signal Corp won two straight falls from our own wrestler Philip Brodsky," noted Barlow. And two days later, the company established a baseball team, managed by Hugh Lawler.[61]

Several former members of the original 1st Connecticut Ambulance Company, all of whom had seen service at the Mexican border in 1916 and had been demobilized upon returning home, were called up to complete their National Guard obligation in the Company in early August. These ten veterans would contribute some essential "good advice on 'soldiering'" for those whose only experience had taken place in the Bridgeport armory.[62] They included John A. Holzheimer, 23, who had joined the National Guard Ambulance Company in the summer of 1913 and served as a sergeant on the Mexican border; Charles W. Brendel, 20, who had joined in late 1913; William F. Foley, 22, who had joined in 1914; Christopher Cody, 22, and George J. Cormier, 20, who had joined in 1915; and Fred E. Pinney, 19, and Walter L. Scott, 22, who had joined just before the company headed for the border in 1916. Twenty-two-year-old James S. Garvin, a 1914 Rutgers graduate, had been working in banking when he joined just before the company headed for the border. He married just before joining the new company. As one of the two most-experienced members of the entire company, and perhaps as a joking reference to his youth, Brendel would receive the nickname "Pop."

The pace of military life increased the second week in August. On August 7, Barlow noted: "Calisthenics. Non Commissioned officers school started," and the next day they finally received used mess kits.[63] On August 9 the company was out drilling on the field when a heavy rain began. Later they would learn to operate despite the weather, but on this day early in their training, they fell out and "had to run one quarter of a mile to dry out," according to Barlow.[64]

For the first two weeks, Lieutenant Powers had been commanding the company, but he had not inspired the men. On the ninth, Captain Frank W. Stevens arrived in camp and took command. "More pep now and the same proportion of work," remarked Barlow. That day they "signed enlistment papers for the 'Duration of the Present Emergency' Only."[65]

"We have 13 old horse drawn Ambulances for training but the worst training is having to wash our own clothes," Barlow noted.[66] Despite the persistent showers, the men began to practice what they had been training for. "Several calls for Ambulance every day," wrote Barlow on August 10. "Men kicked by horses etc. We can hear the big guns at practice on the Long Island Forts. Reports are that we are to go direct to France. We shall see."[67]

While the ambulance drivers and orderlies practiced tacking and untacking their horses, maneuvering their ambulances, and loading and unloading them,

Dr. Frank W. Stevens had an M.D. from Yale and was entering practice as a gynecologist in Bridgeport when he joined the National Guard Hospital Corps in 1905. Promoted to captain in 1912 and a veteran of the Mexican border expedition, he was 44 when he was assigned to the Company in 1917. He commanded the men, and their respect, through their summer of introduction to the Army, their travel to France, and much of their challenging winter of training there. He would be transferred to the 104th Field Hospital in January 1918. Dr. Stevens submitted this photograph, taken near Verdun on October 11, 1918, with his Connecticut Soldiers' Questionnaire in 1920 (courtesy Connecticut State Archives).

the litter bearers worked on more physical drills. They learned to march with folded litters on their shoulders, and to properly unfold and carry litters with either two or four bearers, making sure to march out of step to keep the litters from swaying. They learned to carry litters uphill with the patient's head forward and downhill with the patient's head at the back. They learned how to hoist litters over fences and other obstructions, and how to load them into an ambulance. They also began to learn the basic first aid practices that would keep the wounded stable during their time on the litter.[68]

As training progressed, they learned the more intricate demands of military drill and inspection. "Tents are furled, cots put outside, blankets, shelter-half and poncho folded in regulation manner for inspection," Barlow noted.[69] Discipline also became more severe. "While we were having inspection, Domico had his throat condition relieved," wrote Barlow, sarcastically, on August 15.[70] And in early September he would note, "Pop Brendel's gang in tent # 19 all slept over and had to run around the camp and then take a shower bath to wake up."[71]

Beginning on August 11, 24-hour liberty passes were issued to 15 men each Sunday.[72] On Sunday, August 24, Barlow noted that some men took their passes and used "blind baggage"—hopping a train without a ticket—"to have another peep at Bridgeport while others were given rides in passing autos."[73] Others, either on liberty or surreptitiously, might jump a train or a trolley for the six-mile trip into New London, where O'Leary's restaurant was especially popular among the men.[74]

As the summer passed, a few men challenged the increasingly strict military discipline. On August 13, Barlow noted, "Burgoyne who deserted, gave himself up." He would not last with the company. Two days later, "Lucas and Doreski were detained at New London as they were away without a pass." And on September 13 Barlow would note, "Bell and Watkins returned from their A.W.O.L. tour and were in time to join the tent, foot and underclothing inspection."[75]

The men were not forgotten at home. Proud to have several employees in the Company, the Columbia Graphophone Company sent the Ambulance Company a Graphophone and records to provide a few sounds of homelife. It would keep them company through their service.[76] And on August 16, after "a shelter tent drill in the lowry weather" the men received "Red Cross bags from Bridgeport, that contained comb, soap, paper, pencils, handkerchief, housewife, tooth brush and tooth paste."[77]

Up in Boston, General Clarence R. Edwards was working to turn the National Guard units into a U.S. Army division. Born in Cleveland, Ohio, in 1859 to a grocer father whose brother would be a Civil War hero, Clarence Edwards was interested in a military career from a young age. After attending a military academy, he entered West Point in the Class of 1883. There he excelled in athletics but not in the classroom, graduating last in his class of 52. (Though he was only 20 months older than General Pershing, he was three years ahead of him at West Point because Pershing had spent two years teaching and studying in college.) Edwards had some army experience in the West but spent much of his career in administrative posts in the east. Prepared for duty in Cuba during the Spanish-American War, he was instead made an adjutant general, and on the staff of General Henry W. Lawton he saw field service in the Philippines in 1899. Returning to Washington, D.C., he then became chief of the War Department's Customs and Insular Division, managing the affairs of the territories recently taken in war. By 1912 he had been promoted to brigadier general and was assigned to Regular Army duty in the West and then Hawaii. In 1915 he went to Panama and organized a defense plan for the Canal Zone. With the declaration of war in April 1917, he was appointed head of the Northeastern Department and came to Boston to arrange the defenses of New England, becoming a popular public figure there. This duty turned into divisional command when he received authorization to form the 26th Division on August 14.[78]

Organized and genial with his men, Edwards would become a very popular commander within the division. But he could be outspoken and critical of other officers in public, and among some Regular Army officers he was considered unreliable and lax in his application of discipline.[79]

As he assembled his staff, Edwards was joined by Lieutenant Colonel James L. Bevans as division surgeon. Born in Wisconsin in 1869, he attended medical school and served as assistant surgeon in the 5th Illinois Volunteer Infantry during the Spanish-American War. In 1901 he was appointed an assistant surgeon in the Army Medical Corps and had risen to lieutenant colonel by 1917. He would command the sanitary train encompassing the division's ambulance companies and field hospitals.

When General Edwards's chief of staff, Major George Shelton, delivered the authorization for the formation of the division, he also handed over advance information on the table of organization and equipment for AEF divisions. With this information, and the close proximity of all of his units, General Edwards was able to announce that the 26th Division was complete and ready for service on August 22.[80]

Back in Niantic, the pace was increasing. On August 17, Barlow noted: "We were routed out at 4–30 this morning for some unknown reason and with the heavy rain every one was sore. New men were still being enlisted here at Camp."[81] Three days later, "we broke camp but orders were rescinded and we pitched tents again," wrote Barlow. "More Ambulances were received and men were inoculated."[82] And the next day he added, "we have two drills per day but many are unable to drill due to the effect of the inoculations."[83]

Born in Massachusetts, Curtis F. Banks was a 20-year-old chauffeur student in Bridgeport when he enlisted in the Ambulance Company in May 1917. He was photographed in campaign hat, shirtsleeves, and canvas leggings, standing in camp near the Niantic River in the summer of 1917. Banks submitted this photograph with his Connecticut Soldiers' Questionnaire in 1920 (courtesy Connecticut State Archives).

By this time, U.S. Army soldiers were routinely inoculated for the most virulent diseases of groups living in unsanitary conditions. The smallpox vaccine had been developed in 1798 and had long been administered in the U.S. Army. The cholera bacillus in excrement-tainted water had killed or debilitated soldiers for centuries before a vaccine was developed in the 1880s and perfected in the 1890s. Typhoid was another waterborne bacillus perhaps even more responsible for soldier deaths through the centuries. A vaccine for typhoid was finally developed in 1896.

When a second inoculation was administered on August 27, Barlow noted, "many sore arms and few at drill." Their third inoculation would come on September 5.[84] With this course of inoculations over a few days, the men would suffer sore arms and slight distress, but they would be spared several forms of death during their service.

Now that they were in unified federal rather than independent state service, the ambulance companies were renumbered on August 20. The 1st Massachusetts Ambulance Company became the Division's 1st Ambulance Company; the 2nd Massachusetts Company became the 2nd; the 1st Connecticut Company became the 3rd; and the 1st Rhode Island Company became the 4th.[85] On August 21, the Rhode Island company—now the 4th Ambulance Company—arrived at Niantic, having spent the previous month in camp at Quonset, Rhode Island. Barlow noted: "The Rhode Island Troops arrived and the hour for retreat was changed to 5–30. There was a terrific wind and rain storm this evening that blew down all tents and drenched all hands."[86]

On August 28, Lieutenant Sprague and the other officers and men returned from Camp Oglethorpe to share their training. But what they found was perhaps not up to their new military standards. As Barlow recorded, "due to rain most everyone was playing cards in the tents."[87] Perhaps they were just acting like old soldiers, as they were a few weeks later, when Barlow noted that they "received our first pay this afternoon and SOME of the boys played craps—for a short time."[88]

At the end of the summer, a few early recruits finally joined the company at Niantic. They found a unit with a great deal of spirit, and they had to pass through rites of initiation to claim their membership. On August 28, Barlow noted, "Paul Crocker given fine initiation, including a hair cut," and on September 19, following his training at Fort Oglethorpe, "Bill Adams was initiated."[89]

Since early August, the 42nd "Rainbow" Division had been expected to lead the AEF to France, while the 26th Division would report to Camp Greene in North Carolina. But it took longer than expected to gather and equip the 42nd Division on Long Island, and it was not prepared to travel when the U.S. Army Transport Service began to organize convoys of troopships. At the same time, General Clarence Edwards sent his aide, Captain A.L. Pendleton, to New York to confer with the transportation officials. Pendleton assured them that the 26th Division was ready, and at the beginning of September he learned that four ships would be available in three days, with no chance that the 42nd Division would be ready to board them. Pendleton notified General Edwards, who arranged to get the 101st Infantry and 1st Ambulance Company to New York on September 7, and the 101st Field Artillery two days later. They would arrive in Europe on September 20 and 21. A second contingent would depart from New York a week later.[90]

Captain Pendleton also visited Montréal to judge the prospects for using British ships from that port, which was served by big White Star and Allen Line steamships. The War Department and the State Department quickly negotiated an agreement, and the division then had a second embarkation point. The 2nd Ambulance Company and 2nd Field Hospital would depart from there on September 16.[91]

This was all done with such secrecy that even units in camp were surprised to find their companion units missing in the morning. With the end of summer they all suspected they were going somewhere, sometime, but had no idea where or when. So the drilling continued.

At the beginning of September, the Niantic camp was bustling. "Our mess included corn on the cob and ice cream to show the many visitors we eat well at camp," Barlow wrote. The black troops of the 1st Separate Company "were leaving camp for parts unknown." The cavalrymen of Troop A and B, soon to be dismounted and assigned to machine guns, "were doing stunts with their horses." Meanwhile, "The 'Fatigue' gang were policing the parade grounds."[92]

On September 4, Barlow noted: "Visitors are allowed to visit Camp between the hours of 11 A.M. and 7 P.M. We had best drill of season and tonight men are watching peculiar lights in the 'Grove' and suspect a spy is signaling to boats in the 'Sound.'"[93] The next day the camp was reorganized. "The Hospital Unit have erected a hospital tent adjoining our Company street and have one case of mumps isolated," Barlow wrote.[94]

"We were issued new style haversacks in the rain this morning," noted Barlow on September 7.[95] Because the army pack/haversack, with its long blanket roll, could not be worn with the new 1916 medical belt, the army had quickly adapted an existing pack for medical use. The pack had been designed and produced as a set of two ration bags or saddlebags for the new U.S. Cavalry Model 1912 Trial Saddle. For dismounted use, the bags would be removed from the saddle, laced together, and worn as a backpack with the attached shoulder straps. These saddles, and the bags, had their most intensive field tests during General Pershing's Punitive Expedition in 1916. The bags survived the field service better than the saddles did, and they were expected to be part of the Model 1917 Service Saddle, a design that was cancelled as the war began. Instead, the ration bags were redesignated as medical backpacks because they were shallow enough to ride above the belt, and the stay straps could be attached to the belt to help hold it up.[96]

At age 36, Dr. Charles H. Sprague made the transition from civilian hospital to military field medicine. Leaving his wife and young son at home, he received basic training at Fort Oglethorpe, Georgia, and then handled much of the training of the Company. The men referred to him fondly as "Doc," and his wife Emma would take a leading role in the Bridgeport Comfort Club that did so much to sustain their morale. After further training in France, "Doc" Sprague would command the Division's equipment for delousing the troops (courtesy Le petit musée du Doughboy).

On September 12, according

to Barlow, "we had our first hike with packs but the dance at the Social Center seemed to be enjoyed the most."[97] Barlow would remember "each day trying to follow Lieut. Sprague or lieut. Nagle out in the country for a few miles with packs on our backs and saying it was a tough war."[98]

Other items of their service uniform also arrived. On August 27, the men received another pair of army shoes and a wool overcoat. On September 11, they formed up to turn in their cotton summer blouses and breeches and draw wool ones. It probably took a bit of trading and stitching to get each of them properly fitted, but they would be ready for winter somewhere.[99]

By the middle of September, a departure seemed imminent. While the daughters of the Bond family of Niantic were entertaining seven of the company at dinner one night, "many others worked loading freight cars until nine P.M.," remarked Barlow.[100] Then one final assessment found a last physical weakness in the company. "Harry Lee sent to New Haven to have his feet looked after," noted Barlow. Lee would be discharged.[101]

Around the first day of fall, "thirty took examination for non commissioned officers and every man ordered not to leave camp as all tents are being taken down," wrote Barlow. "Many slept on the tables in the mess shack."[102] Then, on September 25, Barlow recorded: "HURRAY* We broke camp and hiked to the Niantic railroad station at 4 this afternoon but did not leave by train until 8 in the evening. The train took us through Saybrook, Hartford, Springfield, White River Junction and stopped at Montréal, Canada, where we detrained."[103]

3

To France

October 1917

Already a majority of the 26th Division had embarked for France. Most of the units had departed from the Army's transportation depot at Hoboken on New York Harbor, but the 2nd Ambulance Company and the 2nd Field Hospital had left from Montréal on September 16.[1] The Connecticut and Rhode Island Ambulance Companies would follow in their wake.

When the train rolled across the nearly two-mile-long Victoria Bridge over the St. Lawrence on the morning of September 26, it approached the wharves of Montréal Harbor. There lay the Allan liner *Corsican*. The men had a few moments to disembark and stretch before they formed up for inspection and boarded the ship. While they carried their personal gear on their backs, there was plenty to load. And the volume grew with the arrival of a train from Westfield, Massachusetts, carrying a battalion of the 104th Infantry. The headquarters company of Brigadier General Charles H. Cole, commander of the Division's 52nd Brigade, also pulled up to the ship. As all of these men filed up the gangways and were directed to their bunks, the 24 horse-drawn ambulances of the two companies, plus seven escort wagons were hoisted aboard, as were 322 tons of equipment and supplies, delivered in seven railroad boxcars.[2]

Five hundred feet long, with a beam of 61 feet, the *Corsican* had been launched at Glasgow, Scotland, ten years earlier. Owned by the Allan Line of Liverpool, she had sailed between Liverpool and St. John, New Brunswick, for the Canadian Pacific before the war. Her two coal-fired, triple-expansion engines gave her a top speed of 16 knots. She had four accommodation decks, with a well-appointed first-class dining room, a music room, and a smoking room, radio communications, a modern ventilation system, and full electric lighting. Large tanks held 400 tons of fresh water for the ocean crossings. In case of catastrophe at sea—in 1912 the *Corsican* had struck an iceberg off Newfoundland, as the *Titanic* had—the ship had seven watertight bulkheads and a double bottom with ballast tanks. The *Corsican* also carried 16 lifeboats and 10 collapsible boats. For convoy duty, the ship carried a six-inch naval gun for a bit of protection from visible German U-boats on the Atlantic.

As designed, the *Corsican* could carry 300 first-class passengers, 400 in second class, and 1,500 third-class passengers in steerage.[3] Since commissioned officers were entitled to first-class accommodations, Brigadier General Charles H. Cole, with

The 500-foot steamship *Corsican* of the Allan Line was launched in 1907 for service between Liverpool, England, and St. John, New Brunswick. With two triple-expansion engines, the ship could steam across the Atlantic at 16 knots. The *Corsican* became a troopship for Canadian and then American soldiers during the war, carrying a six-inch gun at the stern for protection. Postcard by C.W. Hunt & Co., Liverpool, ca. 1908 (author's collection).

his two staff lieutenants, 32 officers of the 1st Battalion of the 104th Infantry, and 10 officers of the two ambulance companies, moved into their upper-deck staterooms. Assigned to bunks belowdecks in steerage were the 16 enlisted men of General Cole's headquarters company of the 52nd Brigade, the 988 men of companies F, I, L, and M of the 104th Infantry, and the medical men: 26 members of the medical detachment of the 104th Infantry, and 153 men in each of the two ambulance companies. The total of 1,385 men on board was considerably less than the ship's 2,200 bunks could accommodate.

The men had a few hours to arrange their bunks, find the toilets, the steerage dining room, and the gangways that led most directly to the deck. While they slept the ship's boilers were stoked and by early morning the ship had steam up. Perhaps even before réveille, the *Corsican* left the wharf at 5:30 in the morning of September 27.[4] Heading downriver, it made the 150 miles to Québec and, with all lights extinguished, passed under the Québec Bridge in the night. As they approached open waters, the troops were ordered to keep portholes closed and not to show any lights, even a match or a cigarette, in the dark. To supplement the ship's gun crew, a contingent of men, including Ray Pomeroy, Robert Marston, and William Leonard of the ambulance company, was charged to learn the 6-inch gun drill and stand watch for German U-boats.[5]

After three days of steaming down the St. Lawrence, past the Gaspé Peninsula, and around Cape Breton, the *Corsican* completed the 1,000-mile passage to

Halifax, Nova Scotia. The large, well-sheltered harbor had served the British Royal Navy since 1759. During the American Revolution and War of 1812, it had dispatched and received convoys of merchant ships seeking safety in numbers against raiding American vessels. Now it was dispatching American convoys in the face of German raiders.

The *Corsican* steamed slowly up the harbor, passing the Halifax waterfront to port, and continued through the Narrows. As it was the last day of the month, the officers used the time to muster their companies to sign the pay rolls, though no money was issued. The *Corsican* then found its anchorage in Bedford Basin. This long, wide, well-defended bay had good holding ground and plenty of room for vessels awaiting their convoys. At any time it was full of coasting schooners, naval vessels, ships loaded with provisions for Great Britain, France, and Belgium, troop ships, supply ships, and ammunition ships. When Leslie Barlow looked out as the *Corsican* came to anchor he saw "battleships, destroyers, Belgian Relief Ships and Square Riggers."[6]

The narrow approach to the basin, defended by two sets of anti-submarine nets and coastal fortifications, kept the location secure from attack. But just two months after the *Corsican* passed through, a French ship loaded with ammunition for France and an empty relief ship bound for New York would have a low-speed collision in the Narrows. The ships were not damaged, but a fire broke out on the French ship and twenty minutes later the ship blew up with the largest explosion created by humans to that date. More than 1,600 people were killed instantly and 9,000 were injured as a 400-acre section of Halifax and a portion of Dartmouth, across the Narrows, were leveled by the blast. But here in October the tight maneuvering of ships, large and small, continued uneventfully.

The next day a two-masted schooner came alongside with a hold full of coal for the *Corsican*. As the crew hoisted the dirty fuel on board, the soldiers on deck amused themselves by playing post leap, which was "almost like leap-frog only rougher," according to Barlow. If they looked up, they might have noticed another vessel come to anchor to join the convoy.[7]

Sitting at anchor was harmful to both morale and fitness of the men, so on October 4 General Cole ordered that all 1,300 men on board would go through an hour of calisthenics every morning.[8] But exercise was not enough to settle the troops. The next day the *Corsican* hoisted the anchor and steamed through the Narrows to moor at the Inter-Colonial Railway Wharf on the Halifax waterfront and take on supplies. When the gangways went out and guards were posted, a number of men tried to rush the guards to get ashore. Turned back, they still managed to engage with wounded Canadian soldiers in the hospital on the wharf. Barlow reported that many of them "were terribly wounded and are giving us our first real War information and our troops are gladly trading many small articles for souvenirs with them."[9] When he wrote the history of the sanitary train, Earle Radikin remembered, "the exchange of cigarettes and patter with Canadian wounded on the docks and their laughter in spite of wounds were not soon to be forgotten."[10]

While the *Corsican* lay on the waterfront, four more transports steamed past to anchor in Bedford Basin. From New York came the 520-foot *Aurania* with the rest of the 104th Infantry and the 101st Ammunition Train, and the 700-foot *Cedric*, with the division commander (Major General Edwards), his staff, the 3rd Field Hospital, and the 103rd Machine Gun Battalion.

Four more large transports came in, all heavily loaded with troops.[11]

At 5:30 on the morning of October 6 the *Corsican* took aboard the mooring lines and was tugged away from the wharf to take its position in a convoy of nine vessels. As the convoy headed down the harbor, "bands upon the decks of two British cruisers played our national anthem," reported the historian of the 103rd Machine Gun Battalion's Company A, on board the *Cedric*. It is likely that, aboard the *Corsican*, as on board the *Cedric*, "every officer and man of our ship snapped to attention and held the salute until the last strain had died away." The ships then steamed out into "a rather choppy sea."[12]

Offshore, the convoy turned northeast for England. The next day, Barlow noted: "a camouflaged converted cruiser joined our convoy which is making about ten knots per hour. The men are enjoying the beautiful sunsets, but not the raw wind." The ship had a canteen where the men might purchase candy, cigarettes, and other small treats during certain hours of the day. They found the prices to be "about double prices in the U.S.," but that hardly mattered as they had not been paid at Halifax and most of them were out of money.[13]

What had started as an adventure soon turned into an ordeal in the rising seas. "The food is not good and consists mostly of fish and many are seasick," complained Barlow. "Dishes crash off the table in the heavy sea. The ship has no hot water and often no cold water for the use of troops. Toilets are out of order. WHY did we leave home?"[14] Many of the men were not bothered by the constant motion, but a few, including James Peck, were "sick during nearly the whole voyage."[15] On October 10, one of the infantrymen died. In a solemn ceremony with the troops at attention, he was "tied to weighted planks, draped in the American flag and buried at sea."[16]

During the zig-zag crossing the officers kept the men busy with calisthenics and boat drills, in addition to standing guard at companionways and keeping watch for German U-boats. Two were reportedly sighted, but the ships maneuvered away safely.[17] "We have slept with life belts around the waist," noted Barlow, "and must now sleep with all clothes on as we are in seas said to be seething with submarines and 12 destroyers have been sighted in the distance, acting as our escort and seem to dive into and out-of the rough sea like birds in a wind storm."[18]

"Well, we went on and on, always keeping a look out for subs, but we were not afraid, for up there on one of the gun crews were Pomeroy, Marston and Leonard of our own gang," recalled Barlow.[19] He also recalled trying to sleep as the *Corsican* pitched and rolled through the heavy seas. "At night when trying to sleep, that old propeller would come out of the water and w-o-a how it would spin, then as the ship went back in that abyss that propeller shaft would ripety rip slam bang into that thrust box, as though the barge were going into steen pieces and we all prayed as we never prayed before that 'twould hang together till we made our port and we could unlimber from those life belts."[20]

After a week at sea, on Sunday the fourteenth, "troops in both Catholic and Protestant services thanked the Lord, amid showers, that we were through the section of the sea, known as the Devils Hole and waves seemingly mountainous high had subsided," noted Barlow.[21] The next day, the *Cedric*, *Aurania*, and *Corsican* left the convoy to steam north around Ireland on the way to Liverpool. The men had been on board for a full 20 days since boarding in Montréal when they sighted land on October 16. At 5:00 the next afternoon the ships steamed up the Mersey and tugboats nudged them into their berths at the Prince's Landing Stage at George's Pier Head on the Liverpool waterfront.

Now accustomed to maneuvering in groups on the ship, the men shouldered their packs and formed for roll call before disembarking. As the tons of gear and the ambulances were hoisted out of the hold, the men were marched ashore from the landing stage, across the Princes Parade roadway on the quay, and into the long, covered Riverside Railway Station.

While the men carried their packs, blankets, and overcoats, they were leaving without the barrack bags of personal possessions that had been carried in the ship's hold. Those would be unloaded, sorted, and sent on after them. Private Thomas Bale was assigned to remain and oversee them in transit.[22]

Men with any money remaining paid a quick visit to the food vendors at the station. "I bought some pork pies in Liverpool and they were great," remarked Herbert Beers.[23] Then they formed to board the waiting trains. Before they boarded, the men each received a day's rations: a loaf of bread, a piece of cheese, and a can of "corned Willie," the soldier's term for corned beef. By 9:00 that evening, the ambulance company men had taken their seats and the train pulled out.[24]

The train gave them another reminder that they were in a foreign land. At home they were accustomed to an open car with seats on either side of the aisle and a lavatory at one end. Here they were loaded into compartment coaches with side doors. Each compartment held eight on facing bench seats without armrests. Third-class coaches often had no lavatory. "Riding day and night in a third class coach, eight men to a compartment, was far from pleasurable," remarked Earle Radikin in his history of the Division's medical units.[25]

The next morning, they clambered off the train to stretch and gaze around. They found themselves at the village of Bordon in the middle of a rural landscape, where a British Army band serenaded them as they formed up and marched to the military camp at nearby Oxney Farm.[26] The camp at Bordon had been used by the British Army since 1903. Located on the sandy, scrubby heath of Hampshire, it was about 50 miles southwest of London and 40 miles northeast by rail from the seaport of Southampton. The camp had only a few permanent barracks. Barlow remarked: "This is a tent camp and men sleep cold due to the fog. No camp fires are allowed after sundown."[27] A good reason for that was that the camp was within range of German night bombers. From the camp, Herbert Beers informed his mother: "They had an air-raid there [London] the other night and killed a few. Aeroplane scouts go over the camp two or three times each day."[28]

Earle Radikin remembered: "Slum and roughing it came into excellent social standing in Rest Camps—everybody did them. Two meals a day—both slum, with coffee in the morning and cheese and tea in the afternoon—a circular wooden floor ten feet in diameter for a dozen men to make themselves comfortable on and MUD:

The rest camp at Oxney Farm near Bordon, England. The ground has not fully turned to mud, but the circular wooden floors of the tents can be seen in this image of a group of British Officers' Training Corps soldiers at mess, ca 1914. Photograph postcard by Gale & Polden, Ltd. (author's collection).

Such is every man's mental picture of the Rest Camp."[29] The "slum" or slumgullion stew, made of whatever canned goods were available, was stirred and heated in large pots. It would become the standard fare for the troops in France. But here in Britain, there were a few amenities. "All churches are open and sell small cakes at reasonable prices and have installed baths for the use of soldiers," noted Barlow.[30]

On Sunday the twenty-first, Herbert Beers had a chance to write home to his mother in Newtown. "We are having so-called good weather here in 'Merry England,' sunshine through a skim of clouds," he wrote. "Am feeling fine and hard as a rock, but short on money—in fact dead broke. We haven't been paid since we left Niantic. I wrote you a letter on the boat and finished it in camp. This is the second. Expect we will be here for a week or two before we leave for France. Lieut. Sprague says we will get paid as soon as we get there; all our mail will be there also." Although others complained that the British only served them two meals a day, Beers was enthusiastic about the food. "In the Y.M.C.A. they sell buns and a cup of coffee for two pence. The bread they give us in camp for mess is great. I could eat two loaves a meal. They cook in pots that are oval shaped and call them 'Dixies.'" He added: "When you go out on the roads here you turn to the left instead of the right. I wouldn't like to drive a car here for I sure would plunk some one. A great many people here ride bicycles. Tell Henry he could make a fortune here selling wheels. The roads around the camp are simply great; the U.S. had better come here and take a few lessons on road building." And he concluded with a request for pipe tobacco and Turkish cigarettes: "Send me over a dozen tins of Prince Albert, a few Rameses and some Fatimas.... I hope you are all feeling the finest at home. Remember me to everybody. Tell John Beers I saw a Buick yesterday. Love to all."[31]

Barlow understood that their "stay in England has been sort of a quarantine, to make sure there was no infectious or contagious disease among the troops before mingling them with so many thousands in France."[32] Despite cold nights and slum, they had enjoyed their interlude in England. "We were becoming used to the London papers, short hikes, seeing heath and holly," wrote Barlow.[33] But they had also noticed the effects of war. "Many women were noticed doing the work ordinarily done by men," continued Barlow.[34]

After five days at Bordon, on October 23 they were ordered to don their packs and form up. Marching back to the railroad station, they boarded a train bound for Southampton. They disembarked on the waterfront, and once night fell they were ordered aboard the steamship *Lydia*.[35]

The 253-foot steamship *Lydia* had been launched in 1890 for swift mail service between Southampton and Britain's Channel Islands off the French coast. Designed for speed, she could make 19 knots with her designed complement of 170 first-class passengers and more in second class and steerage. But as a troop transport all niceties were ignored and the men were simply herded aboard for the 130-mile run across the English Channel to Le Havre, France. A night-time crossing was safest, but many were aware that U-boats were perhaps a greater threat in the Channel than in the North Atlantic.

The men had become quite self-sufficient, especially in the interests of their stomachs, and Barlow reported that they "stole most of the food supply that had been provided for the ship's crew." But a few may have regretted that action. According

The 253-foot Royal Mail Steamship *Lydia* was built in 1890 for fast service between Southampton and the British Channel Islands off the French coast. War changed its duty to troop transport, and with its 19-knot speed, it could make the 130-mile run to Le Havre, France, in about seven hours (normally at night). J. Welsh & Sons postcard, Portsmouth, ca. 1905 (author's collection).

to Barlow, "some men who had not been sick on the way across the ocean were extremely sick on this short trip and men lay sprawled on the deck in all positions, so sick they almost hoped they would die, while others were planning what they would do if struck by a torpedo from a submarine."[36]

On Wednesday, October 24, the men of the 3rd Ambulance Company disembarked from the *Lydia* at 10:00 in the morning and set foot in France for the first time. Shaking off the residual effects of their seasickness, they shouldered their packs and formed up. And then they were on the march. Eight kilometers (five miles) of uphill hiking brought them to a rest camp where they expected to stay. But orders caught up with them, directing them back to the harbor to unload the *Lydia*. Back down the hill, they spent the afternoon unloading their own supplies, possibly including their ambulances. In the evening they were directed to trains, destination unknown. "Beware of 'Rest Camps'" was Leslie Barlow's conclusion.[37]

4

A Winter of Training

November 1917–January 1918

With a few moments to look around at France, their eyes were drawn to the familiar. "Tell John Beers the first car I saw in France was a Buick," remarked Herbert Beers. "They were putting a great many Pierce Arrow trucks together on the wharves."[1]

With their duties as longshoremen finished, and their equipment loaded on a train, the men lined up to receive rations. Then they climbed into their assigned cars. Some got into the French version of the third-class compartment coaches; others had a new experience. As Earle Radikin wrote in the 101st Sanitary Train history: "riding à la natural in the now familiar 'Hommes 40: Cheveaux 8'—box cars—and having the forty stretch to 41 in some cases—hasn't become a joke yet. 'Chow' consisted of English hardtack, American corned Willie, occasionally cold canned beans or cold canned tomatoes and some units had goldfish issued along with the rest."[2]

Many of the ambulance company men squeezed into third-class coaches and the train crept forward, as Leslie Barlow recorded, "the train kept just about moving all day, eight men were ordered into each compartment and tried to sleep sitting up but after eating the corned willie, hardtack and jam that had been issued as train rations, they took time at several stations to drop off the train and wash up by sticking their head and hands under a hydrant, which in this Country are operated by pushing a knob at the top."[3]

The route southeast from Le Havre skirted Paris then continued through Chaumont to Liffol-le-Grand and Neufchâteau. As a Connecticut farm boy, Herbert Beers had his eye on the countryside. "I would like to spend a week hunting with Henry but I guess I will have to call it off this year. I saw a good many quail in the fields as we rode along on the train. There is lots of good land here and they raise acres of sugar beets."[4]

The Y.M.C.A. secretary who served the company would tell the families back in Bridgeport, "the contempt of the American boys for the French traveling facilities and the toot of the French engines, is genuine after they have traveled about 200 miles."[5] About 36 hours after departing Le Havre, the train shuddered to a stop at the station just south of the center of the town of Liffol-le-Grand at four in the morning of October 26.[6]

The French Army had made arrangements for the arriving American divisions to occupy its training areas along the Meuse River in the Vosges region, about 240 kilometers (150 miles) east of Paris and 32 kilometers (20 miles) behind the lines in the Toul Sector. General Pershing had established the American Expeditionary Forces headquarters at Chaumont, about 64 kilometers (40 miles) to the southwest of this area. The 1st Division occupied the 1st Training Area around Gondrecourt, about 32 kilometers (20 miles) southwest of Toul and 20 kilometers (13 miles) northwest of Neufchâteau. The 26th Division was assigned to the 2nd Training Area around Neufchâteau. In November, the 42nd Division would settle into the 4th Training Area around Rimacourt, 24 kilometers (15 miles) southwest of Neufchâteau. In this area, the French had dug training trenches and set up ranges for rifle and machine gun fire. Under French instruction, the men would learn the routines of trench warfare and the use of the machine gun. While excellent preparation for war as it had been fought for the past two years, the emphasis on the trench conflicted with the concept of open warfare that Pershing and his commanders had in mind for the AEF. The ambulance companies and field hospitals would learn through experience as they transported and treated the sick and injured soldiers.[7]

From the station at Liffol-le-Grand, the street led north, crossed the main road between Neufchâteau and Chaumont, and entered the town. It passed between the tightly spaced stone houses, crossed two of the streams that came together in the area and several side streets, then forked at the town center, with its church and town fountain. Leslie Barlow would note: "Liffol-le-Grand is a small town of stone houses with barns attached, with no space between buildings. The cattle are taken to pasture on the outskirts of the town and watched over by children or aged men or women as all able-bodied men are in the Army. There are no fences to keep the cattle from roaming. Three or four French men in town are expert wood carvers and engravers. Roads are good and highways between towns have a row of tall poplars on each side and must make a fine roadmap for aviators."[8]

Near the railroad, the French had built Adrian barracks to house troops. Developed by French General Louis Auguste Adrian in 1915, the Adrian barrack became standard for French and then American winter use. A hundred men could be accommodated in one barrack, which measured approximately 100 feet long and 24 feet wide. Built with simple post construction and sided with boards or tarpaper panels, the Adrian design was distinguished by its sloping side walls below the wide, narrow windows under the eaves. The sloping side timbers added strength and stability to the simple prefabricated framing structure. Inside, ranks of heavy double-deck wooden bunks filled most of the space. One or two small wood stoves provided some heat.[9]

Barlow reported that the Company "marched to some wooden barracks at the edge of the town, through several inches of mud and after throwing off their packs went over to a brook to 'wash up.'"[10] Among the first orders they received as they settled into the barracks was that they should not mention their location in correspondence, "but simply state that we are 'Somewhere in France.'"[11]

Herbert Beers immediately sat down to write to his sister, heading the letter "Somewhere in France, Oct. 26, 1917." Eager for tobacco and chocolate, he wrote, "we are in good barracks and guess we will be comfortable.... Probably I write about the

The main square, post office, and public fountain at Liffol-le-Grand. French postcard (author's collection).

same stuff each time, but if we were allowed to tell where we had been I could say a whole lot more. Send me some Rameses, Fatimas and Prince Albert. I tell you this each time so if you get one of my letters you will send some, because I don't know whether my letters will reach home or not. I would like some Peter's chocolate, Hershey's bars or Baker's or Huyler's sweet chocolate. Bud says send Huyler's as it won't melt, but I don't believe Peter's will in this weather. I probably seem to want a lot of tobacco and chocolate but the stuff you get here is pretty cheap, and also it costs pretty well, and the French tobacco is so green and strong you can hardly use it."[12]

The next day Barlow complained that his barracks roof leaked, and they only had candles for light. But they were settling into military routines, posting guards and digging latrines "150 feet from barracks and through a plowed field."[13]

With the other ambulance companies settled at Liffol-le-Grand as well, there were plenty of medical officers who combined a desire for an American level of sanitation with a need to keep their men occupied. As Earle Radikin recalled: "Sanitation was a thing unheard of among those French. Manure was piled high in front of each and every house, and was ankle-deep, and the civilians drank only wine because experience had taught them that water would kill them."[14] The companies sent details to remove the manure and scrape the mud from the streets. With the ingenuity of the American doctors, the water was purified or treated for drinking. "The inhabitants must have thought Americans a crazy lot of people," wrote Earle Radikin, "but before many weeks the French agreed that American ideas were good ones and joined in the work."[15]

With the camp and town organized but no ambulance duties to perform, the ambulance companies resumed their daily first-aid, litter, and close-order drilling.[16]

And there was plenty of daily fatigue duty, mixed with sightseeing. "Details from this Company have to hike eight miles each day for our supply of wood," up in les Hauts Bois north of town, "but take time to watch the French women washing clothes at the public fountain, using a flat paddle, a large bar of soap and cold water," wrote Leslie Barlow. "The women wear large wooden shoes."[17] The French forest service supervised the woodcutters. Division historian Emerson Taylor recalled, "it was a curious sight to see the men come in at nightfall, each carrying a long branch or sapling to be split into logs at the company kitchens."[18]

Those left in camp had plenty of duty as well. "Many are kept busy digging incinerators and hauling water," noted Barlow.[19] He explained: "The people of this town have no running water in their homes. They all go to the corner hydrant. We fill a canvas bag with spout attached and chlorinate all water used for drinking purposes."[20] Some were more adept at this task than others. "Who ever chlorinated the drinking water made it so strong it tastes and smells like a doctor shop," noted Barlow one day.[21]

Encouraged to hike to maintain their fitness, quite a few men made the 40 kilometer (25-mile) roundtrip to Domrémy-la-Pucelle, north of Neufchâteau, to visit the birthplace of Joan of Arc.[22] Born there about 1412, the teenage Joan had visions and, after inspiring the young French king, rallied and led the French troops to defend France from one of its many invasions, this one by the English in 1428. After several successful campaigns, she was captured in 1430, tried, and burned at the stake. As a martyr, she became a symbol for France, particularly in wartime. In the little town, the men could see the house where she was born and the church where she was baptized, small but sacred bits of French history.

Besides regular drills and "physical exercises down in the lot," sports kept the men occupied.[23] "We played football yesterday against Rhode Island and defeated them 42–0," wrote Herbert Beers, referring to the 104th Ambulance Company. "I played center and got only one bump. We are going to play every Saturday."[24] By January, they had turned to basketball. "Company won a basketball game from the 103 Supply Company," noted Barlow.[25]

With all of the duty and hiking in the army marching shoes they had worn for three months, many men had worn holes in their soles. These shoes had proven inadequate during the Mexican border campaign, so the Army developed a new, heavier model in the spring of 1917. But until they could be produced in sufficient numbers, the old, thin-soled shoes had been issued throughout the army.[26] Since the quartermaster department had not yet fully organized its supply train and had no boots to issue, the men had to improvise, sometimes cutting tarpaper insoles for their old shoes.[27]

Finally, in early November the Company received a first issue of 50 of the new trench boot designed for Army use earlier in 1917. These were, according to Barlow, "heavy shoes with a large metal piece shaped like a horse shoe on the heel and hob-nails in the soles," A few weeks later another batch arrived.[28]

Socks also wore out. "Some of the men are out of stockings and are wearing wristlets for stockings," noted Barlow.[29] In mid–November he noted the consequences: "Many are sick, due to their feet being wet all the time and from hiking in the mud." But only a day or two later, "the Red Cross beat the government by coming to our rescue with a supply of socks, real heavy, woolen ones."[30]

Major General Edwards admitted the challenges his men faced. "There were many articles of equipment which they could not get," he wrote. "Frequently there would be a deficiency in the rations. I never saw so much mud and rain in my life. Their feet were generally wet and we were experimenting with the shoes." He remarked with a bit of sarcasm, "we turned the leather wrong side out and fixed the pores so that they would act like syphons—and fill our shoes with water. I never saw men put up with so many discomforts in my life."[31]

Footwear would remain an issue through the winter. Quartermaster troops, and eventually ambulance company men, especially ambulance drivers, were authorized to receive thigh-high "half-hip" rubber boots, but they had not been issued. Thinking of the kind of rubber overboot he was familiar with at home, in mid–November Herbert Beers wrote his sister: "Send me a pair of eight and one-half four-buckle arctics. They don't have them over here. I guess I must be a pretty expensive brother, am I not?"[32] But just after Thanksgiving he would write: "We have all had hip rubber boots issued to us and they are great to walk in the mud with. It isn't very cold yet; the ground freezing up only once. The other morning the ground was white with snow but it soon melted."[33] Beers may have been speaking of the ambulance drivers and orderlies as, just before Christmas, Barlow noted that Sergeant Brendel "has bought the only pair of boots in France (that is as far as we know). He is the most popular man in the AEF as everyone is allowed to borrow his boots and very few have shoes that are not worn out or soaked through every day."[34] He continued: "Our shoes are so wet each day that men burn paper in them each morning before they start out. Socks are damp all the time and are dried out by sleeping upon them."[35] With wet, cold feet day after day, many men developed the painful inflammation of chilblains, which the British called trench foot.[36]

In early January came an issue of leather moccasins for wear in the half-hip rubber boots. The men also turned in their worn canvas leggings for the wool spiral-wrap leggings or puttees worn by the British and French. Wrapped tightly over the boot tops and up nearly to the knee, these wool wraps offered a little bit of warmth while resisting the wet and mud in which the soldiers operated.[37]

Despite some improvements in footwear through the winter, on January 24, Barlow would write: "THIS IS GOOD, so few men now have shoes to wear that orders were posted, that if we have shoes we must post our name and size of shoes worn, on the door so that if a man is picked for guard duty and has no shoes, he must go to the list and borrow from the one who has his nearest size and that soldier must take a turn at staying in the barracks. Many sleep with their wet shoes on as they have found, if they take them off they can not get them on again in the morning."[38]

Their headgear would also change. The Division had arrived wearing the Army's wide-brimmed campaign hat, but between November and February these were turned in for the simple, brimless wool caps worn by British and French soldiers. The American soldiers called these overseas caps, and the Division generally received the symmetrical French design.[39] More ominously, on January 22 the Company would receive orders that "steel helmets must be worn at all times from this date."[40] At this stage of the war the 26th Division received the British Brodie helmet. The Allies had gone to war without protective headwear, but it quickly became apparent that there must be protection from head wounds, especially during trench warfare. Patented by John L. Brodie in 1915 with a rounded crown and about a two-inch brim, the helmet could be pressed from sheets of manganese steel, with a padded liner and chin strap attached. The helmet weighed a little more than two pounds and was painted with drab, sand-textured paint for low visibility. Before beginning to manufacture a U.S. version of the helmet in 1918, the War Department purchased 400,000 of the British helmets and issued them to the first divisions to arrive in France.[41]

By January, the standard issue of clothing per man among the divisions in France was supposed to be two pairs of wool breeches, three pairs of wool drawers, two wool blouses, two wool shirts, three wool undershirts, five pairs of wool socks, two pairs of puttees, two pairs of shoes, one wool overcoat, one waterproof slicker, three blankets, one hat or cap, and one pair of gloves. This was specified in an order from AEF Headquarters on January 4, which implied that the men were hoarding clothes, contributing to whatever shortages there might be. While they would eventually reach their allotted quantities, the ambulance company men could attest that their shortages were due not to hoarding but to continued lack of access.[42]

As with equipment, it took some time to establish a food supply system for the Division. At first, the cooks improvised. "Our food is not good and supplies of French stores are costly," Barlow wrote a few days after they arrived.[43] Beers remarked: "The people over here seem to make a great deal of jam from all kinds of fruit and it is fine to put on bread. We have got a dandy mess sergeant and he can sure cook up food in good style, when he gets hold of some."[44] Barlow agreed: "And maybe that man Carter of ours and his gang of stevedores, can't turn out some feed, if he gets the wherewithal."[45]

Ten days after arriving, the Company "was issued its first rations from the U.S.A."[46] Thereafter, the men looked forward to their army food. "Mess serg't Carter started off by serving pan-cakes," Barlow noted one day.[47] "I am feeling fine and certainly am having a wonderful experience," wrote Herbert Beers. "Jimmie Peck and Lodrick James are always up in front for mess and you can just bet I'm not very far behind—mostly in front if anything."[48] "At supper several have a habit of crashing the mess line as the mess shack is in darkness," noted Barlow on November 15.[49]

Beyond army food, they looked to home for accustomed treats. "Anything from home that is sweet is very acceptable over here," Herbert Beers told his sister. "I guess you have gotten some of my letters asking for stuff by this time. But send me some nuts and sweet chocolate, only be sure and pack the chocolate well. Apples would be smashed. Can't you plan out a way in which to send me some mince pie meat?"[50]

Although the barracks were cold and dark, the men made the most of them in their off hours. "Groups surround each small stove in the barracks to sing each evening," noted Barlow.[51] Occasionally, they organized events to show off their talents. On November 15, "there was an entertainment in the barracks by men of the Company, which included boxing, a recitation by Radikin and clog dancing by Ezra Garvin."[52] Shortly before Christmas, Paul Crocker would organize a glee club.[53]

And after lights out, "we have plain, fancy and even professional snorers," remarked Barlow.[54]

Just as they had found the sanitary conditions of Liffol-le-Grand did not meet their standards, they would find it difficult to maintain their own cleanliness. At the beginning of November, Barlow noted, "many took their first bath in several weeks, over in the brook."[55] In mid–November, Barlow would comment, "several took hot baths (two men to a bucket)."

But in December he would complain: "We have no place to wash. Men go over to the brook and break a hole through the ice."[56] By the end of January, bathing was mandatory. "Orders were issued that all MUST take baths and all names are checked to see that this order is obeyed," noted Barlow.[57] One way to improve their cleanliness and try to avoid the body lice that plagued soldiers was a good haircut. "Mike Kwasniski has proved to be a barber and every one is having a convict style haircut," Barlow noted at the end of November.[58] As they became more familiar with Liffol-le-Grand they discovered a service that contributed to their cleanliness. "Men are finding French women will do their washing if paid a moderate sum," noted Barlow.[59]

Dr. Paul G. Waterman received his M.D. at Cornell in 1902 and became a physician and psychiatrist in Hartford. He joined the National Guard in 1911 and served as a regimental surgeon on the Mexican border. Drafted into service as a major in August 1917, he was director of the Division's ambulance companies from September 1917 to March 1918 and then commanded the Sanitary Train from March to October 1918. He submitted this photograph, which depicts him as surgeon of the 4th Division, with his Connecticut Soldiers' Questionnaire in 1920 (courtesy Connecticut State Archives).

In early January, after Major Waterman inspected the barracks, Barlow reported, "several were busy digging holes to erect poles and wires so that all blankets may be aired out, if we ever have a sun-shiny day."[60] After the war, Barlow would remark, "no little credit should be given to Major Paul Waterman, although we considered him almost a Kaiser and dreaded his weekly inspections, peeking under our bunks and other places where we were apt to be poor housekeepers, our fear of him made the men keep neat and clean and help to prevent any sickness from breaking out among the men."[61]

The Company had already encountered the Y.M.C.A. at the "canteen" in Niantic. In France, Y.M.C.A. representatives, or "secretaries," would set up their relief huts as close to the front as possible, earning great respect and appreciation from the soldiers. The Rev. William B. Lusk of St. Stephen's Church in Ridgefield, Connecticut, west of Bridgeport, had decided to go to France as a Y.M.C.A. secretary as the 26th Division headed over. When he announced his plan to his congregation, they offered him a six-month leave of absence and raised $16,000 in just three days to underwrite his Y hut. At a brisk 48 years of age, he left his wife and eight-year-old daughter at home and arrived at Liffol-le-Grand in October.[62]

"They are putting up a new Y.M.C.A. here," Herbert Beers reported in November. "It is only 500 feet from the barracks. Makes it pretty handy for us fellows. They are going to have moving pictures twice a week."[63] It appears that the Reverend Lusk had obtained the use of one of the Adrian barrack buildings for his Y hut. While spacious enough to squeeze in several hundred soldiers for events, it was not designed for comfort. "In our Y.M.C.A. huts we had some funny little French stoves," remarked Lusk. "They are tiny little things and no one can imagine why they were ever invented. They were the worst little things, but the boys used to sit huddled around them in the huts."[64] While not much warmer than their barracks, the hut was a very popular destination for the men. In their off-duty hours, they could go to the hut to drink coffee and perhaps to get some candy or tobacco, to play checkers or chess, to obtain stationery and write home, to read books and magazines, to hear lectures or to see movies.

Known as "Daddy" to his parishioners, Lusk would play that role for the young soldiers. "In my Y.M.C.A. hut, I used to pack it with men and serve hot chocolate to them before they started out on their duty," he told their parents.[65] Lusk also kept a supply of cash on hand, "so when a soldier came along at Christmas time, who had not been paid in three months, as some of them did, I could hand him the money and not have to do it out of my pocket. I told them if they ever paid it back it would be appreciated, and if they didn't, it would be all right."[66] The Reverend Lusk also scheduled lectures by passing ministers. On November 11, "Bishop Israel spoke at the 'Y' and announced U.S.A. had been in this 'War' 222 days," noted Barlow. "The mess sergeant celebrated by serving pan-cakes."[67] In addition, "one of the U.S. Military Bands gives a concert most every evening," at the Y hut, according to Barlow.[68]

In the middle of January, the Y hut would have three special visitors, American women selling candy and chocolate cakes to the soldiers. Barlow reported: "There are two or three American girls over at the 'Y' Hut. One or two of our men are so smitten they have forgotten they belong to this Company, but no one blames them very much for this is the first time in three months we have heard the voice of an American girl."[69] Jesse Bailey of the Sanitary Detachment of the 103rd Machine Gun Battalion, and part of the "Newtown Club" with Beers, Peck, and James of the Ambulance Company, was there when the women arrived. "They surely made a hit in town," he wrote to his wife. "The night they arrived in the Y.M. the boys were all there having a boxing match & when they came on the stage & were introduced, I doubt if a girl or 3 girls ever got such a cheer before. It came from about 500 fellows in a low closed hall & you can imagine."[70]

The Y.M.C.A. was not the only support group for the soldiers. Back in Bridgeport, Lieutenant Sprague's wife Emma and a number of the mothers of young men in the Ambulance Company joined together to form the Bridgeport Mother's Comfort Club in November. They would send letters, money, toiletries, tobacco, candy, and gifts to the men.[71]

Such items were becoming essential. Two months after boarding the train at Niantic, Barlow wrote: "We have not been paid since we left Niantic. The men have no smokes, tooth paste, soap or money for same."[72] Finally in early December Barlow could finally exclaim, "how-de-dow, we were paid."[73]

The War Risk Insurance Act of October 6, 1917, authorized the government to underwrite term insurance for members of the military. Coverage ranged from $1,000 to $10,000. Within five years after the end of the war, the insurance could be converted to normal commercial insurance. The allotment system set up by the War Risk Insurance Act of October 6, 1917, authorized compulsory distributions from a soldier's pay to his wife (or ex-wife) and children, and voluntary distributions to his parents and siblings. The soldier was required to contribute at least $15.00 but not more than half his monthly pay. The supplementary government allowance was based on the number of dependents. In early December Barlow would note: "The men were busy filling out blanks for government insurance. Most of the men have taken out $10,000 worth."[74]

As Herbert Beers made clear to his sister, tobacco was an important connection for the men to their homeland. "Men are curiously picking fleur de lis in the rain and seem to enjoy the cigarettes sent from the fund of the New York Sun," recorded Barlow in early November. "All non-smokers friendship is sought. No American or even French tobacco is for sale in this town."[75] When he received a box of cigarettes from a neighbor at home, Beers wrote: "Received the tobacco that you sent me in first class condition. I just can't tell you how glad I was to get it. Thank you, Mr. Morris, and I guess nearly a hundred fellows would say the same thing to you if they could. American tobacco is as scarce as hen's teeth over here. When that tobacco came, I took it into the barracks and anybody that wanted a smoke had one. I've been smoking cigarette butts and giving them, when I had them to give. Something I've never done before in my life."[76]

The road between Neufchâteau and Chaumont that passed the barracks was a major thoroughfare. One day the men watched a car full of visiting U.S. senators pass by.[77] Another day a French division marched through, which "made Barnum's Circus Parade seem small."[78] In mid–December the 42nd Division would march through on its way from the railroad station in Neufchâteau to its training area near Rimacourt.[79] On November 11, General Pershing came down the road, making a quick inspection of the Division's quarters, but not its men.[80] And on November 12, the road brought General Edwards himself, from his headquarters in Neufchâteau to inspect the different units in Liffol-le-Grand. He had just returned from ten days on the British and French fronts to observe organization and frontline tactics. Edwards was busy getting the Division organized for its winter of training with a more efficient supply system. "Continually he visited battalions, and talked to the men in the most informal, personal manner," wrote the Division's historian, Emerson Taylor.[81]

Perhaps taking a cue from General Edwards, "Lieut Sprague gave the Company a lecture this afternoon," noted Barlow.[82] While the Company seemed to be settling successfully into its duties, a few weeks later Corporal Barlow would report, "all the non-coms received a bawling out from the Captain." Captain Stevens now had ten years of command experience in the Medical Corps, while some of the noncommissioned officers had only been in their posts since September and did not fully know their formal duties. Barlow had been a corporal since May and would be promoted to sergeant on December 19.[83]

In October, as the Division settled in France, the 101st Sanitary Train had redesignated its units to conform to AEF enumeration. The 1st (Massachusetts) Ambulance Company became the 101st, the 3rd (Bridgeport) Ambulance Company became the 102nd, the 2nd (Massachusetts) Ambulance Company became the 103rd, and the 4th (Rhode Island) Ambulance Company became the 104th. The field hospitals were renumbered in a similar manner.[84]

"And so, after encountering almost every conceivable difficulty—mud, filth, bad water, lack of drugs, and irregular delivery of food—the Sanitary Train began to do its work," remembered Earle Radikin in the Sanitary Train history. "At first good hospital men were driving ambulances and good mechanics were caring for sick men in the hospital, but training and transfers soon gave us a trained man in every job."[85] Soon the Company began to lose familiar men and gain new faces. After the 104th Field Hospital moved into a convent in Neufchâteau on October 22, 18 men of the 102nd Ambulance Company were detailed on November 11 to work at Neufchâteau.[86] Then, at the beginning of December, "during the light snow 18 men were transferred to other units." Fifteen of them would return six weeks later.[87]

On November 20, the 101st Field Hospital had moved up from Bazoilles to Liffol-le-Grand to occupy a French convent not far from the Ambulance Company barracks. "The place was in bad condition upon arrival there, but two weeks of scrubbing and cleaning 'American style' made a great improvement and, on December 7th the hospital was opened," wrote Earle Radikin.[88]

In mid–November, the Company received notification that it would be assigned motor ambulances rather than horse-drawn ones. According to the AEF prescription, divisions were to have three motorized and one horse-drawn company, so three companies would turn in their horse-drawn ambulances and send men to fetch motor ambulances. Although the Army had settled on General Motors ambulances, those had not yet arrived in France, so the Division was provided with some of the Fords being produced in the U.S. for the American Field Service.

On October 18, the 101st Ambulance Company had sent men on the 720-kilometer (450-mile) trip to the port of St. Nazaire, where the bulk of AEF supplies were landed. They returned with a first batch of Fords, but the Division's quartermaster department, which had only three trucks to distribute rations to the 20,000 men encamped around Neufchâteau, requisitioned them. The 103rd Ambulance Company then sent a detachment and brought back 12 Fords, and the 101st Company went back for 36 more. Then the sanitary train commander had to decide whether the 102nd or the 104th would get the final motorized designation.[89]

On November 17, Barlow noted, "rumors are, we are to be motorized—Our

Company won from Rhode Island in football by a score of 42 to 0." Indeed, they had won twice, as the 104th (Rhode Island) Company would be burdened with its horse-drawn ambulances for the duration.[90]

The officers then decided who would make the transition from driving horses to driving Fords. On November 18, Herbert Beers wrote to his sister: "Say send my big winter mitts over for I am going to drive an ambulance. I have been appointed… I expect to go to Paris or somewhere near there in a day or two after ambulances with some other fellows."[91] Two days later Barlow noted: "Ten men have been sent to a sea-port to bring automobiles to us to replace our horse drawn ambulances."[92]

While Beers was away, his childhood friend Arthur Fairchild, a member of the Sanitary Detachment of the 103rd Machine Gun Battalion, had a great surprise on November 23. "I was walking down the main street this morning when whom should I meet but Lodrick James. Come to find out the Connecticut Ambulance company to which he belongs is here in this village and has been as long as we have. They are in barracks a stone's throw from the hospital, but about a mile from where we are billeted. Isn't it funny that we didn't meet before this. Jimmy Peck is sick just now with laryngitis in his quarters, so I took him up some chocolate this afternoon and talked over old times with him. Herb Beers is away for a few days. He has gone to _________ with some others to bring back their Ford ambulances. So I haven't seen him yet, but will on his return in a couple of days. So it seems like old times to get the old crowd together again."[93]

While the ambulance men were away, the rest of the Company attended lectures on camp sanitation. They also received the red-cross sleeve brassards that would identify them as noncombatants.[94] And they began to see the kinds of injuries they would treat at the front. "A sergeant from Massachusetts was killed near us as the result of a motorcycle accident in the rain," wrote Barlow in late November.[95] A few days later, "a hand grenade blew up in a man's hand at drill in infantry tactics, giving us our first real case to supply first aid."[96]

On November 27, a train pulled in and discharged some familiar faces. After a month in transit, Private Thomas Bale was arriving with the Company's barrack bags, which he had been watching since they were unloaded from the *Corsican* on October 17. Also on the train were the ten men who had been sent to get the first of the Company's Ford ambulances.[97] Later that day, the ambulance drivers and their orderlies learned what their duties would be, and the Red Cross representative handed out gloves.[98] The next day, the men unloaded their barrack bags. According to Barlow, "the men were sorting over their personal property and were ordered to unload 12 French flat cars of Ambulances and escort wagons."[99]

The ambulances arrived in "boxes hardly larger than a piano box but in which are two knocked down Fords," and it took two days to unload them.[100] Mechanics Honeck and Edes, probably assisted by the Company's several machinists and the drivers and their orderlies, got the vehicles assembled in short order. Just four days later their friend Jesse Bailey in the 103rd Machine Gun Battalion wrote, "Hub Beers and Jim Peck have their Fords all tuned up and I hope to go for a ride with one of them."[101]

But the ambulances were not sufficient for all of the work the Company had to do. "Our Company borrowed some mules from another outfit and are using them to haul freight," Barlow noted at the beginning of December.[102] Barlow was probably referring to the departure of the Company's original horse-drawn ambulances when he noted on December 11, "our Ambulances were sent to Nancy."[103] The next day they received 16 horses, which might have been intended for the horse-drawn ambulances but could be used for hauling supplies or as riding horses for officers.[104] The following week the Company's motor pool was filled out when "Three motorcycles and two G.M.C. trucks were assigned to us."[105]

Thanksgiving arrived two days after the Fords did, and the Company celebrated it in American style. "Well, I had the best dinner you ever ate in your life, at least it tasted that way to me," wrote Herbert Beers. "Perhaps I didn't have as many different kinds of pies and candy, nuts and the like and served up in style, but—turkey and dressing, white and sweet potatoes, giblet gravy, prune pie, bread and butter, cream onions and cranberry sauce. It was as good a dinner as I ever ate. The turkey was fine!"[106]

George Herbert "Hub" Beers was a 23-year-old farmer from Newtown, Connecticut, when he joined the Company in May 1917. His letters home, published in the local newspaper, offer insights into the life of a wagoner. Here he poses in his yard at home, wearing his National Guard summer uniform. He submitted this photograph with his Connecticut Soldiers' Questionnaire in 1920 (courtesy Connecticut State Archives).

Beers was enthusiastic about his new duty. "I am driving an ambulance now and certainly am seeing a lot of France. No active service yet. I have been to Paris and spent about four hours there. It is a fine city, but I had rather go to any old city in the U.S. I have been in several other large cities besides.... France is a wonderful country and I certainly would like to drive through it—I have some of it."[107]

With ambulances assembled and running smoothly, the Company could take up its duty in delivering sick and injured soldiers from their regimental infirmaries to the hospitals in the area. The 101st Infantry was scattered from Rouceaux north of Neufchâteau to Villars and Circourt south of it. The 102nd Infantry and 102nd Machine Gun Battalion were to the southeast, near Landaville, Rouvres-la-Chétive, and Certilleux. The 103rd Infantry and 103rd Machine Gun Battalion were near Liffol-le-Grand. The 104th Infantry was farther south, near Harréville and Sartes.[108]

The hospitals were also scattered through the training area. The 101st Field Hospital had moved from Bazoilles, six kilometers (four miles) east of Liffol-le-Grand, to the convent on the outskirts of Liffol-le-Grand, near the Ambulance Company barracks. The 104th Field Hospital had settled in a convent in Neufchâteau. Contagious cases were taken to the 104th Field Hospital, while injuries and noncontagious cases were taken to the 101st Field Hospital.[109]

Severe cases would be evacuated to one of the base hospitals in the region. The AEF had immediately outgrown the army medical department's ability to treat its sick and casualties. So, like at the American Hospital in Paris, American medical schools worked through the American Red Cross to establish army hospitals in France. These stationary base hospitals combined the expertise of American medical professors and a sort of apprenticeship for medical students who got practical experience while providing care. And most of them had a contingent of American female nurses.

At Chaumont, where General Pershing had established the AEF headquarters, Base Hospital 15 was 45 kilometers (28 miles) southwest of Liffol-le-Grand. Organized at Roosevelt Hospital in New York City in April 1917, Base Hospital 15 became the first U.S. Army hospital unit to arrive in France when it disembarked in July 1917. The hospital had 20 physicians from Roosevelt Hospital, 65 nurses, and 150 enlisted men whose training fitted them for hospital duties. Serving both French and AEF soldiers, Base Hospital 15 had about 3,200 patients by January 1918. Major Charles H. Peck of Newtown, Connecticut, served as senior consultant in general surgery there and eventually directed the hospital. He and Percy Platt, another Newtown native at Base Hospital 15, were old acquaintances of ambulance driver Herbert Beers and his orderly James Peck.[110]

Six kilometers (four miles) east of Liffol-le-Grand, at Bazoilles-sur-Meuse, the Johns Hopkins University medical staff had established Base Hospital 18 in the Château de Bazoilles-sur-Meuse at the end of July 1917. Organized in November 1916, the Johns Hopkins Unit brought over 32 third-year medical students and after a year graduated them as M.D.s and commissioned medical officers. The hospital had 1,000 beds.[111] At Vittel, about 40 kilometers (25 miles) by road southeast of Liffol-le-Grand, the University of Buffalo Medical School had set up Base Hospital 23. Finally, the American Red Cross had placed its Military Hospital Number 1 in Neufchâteau as Base Hospital 66.

Sergeant Barlow suggested the Company's role. "Our 26th Division is scattered through many towns in this area and an Ambulance must call for sick and injured each day. Many are injured at drill. Guns are booming at practice all through this section. There is severe training under advice of French soldiers skilled by experience in their respective branches.

"One of the ambulance routes covers the French towns of [Certilleux] and Landaville while the route known as 4b, covers Base Hospital # 66 at Neufchâteau, Monecourt and Gironcourt."[112] Earle Radikin noted, "The Ambulance Companies covered the whole of the area each day, and evacuated from our divisional hospitals to Vittel and Chaumont."[113] But by the end of January Barlow could write, "there are three more Ambulance Companies in this town but we do the evacuation work for the entire division of about 25000 and there are a large number sick."[114]

Ambulance duty could be dangerous, especially in winter. "Ed Ashley was thrown through the windshield in an accident," reported Barlow on December 31.[115] And cold weather made the usually reliable Ford ambulances temperamental. The starting operation required teamwork between the driver and orderly. The driver adjusted the gas flow and sparkplug timing with levers on the steering column. Then the orderly at the front closed the choke with a lever and took hold of the crankshaft crank. He would lift the crank a quarter turn and release until the flywheel magneto passed a charge to the sparkplugs and ignited the gasoline. With a very cold engine it might take multiple quarter-cranks, or even whole turns of the crank to get the engine to fire off. The orderly then quickly adjusted the choke for the right gas mixture and jumped into the ambulance. But he had to crank carefully, usually with the left hand, as when the engine caught it snapped the crank with the power to break the orderly's right wrist or arm.[116] "Bill Adams broke his wrist cranking an automobile," Barlow noted on December 31.[117]

By the end of January, it was so cold that the motor oil congealed and made cranking almost impossible. But the ambulance men were ingenious. "The automobiles are left out and drivers have to take turns towing one another to get them started," noted Barlow on January 24. It must have amused the men to see the vehicles jump when the engines caught.[118]

These U.S.-built Ford ambulances had the rudimentary heater specified by the War Department for the patient compartment. With the exhaust line run just below the floor, the compartment could be kept warm. But if the vibrations of hard use were to crack the exhaust line, it would both warm the compartment and fill it with carbon monoxide. On January 23, Barlow noted, "mechanics are making one inch holes in the tail-boards of all motor ambulances as one wounded soldier when being transported was overcome by the gas fumes coming up from the exhaust."[119]

Even with the generally good roads in the area, the Fords were accumulating a lot of miles and sometimes needed replacement parts, which were hard to obtain. "Williams lost out in trying to win some badly needed auto parts over at the railhead," noted Barlow on January 20.[120]

By December the men were feeling at home in Liffol-le-Grand, even though "the rumble of the guns at the 'Front' can be heard in this town."[121] There, "an aged French man announced he had arrived and had for sale a one sheet American Newspaper."[122] For everyone else, "a Town Crier with a drum announces the War news and change in prices of supplies each day."[123] Some of the men were pleasantly surprised to find that "saloons are open on Sunday."[124] "Men are enjoying a few days good weather by making rings out of French coins, buying feeds of des [œufs] and [pommes] de terre frites at French homes at reasonable prices," noted Barlow on December 15.[125] "Saturday the 15th was Hub Beers' birthday (24th) and we 4 Newtownites celebrated with a rousing good feed down at a little French house," reported Beers' friend Jesse Bailey of the 103rd Machine Gun Battalion. "The madame cooked us 17 eggs, steak, French Fried Potatoes, Chocolate and cakes. Also had pickles (beer) and cheese to burn."[126] Later Barlow would report: "Many have found French homes where tasty waffles are made. The Richume family who live near the drug store seem to be most popular and are the finest peasant type. Drug stores over here sell only drugs."[127]

The men might also try to buy things in the local shops. Barlow remembered that "Jim Morrell took ten minutes to buy a wash basin; after he made all kinds of motions, like splashing water, etc., you know then the lady said in fine English, 'Oh, you want a wash basin.'"[128]

But evening trips into Liffol-le-Grand could get rowdy. "One or two of the boys try to drink up all the liquor in town each evening and then give a Company lecture after taps, about being an Irish-American and proud of it or about the conditions they met when on the west coast of Spain," wrote Barlow shortly before Christmas.[129] The Company's officers were billeted in houses in the town, which meant that the men in the barracks were free of tight supervision there, but might have off-duty interactions in the town. Barlow remembered that "Major Waterman used to make us 'snap it up' by shouting 'Run' 'Soldier Run' and when at Liffol-le Grand one dark night, a soldier stuck his head in the Major's billet and shouted 'Run Soldier Run' and then he 'Run.'"[130]

Heading back to their barracks they would find "guards are posted by all Companies every night. They slush around in three inches of mud and sleep in a barracks used as a guard house."[131] One night, "Gariepy when on guard, at midnight became unduly alarmed and woke everybody up by shouting 'Airplane.'"[132]

Shortly before Christmas, Barlow noted, "we were given some serious talks about just what we are to be up against and told we were to be a sacrifice division."[133] It is not clear if AEF headquarters had determined that it would throw the Division into sacrificial situations, or if it was a simple fact acknowledged in the division that it would have to bear much of the fighting until the balance of the AEF arrived. After the war, the veterans would adopt the term "sacrifice division," but Barlow's remark suggests that there was intent as well as circumstance in the term. But there was good news as well: "We received some more mail and 'BOY' [it's] better than nine bottles of medicine to hear from the folks at home."[134]

As Christmas approached, the men began to receive packages from their families and from the Bridgeport Comfort Club. The Company also planned a Christmas festival for the children of the town. Captain Stevens went to Neufchâteau and bought all the toys he could find, and "Harry Edes and others decorated one end of a barracks, with automobile tires, lanterns etc.," noted Barlow.[135]

On Christmas Eve, Herbert Beers wrote home: "Dear Mother: To-day is the day before Christmas and it has been a fine day. Pretty cold but a good day, Lodrick James and I have been out all day and have seen a bit of France. Tonight we are going to have a Christmas tree at 7:30. I expect we will have a good time.

"Ella Beers sent me a nice muffler and some chocolates. Mary and Hope sent a Christmas card; also young Hope. Caroline George sent a card. Frances Paine sent a fine letter. In fact every one has been writing to me, Lillian and Sarah, too. You should see our turkeys, beautiful birds. Mince and apple pies, nuts, figs and lots of good things. The boys are all singing and dancing. We have some dandy singers....

"Sergeant Bob Stewart and I have been reading the New Testament and made quite a hit."[136] Beers continued: "we had a Christmas tree and all received presents. Capt Stevens acted the part of Santa Claus and gave them out. Dancing and singing was part of the program."[137]

"CHRISTMAS—3000 MILES FROM HOME, made all sober minded," remarked Sergeant Barlow.[138] The holiday could not interrupt the duties of the Company, so the ambulances made their regular rounds between the camps and the hospitals. "I rode about 45 miles this morning and didn't have to change a single tire," wrote Herbert Beers. "The hob-nails that come out of the shoes are very plentiful in the roads. You can pick them out of the tires any old time. Tell Jimmie Nichols I've got a car that will trim his old Ford any day; and Frank Blackman's too."[139] Barlow noted that "several hiked up to the German prison camp at Liffol-le-Petit, one mile from this town and all had to fill out occupation blanks."[140]

That afternoon the celebration began. Beers told his mother: "My first Christmas away from home and it has been a very pleasant one. Of course there were a few drawbacks, but I am used to them, and 'grin and bear it,' as grandfather used to say. We had the finest dinner: turkey, potatoes, cream onions, gravy stuffing, pie, figs, nuts, bread and butter and coffee.... It snowed a little last night, about an inch. Tonight it is snowing again. Sergeant Bill Foley took up a collection for the small kids this afternoon, 52 francs in all; Bill, Harry Worley and myself went down to the Y.M.C.A. We bought chocolate, figs, cakes and nuts. Then we collected about 50 of the kids and gave the stuff out to them, along with some other trinkets. Sambo, a member of our company, acted as interpreter. The kids sang for us, spoke pieces and then we sang for them. We all had a great time, especially the kids. All the fellows were there so you can bet there was some noise."[141] Barlow added: "All the French children in town had been invited as our guests and were given toys, nuts, and candy, and they showed in many ways that this was about the best work of Santa Claus they had seen since the war started. Much of the credit for this party should be given to the Bridgeport Comfort Club for they had sent us many articles as gifts and gifts of money."[142]

In November, the first major personnel changes had taken place in the Company. Although much of the company's spirit was derived from the bond of shared origin and mutual experience, that went against the spirit of the AEF. General Pershing's ideal was an interchangeable army, where the men's loyalty was to the mission, not to their unit. He was also skeptical of the National Guard citizen soldiers, whom he considered to be unprofessional and too tied to their home networks. He preferred to have officers and men reassigned to avoid developing too much familiarity between officers and men.[143]

At the same time, Majors Waterman and Adams were finding the officers best suited to the expected duties of the different units, even as they pruned weaker officers. They may also have intended to give officers experience in both ambulance companies and field hospitals to improve coordination once they were operating in the field. "The hardships helped to discover and form the likely officers as nothing else could," wrote Emerson Taylor in *New England in France*, a sentence Lieutenant Sprague later highlighted in his copy of the book.[144]

In November, the two popular Lawlers, Lieutenant Daniel and Private Hugh, were transferred to the Sanitary Detachment of the 102nd infantry.[145] Lieutenant Sprague departed for an officers' school, "Somewhere in France," at the end of November.[146] When he returned at the end of December, Barlow remarked, "Lieut Sprague returned from officers training school and must have had some hard life for he looks grey."[147] Lieutenant Frederick Gregory of the 101st Field Hospital was transferred into the Company in early December and drilled the men for the first time in the use of gas masks. He would be transferred on to another unit at the beginning of January, but he would come back to visit the men.[148] On January 9, Lieutenant Thomas V. Daley of the 104th Ambulance Company and Lieutenant James F. Cobey of the 103rd Field Hospital were transferred into the Company. Just 25, Cobey was the son of an Irish-born sheet-metal worker. He grew up in New Haven, Connecticut, and attended Yale University for his undergraduate and medical degrees. He was interning at St. Francis Hospital in Hartford when he was drafted for medical service on October 5.[149]

In early January the Company's original captain, Frank Stevens, was transferred to the 104th Field Hospital and gave the Company a farewell address.[150] Barlow remarked that Stevens "was not only an officer but a father to us all as well."[151] He would be replaced by Captain Clyde C. Johnston, 32, a Nebraska native who had gotten his medical degree at the University of Maryland and was practicing in Springfield, Massachusetts, until the war. Johnston was transferred into the Company from the 104th Infantry. Barlow immediately noted that Johnston "surely is a nifty dresser."[152] When the Reverend Lusk addressed the people back home in Bridgeport a few months later, he remarked: "They say take a doctor who has achieved a degree of success and put a uniform on him and give him the authority and you have spoiled a perfectly good human being. There are some exceptions of course, but mostly they have no more regard for a man than a dog." Barlow and his friends in the Company would soon share this assessment of Captain Johnston.[153] By January 15, Barlow could say, "all except one of our original officers have been transferred to other units."[154] A few weeks later there was a change at the top of the enlisted ranks when Sergeant Harcourt Grant, a National Guard member since 1915, transferred in from the 104th Field Hospital and was appointed first sergeant in place of "Pop" Brendel. But Grant barely lasted two weeks before a truck crushed his hand against a stone post.[155]

On New Year's Eve, Herbert Beers' ambulance orderly, Lodrick James, wrote his sister: "We received the boxes from Newtown Red Cross, and believe me, they were some boxes. The persons who got up those boxes certainly were clever and understood our desires and needs. I have seen a great many boxes over here, but those from Newtown had them all beat to a standstill. The plum puddings from Mrs. Tiemann also came and were fine. I hadn't tasted anything so good in a long time.

"Some French musicians came to see us just now and [Red Worley] bought the violin-player's instrument for 100 francs. It seemed rather funny to me to see him buy the violin just after they had gotten through taking up a collection. He is having a great time playing it now.

"Arthur Fairchild, Jesse Bailey, Herb and I are going to have a New Year's party to-night. Herb bought a goose for 25 francs this afternoon, for the supper. I thought that it was a lot of money, but you know the old saying, 'We are a long time dead.'"[156]

Herbert Beers was only being slightly hyperbolic when he told his mother in December: "Our company has the reputation of being able to do anything from building roads to making airplanes. When anything special is wanted they send for the 102d Ambulance Co., and we always fill the bill."[157] Reflecting their pride, Private Earle Radikin wrote and posted a Company motto in early January: "'Our Origin' Made in Bridgeport and proud of it—'Our Ambition' To be the best Ambulance Company in the Best Section in the Best Division of the Best Army in the World. 'Our Motto' To do anything and everything anybody asks of us and to do it better and quicker than any one else—There is no such word as 'can't' in the 102nd Ambulance Company."[158]

Already a detachment from the Company was providing an essential service to the Division. "Cooties," or lice, had made their appearance as soon as the men began living in the barracks, and "sorting Cooties"—digging them out of the seams of their clothing and crushing them—had become a regular pastime to fight the itching and discomfort of lice running and biting under their clothes. Perhaps as early as the beginning of December, eight members of the Company were assigned to operate "horse drawn cootie machines" that were "kept busy going from camp to camp." These will be described in the following chapter.[159]

At the beginning of January, the Company had a chance to expand its expertise when Crocker, Doreski, Edes, Foley, Hough, P. Johnson, Klingel, and Willis "were sent to a school where feet will be treated." Sergeant Lieberum would join them.[160] Soldiers' feet were prone to general soreness, chafing, blisters, chilblains—trench foot—or even frostbite in winter, and twisting and crushing injuries in any season. In the winter rain and mud of France, it was difficult to maintain the "clean feet and clean, dry socks" prescribed in the sanitary handbook. The ambulance company supplies contained foot powder, plasters, petroleum jelly, and even whale oil with which to treat feet, and sanitary troops were expected to conduct regular foot inspections.[161] "Graduates" of the foot school would also have the knowledge to correct flat feet and bad posture to improve the readiness of the soldiers.[162] Doreski, Edes, Hough, and Lieberum came back from the foot school at the beginning of February, able to apply their new knowledge of treatments for the soldiers' foot ailments.[163]

For the most part the men remained healthy despite the wet, cold conditions. Mild colds were common, but the only contagious disease to spread among the men appeared late in their training. "Several cases of mumps have been found in this barracks," wrote Barlow at the end of January. "The only means of isolation we have is to put them in one corner of the barracks and QUARANTINE them."[164]

In an isolated case, William Cumming came down with measles in December, and this led to mastoiditis and then meningitis. He reported sick on the last day of 1917 and was evacuated to the contagion hospital run by the 104th Field Hospital in Neufchâteau. Until antibiotics and antiviral drugs were developed decades later, measles might be managed through quarantine, and mastoiditis through surgery, but meningitis was a largely a mystery. The combination of all three proved lethal, and Cumming died on January 5.[165] The next day he was buried in the city cemetery at Vittel.[166]

Joseph Wellwood was one of those transferred to work in the 104th Field Hospital at the beginning of December. He developed an ear infection that progressed into mastoiditis. He was evacuated to Base Hospital 36 at Vittel on December 31, and surgery relieved the mastoid abscess on New Year's Day. But during his recuperation he contracted scarlet fever. He lingered in the hospital for a month and a half, eventually developing nephritis (what became known as poststreptococcal glomerulonephritis). He would die in an ambulance on the road between hospitals on February 17.[167]

Probably in response to one of these deaths, and the pall that losing friends brought over the Company, one of the members—probably Earle Radikin—composed a poem, which eventually made its way back to Bridgeport.

One more of Death's grim toll
A volunteer in his country's cause,
A name for the honor roll.
No Eulogies have we to speak

All words are empty—vain.
The sacrifice supreme he made
Gladly—and no thought of gain.
Our hearts are far too sad for words,

We countless friends who mourn.
But silent prayers must reach the stars
And him who is now gone.
And never shall his memory die

But rather always live
In hearts, though saddened, still inspired,
That we in turn, may also give.[168]

American soldiers had not yet entered the trenches, but they were given an opportunity to improve conditions for Allied troops in the trenches. In 1915, British soldiers began to come out of the trenches with headaches, leg pains, and an intermittent fever. While not lethal, the symptoms were debilitating enough to keep men in the hospital for extended periods, and the strange ailment affected enough men to weaken the battle strength of their regiments.[169]

By the middle of 1916 British Army medical authorities had concluded that the body lice that infested every man in the trenches were probably responsible for trench fever in some way. As research continued, the Medical Research Committee of the American Red Cross met in October 1917 and proposed funding research on some problem affecting Allied soldiers. Realizing that the exact linkage of the louse to trench fever was still unknown, and that U.S. soldiers would soon be exposed to conditions fostering trench fever, the Red Cross agreed to support an American trench fever experiment.[170]

In the British Royal Army Medical Corps, the equivalent of an American base hospital was a general or a stationary hospital. Number 12 Stationary Hospital had originally been established at Rouen in February 1915, but was relocated in June 1916 to Saint-Pol-sur-Ternoise, about 32 kilometers (20 miles) behind the British lines around Arras, it was close to the source of trench fever sufferers, research had begun there in the summer of 1917. Authorities agreed that it was the best site for the American project as well.[171]

The British proposed that the American experiments attempt to determine the exact method of transmission from louse to human and also to see how blood was involved in spreading the infection. In January, General Pershing agreed to the use of volunteers from the AEF, possibly encouraged by his secretary, Colonel Frank McCoy, who had been an aide to General Leonard Wood when Wood permitted the use of Army volunteers for yellow fever experiments in Cuba in 1900. Pershing required that the volunteers understand the nature of the experiment and sign a consent form. Pershing had specified 60 men, but 66 were actually selected.[172]

As the National Guard division furthest along in its training, the 26th Division was a logical source for the trench fever volunteers, and the sanitary units were best suited to contribute men for a medical experiment. When the experiment was announced on January 6, everyone in the 102nd Ambulance Company volunteered.[173] But the other ambulance companies and the field hospitals also volunteered with enthusiasm. To spread the honor, and the burden, across the Division,

The Royal Army Medical Corps established No. 12 Stationary Hospital at Rouen, France, in February 1915. It was moved to Saint-Pol-sur-Ternoise, behind the British lines around Arras, in June 1916, and the Medical Corps began trench fever research there in the summer of 1917. This is how it looked, under a layer of snow, in February 1917 (© Imperial War Museum, Q 4723).

volunteers were drawn from each unit. The 102nd Ambulance Company was proud to contribute eight men, with another seven of its original members also participating from other units. The 101st Ambulance Company also offered eight (including Etheridge and Turner), the 103rd Ambulance Company gave ten, the 104th Ambulance Company provided seven (including Elliano and Lambert), the 101st Field Hospital contributed four, the 102nd Field Hospital offered fourteen, the 104th Field Hospital gave three, the 102nd Infantry's medical detachment provided the Ambulance Company's former members O'Connor and Vassel, the 104th Infantry's medical detachment gave one, and the Division's Sanitary Train headquarters provided the Company's former member Alfred Noren. The balance of eight men came from Base Hospital 15 in Chaumont.[174]

On January 28, the men were mustered at Liffol-le-Grand under the command of Lieutenant Rapport of the 101st Field Hospital and put on a train. The route led around Paris and then northeast to the British sector, possibly taking a roundabout path to the coast and then up the Ternoise River past the British base camps to Saint-Pol. There they settled into the wards prepared for the experiment.[175]

Thirty-four of the men were chosen for the blood experiments and moved into a ward for those. British doctors drew blood from seven British soldiers who had developed trench fever at the front. Some of the blood was kept whole and some was separated into plasma and proteins and other solids. Sixteen of the volunteers were inoculated with whole blood from the British soldiers. The other eighteen men received different elements of the blood components. Then they waited. Within five days, a few of the men began to experience symptoms of trench fever. The last of the group developed symptoms at 20 days. In the final count, 15 of the 16 who received whole blood developed trench fever, while 8 of the 18 who had received blood parts came down with it. All five who received unfiltered blood plasma, and three of four who received washed blood corpuscles, contracted the fever, while those who received filtered plasma or filtered ground corpuscles did not. Two men were also injected with a filtered suspension derived from the urine of trench fever sufferers, and one of them developed trench fever.[176]

Twenty-six men were chosen for the lice experiments and placed in their own ward. There, the "louse expert" walked around with lice in his pocket. To administer them, he placed 25 to 100 lice on the subject's arm and contained them within a calico "cell," which held them in place for the 30-day duration of the experiment.[177] Lice that had fed on British soldiers infected with trench fever were placed on 22 of the men. To determine whether lice feces were involved, two of the men had a chiffon covering on their arm so lice, hanging upside down, would bite through the cloth and the feces would never contact the skin. Another four men were bitten under the same conditions by uninfected lice. The final eight men were chosen as a control group to live under the same conditions as those exposed to lice.[178]

Neither the control group nor those bitten by uninfected lice developed trench fever. Of the 22 men bitten by the infected lice, 12 (54 percent) came down with trench fever. It took a bit longer for trench fever to develop from lice bites. The first man began to show symptoms at 16 days, while the last developed them at 25 days.[179]

"The fever seemed to come on the men at night," reported correspondent Frank

Sibley. "A man might go to bed feeling well, only to wake in the morning with a high temperature, a splitting headache, and pains in his legs and muscles generally. He would very likely break out in pink spots all over his body, and suffered from pink-eye in many cases." The symptoms would subside in a day or two, but then might recur up to eight times in three- to five-day intervals.[180]

The clear evidence that the louse transmitted whatever caused trench fever was considered a "triumphant conclusion" to the experiment. However, it would require another six months of research before British doctors could conclude that trench fever was caused by a Rickettsia bacterium.[181]

Once the results were tallied, the eight men in the control group, and most of those who never developed trench fever, could go back to their units. Most of the infected men had lost 20 to 25 pounds through inactivity and debility.[182] They remained in convalescence for as long as necessary. John Noren was sent to the American Ambulance Hospital in Paris on March 1, whereas Howard Etheridge was sent there on March 27, and Vernon Peck may have been held at St. Pol until May 1. Most of those who had developed trench fever spent at least two months at the American Hospital in recuperation, regaining their weight and some of their strength. Noren went back to the Division on May 5 and was transferred to the 103rd Field Hospital. But some would never return to frontline service. Howard Etheridge would arrive at the American Ambulance Hospital on March 28, but not until July 5 was he ready for release, and then he was sent for further recuperation at Base Hospital 17 in Dijon. Etheridge would not be released from the hospital until November 8.

John Elliano is a puzzle. He had been transferred to the 104th Ambulance Company just before the trench fever experiment, and he later claimed that he spent the

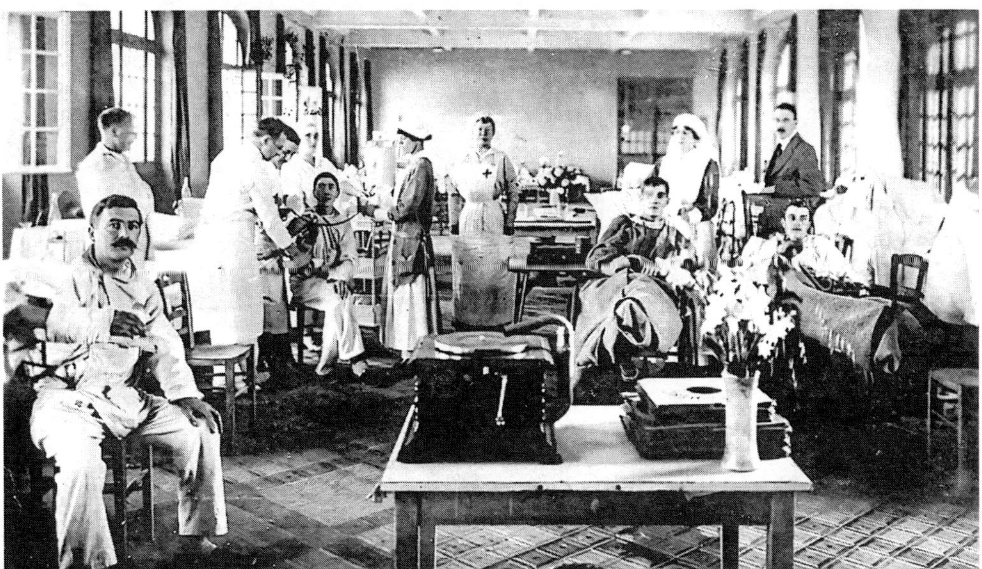

Most of the Company's volunteers who contracted trench fever recuperated in wards like this at the American Hospital in Paris. Notice the female nurses and the flowers and phonograph on the table in the foreground. French postcard (author's collection).

month of March in the British trenches on the Somme rather than in Number 12 Hospital at Saint-Pol. He then recuperated at the American Hospital in Paris from April through July, but still required further recuperation at Base Hospital 17. There, from August to October he would serve as acting sergeant of the military police at the Base Hospital 17 annex at the seminary at Plombières-lès-Dijon.[183]

Major Richard Strong, who was instrumental in promoting the American participation in the trench fever research, would propose that each volunteer who came down with trench fever during the experiment be awarded a Distinguished Service Medal. Based on the postwar notations of MCC awards, it appears that David Turner, William Murphy, Frederick Pill, Victor Schaeffer, John Vassel, Arnold Watkins, and Harry Worley were also among the infected.

The Division was also preparing for a form of warfare the U.S. Army had not experienced before: the use of chemical agents. The German army had initiated the use of chlorine gas against the British in the frontline trenches near Ypres on April 22, 1915. When inhaled in high concentrations, the chlorine irritates the lung tissues so badly that after a few hours the lungs fill with fluid and the gassed man essentially "drowns in his own serum."[184]

Born in Italy, John T. Elliano was seven when he arrived in the U.S. and was an 18-year-old employee of the Columbia Graphophone Company when he enlisted in the Company in March 1917. He was transferred to the 104th Ambulance Company in January 1918, just before he was accepted as one of the trench fever volunteers. He claimed that his trench fever exposure took place in the British trenches rather than at No. 12 Stationary Hospital. He would recuperate at the American Hospital in Paris and Base Hospital 17 in Dijon and would only get back to his unit for a month in the fall. He submitted this 1919 photograph, showing him in his helmet with gas mask at the ready, with his Connecticut Soldiers' Questionnaire in 1920 (courtesy Connecticut State Archives).

Using the wind to deliver the gas, the Germans first projected clouds of chlorine across the lines, but that uncontrollable approach was soon replaced by the use of artillery shells filled with gas. The targeted use of gas could place it well behind the lines and made it a very effective weapon. The British retaliated with chlorine in September 1915, and at the end of the year the Germans introduced phosgene (carbonyl dichloride), which was ten times more lethal than chlorine, despite its pleasant odor of new-mown hay. Like chlorine, phosgene badly irritated the lungs, but it also burned eye and even skin tissue. Because the symptoms of inhaling phosgene were often slow in appearing,

Born in northern Maine, 40-year-old David P. Turner was working in Bridgeport when he enlisted in the Company on the day of draft registration, June 5, 1917. He served as one of the Company's cooks that fall. He was transferred to the 101st Ambulance Company in December, shortly before being accepted as a trench fever volunteer. After his recovery, he was assigned to the 319th Infantry of the 80th Division and was returned to the Company in March 1919 (courtesy Le petit musée du Doughboy).

the lung damage was often irreversible and even fatal. Again, the Allies retaliated. Then, with the AEF about to go into training in the U.S. in July 1917, the Germans introduced the vesicant mustard gas (ethylene and sulfur chloride), which caused severe blistering of the skin, at least temporary blindness, and severe inflammation of the respiratory system. The heavy, semi-liquid gas, which had a slight mustard odor, could persist for days in low-lying areas. The Allies developed their own mustard gas, and both sides may have used simple tear gas. The Germans also threw over shells filled with "sneezing gas" (diphenylchloroarsine), which in dust form could penetrate gas masks, forcing soldiers to remove their masks and inhale the accompanying phosgene. The Allies would come to know the gasses by the symbols painted on German gas shells: blue cross for sneezing and tear gas, green cross for phosgene, and yellow cross for mustard gas.[185]

As soon as they faced gas attacks, both sides began to develop masks to neutralize the gas. After several approaches, the French issued the M2 full-face mask in March 1916. The wearer breathed through a cloth pad that was impregnated with castor oil and sodium ricinate, which neutralized phosgene for up to five hours. The mask was uncomfortable, hard to breathe through, and subject to fogging of the eye pieces, but it was easy to carry and to put on. The ambulance companies would receive these masks, mostly for use behind the lines.[186]

After designing a cloth helmet impregnated with neutralizing chemicals in 1915, the British took a different approach, with air-filtering materials in a small metal canister that was attached to a full-face mask with a flexible breathing hose. Introduced as the large box respirator in 1916, it used layers of lime-permanganate, pumice soaked in sodium sulphate, and bone charcoal to filter the air. The entire unit was carried in a shoulder bag, which would hold the filter canister when the mask was put on. The hose was connected to a mouthpiece in the mask, which the wearer would grip in his teeth. Prongs above the mouthpiece pinched the nose shut, and an external valve on the mouthpiece would open upon exhaling. Later in 1916, the British developed the similar small box respirator, with lime-permanganate granules between two layers of bone in the canister, and the bag designed to be worn on the chest for quick use.[187]

In 1916 the French issued a version of the large box respirator, with the canister worn on the back and the airflow passing across the eye pieces to keep them clear, rather than through a mouthpiece. The filtering system of this mask, devised by Dr. Jules Tissot, was then added to a modified German design with the filter canister attached directly to the facemask. In 1917 the French issued the Tissot Appareil Respiratoire Spécial (ARS) mask. Because these masks without a mouthpiece allowed the wearer to speak, they would be issued to artillery and medical units where communication was necessary.[188]

The Company was first introduced to gas masks when Lieutenant Gregory drilled the men in the use of the British small box respirator about December 10.[189] At the beginning of January Barlow remarked, "we have hikes, gas mask drills and received mail from the good old U.S.A. dated as late as December 5th, 1917."[190] Gas mask training continued, and on January 17 Barlow noted, "all are now drilling with gas masks, which must be put on in six seconds."[191] And the next day, "we now have a Gas School to attend and had to hike forty minutes with respirators on and then be able to change from respirator to French mask in a chamber filled with gas."[192]

As well as learning to function while wearing gas masks, ambulance companies also learned to provide first aid to those who had been gassed. In addition to litters, splints, bandages, and medications, the equipment for an ambulance company dressing station would include some special "gas appliances." Those assigned to handle mustard gas cases wore rubber coats and gloves to avoid contamination, and might wear a Tissot ASR mask, which would allow them to speak to their patients.

Because the first step was neutralizing the acidic gas, the dressing stations had large quantities of chlorinated lime and sodium bicarbonate. Earlier in the war, the Allies had discovered that the best way to neutralize gas residue was to apply a wash of chlorinated lime. The French found the perfect applicator in use in fruit orchards. The tank sprayer developed by the Vermorel company before 1900 for applying insecticides was readily adapted to applying a lime wash. The attendant would wear the copper tank on his back, with the pump handle in one hand and applicator hose in the other. Each AEF dressing station would be equipped with a Vermorel sprayer.[193]

The pace of training had picked up, but the men continued their social routines as possible. Although they received orders that "we must not mingle in groups, for fear of an airplane bomb killing or injuring more than need be," they still enjoyed themselves out of sight.[194] "We had another Newtown meeting last night only three of us being present, as Art was off on a hike and 'Hub' Beers on an ambulance call," wrote Jesse Bailey of the 103rd Machine Gun Battalion on January 30. "I bought a dozen eggs, Chunkie [James] a slab of steak and Jimmie [Peck] some cheese, bread and light beer (that's the only kind they have here—water in a beer bottle). We took these down to the ladies (Madame's) house I should say where we so often go, and had them nicely cooked. I think I must have eaten over half the eggs and a goodly am't of the rest. Oh! It's a hard war but it has its bright spots."[195]

But discipline increased as well. "Men are punished for minor infractions by having to hike with full packs for two or three hours," reported Barlow around January 20. "Mackey and Carleton were thrust into the guard house for being forty minutes of[f] their post when doing guard duty."[196]

At the beginning of February, it was clear that the Division was about to get closer to war. "Infantry, artillery and other branches are taught to KILL," wrote Barlow. "Big, two fisted men are becoming serious about their religion, ask to be baptized and take communion. We saw one preacher use a mess kit to hold water for a baptismal service. It is plain to be seen we will soon be thrust into our HELL for that's what they say it is up there. One's heart aches for the men in the fighting units, when we see them coming home in the morning after drilling in training trenches and snow all night under conditions as near like the Front as they can be made."[197]

At the same time, the Ambulance Company was also preparing for action. "All of our horses and mules have been sent to other units," noted Barlow. Although sanitary troops were noncombatant neutrals, defended by their red-cross brassards rather than arms, sidearms were occasionally issued, especially to defend equipment and gasoline supplies. "All non-coms have been issued 45 calibre Colt automatics," Sergeant Barlow remarked. And in addition to carrying the ill and injured to the hospitals, "our Ambulances are being used to transport officers to various schools of training."[198]

Then came the sure indication of a departure. "Six sandwiches issued to each man were supposed to be rations for twenty four hours," remarked Barlow on February 8. "Men are buying up about all the eatables left in the stores." Wherever they went, they would be comfortable en route.[199]

5

Under Fire on the Chemin des Dames

February–March 1918

The French had devised a highly structured, three-part training program for the American divisions as they arrived. The 26th Division had just completed the first part, with drills, officer and enlisted schools, weaponry training, and finally some time in practice trenches far behind the lines. After three months there, now they would embark for a "quiet sector" of the front lines, where they would be integrated with French frontline troops to learn to work under fire. The infantry and machine gunners would learn to shoot, avoid being shot, and even to raid enemy trenches. The artillery would learn to target and coordinate their fire and experience return fire. And the sanitary troops would learn to set up their field hospitals, aid stations, and dressing stations, and make ambulance runs under barrages of high-explosive and gas shells. A month and a half here would prepare them for taking over another quiet sector all on their own and taking on whatever frontline duty AEF headquarters demanded.

On February 9, the "Company was routed out early, loaded into French freight cars in the dark and traveled all day and all night, passing miles and miles of old trenches, bomb shattered houses and dugouts at all railroad stations," remarked Sergeant Barlow.[1] The destination was Soissons, an ancient city about 95 kilometers (60 miles) northeast of Paris, located in a bend of the River Aisne. Across the river to the northeast, low ground extended back about a mile to the steep slopes of the limestone ridge known as the Chemin des Dames (*ladies path*), named for the road improved for the use of two daughters of King Louis XV—"the ladies of France"—in the 1760s. A few steep valleys led up to the crest of the ridge, which then sloped down to the Canal de l'Oise à l'Aisne and the open land beyond. For centuries the soft limestone of the ridge had been quarried for building blocks, and in the valleys were many quarry caves, some extending for thousands of feet underground.

After the German First and Second Armies were stalled in their drive on Paris in September of 1914, the British and French had attacked the retreating Germans along the Aisne. Holding the ridge, the Germans used machine guns to drive off the British. The lines then settled on the far side of the ridge, along the Canal de l'Oise à l'Aisne, with the Germans 500 yards away on the far side and the French on the near side. A few hills offered strategic machine gun posts, with infantry in trenches between, and artillery miles to the rear had gotten the range of every point along and behind the lines. While there was little likelihood of a major assault here, the Division would receive an immediate and intense introduction to frontline service with the French 11th Corps, just as the 1st Division had in the month previous.

The Company climbed off the train at Soissons before daylight and unloaded its equipment, including the ambulances. "The ambulance companies did really good work in unloading their machines at night for the first time without the aid of lights—which were, of course, forbidden because of hostile airmen who continually crossed our lines," remarked Earle Radikin in his Sanitary Train history.[2] But he continued, "we tried our best to let the descriptions satisfy us and to act in an unconcerned, 'veteranish' sort of fashion, but curiosity got the best of us as curiosity will, and a greener looking bunch of rookies than we were never marched to a front in France."[3]

Now that it was in the field, the Division would assume its tactical structure. The 51st Brigade, made up of the 101st and 102nd Infantry would take the right of the line, supported by the 101st and 102nd Ambulance Companies. The 52nd Brigade, composed of the 103rd and 104th Infantry, would take the left of the line, supported by the 103rd and 104th Ambulance Companies. This might change in open-field fighting, or in contingencies, but it often meant that the men of the 102nd Ambulance Company would be serving their fellow Connecticut residents in the 102nd Infantry.

The sector of the Chemin-des-Dames front where the Division was assigned to work with the French stretched from beyond Filain on the right for more than ten kilometers (six miles) to beyond the heights of Pinon on the left. Directed to the right, the 102nd Ambulance Company men shouldered their packs and "hiked in heavy marching order to Vailly a distance of about ten kilometers and were there billeted in cellars of this once most beautiful town, now but a mass of torn and twisted debris," wrote Barlow. Although the hike was along the flat, heading upriver (east) from Soissons, "several men fell out on this hike and were picked up by the Ambulances."[4]

The September 1914 British attack had met German resistance at Vailly-sur-Aisne, and Barlow remarked: "A small bridge is near us on which the British lost thirteen men, one after another, as volunteers, before a fuse could be set off to blow up the bridge so that the Germans could not cross it. We heard an English soldier recite a poem about this bridge when we were at Borden, England, but did not at that time suppose we were going directly to it."

Barlow refers to the poem, "The Hell-Gate of Soissons" by Herbert Kaufman, in his diary on February 9–10, which concludes, "By the valour of twelve English martyrs, the Hell-Gate of Soissons is won!"

The area had been devastated during the 1914 fighting and by artillery ever since. "Trees in this section have been chopped off short by the Germans. Factories are marked 'Gott Strafe England,'" wrote Barlow.[5] "I have seen what shells can do and what they are likely to do," Herbert Beers told his mother. "Towns all shot to pieces. You know all the houses and buildings over here are all stone, except the window casings, doors and rafters. Can you imagine a town like Newtown built of stone and cement, all leveled to the ground, the hills all criss-crossed with trenches, and every square foot of ground full of shell holes, the trees all shot and torn to pieces, and every once in a little ways a dugout or dressing station? This is the kind of country I am in now."[6] But Barlow noted certain benefits of the earlier German occupation. "The Germans before being driven from this town had rigged up a large Douche (Showerbath). We are putting it to good use."[7] And with either light rain or light snow falling almost daily, the men were encouraged that "several pairs of [half-hip] boots have been issued and are worn all the time as the roads are always wet and muddy."[8]

From the headquarters at Vailly, a road wound up the valley, then forked on the way up, the left fork leading up a narrow valley to Aizy-Jouy. Another road led about two kilometers (a mile) upriver, where a left turn up a wide valley led three kilometers (a mile and three-quarters) to the shattered town of Ostel, which was a few kilometers in rear of the lines at Braye-en-Laonnais. Dressing stations were set up at Ostel, Zele, and Caiu.[9]

"Captain Johnston asked for volunteers to go up to the 3rd line trenches to act as stretcher bearers," reported Barlow on the day they arrived. "Every man in the Company volunteered but only 16 were picked and sent up."[10] The litter bearers would find that even a quiet sector was beyond imagining. "No lights are allowed. Trenches are filled with rats. There are barb-wire entanglements galore, shell holes, unexploded shells, etc. The rats eat your hardtack in your pack while you are resting on it," described Barlow.[11] "Up at Ostel post, our men are billeted with the French in a dugout built by the French and which is reached by going down 26 steps into the ground," he noted. "Shells from German artillery go over these towns and … ten kilometers to the rear of where most of this division is billeted in cellars and in holes dug in the banks."[12] Herbert Beers wrote home from Ostel, "about two miles from the first line trenches. I am writing in a dugout about 30 feet underground. It is very comfortable. It is pretty lively work to say the least."[13]

In several places, the dressing stations were in the limestone caves, where the doctors could stabilize the wounded and the litter bearers and ambulance drivers could shelter between runs. Ambulance Driver Earle Radikin, in his 101st Sanitary Train history, described one of them on the left, above Soissons and behind the 52nd Brigade: "Mont Leury was the advanced post, 5 km from the front lines, with a dressing station and litter-bearer station in a limestone cave with electric lights, but damp and with plenty of rats. Litter-bearers were sent by detachments to learn as they served along the French lines at Les Tueries."[14] Radikin also described another cave: "I was stationed 'way up in a cave near the front lines, a mammoth place holding some 60,000 men. The road leading up is exposed for about——kilometers, so that during the day you just hang around, only going out with extremely serious cases."[15]

The litter bearers were getting practical training at several stages among the French on the line. Some were assigned to dugouts in the trenches, from which they would venture out to carry wounded back to the aid station. In the trenches, the standard litter was too long and awkward to navigate the narrow, winding trenches, so some were equipped with litters having flexible bamboo bars. Another model was the snowshoe litter, with a shallow metal basket frame with rounded ends that fit

At the village of Ostel, the main street ran uphill from Vailly-sur-Aisne to the Chemin des Dames. The village had been largely destroyed during the September 1914 fighting along the Aisne. In conjunction with the French, the Company had a dressing station in a deep dugout here, and the Company's ambulances ran the wounded down this narrow road and across the Aisne to the field hospitals. French postcard, 1917 (author's collection).

around tight corners. But from the aid station back to the dressing station, where patients were prepared for the ambulances, the standard litter was used.[16]

Litter bearers also began to use an essential tool for tracking the wounded from the point of collection to the hospital, the diagnosis tag. Each litter bearer carried a booklet of tags, and if he was the first to attend to a wounded man, he filled out and affixed the man's tag, wiring it to a button. As Barlow indicated: "A diagnosis tag is pinned to every wounded man before being sent to the rear. Tags marked G.S.W. mean gun shot wounds. Those marked N.Y.D. mean the condition or fever is not yet fully diagnosed and those few marked S.I.W. mean self inflicted wounds."[17]

After the first group of litter bearers had been on post for a week, "29 of our men were sent to the lines to act as stretcher bearers and to relieve our men who have been up there," Barlow noted. They would continue to alternate for the 45 days the Division spent on the front.[18]

The first contingent of the 102nd Infantry entered the front lines on February 8, and the battalions cycled through on a 10-day rotation. On the night of February 28, under an intense artillery barrage, the Germans attempted a raid on the front line but were repulsed. Barlow recorded: "The 102nd Infantry are in the lines," meaning that the litter bearers would now be evacuating some of their fellow Nutmeggers, including the two killed and others wounded or burned by mustard gas that night.[19]

A few days after they arrived at Vailly-sur-Aisne, Barlow reported: "Ambulances are collecting the wounded from Posts at Ostel, Caen and Zelle, that have been brought from the scene of action by stretcher bearers from this and other Companies." Having already performed more than two months of winter work around

Liffol-le-Grand, "most of the Ambulances are out of repair and no new parts are available."[20] The next day, "four Ambulances broke down all at once."[21]

Herbert Beers told his mother: "Our work at the front consists of going up to a dugout between the second and third trenches where they have a dressing or clearing station. We stay there a day and then another ambulance comes and relieves us. We carry the wounded from the post back to a camp, where their dressings are fixed over if they need it—and then go back to the post again. There is a sort of a hospital at the camp. From the camp the patients are carried further back to some hospital. We don't have much to do just now, but expect to have lots of work soon."[22]

Telephone wires linked the infantry battalions on the front lines with regimental headquarters and on to the artillery and supporting units in the rear. While the wires were occasionally broken by artillery barrages, the telephone allowed the officers at the front to quickly request artillery support or to summon an ambulance to evacuate wounded. All telephone communication was supposed to be conducted in code, so at one time the message "HAVE WOODCHUCK SEND HOT DOG TO CHICAGO.—MUSKRAT" indicated the need for an ambulance. Each unit has its own

Titled "Repairing a Flivver within range of the German guns" and taken near Vailly-sur-Aisne, this image suggests how self-reliant the drivers and their orderlies became in keeping their ambulances on the road. About the time this Signal Corps photograph was taken in February 1918, Sergeant Barlow wrote, "most ambulances are out of repair and no new parts are available," and "four ambulances broke down all at once." The man in helmet and half-hip boots wears a Colt .45. This suggests he could be someone like Mechanic Harry Edes, whose duty was to keep the ambulances running and to protect their gasoline, parts, and supplies. This Ford ambulance's canvas roof and windscreen have been rolled up and strapped out of the way. The small window allows the orderly to keep an eye on the patients in the rear (National Archives, photo no. 111-SC-7022).

code name; "Codeine" was the name for the 102nd Ambulance Company at one point.[23]

"One of the Ambulances has had several wounded die in it and is now known as the Black Maria," Barlow recorded in mid–February.[24] A day or two later, "some one burned the Black Maria."[25]

Barlow noted that the ambulance drivers never knew who they might be carrying. "U.S. Troops are working with the French in this sector. Thirty Germans were captured and brought through our dressing stations. Our Ford Ambulances will hold three wounded on stretchers. In a recent load, Goodnow had a Frenchman, a German and an American."[26] A few days later, "five trips were made with various Ambulances to remove dead bodies at the front."[27] And soon the evidence of a steady, low casualty rate began to be evident. "The French Cemetery in Vailly is now being used for U.S. Soldiers and is growing very fast," wrote Barlow in early March. "Each evening there are a few horribly wounded cases added to the morgue at the edge of town."[28]

Much of the evacuation work had to be done at night, as ambulances were targets of daytime artillery despite their neutral status. Night driving was not easy. "The flashes from the artillery at night, blinds the Ambulance drivers, as the poor devils have no lights," reported Barlow.[29] Perhaps that is why "Drury had a smash up with his Ambulance" on February 28.[30]

The Company's ambulance men carried patients to several evacuation hospitals. One was the large French Evacuation Hospital 18 between Vasseny and Braine, about 10 kilometers (six miles) across the Aisne and Vesle Rivers from Vailly. It was "a monster hospital," with about 40 Adrian barracks, 16 ward buildings, and four double-wall Bessonneau hospital tents, operated by "3 Auto-chiro, 58 nurses, and 600 men," according to Earle Radikin, who probably delivered patients there. The 104th Field Hospital was attached to the complex for practical experience.[31] The other evacuation hospital "for slightly wounded and slightly sick" was in an old château at Muret-et-Crouttes, about 25 kilometers across the Aisne (13 miles behind the lines), by way of Braine. This hospital was operated by the 103rd Field Hospital, and six of the Company's ambulances were initially assigned to serve it. Originally set up by the French, this hospital had about 350 beds in the château, two Adrian barracks, and two Bessonneau tents.[32]

While the ambulance drivers were simply following orders from the dressing stations when they arrived at a hospital, their patients were not necessarily accepted. If the "slightly sick" patient sent to the 103rd Field Hospital turned out to have a contagious disease or a venereal disease, the officer of the day would redirect the ambulance to the evacuation hospital.[33]

To reach either hospital, the driver had to remember several turns or would go far astray. Herbert Beers described the difficulties: "Two or three nights before I went to the hospital one of our ambulances answered a call; they were gone for two hours. I was first on call, and a call came in saying that our ambulance was stuck; so I had to go out and take two side fellows. They were to go to different hospitals. I had never been to either one and it was 11 o'clock. Art Best, you remember Alma Best, he is her brother—was with me. We traveled until about 2, found one place, and then started out for the other. We went through all kinds of villages, but couldn't find it so had to go back to our place and send another crew out. It was just six o'clock in the morning and I had been going since 5 o'clock the morning before. I sure was tired. You know all the men we carry from the trenches are not wounded; some of them get sick."[34]

Barlow described another affliction of the men on the front lines. "Many of the soldiers are developing scabies and have to be removed from their units, sent to the rear in Ambulances or trucks, rubbed, scrubbed and scoured until sore, in some field hospital and then after a few days are sent back into action."[35] He noted that most of these cases "we had to transport to the hospital in our big trucks."[36]

Earle Radikin had gotten pretty cocky and told his father, "driving up a road that is being shelled, for instance, is not so tough as it sounds really—just time them and sneak through them. Of course, you mustn't stall the motor."[37] But it was not child's play. "A shell burst just ahead of an Ambulance driven by Spencer Wills and killed two men," noted Barlow in mid-March.[38] Leland Gilbert was a Bridgeport jitney owner and driver before the war. He wrote back to his landlady, reporting that "he needs no destination signs on his 'jitney' on the other side as he knows where he is bound and the passengers do also, if they are conscious at the time."[39]

During these weeks under fire, the drivers developed their own esprit de corps. "The Ambulance drivers have formed what they call 'The Forty Thieves Society,'" reported Barlow. "Radikin has drawn a large picture on the wall of one of these ruined houses and drawing purports to show the Club Rooms this Company is to have at Seaside Park when we return to the U.S.A."[40] Barlow later called it "a dugout to be made in Sea Side Park, [with] special pipes to the different soda fountains. We have often wondered what Heinie thought, when he captured that same little town and saw this drawing on the wall."[41]

Like the other companies in the AEF, the 102nd Ambulance Company had a "rolling kitchen," a two-wheeled iron box with sheet-metal stovetop, an oven, and holes for several large canisters for boiling food in large quantities. The cooks kept it fired up with wood, and its tall smokestack provided a strong draft and hot fire. The kitchen would be towed behind the Company's truck on the march (or carried on a railroad flatcar), and might be placed under a temporary roof when in position at a place like Vailly.[42] The supply line by rail to Soissons and by truck to the various quartermaster depots was more efficient than that to Liffol-le-Grand. But in the beginning Barlow complained, "we have only slum to eat and might as well throw away our knife and fork."[43] But on February 2, "one of the G.M.C. trucks broke down when after rations, and could not be located until late in the evening and this meant no chow," wrote Barlow.[44]

For those nearer the front, "food is sent from the cook shack at Vailly to Ambulance Posts and from there relayed to the stretcher bearers," explained Barlow.[45] The Army had large, insulated "marmite" cans in which to carry the hot food to the dressing stations and into the trenches.

Back in Vailly, with a Y.M.C.A. hut nearby, the men could also supplement the army diet. "All soldiers seem to be developing a sweet tooth," noted Barlow on February 20. "They buy condensed milk at forty cents per can and eat half a can at a time on slices of bread."[46]

As challenging as duty on the Chemin-des-Dames front was for the sanitary troops, "on the 26th we had Turkey for dinner, that was sent from the good old U.S.A.," remarked Barlow. "It was intended for Washington's Birthday, but what is a few days among friends? 15 French planes were over this town. May be they smelled Turkey."[47] But that fine meal soon exacerbated bad feelings among the men against their new officers. The next day Barlow complained, "men have found that the officers took 25 percent of all turkey issued to this Company."[48]

Now feeling that the officers were out for themselves, the men became more attuned to their exclusive behavior. The next day Barlow remarked: "The men of this Company who are acting as orderlies, are seen every few days taking large quantities of empty bottles back to the French Commissary, in a U.S. Mail sack. More for 'Officers Only' stuff."[49] And Captain Johnston's demands for special treatment only continued. At the beginning of March, Barlow reported: "Our officers are demanding steak for their mess, from the mess sergeant. He has such a small amount of meat left that all he can issue to the Company is stews and soups. When the mess sergeant protested he is reported to have been told 'To Hell with the Men.' 'I am ordering steaks.' We know he is entertaining many officers of higher rank than himself and we suppose he is in hopes of being promoted."[50]

Later in March the enlisted men would retaliate. "The food is poor and the men are discouraged to such an extent they raided the mess shack, stole enough steaks for a mess and spent half the night cooking them in a cellar," recorded Barlow, who may have been in on the raid. "All enjoyed the party. The first report of an investigation was that all involved in the steak raid were to be shot at sunrise. Sorensen was one of the first to be questioned and his answer that 'he did not know and if he did he would not tell,' rather put a damper on the investigation."[51] At the same time, Barlow reported, "a group of the Company, known as the Foreign Legion swiped a barrel of wine from a French commissary wagon but it was found where they had hid it awaiting nightfall." Such hijinks showed that the men were still spirited, but their sense of discipline was diminished by their lack of trust in their officers.[52]

The men had been trained to use gas masks at Liffol-le-Grand, but at Vailly and points closer to the line they frequently encountered actual gas. The Germans knew an inexperienced division was opposite them and tried to make their lives as difficult as possible. "It is rather quiet at the Front and it snows a little every few days," remarked Barlow. "Gas alarm is blown almost every night. All sorts of horns are used when gas is being sent over," he continued. "Each unit warns the other and the alarm is passed for many miles to the rear."[53]

The French taught the Americans the correct hierarchy of gas-mask use. Within two miles of the front lines, both the British small box respirator and French M2 mask were to be kept on the body, with the respirator in the "alert" position, high on the chest with flap open, ready to be put on in six seconds. In the zone five miles behind the front, both masks were to be worn slung, with the French on the right hip and respirator on the left hip. Between five and 12 miles from the front either mask could be worn.[54]

In addition, Barlow observed that "horses have a gas mask fastened to the harness for emergency and have many severe gas burns" from mustard gas.[55] Two weeks later he noted: "Gas curtains are being placed on all doors, where troops are billeted as the gas hangs close to the ground and seems to search out all holes in the ground. The curtains are simply horse blankets in most cases. The idea is the same as a storm door on a house."[56]

At the same time, "the French sixteen-inch railroad guns were moved into Vailly and this is going to be a nice place to try and live, when Heinie finds this out," warned Barlow.[57] Sure enough, "Heinie was not long in finding out about the 16-inch guns of the French for we had 175 wounded through our dressing station in 24 hours and most of them were also gassed."[58]

Earle Radikin described his ordeal that evening: "It was the day before St. Patrick's Day and I managed to convey the information to poilus (I speak pretty decent French now) that in the states we had two big holidays, Fourth of July and the 17th of March. So we fixed up a party that night. Well about 9 o'clock at night the Boche began heaving over mustard gas shells—it rained shells. Right off the reel we got a couple of patients, in serious condition. It was absolutely impossible to get out though, so we simply had to wait.

"About 1 o'clock there was a lull and I started out. I'll never forget it, never. The litter bearers (all French) shook hands with me, wished me 'bon voyage,' three priests blessed me, and someone speaking English told me to drive like hell. I did. It was the blackest night I can remember—a thousand shell holes—and you could smell the gas even through the respirator.

"Anyway, it happened that I got away just before the second bombardment, which lasted two hours, after which I went up again. In fact, I worked 48 hours straight."[59]

The Company's former lieutenant, Daniel H. Lawler, was then on the front line with the 102nd Infantry. On March 16, "he rendered first aid to more than 100 cases during an unusually intense gas bombardment in sector occupied by 102d Infantry, not only in his aid post, but going out to a point where a large number of casualties had occurred due to the concentration of German fire," noted his official citation. "This trip was made to render relief to men before they could possibly be brought to any aid station. Throughout the night, he went all over the shell area, giving aid. He was gassed in comparatively mild form, but later was evacuated to a hospital." He would spend about three weeks in the hospital, returning to his regiment on April 12. For his actions he would receive a Silver Star and be promoted to captain.[60]

"If you could ever see a man who has been mustard-gassed, perhaps you could appreciate my feelings," Radikin wrote. "Of all the inhumane, barbarous instruments of war, that's the worst. Blinded, nose, throat and ears burning and even sometimes the whole body, it is simply wicked. I felt like grabbing a gun and starting after the barbarians myself."[61]

And perhaps having survived so many close calls had Radikin feeling invincible. A few days later Barlow noted: "Rad picked up a six-inch unexploded shell that has been sent over by the enemy, and all ran away from him."[62]

The mumps that had developed at the end of the Company's stay at Liffol-le-Grand spread among the ambulance drivers and orderlies during their time on the Chemin-des-Dames. The surgeon general would later report, "of the less important communicable diseases, mumps hold first place.... No measures applicable under existing conditions appeared to have any effect in controlling this disease." He suggested that exposure was probably universal, and only those previously exposed did not contract mumps.[63] "Deutsch is over the mumps. West was sent to the hospital with the mumps," Barlow wrote on February 24.[64] A few days later, "C. Morgan and Gus Hannon were sent to the hospital with mumps."[65]

Herbert Beers also ended up in the hospital with mumps. On March 9, he remarked to his mother that her letter "came while I was in the hospital with the mumps. Still there. I guess it takes about three weeks for the swelling to disappear. I am feeling fit as a king, but the French doctor still keeps me in. All he says is 'bon.' Last night there was a deuce of a noise going on outside. It was a Boche air raid going on some where. The guns were firing at them and it was some noise. It's a fine day out; the sun is shining and it is hotter than the deuce. Real spring weather. The nurse brought in some violets this morning and some pussy willows."[66]

Here at the front, the men were fascinated by the air war overhead. "We witness many fierce air battles," wrote Barlow in mid–February. "Four Huns were shooting at one French aviator today, but he sailed away without being harmed. After that there were twelve planes over this town and we ducked out of sight to watch them scrap it out, and we are learning the value of not congregating in groups."[67] "It gets pretty exciting when they get to firing at the Boche planes," agreed Herbert Beers. "We all stand out and watch the fun. Saw a German airplane fall; was shot down by the French. The engine went 12 feet into the ground. Of course both the Boche were killed. It was some smash. They have air battles every clear day."[68]

Both sides sent up large, tethered balloons, below which a man suspended in a basket would phone down his observations of activities behind enemy lines and direct artillery fire. The balloons were frequent targets of enemy aircraft. "Observation balloons are up and our planes are trying to get them," noted Barlow on February 12. "One French aviator's plane was set on fire but he came down in a parachute with shots bursting all around him."[69]

At night, reported Barlow, "scores of searchlights scour the sky for airplanes. This gives the appearance of an Aurora Borealis. Now and then the French machine gunners rip off a stream of lead into the sky in the direction of an enemy plane."[70] Beers also remarked on the antiaircraft "artillery shooting at the Boche. They get one once in a while. We were all very much excited at first but it is getting to be common now."[71]

At the beginning of March, the Army began to distribute individual service numbers to all the men in uniform. The divisions already in France received the lowest numbers, and the sanitary troops received the lowest of all. In the 102nd Ambulance Company, the numbers, issued to noncommissioned officers and then alphabetically to privates, numbered in the 3300–3450 range. The name and number was stamped on a pair of aluminum disks worn on a cord around the neck, as Barlow explained: "Blanks for identification tags have been issued and are being marked with the name and serial number of the wearer and to be worn around the neck. The name of the unit must not be on the tag for in case of capture by the enemy, they would then know what unit or division was fighting them."[72] Barlow's number was 3301.

The Rev. William Lusk of the Y.M.C.A. told the families in Bridgeport: "All the boys have cooties and they sing a song worded like this after the popular American song; 'They go wild simply wild over me. The cooties are in France. They run up and down my pants. They go wild simply wild over me.'"[73] The 102nd Ambulance Company would lead the Division's attempt to subdue the wild cooties.

In 1895, the British doctor John C. Thresh had patented a steam boiler to treat clothing and bedding with pressurized steam in the theory that insects, bacteria, and even anthrax spores would be killed by extended exposure to steam at a higher temperature than the boiling point. After much testing, debate, and refinement, Thresh patented his first commercial unit in 1904. One horse-drawn model was designed for mobile use in small communities. It contained a chamber five feet long by three feet in diameter with two metal baskets to hold clothing and bedding. When the door was sealed shut, a slight vacuum was induced and steam produced by the small coal-fired boiler under the unit was admitted to the chamber. After about 20 minutes of exposure to the pressurized steam, all of the infesting organisms were dead. The contents were then dried by a flow of hot air. The British Army adapted this model for military use, although its capacity was small. The AEF had purchased 24 of these horse-drawn units in September 1917, and the 26th Division was issued two of them, which had made their appearance in the winter camps near Neufchâteau, operated by eight men assigned from the 102nd Ambulance Company.[74]

On March 10, Lieutenant Sprague was transferred to Division headquarters and given a new assignment. He would command the Division's new mobile disinfestation unit, which would be operated by nine men from the 102nd Ambulance Company. The Division's disinfestation, which was already being done on a small scale with the horse-drawn units, would now use the most modern technique, adapted from the British Army.

The two vehicles Sprague would command combined the pressurized steam treatment of clothing in large Thresh laundering units with steam-powered trucks developed by the Foden company. After perfecting the small, mobile units for community use, Dr. Thresh had designed large, stationary model QQ "Quest" units with piped-in steam for industrial use. About 1915, the British War Department developed a plan to mount these large units on the steam-powered lorries (trucks) that it was purchasing in large quantities from the Edwin Foden & Sons Company. Edwin Foden had begun as a partner in a British company that built large industrial steam engines, small stationary engines, and eventually agricultural steam tractors. In 1887 the firm became Edwin Foden Sons & Company, and it began steam lorry (truck) production in 1898. One of its lorries performed very well in a War Office test of self-propelled vehicles in 1901. Foden introduced a 5-ton vehicle in 1911, and in 1913 the War Department began to purchase them. With the outbreak of war, the War Department greatly increased its purchases of Foden 5-ton steam lorries and Foden then devoted all production to the War Department, producing about 800 by the end of 1918.[75]

The 5-ton Foden steam lorry was an "over" type, with the steam engine mounted above the chassis. The horizontal fire-tube boiler produced 200 pounds of pressure, and the compact two-cylinder engine developed about four nominal horsepower or

40 brake horsepower. The vehicle had two forward speeds and a reverse, with power conveyed to the rear wheels by a heavy chain drive. The driver sat behind the steering wheel on the left, but the seat was designed so that he was half outside the cab, with his left foot on the frame as he leaned out to see forward beside the boiler. With its hard rubber tires, the Foden lorry was restricted to a top speed of eight miles an hour to avoid vibration damage. The driver was expected to have "a moderate idea of speed" to avoid going too fast. To slow or stop, he used a foot brake for the engine flywheel to slow the engine and drum brakes for the rear wheels to stop the vehicle.[76]

The driver's assistant managed the coal and water. To get the engine up to steam took about 110 pounds of coal, and to operate the vehicle or the Thresh units required about 70 pounds per hour. In addition to a coal bunker, the vehicle had a large water tank with a pump and long hose so water could be drawn from wells or streams, which provided enough water for 20-miles of steaming. Fully loaded, the vehicle weighed about nine tons. For night operation, each Foden was fitted with a locomotive lantern. After a 1917 accident that damaged a boiler, they were also fitted with railroad-style front bumpers on the chassis.[77]

The British Army fitted out at least 98 of the 5-ton Fodens with Thresh units for mobile disinfestation behind the trench lines. As the AEF prepared to arrive in France, the chief surgeon concluded that steam was the best treatment for the unavoidable infestation of uniforms by lice and other organisms. Expecting that ten American divisions would soon arrive in France, he ordered the purchase of 20 Thresh-Foden units, believing that two, along with one horse-drawn unit, would be sufficient to treat the clothing of a 28,000-man division. At least 17 units were finally delivered to the AEF in January and February 1918, and the Motor Transport Service distributed them to the divisions in the field.[78]

Not only did the men assigned to them have to learn to operate and drive a steam truck, they also had to learn to "cook" the vermin out of clothing and blankets. Behind the cab of the Foden steamers, two Thresh QQ units with doors at both ends were mounted side by side. Measuring three feet, seven inches in diameter and six feet long, they each had a volume of 60 cubic feet. Two men managed the units. They would load each metal basket with either 60 blankets or 35 "kits" of clothing (not including overcoats). They would then seal the doors and open the steam lines, feeding in steam at five to ten pounds pressure to raise the temperature to 238 F. While they could watch the gauges, most operators learned to watch the outlet pipe for a wisp of steam to know the unit was up to temperature. After approximately 20 minutes of steaming and ten minutes of hot-air drying, the wool blankets or uniforms would be dry and were shaken out and handed back to the waiting soldiers. The whole process took about an hour.[79]

It appears that Sergeant William Cowie was put in charge and drove one machine and Corporal Rocco Francolini took the other. Each had an assistant to feed the boiler with coal—often in the form of compressed briquettes—and to refill the water tank. Two men operated the Thresh units on each vehicle, and one man drove a 3-ton General Motors truck with supplies and extra clothing for issue. This detachment went off to learn their new specialty, then would make their way around the Division to disinfest its lousy troops.[80]

The details of the Thresh-Foden disinfectors are displayed in this view of the Division's unit 502. The driver—probably the noncommissioned officer in charge—sits at the wheel with his left foot on the step, which was the normal driving position. Each wood-sheathed cylinder accommodated two baskets of loosely bundled clothing. With the full baskets in the cylinders, the doors were dogged down to be air-tight, and steam was introduced. The operators could monitor temperature and pressure gauges or watch the vent pipe above each cylinder for a wisp of steam to know the unit was operating properly. After about 20 minutes of pressurized steam and ten minutes of hot air, the clothing was considered rid of lice and the doors were opened. Each bundle was given back to the appropriate soldier, then the next group arrived to deposit their lousy clothing. The men have hung their helmets on top of the front Thresh cylinder and their French M2 gas masks behind the cab door, and have placed their mess kits under the cylinder. Private C.E. Painter of the Signal Corps photographed the unit at Raulecourt on June 6, 1918 (National Archives, photo no. 111-SC-14610).

Two days after the heavy gas bombardment, the Division reached the end of its training session with the French Sixth Army and was withdrawn from the line. The orders called for a move to Brienne-le-Château, more than 100 kilometers to the southeast, where it would engage in open-warfare training. At the same time, the Germans launched their spring assault on March 21 north of Soissons, where the British and French lines converged. The German plan to overwhelm the British and French armies before the American divisions arrived in force would bring an end to the 26th Division's training.

On March 22, "all were routed out early this morning," reported Barlow. They shouldered their packs, then crossed the river and hiked the eight kilometers to the railroad line at Braine.[81] Y.M.C.A. secretary William Lusk stepped up to support the departing troops. "When the 26th Division was leaving [Braine] I served coffee to

30,000 or 35,000 men and an apple for each. I brewed 1,000 pounds of coffee and had to make it in a shed and be ready to put out the lights at a moment's notice to keep from the raiders."[82] While they loaded the trains and waited to depart, "quite a number of large shells landed in this town during that time."[83]

Born in England, James W. Clark, 30, was married, worked as a clerk for a Bridgeport printer, and had his first naturalization papers when he enlisted in the Company in June 1917. Elevated to private 1st class in December, he would be assigned to duty with the Thresh-Foden disinfectors. In this photograph from the summer of 1917, he wears his cotton National Guard uniform (courtesy Le petit musée du Doughboy).

The route led them on arc to the southeast and then southwest through La Ferté-Milon, then across the Marne and east through Nogent. Further east, "the train was held up during a most wicked air raid at [Chalons-en-Champagne]. There is nothing that puts the fear of God in a man like those cussed bombs dropped from an airplane," exclaimed Barlow.[84]

On March 23, the Company arrived at Brienne-le-Château, about 60 kilometers south of Chalons-en-Champagne and 60 northeast of AEF Headquarters at Chaumont. At Brienne-le-Château the Company was billeted "in a large barn just outside the town and the natives seem delighted as only a few U.S. Soldiers have been billeted in this town before," reported Barlow, who correctly noted that it was "the town where Napoleon received his early military training."[85]

With the Division's entire Sanitary Train gathered at Brienne-le-Château, "members and ex-members of this train are renewing acquaintances" since the different units had exchanged so many men during the past five months. In the 102nd Ambulance Company, there were also changes among the noncommissioned officers. "Holzheimer is now top-sergeant, Levasseur is quartermaster, Barlow is sergeant of stretcher-bearers and Northrop goes back to the automobile school," noted Barlow.[86]

But two days after arriving, "we are on the move again," marching east to Crespy-le-Neuf, where they "had lunch at a cross roads," and then on through Morvilliers, explained Barlow.[87] This was part of a "march problem," a training exercise in moving a division cross-country.[88] "This move gave the Medical Department its lesson of functioning while coming long distances by train, by truck, and by marching, with coincidental sanitary activities, long runs to hospitals and care of transportation," wrote the Division Surgeon. "It was well done. Here was shown the uselessness of horse-drawn transportation as compared with motor, and here our horse-drawn ambulances should have become a thing of the past," as the 104th Ambulance Company struggled to keep up.[89] After a 15-kilometer (nine-mile) hike, the men "were billeted in a hay barn at Soulaines[-Dhuys] and were quite cheered up by the concert of the 101st Infantry Band and by the town character who was doing the funny dancing when the Band played."[90]

On March 26 they "left Soulaines in trucks at noon," heading east, "but did not arrive at Joinville until nine at night and slept in a one-story French billet that was equipped with double deck bunks and plenty of lice."[91] The next morning, "we had to poke about with candles and get up early (4 A.M.) and were taken in trucks to [Lafauche] and billeted in barns about the town." They were now back within a few miles of Liffol-le-Grand, but their next move was not obvious to the men.[92]

On March 28, "we were paid at ten o'clock at night in a barn," noted Barlow. But, he continued, "there is very little for sale in this town. BOY. What we would not give to see a newspaper."[93] "So this is GOOD FRIDAY?" he asked the next day. "The Town crier announced in the rain that no more liquor is to be sold to American soldiers."[94]

Barlow also documented further changes in the Company. Their longtime junior lieutenant, William Nagle, received transfer orders. He would be missed. "He was a friend of the soldier and a good fellow," wrote James Peck. "He is a very smart young doctor."[95] Eight enlisted men were also transferred. George Oppenheimer "was sent to a hospital with an infected toe," and "Artie Best is down with pneumonia." A trip to the hospital meant a likely transfer to another unit once one recovered, which would be the case with both Oppenheimer and Best. G. Spencer Wills seems to have been the last of the ambulance drivers to come down with the mumps, but his illness did not immediately take him away from the Company.[96]

With the Division on the march, followed at various intervals by the ambulances, the drivers had a bit of discretion. "I've just pulled into the hospital here after doing about 100 kilos and as it is late and raining pretty hard, I reckon I'll spend the night here, treat myself to the luxury of crawling in between two clean white sheets, on a real mattress. Some sensation, believe me," Earle Radikin wrote his father on March 28. He continued: "Well, I told you my stretch was finished and I was back in repose. Yes, I've been in repose, or the division has, for about two days. And tomorrow—goodbye repose, goodbye 10 days in Paris—they need us on the line. C'est la guerre. And the sooner we get back the sooner it will be over. You know the Germans are pulling off a big drive and I think it is their last one. After the beating they are going to get they may get it through their thick skulls that they cannot win.

"Met a bunch of boys from home [Pawcatuck, Rhode Island] the other day, the first time since I've been over here, although we are all the Yankee division. Had one funny experience when I stopped on the road to get some mess. Somebody introduced me to the mess sergeant. After shaking hands, he said, 'Oh yes, I used to work for your old man; I worked one day and he fired me. Now I get even. Go up and get your stew.' And from what I mean he did get even. That stew was all right in its way, but somebody must have stolen the meat. All I could find were carrots. Better not fire any more guys that threaten to become cooks. His name was Spirnthall. I also met Jack Little, plugging along on an old skate, and Ned Eaton, Jack Chandler, Crowe and all the artillery boys." He concluded: "But it's time to turn in and I'll have to call it quits for a while. It may be quite some time, because I fear I shall be very busy these next few weeks in the trenches."[97]

6

Running Dead Man's Curve

April–June 1918

Since 1914, the battlelines south of Verdun had extended southwest to near St. Mihiel, then turned roughly east, from the high ridges near the Meuse to the Woëvre plain across which the Germans had attacked at the outbreak of war. In this salient, the Germans had entrenched on high ground above the Rupt de Mad stream, with the peak of Montsec just behind the line to provide a clear view of the opposing French trenches in the boggy valley and lower hills to the south.

As a relatively quiet area, the French considered the Toul Sector (named for the city behind it) an ideal location for American divisions to learn to operate in the lines on their own. In January the 1st Division had occupied the lines with the frontage of a brigade (two regiments), with French divisions on both sides. Now ready for combat, the 1st Division was being withdrawn to support the French resistance to the German assault across the Chemin des Dames. As its successor division in training, the 26th was moved into the sector to occupy the lines. However, with the urgent need for troops to defend Paris, a French division was also withdrawn, leaving the 26th with a 10-mile-wide sector to occupy.

The line ran from the Bois Brule and Apremont on the west, then in front of Bouconville, Xivray, and Seicheprey (later shifting right to cover Flirey as well). An east-west ridgetop road from Bouconville through Beaumont to Flirey linked the positions. A north-south route connected both Apremont and Bouconville with Jouy on the west side of the sector, and on the east side another ran from Seicheprey and Beaumont, south through Mandres and Ansauville, to Ménil-la-Tour. Between those roads was the large La Reine Forest, where troops could shelter when in reserve. An extension of the forest across the road between Ménil-la-Tour and Ansauville, called the Bois de Réhanne (or Réhanne Woods), provided additional shelter. Division headquarters would be established at Boucq, south of the forest on a road connecting Jouy and Ménil-la-Tour. Further south was the city of Toul, near which the 94th Squadron of the U.S. Air Service's First Pursuit Group would arrive on April 9 to begin offensive patrols over the lines.

On March 30, the men of the 102nd Ambulance Company were loaded into trucks at Lafouche and were driven about 80 kilometers (50 miles) north, through Neufchâteau, across the Meuse River at Toul, and on to the crossroads village of Ménil-la-Tour. "There are a few old natives in Menil," remarked Sergeant Barlow.

"The town has not been knocked down by shell fire. All houses are built of stone and joined with the barn. Manure is piled between the kitchen and the road."[1] On their first night in the sector, the Ambulance Company men "slept on the ground in some partially completed barracks," and received strict orders "in regard to no smoking or using of lighted matches, automobile lights or fires of any description."[2]

With all of the 26th Division trucks arriving in the sector, and the 1st Division trucks beginning to move out, "Cooper and Goodnow had smashups with their Ambulances in moving in the rain," remarked Barlow.[3] "All roads are jammed as 1st Division is now being relieved by the 26th Division," he noted the next day. "Mules and horses drop dead from exhaustion or are killed by shell fire, are pushed part way off the road and left there. Trucks of tremendous horse power get stuck in the roads and ditches and are pulled out by other trucks. Sometimes it takes two or three to pull the first one out."[4] And there was confusion in the Company as well. "We were shifted into and out of three different barracks while it was raining," Barlow wrote on that Easter Sunday. "There is nothing to eat because our stove was lost in the shuffle. Each billet was worse than the other. We wound up in the loft of a barn."[5]

Except for a few high points, the trenches here were low and boggy, often with standing water. As was normal military practice, the 51st Brigade (101st and 102nd Infantry) of the Division took the right of the line, in front of Seicheprey, supported by the 102nd Machine Gun Battalion. The 52nd Brigade (103rd and 104th Infantry) took the left, near Apremont, supported by the 103rd Machine Gun Battalion. The troops moved into position and waded into the trenches as the 1st Division filed out. On the ridge, the 103rd (Rhode Island) Field Artillery occupied the gun positions along the road.

On Easter Sunday, "twenty were sent to operate a dressing station at Mandres," which was being vacated by the 1st Division Sanitary Train. The Germans already knew that a less-experienced division was moving in, and "there was a fierce barrage there at night," noted Barlow.[6] With the 26th Division infantrymen already in the trenches, the 1st Division began to retire in the night and were caught by the artillery barrage. By the time they had withdrawn from range, more than 200 had been wounded. "The 102nd Ambulance Company, which had gone into position only that day, immediately started working 'full speed ahead' and dressed and transported all of the wounded," noted Earle Radikin in the Sanitary Train history.[7]

While the Mandres dressing station stabilized the wounded and the ambulance drivers brought them back, the men in Ménil-la-Tour "found the cook stove and celebrated by having pan-cakes and signing the pay roll," noted Barlow. "All watched the six German observation balloons that were up viewing the movements of Allied troops."[8] The dressing station at Mandres remained under fire. "A shell hit the stove being used at the Mandres dressing station," remarked Barlow. "The explosion knocked a can of tomatoes from a shelf and into a side of beef so far it had to be cut out."[9]

Despite the chaotic beginning, the Sanitary Train units found their coordinated positions. The 104th Ambulance Company established a dressing station to the right of the 102nd station in the Bois-de-Renderes [Réhanne], while the 101st and 103rd supported the 52nd Brigade on the left.[10] "Sifting" or triage for the patients of the

A group poses by a Ford ambulance at Ansauville, April 1918. The two men at left have not been identified, but at center is Corporal Ray E. "Pinaud" Pomeroy, wearing a British Army tunic, then Orderly Charles D. "Dud" Mills, and Wagoner Benjamin B. "Dynamite" Wyrtzen sitting on the running board. Most of the men have a French M2 gas mask on their right hip, but Wyrtzen has his preferred small box respirator on his left hip. Photo by Merritt Learned, 102nd Infantry (courtesy Connecticut State Archives).

51st Brigade, brought back by the 102nd Ambulance Company, was performed at the 102nd Field Hospital in an Adrian barracks at Ménil-la-Tour. On the left, the 104th Field Hospital performed the same duty for the 52nd Brigade. Farther back at "Caserne," a large military barracks in the historic fortifications of Toul, the 101st Field Hospital treated the ordinary ailments of the soldiers and the 103rd Field Hospital handled skin conditions and contagious illnesses. With both field hospitals together, and with 15 female nurses supporting their operations, they acted like a base hospital for the Division.[11]

Nearby, at Sebastopol, Evacuation Hospital 1 provided the next level of service.

The portion of the Company at Ménil-la-Tour undertook its frequent work of cleaning up the town it was billeted in. "Whenever the opportunity afforded the men were ordered to work cleaning up the streets and billets of the town where they were billeted and we were sometimes called the medical engineers," recalled Barlow.[12] "A detail of men were sent to bury dead horses and mules as most of our stretcher bearers have been relieved by the Rhode Island [104th] Company," Barlow noted on April 5.[13]

The 102nd Company ambulances would make the run from Mandres to Ménil-la-Tour and also from Ménil-la-Tour to the Caserne hospitals. On the run from the dressing station at Mandres, the drivers had quickly noticed "a sign on a tree near the road from Ménil-la-Tour toward Mandres and Seicheprey, reads

'L'enemi vous voits' The enemy sees you."[14] A German observation post on Montsec was just two miles behind the lines, so between that and the observation balloons there was a clear view for artillery spotters to identify targets. Between the dressing station at Mandres and the dressing station and ambulance head, or forward ambulance position, at Beaumont on the ridge above Seicheprey, was a stretch of road and fields clearly visible to the Germans. The soldiers called the ground Hell's Half Acre. Next to Hell's Half Acre, "where the back road from Mandres to Beaumont makes a sharp turn when it joins the road from Bernecourt and goes up the rise to Beaumont, was the soon-to-be-infamous Dead Man's Curve."[15] "This corner is shelled constantly," noted Barlow. "Serg't Northrop is at Mandres and times the Ambulances to try to be just ahead of the shells, as he studies the intervals between shells, but sometimes the Ambulances lose out."[16] For his work at the Mandres dressing station, Captain Johnston would nominate Lieutenant Robert Durham for his "untiring efforts during an enemy bombardment April 8th to 9th administering aid to the wounded being the only Medical Officer present and after being badly gassed himself refused to be evacuated until such relief came."[17]

As the Division settled in, and received "tons of mail," the Y.M.C.A. men,

The Y.M.C.A. provided moral support and a morale boost in each of the Company's sectors. One of the "Y huts" that might be frequented by members of the Company was in Hamonville, on the road between Mandres and Ansauville. Here, off-duty soldiers wearing their gas mask bags play checkers, catch up on newspapers and magazines from home, and write letters. The stove provides a steady supply of coffee or hot chocolate, and boxing gloves and baseball mitts offer more energetic amusement. Signal Corps photo by Corporal Keen Polk, May 3, 1918 (National Archives, photo no. 111-SC-13331).

including the Reverend Lusk with his Y hut, were right behind. Barlow remarked, "there is a grey whiskered Y.M.C.A. man said to come from Stamford, Connecticut, assigned to work in this area. He is surely a regular humdinger for he goes up into the lines with cigarettes every time they will allow him and walks along as though he were at home."[18]

In this sector, the Y.M.C.A. was joined by the Salvation Army. "The Salvation Army girls have dared to put up a tent at Ansauville and are being highly complimented," noted Barlow in the first week of April. "This hut is operated by the McIntyre sisters who are so well known and liked by the men of the Division."[19] Established in London in 1865 to feed and assist the poor, the Salvation Army acquired its name in 1878 and took on a military structure in its organization while espousing an informal approach to its missionary work. It spread to the United States, where one of its early champions was William A. McIntyre. After working among the Labrador and Newfoundland fishermen, McIntyre had taken the family to California for his health and more recently had been assigned as commissioner of the Salvation Army programs in the Northeast. Among his children were sisters

Wearing helmets and gas masks at the ready, Gladys and Irene McIntyre, Muriel Turkington, and Stella Young make pies at their rudimentary Salvation Army hut in Ansauville. The soldiers gathered around them confirm Barlow's remark, "we love those McIntyre girls almost as much as we do the cruellers, only we tell them about the cruellers." Signal Corps photo, April 9, 1918 (National Archives, photo no. 111-SC-10444).

Irene, 26—who had graduated from Mount Holyoke College in 1913—and Gladys, 23. Irene had seen the outbreak of the war when she accompanied her father to a peace conference scheduled for Switzerland in July 1914. With the U.S. entry into the war, Irene and Gladys requested their father's permission and assistance to go to France as Salvation Army volunteers. They were accepted in November and Gladys went over immediately, followed by Irene in March, with 15 other Salvation Army personnel. They had been assigned to the 1st Division in the Toul Sector, and they remained when the 26th Division replaced the 1st.[20]

By the time they began serving the 26th Division, the McIntyre sisters had been joined by Stella Young, 22, of Everett, Massachusetts, and Myrtle Turkington, 25, of Manchester, Connecticut. They fried doughnuts, made pies, and served coffee and chocolate to the soldiers, often at their rudimentary kitchen in a ruined building at Ansauville, within range of German artillery. They often wore helmets and gas masks like the men they served. "The Salvation Army workers are always right there where they are needed most," reported Charles Johnson. "The best ones greet you when you come from the front standing ready to give you a hot cup of coffee, and a hot cup of coffee certainly tastes mighty fine to the boys at that time."[21]

"Those who are not on details are busy eating crullers over at the Salvation Army hut," remarked Barlow in June. "Most every one gets over there in the evening. We love those McIntyre girls almost as much as we do the cruellers, only we tell them about the cruellers."[22]

Barlow recognized the incongruity of the young women offering a domestic

Off-duty soldiers fill the street of Ansauville, where Gladys and Irene McIntyre, Muriel Turkington, and Stella Young serve up coffee and doughnuts. Signal Corps photo, April 8, 1918 (National Archives, photo no. 111-SC-10444).

treat so close to the frontlines. "Here surely is a study in Mob Psychology. The men eating cruellers have been busy killing other human beings for many months and their minds have been through the tortures of the damned but the sight of these women, takes their mind to the loved ones at home and they wander around in the mud with tear drops in their eyes and answer 'Yes Mam' and 'No Mam' like so many school children but would arise like wild men in an instant and almost tear asunder the man who dared to utter an oath in the presence of these ladies."[23]

About April 15, a section of 12 ambulances from the U.S. Special Sanitary Unit (SSU) 647 were attached to the 102nd Ambulance Company. The added Ford ambulances both increased the number of wounded and gassed who could be evacuated and anticipated the replacement of the 102nd Company's nimble Fords with the bigger GMC ambulances authorized for use by the AEF.[24]

SSU 647 had been created at Sandricourt, north of Paris, in the fall of 1917 from former volunteer drivers with the American Field Service and other units that were being superseded by the arrival of U.S. Ambulance Service companies from Allentown. The unit made several trips convoying Ford ambulances until it was ordered to Neufchâteau in February to work with Base Hospital 66. That was the extent of its service when it was ordered forward to Vignot on April 15. Immediately, a portion of the unit was ordered up to support the French division on the left, and another section of 12 was assigned to the 102nd Ambulance Company, which sent half of them forward to Mandres, "where a dressing station had been set up in an abandoned house at the Beaumont end of the village," wrote the unit's historian, Robert Bodfish. "The cars were lined up in the yard and the men utilized the second story of a nearby house for their quarters."[25]

The SSU drivers mostly covered the aid stations along the ridge to the west, from Rambaucourt to Bouconville, and at night they ventured down to the 102nd Infantry aid station at Seicheprey. "The road to Seicheprey was very narrow and it dipped sharply as it led into the destroyed town," remarked Bodfish. "Here the men found shell holes and evidence of war in plenty. In fact they were forced to shut off their motors at the aid station lest the Germans hear them."[26]

On the Division's left, the Germans tested the 104th Infantry with barrages and raids by *stosstruppen* (specialized assault forces) From April 10 through the 13.[27] The litter bearers and ambulances of the 101st and 103rd Ambulance Companies evacuated more than 200 wounded during the action.[28]

As he watched "miles and miles" of big French 155 mm. cannons going forward to the 103rd Field Artillery positions, and noted, "this section is honeycombed with all width of railroad and more are being built, leading to the front lines for the transportation of ammunition and heavy guns," Barlow remarked, "we imagine there is going to be SOME FIREWORKS soon," and in anticipation the hospitals in the rear sent forward "an army of litter bearers," surgeons, dressings, splints, and 1,500 units of anti-tetanus serum.[29]

Charles Johnson recounted that he and Frank Crump left the dugout where they were supposed to sleep that night to enter an officer's house, where they "took advantage of some beds there. It was at this time that a mustard gas shell landed over the roof and Private Crump was seriously gassed."[30]

"On the 20th there was a gas alarm at 4 A.M. followed by an attack on the 102nd Infantry at Seicheprey," wrote Barlow.[31] The German artillery placed a box barrage around the two companies of the 102nd Infantry holding the lines at Seicheprey to prevent supporting troops to advance. Then they attacked with specially trained *sturmtruppen* (storm troopers), flamethrowers, and *stosstruppen* to drive the Americans out of the trenches and seize prisoners. The outnumbered New Englanders fought fiercely and eventually retook their positions, but they would lose about 150 prisoners.[32]

During the intense fighting in the trenches and in the remains of Seicheprey, litter bearers were sent forward to evacuate the wounded. They ran across "Hell's Half Acre" next to "Dead Man's Curve" and took shelter in Beaumont, on the ridge above Seicheprey. When the shelling eased up slightly, they "made a wild dash between shells into the communication trench" that led downhill to Lieutenant Comfort's 102nd Infantry aid station in Seicheprey.[33]

The fighting continued as evacuation began. As Earle Radikin described it in the Sanitary Train history, "the route of conveying patients was through the communication trench back to Beaumont, which was the ambulance head. The trench was extremely narrow, knee deep with mud, and at various places it was levelled from concentrated fire upon it. The trench was also strewn with bodies." Radikin continued: "In carrying litter patients through this trench the hands of the men were torn by the sharp stones that projected from the walls, because of insufficient width, but they kept on. Some places were so narrow and caved in by the bombardment that in order to pass, it was necessary to lift the stretcher and patient above the trench, this being especially so when turning sharp corners, although this imperiled the life of the patient. On occasion a litter squad and patient were partially buried by the bursting of a shell on the parapet of the trench, but fortunately all escaped injury."[34]

In the beginning, ambulances were also sent down from Beaumont to Seicheprey to evacuate wounded. Herbert Beers told his mother: "I never thought I should see such exciting times. I got up to answer a call at 5 a. m., and from then until the next day I realized I was in a war. Gas shells and high explosives were coming over about as fast as the Boche could pull the trigger, I guess. Two pieces of shrapnel went through my ambulance and knocked the front tire off; it didn't hurt the tire any. I changed it and it has been on ever since. I was following one ambulance down into a town and a shell came along and pushed it clean off the road."[35]

Beers was following the SSU 647 ambulance driven by Leo McGuire.[36] Stan Glover of the Company was acting as McGuire's orderly, perhaps because Glover knew the roads. McGuire's ambulance was "flying like a bat out of the bad place" as they came down the hill to the aid station in embattled Seicheprey. But, "a shell struck right at its tail-board; the ambulance slewed round, its whole rear end gone, and rolled over upside down in the ditch. At the Seicheprey aid station, under command of Lieutenant Charles Comfort of the 102nd Infantry, Dr. Comfort, who happened to be watching it come, saw the driver and orderly come out of the wreck and started up the road to see if they were hurt. But the shells came nearer and nearer, and he had to abandon the road for the trench alongside. And when he got into view of the wrecked ambulance there was nobody there. They had beaten it up the road." The two made it back over the hill to the dressing station in Beaumont. Glover "asked the attendant there to look at his shoulder which 'felt bruised.'"

"'And get a move on,' said he, 'because I've got to get back.'"

"The slightest examination showed that he had a smashed clavicle. 'You for the hospital,' said the sergeant, and away he went, grumbling, in another ambulance."[37]

Two other ambulances were struck that day. In one of them Russell Drury was rounding Dead Man's Curve with Frederick Keller as orderly and four wounded soldiers in the back when a shell blew the ambulance off the road, killing two of the wounded men. "Keller pulled the two wounded doughboys out of the Ambulance and into a trench near the road but Drury received the only citation," remarked Barlow.[38]

Corporal Charles Boucher of the 102nd Infantry was severely wounded in the leg. He and a friend were carried on litters to the aid station, where they received morphine for their pain and a hot drink to allay shock. They lay joking through their pain when the friend suddenly died. Finally ready to evacuate him in the middle of a gas attack, the ambulance driver asked Boucher if he had a gas mask. "No

This is probably the remains of Russell Drury and Frederick Keller's ambulance, which was blown off the road by a shell at Dead Man's Curve on April 20, 1918. Two of the four wounded were killed in the blast. Keller rescued the other two, though Drury got all the credit. The trees in the distance stand along the road on the ridge, running from Beaumont to Flirey. Note the narrow-gauge railroad tracks in the foreground and the motorcycle with sidecar in the background. Supplies and field artillery are camouflaged by netting along the road. Signal Corps photo by Corporal Keen Polk, April 30, 1918 (National Archives, photo no. 111-SC-13371).

but for God's sake put yours on and, I will cover my head with my blanket," Boucher answered. "Dead Man's Curve was one *Hell of a Place*," he wrote, "but our good old Ford Ambulance plowed through the shell holes and bombardments and didn't let up till we arrived at the One Hundred and Second Field [Dressing] Station where I was given more shots, a cup of hot cocoa, and cigarettes."[39]

Promoted to wagoner on April 16, 1918, Curtis F. Banks would earn the nickname "Barney Oldfield," perhaps for being a fast driver like pioneering racecar driver and celebrity Berna "Barney" Oldfield. Four days after taking the wheel, Banks was gassed during the Company's evacuation of the wounded from Seicheprey. He would later be cited three times for bravery in action. In this 1919 photograph, he is back home and wears three service chevrons indicating 18 months in the zone of advance. Banks submitted this photograph with his Connecticut Soldiers' Questionnaire in 1920 (courtesy Connecticut State Archives).

The shelling continued after the Germans were driven out of Seicheprey, and the Mandres dressing station came under continuous fire. Sergeant Gerald Northrop and Cook Frank Doreski were both overcome by gas there, and by the end of the day drivers Curtis Banks and Russell Drury "were so badly gassed they had to give up" also, noted Barlow.[40] Leroy MacKinnon, who had been elevated to driver just five days before the battle, also was put out of action by gas. Robert MacDonald was riding as orderly on one of the SSU 647 ambulances when he was overcome by gas. At the Mandres dressing station, Ralph Carlton was overcome by gas. Corporal Ray Pomeroy was also evacuated for gas exposure. Litter-bearer Charles Johnson suffered heavy exposure to gas during his work. Evacuated, he would spend the rest of his military service in the hospital before being discharged with a 15 percent disability rating. Clayton Bell received such a dose of gas that he panicked and suffered from "shell shock." Several of the men of the Company who had been transferred to the 104th Ambulance Company also suffered gas "wounds."

When the shelling resumed around seven that evening and the dressing station was hit, Lieutenant Cobey decided to move the dressing station back to the Bois de Réhanne for the night, leaving the ambulances to make a longer run from the front.[41] Radikin wrote, "it required steady nerve on the part of the ambulance drivers who transported the personnel to the new station," where they arrived around midnight.[42] George Wright remarked: "Our company's boys worked like Trojans through the whole attack. I was busy loading and unloading ambulances and carrying patients steadily for 40 hours. Some work." He continued, "during the attack we were shelled out of our original dressing station. We had to abandon and set up our station a few kilometres back. It was terrible but we won. I'll tell you what the old New England boys are right there with the pluck."[43]

Sergeant Gerald C. Northrop was in charge of operations at the Mandres dressing station in early April 1918 and tried to time the German artillery in order to send out ambulances between shells. He was awarded a Croix de Guerre for exceptional bravery during the action at Seicheprey on April 20. In this photograph, probably taken in early 1919, he wears his Croix de Guerre and two service chevrons, indicating a year in the zone of advance (courtesy Le petit musée du Doughboy).

Ted Wall described what litter bearers experienced in such an action. "When a little scrap is on and shells are bursting all over without letting up; gas shells and high explosive, machine guns and that thunderous barrage fire; whistles going peep-peep; gas alarm signals and everything a regular bedlam; German artillery and our own barking back in defiance; wounded men groaning, etc., there is no time to even think but after it's all over is when you feel it. You start to feel hungry and tired and your eyes are all red from gas and smoke and your face looking haggard; then is when it's hellish."[44]

The day after the battle, Barlow wrote: "Our litter-bearers again worked all night in removing wounded near Seicheprey. Captain Durham was assigned to this Company as Lieut Gregory had to be sent to the hospital from exhaustion as did Captain Blair of the 104th Ambulance Company."[45] The 101st Ambulance Company litter bearers relieved those of the 102nd in the afternoon of the twenty-first.[46]

Barlow suggested that the 102nd Infantry "showed the Germans that although they had been outnumbered and it was really their first baptism of fire, they were units to be dealt with in a far more serious manner than the Germans evidently supposed."[47] George Wright put the Seicheprey action in patriotic words for his parents back home. "We are making a name, if I say it myself," he wrote. "Without blowing a bit, our division is doing great work. You know we had quite a sharp battle here at our sector. The Boches started it with a stiff barrage on the 20th of April at 3 a.m. They bombarded our front lines, in fact the whole area, front and back for five hours (Gee, some shells) and then they came 'over the top' and our boys were right there when they arrived." Wright put it simply: "The Fritzies managed to push our fellows out of a little village, but our boys came back strong and recaptured the town and sent the Huns back again without a foot's gain. And Fritz lost more men than we did, too. It was terribly wonderful."[48]

Sergeant John A. "Andy" Holzheimer began his ambulance company service with the Connecticut National Guard Company in 1913. Called back into service with the 102nd Ambulance Company in the summer of 1917, he was one of the most experienced members. In this postwar photograph he wears the Croix de Guerre he received for bravery during the action at Seicheprey on April 20, 1918. He would also be cited in orders for bravery in action. This 1919 photograph depicts him with his Croix de Guerre with two stars, his sergeant's chevrons and whistle on a chain, and three service chevrons and discharge stripe. Holzheimer submitted this photograph with his Connecticut Soldiers' Questionnaire in 1920 (courtesy Connecticut State Archives).

For days afterwards, the German artillery continued pounding the 26th Division positions. "There were three Ford Ambulances and a W.D. truck blown off the road at Hells-Corner, without much chance of getting them," commented Barlow on April 22. "The little Dinky railroad that was built at this point was blown to pieces. Gas shells thrown over into all towns within several miles of the front and the air seems never to be free from it."[49]

Ambulance driving had generally seemed like sport before the drivers got to the Toul Sector. Now, with high-explosive and gas shells flying at all hours, and the Germans targeting Dead Man's Curve, it became an ordeal. "Ambulances pass through several towns each 24 hours and at night the only way they see to drive is to remove the face piece of the gas-mask and leave only the clamp on their nose," commented Barlow. "This of course allows the eyes to be burned by gas but the air by being sucked up through the gas box is purified."[50] Whether or not their eyes were burning from gas, "all drivers not being able to use lights at night are developing a sixth sense, that of being able to see in the darkness," Barlow continued. "Each Ambulance has an orderly who, when not busy caring for the wounded in the car, must listen for the slightest noise ahead, such as the rattle of a chain, which might mean they were running into an escort wagon or other vehicle. An Ambulance is a very light car (we still have Fords with pressed paper tops)." At the same time, "roads are muddy and full of shell holes and the artillery flashes in all blind the eye so that those not used to this work have most vivid nightmares. Often the Artillery is near the highway and shoots over the traffic toward Germany and the concussion seems to almost blow the Ambulance off the road to say nothing of scaring a man half to death."[51]

Sentries guarding the roads at night provided another obstacle. Barlow recalled: "To get up to the lines at night in the Toul Sector, the Ambulance drivers had to have a pass word and also a check word and were often halted by a glistening bayonet, sometimes so suddenly that it took a minute or two before one could get their senses together and get both words out and roads usually open by day were cut off by barb wire entanglements at night. In some points this was done for weeks, the entanglements being removed just before daylight each morning."[52]

At the beginning of May, Barlow noted, "Martin Clarke is busy painting large Red Cross signs on all Ambulances."[53] However, it appeared that the red cross might be more target than shield. The Reverend Lusk told the people at home in Bridgeport: "The Germans shelled the ambulance deliberately. Your boys no longer wear these Red Cross insignias [sleeve brassards] … they are targets for the Germans to shoot at."[54] And Barlow remarked, "the Red Cross flag on the dressing station at Mandres had to be taken down as it seemed to be drawing fire from the enemy, but later we concluded they were aiming at some artillery to the rear at Mandres."[55]

It may have been at this time that each ambulance company also painted its distinctive insignia on its ambulances. Barlow did not mention a date, but he noted that the 102nd Ambulance Company chose a silver eagle and painted that on the sides of its GMC ambulances. The 101st Ambulance Company reflected its Massachusetts origins with two codfish. The 103rd had northern New England origins and painted a beanpot on its ambulances, and the 104th, from Rhode Island, identified its ambulances with a group of Narragansett Bay quahogs or hard-shell clams. With the ambulance companies increasingly working in coordination, this was a way to identify them at a glance while proclaiming their individuality.[56]

Behind the front, things settled down at the end of April. "We were paid," noted Barlow. "Many sent in subscriptions for the Stars and Stripes our AEF newspaper. Men are resting up as there is not much fighting."[57] The weekly military newspaper *The Stars and Stripes* had been established in 1861, during the Civil War, and resumed publication as an eight-page weekly in France on February 8, 1918. With articles by both soldiers and journalists, it was valued by the soldiers as the source for Army news. At Ménil-la-Tour and further behind the lines, Barlow was surprised to discover that "women storekeepers and others seem to think nothing of selling nude postcards."[58] He also noted, "a French woman comes through these towns selling eggs (also liquor)."[59]

Being temporarily settled, the men also indulged in a pet. "We now have a big bull dog for a mascot," Barlow had commented early in April. "He has been given the name of 'Pat.' It appears every unit is anxious to have a pet and swipes the first one found at large."[60]

They also sharpened their soldiers' humor. Clifton Fulton wrote home, noting that German Kaiser Wilhelm, or "William Hohenzollern is familiarly known as 'Billy' to the Potsdam gang," meaning the German administration in the city of

Potsdam where Kaiser Wilhelm lived. "But," said Fulton, "we are the boys that will put the 'ill' in 'Billy' and the 'dam' in Potsdam."[61]

There was also time for sports again. "Eddie McLaughlin boxed over in the outdoor arena," noted Barlow around May 10, and two weeks later, "Ed McLaughlin boxed four round draw with Jenson."[62] "The German balloons are always watching these towns but the men back at [Ménil] spend their leisure time playing ball in full view of the balloons," he added.[63] "I have been playing ball today, and enjoying myself in general," wrote Herbert Beers on May 1. "I think when the sun comes out and shines all day a lot of us fellows will have sun-stroke; it hasn't shone for over an hour at a time in the last three months. Mostly rain. It is probably all right, but I don't like it; nevertheless I am going strong and in 'goot' health. At this moment we are having regular April showers. James [Peck] and I have had some new pants issued to us and they are 'fine.' I have to stand up all the time for fear I will bust mine; can't fasten the three top buttons. James says he hopes he doesn't sneeze in his. I hope I don't. We washed the car yesterday and to-day shined it up with kerosene and oil; then we went back to camp and got it all mud. I suppose Father is plowing and doing all kinds of farm work. If he only had a farm over here, all he would have to do would be to let the Boche plough it up with shells."[64]

George Wright wrote his parents: "I am sitting on a bag of potatoes in one corner of the kitchen, all mixed up with the utensils trying to dry out my shoes. We've had rain for about two days. You know Frank Phillips is cook here now and I can do anything I want in the kitchen. Ordinarily, a private can't stick his nose inside the door of a kitchen. So I stand in here, while Frank is cooking."[65]

"When there was no scrapping at the front, why, we would start a fight of our own, to see who should have the Victrola, that the Graphophone people gave us," wrote Barlow to the Bridgeport Comfort Club. "There was surely a gift far greater than they knew, for it has even toned down men who were severely shell shocked. I understand this treatment is used extensively by the English."[66] "A shell burst near the Graphophone that was given to us and covered it with dirt so it is now entitled to a wound stripe," Barlow had written on April 23.[67]

The wound stripe was part of the AEF's effort to raise morale by giving soldiers visible symbols of their service. The wound stripe was a gold chevron issued for documented cases of wounding by bullet, shell, or gas and worn on the right lower sleeve.

The other service stripe issued to the AEF was a similar chevron, worn on the left lower sleeve, to mark each six months of service in the "zone of advance," or war zone in France. "Mother I have now put in over six months in the zone of advance and am sending you one of the service stripes, the like of which I proudly display on my left arm as I walk about, keeping that arm proudly showing," wrote Ted Wall at the end of May. "The gold chevron is for six months' service in the zone of advance or line of communication and there are few Yanks wearing it as yet."[68]

Mother's Day was May 12, and General Pershing had declared his wish that every soldier write home to his mother. Spencer Wills obliged: "My own Mother: Today, over here, is one of the most important days, if not the most important day, in the history of the overseas forces, as on this day every cog in this vast machinery is working overtime. No matter how important the battle or how strenuous the training, each soldier is thinking of his home, his mother, and has managed to write to her, telling her of his love—and the poor boys who have no mothers to write to are writing the next dearest one to them.

"From General Pershing down through all the branches of the army, and especially the noble Y.M.C.A. workers, they will all work till every letter is on its way tomorrow morning. That little phrase 'Mother's Letter' on the upper right hand corner of the envelope works wonders and will be sent ahead of other mail.

"Christmas and Easter is dedicated to our Savior, but on this day we who have mothers dedicate it to God, Christ and Mother, and it is equally as important, for nowhere can the spirit of God be brought down to us more fully than through our mother.

"And this blessed day, mother dear, I know you are thinking and perhaps worrying about your boy, but I also know that you are smiling bravely and can put away all fears for he is his mother's son, and rest assured that he will do nothing that would cause her a moment of sorrow or heartache.

"No matter what hardships I have to go through or where I am, I am holding you paramount in my thoughts, and with you in my mind I can go through those hardships and withstand all temptations for your sake.

"And so, mother, God bless you and keep you on this wonderful day, and if it is His will that we be separated, may He give you serenity and contentment throughout our separation. And if it be His will that this war shall continue, may He give us both health and strength to carry on whatever burdens ours will be."[69]

"The U.S. government is doing a great thing, sending letters from the soldiers special delivery for Mother's day, and I'll bet many a mother's heart has been made glad through it," wrote Ted Wall a few weeks later. "I know it is a grand and glorious feeling to get a letter from home because I just this minute received your loving letter. How my old heart beats when I see a letter for me from mother dear. I guess you will be overloaded with my letters this last few weeks, knowing a mother's heart yearns for news from France.

"I am now sitting at a table on which is placed a beautiful bouquet of wild flowers of France nestled in a polished .75 shell case, a veteran of Verdun. The Frenchmen make nice ornaments of them, and I hope to get hold of a couple when the war is over. I am enclosing lilies of the valley worn by a French lady yesterday, which was Joan of Arc day. How the flowers pervade the air with their intoxicating perfume. It makes one forget the cruel side of war, which we all hope will soon end. But we boys have the spirit of '76 with us and in realizing the conditions of war now and just how serious it is if allowed to continue, we are will to stand by and do our utmost in bringing peace to everybody.

"The good old U.S. commissary stores have such things as jam, chocolate, cigarettes, tooth paste, biscuits, etc., so that we are pretty well cared for. Of course when we first came over we couldn't get a thing, and we were the pioneers of this army and so paved the way. And how well we know it, too. We endured quite a big lump. Just wait till I am able to state my experiences. It will sound much better, and along with them some good laughs bribed by a good old cup of tea. We boys had chocolate, towels and soap from the good old Comfort club, and how we all appreciate their kindness to us, and we're thankful to say so. Here's luck to good old Bridgeport and the good old U.S.A., and before I blow this candle out I shall start right over and read your letter through again and dream of home."[70]

In the first week of May, clog-dancing James "Ezra" Garvin was badly injured when a heavy truck collided with his ambulance on the road. Carried to Evacuation Hospital 1 at Sébastopol near Toul, he was under care when he developed spinal meningitis. Antibiotics did not exist so there was little possible treatment other than trying to control his fever, and he quickly slipped away, dying on May 16 at age 23. At home he left his widow Katherine, with whom he had spent barely a week of marriage before joining the Company.[71] He was buried at Sebastopol, "in grave # 55," recorded Barlow.[72]

James S. "Ezra" Garvin was born in Toronto and graduated from Rutgers in 1914. He worked in finance but switched to managing his father's property in Connecticut. He joined the 1st Connecticut Ambulance Company in June 1916 and served on the Mexican border. Called back to serve in the 102nd Ambulance Company, he married his fiancée a few weeks before departing for France. A lively presence in the Company and known for his clog dancing, he was badly injured in a collision in early May 1918 and died of spinal meningitis at Evacuation Hospital 1 on May 16. His family submitted this photograph with his Connecticut Soldiers' Questionnaire in 1920 (courtesy Connecticut State Archives).

"All the medico's give you when you are sick or injured is C.C. pills or paint you with iodine and 'Paint it with Iodine' has become a byword," remarked Barlow in late May.[73] Like the infantry and other frontline troops, the ambulance companies and field hospitals had sick call in the morning after réveille. At sick call the doctors or noncommissioned medical staff took temperatures, looked down throats, and dispensed the ubiquitous C.C. pills, a combination of calomel (mercury chloride) and codeine (an opioid) that acted as a laxative, disinfectant, pain-reliever, and cough-reducer. And with their iodine swabs, they painted anything from swollen tonsils to cut fingers and blistered feet with this red disinfectant solution. The aim was to eliminate slackers and provide basic care for those who needed it. But some needed further care. "Goodnow was sent to the hospital with SOME cough," remarked Barlow in mid–April, and a month later Howard Davis was sent there with appendicitis.[74] Around May 10 Barlow noted, "Geer was sent to the hospital with a fever but Goodnow is back from hospital."[75]

In this sector, the soldiers found access to prostitutes, and—like the "heavy drinking" Barlow noted on April 18—this behavior could not be eliminated by punishment. "Prophylactic stations for every battalion," Barlow had commented after the action at Seicheprey. "Kept open night and day. Men compelled to report. These stations would be a Godsend to any city at any time."[76]

At the end of April Barlow had commented, "most of the men who volunteered for Trench Fever tests have returned."[77] However, after a week or so of duty some of them discovered why trench fever had been such a scourge on the British front. The intermittent fever, headache, and muscle pains returned and several of the men had to be sent back to the hospital to recuperate again.[78]

At the beginning of June, the influenza virus apparently brought over by American troops and immortalized as Spanish Flu had reached the 26th Division. "Quite a few have influenza, Ferris, and McGorty have been sent to the hospital and six others have been quarantined," reported Barlow.[79]

While relief from arduous duty might have appealed to some, the reality of life under medical care behind the lines was arduous in its own way. After his recovery from the mumps, ambulance driver G. Spencer Wills told his mother in early May: "At present I am at a casual camp awaiting transportation back to my company, as I have been pronounced physically fit. How I long to be back with the boys. You see, dear, I have been separated from them for over a month and I sure miss them.

"All we do here is lay around awaiting the mess call. No work to do, and I sure would like to get back in harness again.... Just missed Arthur Best by a day at this camp. He went out the day I came in. I told you in a former letter that he was in the hospital with pneumonia."[80]

"The weather is the finest at present but whether the weather is fine or not, I always feel the same as you know," Ted Wall told his mother at the end of May. "Of course a blue streak now and then happens with the best of men. I am not sleeping under ground just now; just finished after three months of it and guess we are entitled to a rest which we are on just now. Don't suppose the cooties will rest though. They are very famous in this world war though they like some people better than others and they surely are very much in love with me. No matter how I snub them they still hang around and keep me on the search all the time."[81]

To keep those cooties at bay, as much as it could be done in a frontline sector, the Company's disinfesting unit had arrived right behind the Division, so Barlow could report on April 5, "a big steam cootie machine is in use trying to rid the troops of vermin."[82] The problem of managing lice had not yet been addressed in an army-wide or Services of Supply plan, so each division developed its own approach. In the 26th Division, administrative staff decided to streamline the process by appointing one officer—Lieutenant Charles Sprague—as assistant sanitary inspector who would oversee bathing, disinfesting of clothing, and the issuance of new clothing as needed.[83]

As the central supply point behind the lines, Ménil-la-Tour was chosen as the site for a fixed bathing facility, and its operation was turned over to the Red Cross. It had a large tent with 40 showers that could accommodate as many as 1,500 men—or half a regiment—per day. After five days of duty in the trenches, an infantry battalion—about 1,000 men—would be withdrawn and sent back to a rest camp in the rear. From there, they were marched or carried in trucks to the bath house, where they stripped and handed over their blankets and clothing to be disinfested in a fixed Thresh steam unit while they passed through the showers. As they moved through the facility, noncommissioned officers scanned them for skin diseases—evidence of which earned them an immediate trip to the hospital—and the Division orthopedist inspected their feet and checked the fit of their boots. After the shower they were dosed with a 3-percent solution of cresol. Derived from coal tar, and having a distinctive odor, cresol could be an irritant to human skin, but it was an effective disinfectant. The clean and disinfected men were then issued fresh underwear and lined up to receive their freshly steamed and deloused uniforms. Fresh underwear, uniform pieces, and boots were issued to those who needed them.[84] The 102nd Ambulance Company was close enough to Ménil-la-Tour to use the large bath house.[85] But Barlow warned: "Be sure to secure underwear when taking a bath at Menil."[86]

Each of the two Thresh-Foden mobile units operated by members of the Company was assigned to cover one of the Division's brigades. One operated from a base at Aulnois-sous-Vertuzey on the left beyond Boucq and the other operated out of Ménil-la-Tour. They rumbled up to the reserve camps where showers had been set up and provided the same disinfesting service as at the central station. Each Thresh-Foden unit was accompanied by a three-ton truck filled with new uniforms to be issued as needed.[87]

One of Lieutenant Sprague's two Thresh-Foden disinfestors rolls into Raulecourt on June 6, 1918. This unit served the 52nd Brigade infantry regiments and machine gun battalion, and the field artillery on the left of the Division's line. Lieutenant Sprague would receive a citation for meritorious service when the unit came under fire at Raulecourt on June 8. Signal Corps photo by Private C.E. Painter (National Archives, photo no. 111-SC-14609).

Sergeant Cowie and Corporal Francolini did not shy away from moving their units close to the front. The one on the left (Number 502) ventured as far forward as Raulecourt, where it came under attack on June 8. Lieutenant Sprague was cited for meritorious service in this attack by German aircraft, apparently attracted by the warlike appearance of a "cootie machine."[88] The "delousing wagon" on the right visited the 101st Machine Gun Battalion at "the Swamp" at La Grand Harcourt, diagonally across the road from the 102nd Ambulance Company's position in the Bois de Réhanne, on April 19. It got all the way forward to Mandres, where the 103rd Field Artillery noted the visit of "the cootie machine" on June 2.[89]

One could not eradicate the body louse, and all those disinfested pieces of clothing would host a new population of lice soon enough, but the Division Medical Director was very satisfied with the operation. "Placing the whole system of bathing and dinfestation, together with the replacement of clothing for the division, under the control of one officer brought about a coordinated service and fine results," he wrote. "Even after other departments were given control or, rather, began to function in the front lines, the Medical Department still felt the weight of responsibility for failure and exercised its energy and interest through the assistant sanitary inspector who remained, really, if not technically, in charge."[90]

The Toul Sector also became the frontline training ground for the U.S. Army Air Service. Like the AFS ambulance drivers, a number of young Americans had gone to France to offer their service as aviators, serving in scattered units but also filling the ranks of the French La Fayette Escadrille, formed in 1916. Among them was the French/American adventurer Raoul Lufbery. Lufbery had grown up in France not knowing his American father. At age 21 he traveled to Wallingford, Connecticut, to find him, only to discover that his father had gone to France. Lufbery served in the U.S. Army and the French Foreign Legion and also became mechanic to a noted French aviator. With the outbreak of the war, he entered the French aviation service as a mechanic but was accepted for pilot training late in 1914. He was recruited into the La Fayette Escadrille in May 1916 and had 16 confirmed air victories when he was commissioned a major in the U.S. Army Air Service late in 1917. He would take command of the 94th Aero Squadron of the First Pursuit Group and bring the squadron to Toul to begin offensive operations on April 9, shortly after the 26th Division arrived in the Sector.[91]

Their presence encouraged the American ground troops. On May 16, Lieutenant Sprague wrote: "Imagine awakening in the morning to the sound of airplanes buzzing over our heads and in the distance to hear the sound of anti-aircraft guns being fired. In this case the airplanes were our own, going over to the German lines. Sometimes they fly low and we can wave to them. It seems good to know that American fliers are with us and believe me they are all right. As soon as a Boche plane appears they get right after him and he is lucky if he gets back."[92]

On May 19, Major Lufbery took off to attack a German reconnaissance plane at low altitude near Toul. When the German fired, Lufbery's plane caught fire and rolled over, and he apparently fell out, landing on a garden fence in the village of Maron.[93] He "was seen to come down out of the sky by many of this Company," wrote Barlow. "The air seems full of planes."[94]

Lufbery's death touched both American soldiers and their French counterparts, as well as civilians. Barlow recorded that Lufbery, "known as one of the best U.S. aviators and whose parents live at Wallingford, Connecticut, was buried at Toul and his grave was covered with the most beautiful flowers. Heaven only knows where they came from or if they could have been purchased for surely there are no flowers within miles of these towns."[95]

A few days later, on the evening of May 23, Lieutenant Sprague continued his appreciation of American pilots. "A Boche plane had just come over our lines and is directly over our heads. But never fear, our brave American aviators are after him and an air fight is on. You can hear the machine guns firing at each other. Our American fighters are wonderful, they carry the fight right to the Huns and as they battle in the night I know who will be successful. Just as I told you the Hun was driven off and brought down. There is no longer the peculiar sound of his motor, but instead I hear only the purring of our motors as the boys return ... here on our own front the American fliers go after the Hun everytime he comes over. God bless those brave boys, they are the finest and the best." Sprague concluded, "one decisive step has been taken towards victory for the Allies, we have the supremacy in the air. With the Americans fast coming in the Hun will be put out of business."[96]

But the Germans were not yet conceding the air. "The Boche planes fly over where Allied troops are at play and seem not to speed up or heed in any manner the shells that burst near them," Barlow noted on June 2. "They are said to be returning from bombing raids on the larger cities in the rear."[97]

With an increasing number of American soldiers moving toward the front lines in France, American entertainers made the trip over to demonstrate support and encourage morale through performances and interaction with the troops. As early as Mother's Day, May 12, Barlow recorded, "five American girls who are providing entertainments at the various camps visited the dressing station at Rehanne Woods and it sure does seem good to see a Gal from Gods Country."[98] He explained, "the camp over in the woods where entertainments are put on in an open air arena is called Camp L'Hermitage."[99]

Soon after, the Y.M.C.A. sent the four guitar-playing Herron Sisters on a tour through the divisions in May. "The [Herron] Sisters from the U.S.A. provided a dandy show for us," recorded Barlow on May 19, when they gave a performance at Camp L'Hermitage. "The crowd cheered so loud the enemy must have heard the noise."[100]

Only a few days later, the more famous Elsie Janis, a star of vaudeville, Broadway theater, and film, came around. An ardent supporter of the soldiers, she and her mother had arrived in France in early 1918 and were making a six-month visit to several divisions, where she told stories and gave lively renditions of popular songs. She spent a week in the sector, performing once or twice a day and even visiting, and firing, the 155 mm. guns of Battery B of the 103rd Field Artillery on May 24.[101]

Barlow reported: "Elsie Janis a well known young lady from the U.S.A. gave us a jim crackin out door entertainment. She is sure some live wire and was greatly cheered. She sure did cheer us up. I will wager the observers in German balloons even enjoyed her entertainment."[102]

Elsie Janis performs for the 101st Machine Gun Battalion at Camp L'Hermitage in the Bois de Réhanne on May 22, 1918. Stationed nearby, the 102nd Ambulance Company also attended one of her "jim crackin" shows here. Signal Corps photo by Private C.E. Painter (National Archives, photo no. 111-SC-14263).

Herbert Beers' friend Jesse Bailey was also a fan and told his wife: "Have seen Elsie Janis in her sketch of songs & stories twice and enjoyed her as we all did. You can easily imagine what one of America's best actresses seems like when we haven't seen a woman of any kind in so long. She had some corking stories and new songs, then ended by dancing with any candidates from the ranks who wished to be her partners."[103]

Elsie Janis herself wrote: "Gave my afternoon show up back of the lines in what is called a *rest camp*. I imagine it is so called because the mud is so deep that if you once step in it you *rest there*. The fellows had just come out of the line. The show was out of doors—the stage two tables 'wished' together. The boys seemed rather shocked to see me at first. I don't wear a uniform, and I'm the only girl I've met who does not. They were fine though. They gave me souvenirs they had picked up, pins, medals, German coins, etc." She continued, "bless their hearts! They are all cheery, and ready to do all they can. They like France, but they love America, and the slogan up here is 'Heaven, Hell or Hoboken by Christmas.'"[104]

Yet, while they were in France many of the men still wished to sightsee. From their deliveries, the ambulance drivers were familiar with the nearby city of Toul, but others were intrigued by the largely undamaged city and its 500-year-old Gothic cathedral and 200-year-old fortifications. "Passes are issued for day time visits to Toul," noted Barlow at the beginning of June. "All are interested in seeing the Cathedral with its towers shot away, the canal locks, the moat that surrounds the city walls with their prison like gateways and the beautiful public gardens."[105]

The regimental bands might perform as well. "The 101st Infantry band gave an outdoor concert and added 16 buglers to their band who have learned the many little tricks used by the French Military Bands," remarked Barlow. "This has greatly pleased the French." And Barlow himself had an affinity for the musicians. "The bandmen have to act as stretcher bearers when needed and plenty of work is found for them when their fighting units are in the lines," he commented. This included washing the socks of the infantrymen.[106]

Such recreation did not deter the Company from its work. "The dressing station at [Réhanne] Woods is in the front of a wooden barracks and men are on duty at all times," noted Barlow at the beginning of May.[107] Soon after he recorded, "92 patients were brought through our station at [Réhanne] Woods, all at night, mostly all were scabies cases."[108] That skin inflammation, caused by a burrowing mite, was especially common in the filthy trenches. Once the itching became unbearable, sometimes in very private places, the soldiers reported sick and were diagnosed at the dressing station and sent to the 103rd Field Hospital for a round of bathing and treatment with sulphur.[109]

Benjamin B. "Dynamite" Wyrtzen was an 18-year-old clerk when he enlisted in the Company on April 3, 1917. Here, he stands next to his Ford ambulance, which has one of the large red crosses painted by Martin Clarke at the end of April 1918. He wears a version of the American Field Service tunic, perhaps obtained from a member of SSU 647, and has his French M2 gas mask over his shoulder (courtesy Connecticut State Archives).

Even a routine ambulance ride to the dressing station could be eventful. "One of the S.S.U. Ambulances with four wounded fell into the ditch at [Réhanne] Woods but was soon pushed out again but boy how it was raining," Barlow noted in early May.[110]

Occasionally, enemy troops were captured or killed in small confrontations between the lines at night. Around May 10, "Bugler Flynn blew taps for several Bosche dead we had buried in the rain," recorded Barlow.[111] This touch of humanity toward an otherwise detested enemy suggested the men now felt themselves the equals of, if not superior to, the Germans. While neither side conducted major assaults in May, the daily sniping, artillery fire, and occasional night raids into the barbed wire entanglements between the lines still found victims. "Plenty of wounded coming through," Barlow noted in mid–May.[112]

With the shift of the front covered by the Division to the right beyond Flirey, "ten men were sent to [Bernécourt] with litter wagons. That is a two wheel cart to which a stretcher is swung," remarked Barlow later in May.[113] Designed by the French, these wheeled litters both smoothed the ride for the patient and eased the job of litter bearers where the terrain permitted their use. At Bernécourt, the litter bearers would serve as adjuncts to the ambulances as they could bring the wounded down the road from Flirey and the 101st Infantry aid station in the Bois de la Voisogne to Bernécourt, or possibly to the sorting or triage station at the 102nd Field Hospital once it moved forward to Minorville.[114]

With the Red Cross operating the bathing and disinfesting unit at Ménil-la-Tour, that service joined the Y.M.C.A. and Salvation Army in supporting the morale of the sanitary troops and the wounded. At the beginning of June, Barlow commented, "the Red Cross send cocoa up for men on duty at the dressing stations and for the wounded."[115]

Even at the Company's dressing station in the Bois de Réhanne, 10 kilometers

Under the supervision of Lieutenant Edward B. Sheehan, a battalion medical officer in the 101st Infantry (left), a litter bearer prepares to use his French wheeled litter to carry a head-wound case from the aid station in the Bois de la Voisognes (in the bunker at right), between Flirey and Bernecourt, to the nearest ambulance head or field hospital. The Company sent ten men with wheeled litters to this area at the end of May. Signal Corps photo by Lieutenant E.H. Cooper, May 31, 1918 (National Archives, photo no. 111-SC-14281).

(six miles) behind the lines, gas shells could be expected to fall without warning. "Gas masks are kept at the 'Alert' even when sleeping and some of the gas smells like ham," Barlow remarked.[116]

By litter and by ambulance, the stream of wounded men brought back from the lines continued. "Thirty-one wounded came through our dressing stations on the 26th," recorded Barlow, "52 came through on the 27th and 64 on the 28th. Every wound and injury imaginable."[117] A few days earlier, Barlow had described "a soldier so wounded by the bursting of a flare that the bandages covered the upper part of his body so that only his eyes could be seen." Barlow was amused that, "after a cigarette was held in the small hole over his mouth he said 'GEE It sure is a hot day.'"[118]

On May 29 he noted, "our records show 1300 wounded have been cared for and transported by this Company since April 1st," which makes an average of 22 men per day.[119] When he looked more closely at the figures on June 1, Barlow proclaimed, "the records show this Company transported 5190 wounded since January 1st. This is two thousand more than any other unit in the entire AEF." The ambulance companies of the 1st Division might have disputed the totals, but it was a clear indication that the 102nd Ambulance Company was among the most experienced ambulance units in the AEF.[120]

This busy dressing station would be wired for a telephone on June 18. "All stations have code name and use code conversation," remarked Barlow.[121] But he was feeling a lack of communication from Captain Johnston. "Our commander has made but one short visit to his boys working near the front," he would comment on June 20.[122]

On June 6, Barlow wrote, "all of our Ford Ambulances have been turned in and the new Ambulances were busy transporting 477 wounded in the last five days."[123] The new ambulances were the GMC Model 16 that the U.S. Army had developed in 1917 as its standard ambulance design. Even though production had continued at 50 ambulances a day, the process of shipping them to France and distributing them to the divisions there was complicated and took months. For the divisions in training, the smaller, more maneuverable Fords, issued as a temporary alternative, had been a fine training vehicle that got the drivers accustomed to managing their own vehicles and could carry them as close as possible to the wounded. However, the Army would have replaced them earlier, but even in April the supply of new ambulances was 40 percent below the number needed.[124]

Barlow had noted on May 17, "ten men were sent to St Nazaire for more Ambulances."[125] Ted Wall was one of these men. "Dearest Pa," he wrote, "how jolly glad I was to hear from you again and a long letter too. I was all bubbling over and had a smile on from ear to ear. I had a regular 'at home day' reading it, not once but three times. Your letter must have been a lucky jinx because just as I had finished it, our skipper came in and said that I was to go on a long journey after ambulances. And believe me Pa, it was some journey; from one side of France to the other and back again in automobiles. I saw some big towns and also beautiful cathedrals of which you will have heard about.... Words cannot express the grandeur. On the trip I met several very pretty girls, one of whom gave me her address. However, she has a fiancé, a French lieutenant. She took me over to her house, a swell affair, and her father brought out some beer and her mother came waltzing in with a bouquet of flowers. Well they kissed me when I said au revoir, even to the old man. Wow France is some affectionate country."[126]

The GMC ¾-ton Model 16AA was just what the Army wanted: rugged, simple, thoughtfully designed, and capable of carrying 8–12 men seated on folding side benches or four patients on litters with the benches folded down. The two upper litters were suspended from hooks and straps that kept them stable. Two 10-gallon tanks held a supply of water for patients, and side racks accommodated four folded litters. The four-cylinder, 30-horsepower engine drove the rear axle through a shaft and bevel-gear. The engine provided plenty of power, but a governor kept the maximum speed to 25 miles per hour. While the engine was still cranked to start and had spark and throttle levers at the steering wheel like the Ford, drivers would have to learn a new gear-shifting method. Unlike the Ford, the GMC's three forward and one reverse gear were controlled with a foot-pedal clutch and gear-shift lever. They would also have to adapt to its handling. With an 11-foot wheelbase, it was almost three feet longer, with a wider turning radius, than the Ford. Mechanic Harry Edes

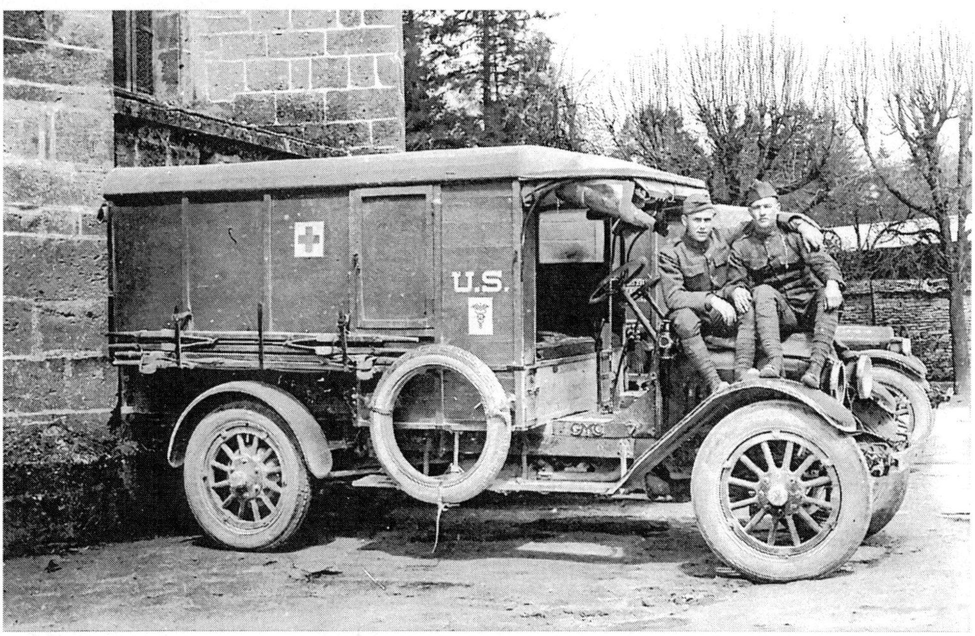

Parked on the ambulance line of an unidentified ambulance company in France, this GMC ambulance shows the details of the Company's new vehicles. The driver and orderly sitting on the hood give a sense of scale. Like Fords, the GMCs had wooden-spoke wheels. Unlike Fords, the GMCs had a gearshift lever for the three-speed transmission, in addition to the emergency brake lever. There is a box for emergency supplies under the orderly's portion of the seat. Racks accommodate two folded litters on each side. This ambulance has a damaged headlight (which would not be used anywhere near the front) and sidelights, which served as convenient hangers for gas masks and helmets. The top is waterproofed canvas duck. The cab has side and front curtains with celluloid windows for possible use in bad weather, and the patient compartment has a rolled curtain at the rear and small side doors for ventilation or access. French real photo postcard (author's collection).

could learn the details of maintaining the new ambulances through the Sanitary Train mechanics who had already learned to service the train's GMC trucks.[127]

After the German assault on Seicheprey in April, the 51st Brigade began to plan for a similar offensive raid on the German line. As Barlow described, on May 30: "The 101st Infantry made their famous 'Million Dollar' raid for which they had drilled for many weeks in trenches supposed to be the same as those occupied at this point by the enemy, but the enemy must have found out the plan for although they were armed with all sorts of clubs, hand grenades etc. they found only one young German boy to capture and he had apparently been left to walk along throwing up a flare now and then to make it appear the trenches were occupied. This boy was about 16 years of age and was given the name of the 'Lamp Lighter.'"[128]

The dash into the German lines was preceded by a barrage of high-explosive and gas shells. When the infantrymen charged through the German trenches they did not notice the residual gas. As Barlow described, "the doughboys were singing as they hiked back from their raid, but soon the gas started working upon them and our Ambulances were kept busy going in all directions, finding them almost dead in the roads, gutters, woods and fields or where ever they had been overcome."[129]

The recent shift to the bigger GMC ambulances proved timely for this operation. "We now have large G.M.C. Ambulances that will hold four stretcher patients or about 12 wounded if they are able to sit up," remarked Barlow. "With these Ambulances we found 250 gassed men and transported them to hospitals at Toul."[130]

Now that the 102nd Ambulance Company was driving GMC ambulances, it no longer served the advanced aid stations, leaving that work to the Fords of SSU 647. On June 19, Tod Gillett of SSU 647 was making a run under fire from the unit's depot at Beaumont toward Flirey with Charles "Dud" Mills of the Company as his orderly. On the return a shell exploded under the right front, lightly wounding Mills but mortally wounding Gillett and one of the wounded in the rear. They were within sight of Beaumont, and several members of SSU 647 scrambled up the roadside ditch under fire to save whoever they could, but Gillett was gone.[131]

As Major Frederic Adams later told it, Mills was struck in the head by shrapnel, but concentrated on dressing Gillett's and the surviving soldier's wounds. Back at Beaumont, he was heading out for another load of wounded, without reporting himself injured, when an officer asked where the blood on his head came from. "I guess I got it from one of the other boys," he answered, but upon inspection he was declared wounded and loaded on the next ambulance for the hospital. He would spend a month at Base Hospital 18 in Bazoilles.[132] Barlow noted Mills' "fifteen stitch scalp wound," remarking that he "showed wonderful nerve."[133]

Two months of service together had bonded the units, and the 102nd Ambulance Company "sent us a note of sympathy that meant much in cementing our already strong friendship for them," remembered the SSU 647 historian Robert Bodfish.[134] Gillett's funeral took place the next afternoon. "The section, with the 102nd Ambulance Company as the guard of honor, marched at half step while an ambulance bore the body to the military cemetery at Ménil la Tour," wrote Bodfish. "The Episcopal service and the fired salutes were the last visible homage to Tod Gillett."[135]

In a sure sign that change was coming, Barlow noted around the first day of

Orderly Charles D. "Dud" Mills (left) and Corporal Ray E. "Pinaud" Pomeroy pose in a Ford ambulance at Ansauville, April 1918. A 33-year-old clerk, Mills was one of the Company's first enlistees and had been trained at Fort Oglethorpe before being assigned as orderly. Pomeroy was a 22-year-old car salesman when he enlisted a few days after Mills and had also been trained at Fort Oglethorpe. He would be gassed at Seicheprey on April 20. Mills received a head wound while riding as orderly with Tod Gillett of SSU 647 on June 19, when a shell struck the ambulance and killed Gillett. Mills would be cited for bravery in attending to Gillett and the other wounded soldier. Notice the gas-mask bags and helmet hanging on the side lamp. Photo by Merritt Learned, 102nd Infantry (courtesy Connecticut State Archives).

summer, "thirty strange officers are inspecting this area. All hope to be relieved. Anyway we hope the doughboys will be."[136] This was the first indication that the 82nd Division was preparing to replace the 26th Division in the Toul Sector. A few days later, as the 82nd Division moved in, Barlow remarked: "Our Company has assembled at [Ménil]-la-Tour and are all ready to move and it is a case of find your own billet. Most all are in a hay loft."[137]

Then, on June 28, GMC trucks carried the Company to the village of Domgermain, beyond Toul. "Most of the old stone houses assigned as billets were found to be so full of vermin that most of the Company pitched pup tents," commented Barlow. And that night, he continued, "the Ambulance men were routed out at midnight and started on a long trip but no one knows where."[138]

7

Forward from Belleau

July 1918

The question of where the 26th Division was headed remained unanswered for several days. On July 1, most of the Division's sanitary units—including the ambulances after all—hiked back to the railroad yard at Toul and clambered into boxcars "marked 8 cheveaux and 40 homme," noted Barlow. "We travelled all night."[1] As they slept, the train rattled south up the valley of the Meuse through Neufchâteau, then west and north up the valley of the Marne. The next day the men had little to do but eat their travel rations and watch as it continued through Joinville before taking the line west through Wassy and Brienne-le-Château to Troyes in the valley of the Seine, where it switched to the main line to Paris. "Scenery is beautiful and people seem glad to see us and wonder at the men being so young," remarked Barlow. Located so far behind the front lines, and never subjected to bombardment or occupation, "these towns are more clean than those we have been seeing," Barlow noted.[2]

By late afternoon of July 2 the train had reached Bondy, in the northeast outskirts of Paris. "Rumors are that we are to parade in Paris on July 4th," recorded Barlow. "Row de-dow, We shall see?"[3] That rumor still had currency on July 3 as they sat in the rail yard within sight of the Eiffel Tower.

Back on June 12, sergeants Holzheimer and Northrop, and ambulance drivers Drury and Wilcox, had been awarded the French Croix de Guerre for extreme bravery on April 20 during the Seicheprey action. The Croix de Guerre had been created in 1915 to recognize acts of heroism. By war's end about 66 men in the Division would receive the Croix de Guerre, but at this stage of the war it was still rare. Barlow would later joke that, here on the outskirts of Paris, "Wilcox, Northrop, Drury and Holzheimer were strutting around like pouter pigeons, so the people could see their Croix de Guerres."[4]

But then the train switched to another track and headed 15 miles east to Trilport. When they were ordered off the train, they mixed with a contingent of U.S. Marines, who were headed from the battlelines to Paris, where they actually would march in the 4th of July parade there.[5] "It was midnight and trucks took us to Villeroy, leaving us at a big farm," continued Barlow. "It was a case of find your own home. Most men were so tired they either crawled into some ox-carts or slept on the ground with their packs for a pillow."[6]

The men may now have comprehended that they were headed for a new battle front, where they would replace the Marines they had just met. The German spring offensive had begun on March 21, just as the Division left the Chemin des Dames, and had continued while the Division held the line in the Toul Sector. The Germans aimed to capture or so-threaten Paris that the Allies would negotiate an end to the war before the AEF's two million men arrived in France. When the 1st Division left the Toul Sector as the 26th Division arrived, it was soon sent to the Cantigny Sector, north of Soissons to reinforce the French there. Late in May the Germans had broken through the French lines above Reims and pushed south to the Marne and then west toward Paris. That advance was stalled on a line running south from Soissons to Château-Thierry on the Marne. Here they were just 95 kilometers (59 miles) from Paris. As the Germans organized a move west from Château-Thierry, the U.S. 2nd Division joined the French Sixth Army and entered the lines on June 1. On June 6, the 4th Marine Brigade attacked into Belleau Wood. It took 20 days of fierce fighting to finally clear the woods of German troops, who withdrew to a line just east of the wood. Having suffered almost 10,000 casualties, including 1,900 deaths, the 2nd Division was in need of relief. The 26th was slated to take its place in the line, which ran west from Château-Thierry to Vaux, then northwest through Bouresches and along the east side of Belleau Wood to the villages of Belleau and Torcy. However, with a German attack expected, the 26th Division would remain in support until it took command of the sector on July 10.[7]

On the 4th of July, the Company "left Villeroy by trucks and passed through Trilport, Meaux, Saacy, crossed the Marne River and into the small town of Mery-sur-Marne," noted Barlow. "All chased down to the river for a swim but were soon chased out by the Gendarmes and later informed by them that there were barbwire entanglements, many dead horses and men, just below the surface of the water." Barlow continued, "we are billeted in homes just vacated by the fleeing French and we enjoyed the pianos, beds, chinaware and even some stew left in the kettle."[8]

The next day, noted Barlow, "the enemy must have noticed this movement of troops for it shelled this town, but we were on the move again and stopped at Bézu-le-Guéry and were billeted in some shelled houses and barns. The town is very dirty. We are relieving the 2nd Division."[9] Bézu-le-Guéry was uphill from the Marne and about eight kilometers (five miles) behind the lines. During the 2nd Division's time there it had been heavily damaged by artillery.

At Bézu-le-Guéry they briefly benefited from the flight of the residents. "We are enjoying the fresh vegetables left in the gardens by civilians who had to flee for their lives. Many odd sights are seen in this movement of civilians to the rear." The Company even corralled an abandoned cow and had fresh milk for a few days.[10]

Even as the infantry and artillery were moving into the positions held by the 2nd Division, the sanitary units set up alongside the 2nd Division field hospital and ambulance companies. The 101st and 102nd Ambulance Companies both had their headquarters at Bézu-le-Guéry, alongside a sorting or triage hospital set up by the 102nd Field Hospital. The 102nd Ambulance Company had a dressing station in the ruined church at the head of the street, but it also set up an advanced dressing station at La Voie du Châtel, about five kilometers forward, behind the 52nd Brigade on the left. The 103rd Ambulance Company dressing station covered the right at

Villiers-sur-Marne, behind the 51st Brigade, and the 104th Ambulance Company operated a dressing station at the Ventillet Farm.[11]

Barlow remembered that, during this time, "Fred Keller motored up to the dressing station at [Bézu-le-Guéry] with two wounded men in the rear seat of an old Ford Touring car with three flat tires and Fred without a helmet or cap. No one seemed to know where he had found the 'Ambulance' or ever saw it after that."[12]

The ambulance drivers had to memorize several routes as they evacuated the sick and wounded from Bézu-le-Guéry. Back down along the Marne, the 101st and 104th Field Hospitals operated a hospital for slightly sick, slightly wounded, or gassed patients at Luzancy. At the next downstream bend in the Marne, the 103rd Field Hospital had surgical teams to attend to the severely wounded, assisted by a group of female nurses, in a large convent at La Ferté-sous-Jouarre. From there, the wounded would be carried about ten miles south to Evacuation Hospital 7 at Château Montanglaust, near Coulommiers.[13]

The drivers were busy, but the litter bearers had little work as the Division settled in. Sixteen of them resumed the role of "medical engineers" and were transferred to the 102nd Field Hospital for several days to help clean up the town.[14] Evidence of the 2nd Division's hard fighting was all around. "There are eight horribly mangled marines over in the shed used as a morgue, at the edge of town," noted Barlow.[15] The men unloading ambulances and working with the wounded at the dressing station suffered the most. "Many have gas burns on their bodies just from handling the clothes of gassed men," he remarked.[16]

On July 10, the enlisted men gathered to meet. They had discovered that Lieutenant Sprague had received a $100 check from the women of the Bridgeport Comfort Club and had sent it on to Captain Johnston three weeks earlier. Johnston had never passed the money on to the men it was intended for. The men concluded that they needed a direct connection to the club.[17]

"There was a double rainbow in the sky this evening and we celebrated by forming the Foreign Chapter of the Bridgeport Comfort Club," joked Barlow. The men elected Corporal Frank Deutsch as president and Sergeant Robert Stewart as vice president. Sergeant Barlow was elected as secretary and treasurer and would soon begin turning his daily notes on the Company's activities into humorous letters home to the club in Bridgeport.[18]

Now that they had an organization and funds on hand, members of the Company decided how to spend some of their money. At the end of March, the soldiers' weekly newspaper, *The Stars and Stripes,* had challenged the men: "Take as Your Mascot a French War Orphan." It was estimated that about 200,000 French children had lost one or both parents to the war, and organizations including the Red Cross were underwriting their care in orphanages across France. For 500 Francs a year, or $87.72, a unit could sponsor a child. "To the elder world we are still an untried Army," *The Stars and Stripes* remarked. "But the youth of France has not suspended judgment. They know us, understand us, trust us. We are their ideals and their idols—everything a man and a soldier ought to be. And now we have a chance to do something for them."[19] Secretary Barlow recorded: "We had voted to spend 1000 francs in the adoption of two French orphans for the duration of the War. These children are made known through the efforts of the Red Cross and the Stars and Stripes. We do not of course have the care of them with us but money is paid through the Red Cross for their care."[20]

The men "also voted to spend 80 francs [$14] in sending five copies of the Stars and Stripes our AEF newspaper, to the Bridgeport Comfort Club." Having addressed the families at home, they turned to a more pressing issue, voting "to spend 200 francs [$35] for some extra food."[21] Barlow specified to the Bridgeport club that they were voting on the use of the mess funds that the club was contributing to. They had agreed to purchase oranges, tomatoes, lemons cauliflower, radishes, a record book, and some needles for their precious Victrola. And for a big meal they purchased baking powder, a case of canned pears, and a case of canned corn.[22] But that did not turn out as they planned. "We were all set for some big eats and the rations did not arrive until midnight."[23]

During its time in the sector, the 2nd Division's ambulance companies had been supported by SSU 502. That unit had been formed at Camp Crane at Allentown in June 1917 and had finally sailed for France in January 1918. After assembling its ambulances at the depot in St. Nazaire it had joined the 2nd Division early in June. Now, as the 26th Division took over for the 2nd, SSU 502 was ordered to remain in the sector with its 20 Ford ambulances. "We have 45 S.S.U. men attached to our Company," noted Barlow on July 10. "They are a fine group of men. The only thing is, we can draw no extra rations for them as yet, but who would not share a can of corned willie with a Buddy."[24]

In this new sector, food was still a concern, as Barlow noted the next day. "Our truck has to go ten kilometers to the rear for each days rations and one of the things brought back are the large round loaves of French bread."[25] As the French holiday of Bastille Day approached, Barlow noted, "the S.S.U Unit now assigned to work with us, donated 70 francs for their share of some extra food for the 14th which in this Country is known as Bastille Day and celebrated as a legal holiday similar to our 4th of July."[26]

The day after Bastille Day, the Germans attacked again, making a two-pronged drive toward the Marne. To the east of Rheims, the French blocked the eastern prong, while the 3rd U.S. Division earned its nickname, "Rock of the Marne," by stalling the German crossing of the river east of Château-Thierry. Even the 26th Division's 51st Brigade had to repel a small attack near Vaux on July 15. This final German advance of the war ended on July 17.[27]

About July 16, the Company moved its dressing station forward from Bézu-le-Guéry to Paris Farm at a crossroads on the Paris-Metz Road near Lucy-le-Bocage, about four kilometers (two and a half miles) behind the center of the Division's line. The 101st Ambulance Company then took over the evacuation of wounded from Bézu-le-Guéry. When it moved forward, the 102nd Ambulance Company left a sergeant behind to show the 101st drivers the routes to the hospitals at Luzancy, La Ferté-sous-Jouarre, and Coulommiers.[28]

At Paris Farm, Barlow remarked: "Enemy observation balloons are watching all the time and no fires must be started, blankets are placed over the windows and candles lighted at night. The men are so worn out that no one seems to sleep. During the day those off duty take a bath in a hog scalding kettle in the farm yard."[29]

In a short story he wrote after the war, Earle Radikin described the interior of the dressing station: "Under the white glare of carbide lamps, doctors and orderlies worked over the endless stream of the wounded. Faces drawn by fatigue, eyes heavy from the loss of sleep they worked mechanically and silently. The wounded men clenched their teeth and puffed cigarettes. They too were silent."[30]

In Radikin's telling, even the GMC ambulances, which were designed to carry between four and twelve passengers, were overloaded by the stream of wounded. "He came back from Vaux with sixteen patients," he wrote. "Four litters in back and the other twelve draped on the mud guard, running boards, the seat and the back step. Another trip and he carried nineteen."[31]

As the Division prepared for action, Division surgeon Porter circulated the code words for communicating by telephone about sanitary matters. So, a request to send litter bearers to a battalion aid station would be "Send Slat to Pup," and to send an ambulance to the dressing station would be "Send Dog to Bid." A request from a dressing station for more dressings and anti-tetanus serum would be "Send Pad and Min to Bid."[32]

"On July 17th, after we had cared for more than 2,000 men in ten days, nothing seemed to shout that there was going to be something doing—'toot sweet,'" remarked Earle Radikin in the Sanitary Train history. But the French had drawn up offensive plans to begin on July 18—though orders did not reach the Division until the evening of the 17th. On the left, the 52nd Brigade would advance north out of Belleau Wood and seize the villages of Torcy, Belleau, and Givry as the French on their left seized the commanding Hill 193 behind the towns. Then the Brigade would pivot to the right and advance east in line with the 51st Brigade, which would take the village of Bouresches. The Division would then fight to the east, in concert with the French on either flank, driving the Germans back from the salient around Château-Thierry.[33]

The French divisions on the left were equipped with the new Renault FT tank, a small two-man armored, tracked vehicle that had entered service at the end of May. Just 16 feet long, and carrying either a machine gun or a small cannon in its turret, it was maneuverable and well suited to the open-field fighting expected during the advance. "Crump and Ferris they both wanted to transfer, soon as they saw those tanks," joked Barlow, "but when they found out they were like a motorcycle, no reverse, well there was a horse of another color."[34]

To be prepared for the attack, the 104th Ambulance Company was ordered to move up to La Voie du Châtel and help the 102nd Ambulance Company operate the advance dressing station there. "It was the darkest, rainiest night in the world and practically all roads were being shelled," wrote Earle Radikin in the Sanitary Train history. "But the company hiked on, in column of twos, with 100 yards between each pair. At two o'clock on the morning of July 18th the station was all ready for work and it wasn't long before their work began."[35]

The attack out of Belleau Wood by the 103rd Infantry against Torcy was scheduled for 4:35 a.m. on July 18, to be followed by the 104th Infantry's assault on Belleau. "At 4:35 o'clock that morning, the zero hour, Allied artillery commenced a smothering fire on enemy position, which told us that the 2nd Battle of the Marne was about to be fought," wrote Earle Radikin. "Almost exactly an hour later patients began to arrive at the dressing station and from that time on there was little rest for litter bearers or for surgeons and assistants."[36]

Litter bearers from all the units assisted the regimental litter bearers in getting the wounded off the field and back to the battalion aid stations in Belleau Wood. From there they carried them to the "Ambulance Head," which that day was located in a culvert under the road between Belleau Wood and Lucy-le-Bocage. "Certain points of the route traversed by the litter bearers from the battalion aid to the ambulance head were under enemy observation and practically all the area between these two points was under shell-fire," remarked Earle Radikin in the Sanitary Train history. "Innumerable were the acts of heroism performed by the litter bearers while carrying patients under heavy bombardment. Often times the shelling was so heavy that in order to protect the patient from further injury they were placed behind large rocks and mounds of sand until the shelling abated sufficiently to allow the litter bearers to proceed with their patients to the ambulance head."[37]

From the culvert near Lucy, ambulances carried the wounded to the dressing station at La Voie du Châtel. From there, they were taken back to the 102nd Field Hospital triage station in Bézu-le-Guéry. By the end of the day, the litter bearers, ambulances, and dressing station had handled 1,648 cases.[38]

In previous sectors, the lines had been fixed and the aid stations generally maintained their locations. Now, as the Division began its assault, locations would change and the ambulance companies had to be updated on the new aid station positions. Earle Radikin described how a driver might be detailed as liaison. "'Here's the dope on the infantry advance. Locate the new aid stations and report back as quickly as possible. Here's something to help you keep going,'" said the liaison lieutenant as he handed over a bottle of cognac in Radikin's fictionalized account. "No one knows beforehand where the new station will be located," continued Radikin. "If the objective is a town it will probably be set up in a house or dugout. But the objective may be a road, a river, any kind of landmark. Then the surgeon chooses some sheltered spot. It may be the friendly side of a hill, a culvert, or it may be necessary to dig. The liaison ambulance locates these stations and informs the officer known as the director of ambulance companies. Prompt evacuation follows."[39]

The Company's Lieutenant Robert Durham was acting as the liaison and transportation officer for the Division's ambulances.[40] With the ambulances all in use at the front, he established a "Provisional Truck Company" to use the Sanitary Train's 5-ton GMC trucks as ambulances to evacuate the slightly wounded from the field hospitals in Luzancy.[41] Barlow speculated that a 5-ton truck, with its solid tires, "must be a rough ride for those with fractured limbs."[42]

The French were delayed in seizing Hill 193, so the advance did not continue until July 20. That day, with Torcy and Belleau now clear—though still under fire—Lieutenant Durham took his 5-ton trucks forward from La Voie du Châtel to secure the wounded who had been stranded there.[43] Among them were about 30 men who had spent the previous two days in an aid station in a wine cellar in Belleau under the care of Herbert Beers' friend Jesse Bailey of the 103rd Machine Gun Battalion.[44]

The renewed advance on July 20 coincided with the German plan to begin a

Lieutenant Robert B. "Bull" Durham's five-ton trucks of the Sanitary Train serve as evacuation ambulances at Belleau, July 22, 1918. The town had been largely destroyed, but many wounded survived in cellar aid stations. Notice that each truck is equipped with a red cross guidon. Signal Corps photo by Sergeant A.C. Duff (National Archives, photo no. 111-SC-16368).

staged retreat to more defensible ground. As they pulled back, they continued to defend the woodlots and villages with machine guns and to shower the French and American divisions with gas and high-explosive artillery shells.[45] That day, Barlow counted 333 wounded coming through the dressing station between four and eleven, "but all the wounded seem to be enthused over the Allies drive."[46]

With the front moving forward, the dressing station relocated again on July 22. "The Artillery is pounding away and the Doughboys can be seen advancing through the wheat fields, shells are bursting all around and surely this is a nervy piece of work, setting up a dressing station in full view of the enemy and on a line with the advancing Infantry," remarked Barlow.[47]

On the gently rolling plain, with scattered woods among the wheatfields, walled farmyards, with stone farmhouses and barns, were scattered along the roads and across the fields. But the bucolic scene had been turned into a wasteland of war. "Dead horses and cattle can be seen in all nearby fields and roads," remarked Barlow. "Airplanes are shot down, German wicker work baskets used by the enemy as shell covers are piled high by the roadsides as the enemy was in this farm house this morning. We dare not drink the water nor touch or remove anything for it may be connected with a bomb."[48]

At Farsoy Farm, "the farm house and barns are enclosed by a high wall with many holes already through it," noted Barlow. "In the center of the court yard is

The Thomas splint was one of the lifesaving devices of World War I. Designed in different versions to stabilize a badly fractured leg or arm, it prevented movement and likely arterial and nerve damage. Thomas splints were generally applied at aid stations, or possibly dressing stations, but ambulance company men were also taught to apply them. Here, a corporal shows two members of the 117th Sanitary Train of the 42nd Division how to use a Thomas leg splint at Bertrichamps on April 26, 1918. The splint is an iron frame with a padded head that rests in the wounded man's crotch. A tape or bandage secured to the soldier's boot is attached to the far end of the splint and twisted to apply tension until the fracture is aligned. Tape and safety pins are then used to secure the leg (or arm) until the patient can be delivered to the dressing station or field hospital. According to the 102nd Infantry supply list, eight Thomas leg splints and four arm splints would be on hand, in addition to a variety of wood splints and flexible wire splints. Notice that the men are wearing their medical belts and their packs with rolled blankets. Signal Corps photo by Sergeant C.H. White (National Archives, photo no. 111-SC-12295).

a muck hole. The wounded who are able to walk are coming in droves."[49] To dress their wounds, the 102nd, 103rd, and 104th ambulance companies worked together in eight-hour shifts. In its first 18 hours, the dressing station handled 1,280 patients. To evacuate them, Captain Johnston was given command of all the ambulances.[50]

In his Sanitary Train history, Earle Radikin singled out the work of the Division's litter bearers. "To the litter bearers undoubtedly the highest praise is due, for they risked more than any others," he wrote. "During these days when our line was constantly advancing—straight into the face of Machine Guns—our men followed unhesitatingly out into the wheat fields targets for machine guns and snipers who little respected the Geneva Cross on their arms, dressing wounded and bearing them to the rear."[51] Among the casualties was Private Ernest Sherman of the Sanitary Detachment of the 104th Infantry, who had been assigned to the Company in the spring. "Sherman transferred from this Company only last week [and] was killed in action with the Infantry when working as a first aid man," noted Barlow. "We seem to have our men only well trained in first aid work when they are transferred."[52]

But there were also moments of dark humor. "The stretcher bearers were bringing in a wounded man at Château Thierry when a shell burst close by and although he was seriously wounded, he became so excited that he jumped from the stretcher and ran away," related Barlow.[53]

The 101st Engineers were planning to use Farsoy Farm as regimental headquarters but moved on when they found the dressing station in operation there. "No one was sorry, for the scenes in and near the dressing station were hardly cheerful ones," noted the engineers' historian. "The wounded were lying all around, waiting their turn. On a crude bench by the light of candles the surgeons were applying the temporary dressings before sending the men back to hospitals farther in the rear."[54]

In his Sanitary Train history, Driver Earle Radikin described the operation: "Immediately upon their arrival at the dressing station at Farsoy Farm every patient who was strong enough was given cigarettes and hot chocolate which was furnished by the American Red Cross." He continued: "After having their wounds treated, the patients were taken from the operating room into the open barn yard where they

Philip O. Palmstrom of the 101st Engineers sketched the Farsoy Farm dressing station. Wounded men on litters fill the walled farmyard waiting for an ambulance to take them back to the field hospitals while the officers and men work furiously to provide care. Palmstrom did not include the shell-shocked, for whom there was no immediate treatment other than perhaps a dose of morphine (*History of the 101st United States Engineers, American Expeditionary Forces, 1917–1918–1919* [Cambridge, MA: Regimental Committee, 1926], 208).

were lined up on litters ready to be evacuated to the rear. During our stay at that station we evacuated and cared for more than twelve hundred patients."[55]

Barlow soon felt overwhelmed by the flow of wounded men. "The men are coming in faster than they can be removed and 70 wounded are on stretchers in the yard, with the most horrible wounds.

"Oh God we shall never forget this scene. Not hardly a moan or a groan from anyone but its just Give me a butt, will you Buddy? Or How did Bill Make Out? And Did Jack get it bad? And then once in a while you might meet one from the old home town and he would beg in a whisper not to tell his mother or else ask you to write her that he was all right."[56]

Under the constant rain of machine-gun bullets and gas shells on the open plain, more men than usual panicked and lost their nerve. Barlow could commiserate: "The shell shocked men are most pathetic, as they duck and moan as the shells scream overhead. Surely they must not be condemned for no soldiers have ever been called up to withstand such shocks to the nervous system and it is a wonder they are not all shell shocked."[57] Some of those who succumbed to shell shock may have been among the many replacement troops in Companies B and D of the 102nd Infantry. These were drafted men, some of whom had not been trained to handle a rifle, and who had only landed in France on July 4. Less than three weeks later they were advancing in the open fields against machine guns and mustard-gas shells.[58]

The historian of the 101st Engineers had noticed the shell-shocked men. "In the courtyard of the farm the shell-shocked were turned loose. There was nothing else to do with them, for there was insufficient room on the 'White' ambulances, which carried the wounded back to the hospitals. It was pitiful to watch the shell-shocked; big husky men who but a short time before had charged onward across the fields of wheat, but who now sat gibbering to themselves or lay moaning on the ground, their arms and legs twitching and jumping as if they had St. Vitus' dance."[59]

Even ambulance drivers occasionally succumbed to shell shock. In his short story, which captures the soldiers' language, Earle Radikin described his protagonist being awakened after 24 hours on duty and one hour of sleep. "Come to, wagoner. You got to go out again," said the sergeant, modeled on Robert "Big Boy" Stewart. "I hate to do it, Jake, old kid but you got to wake up and go out again."

"Don't kid me, big boy. I haven't slept twenty-four hours. You mean somebody but not me," to which the sergeant replied, "you ain't slept but an hour, Jake. But your relief driver, Manklin, cracked on his first trip. So you got to do another twenty-four hours."

"What do you mean—cracked?"

"Well," said the sergeant, "a shell busted alongside and took away a front mud guard and——"

"Can't he drive without a mud guard? Applesauce, guy! Go away and let me sleep."

"You don't savvy. When the mud guard went, his nerve went too. He come in all shakin' and cryin' like a baby. All shot to pieces. Shell shocked proper. The skipper give him a shot of morphine. Get up now. There's still a thousand wounded to be brought in." So, in his overall suit, with his helmet and gas mask hanging from the light bracket on the dashboard of his GMC, the protagonist gets back behind the wheel for another 24 hours.[60]

The wheat fields had long been fertilized with manure, and the soil was full of *Clostridium tetani* bacteria spores. Introduced into the body, the bacteria produced toxins that caused tetanus, or "lockjaw," which had a mortality rate of 85 percent. In the 1890s, a treatment was devised using serum from horses that had developed antibodies through exposure to tetanus toxins. Before the war, anti-tetanus serum was not a regular component of U.S. Army medical supplies, but in France the aid and dressing stations were equipped with several hundred glass vials or ampoules of serum, and sanitary troops were taught to inject it with a hypodermic needle.[61] On the previous fronts the dressing stations routinely administered anti-tetanus serum to the wounded, and here it was essential. "Anti tetanus has to be injected into the abdomen of every wounded and is so painful it seems to be more dreaded than a wound," remarked Barlow. "It makes a swelling about the size of a walnut but the swelling is gone in 24 hours. It has proved very effective."[62] With hundreds of wounded arriving at the dressing station, Barlow reported "three of our men do nothing but inject the anti tetanus and are kept busy, night and day."[63] The application was marked on the patient's diagnosis tag, and often a "T" was painted on his forehead with iodine to make it immediately clear that he was protected from tetanus.

Barlow worried that "many of these wounded will possibly be again wounded before they have been removed far enough to the rear to be out of danger, as the enemy is bombing all roads."[64]

Apparently with the assistance of drivers or orderlies from the Company, including Ted Wall, the Ford ambulances of SSU 502 were used collect the wounded from the infantry battalion aid stations or from where they lay in the fields. "A corporal and I crawled along on a road for an eighth of a mile," recalled Wall. "We had to, there were two big shell holes in the way of the Ford and we couldn't get by, and as soon as we stopped there, why a sniper started with us and bing bing, tried to get us, so we had to drop and crawl to where the wounded men were. We got four and put them on the car and did this with pop, pop flying all around us and those devils shelling the ambulance. Now, mother, talk about excitement."[65]

At the dressing station, Barlow commented: "The small Ambulances are rushing through the fields and returning heavily loaded with wounded. Our trucks and heavier Ambulances are taking them to the rear as soon as they have had their wounds treated or having been recorded, as there is little to be done for gassed men under such conditions."[66] "Traffic was so heavy an enlisted man was detailed to direct traffic," Barlow added.[67]

Like the infantrymen, the ambulance drivers and their orderlies were working to exhaustion. As the 101st Engineers moved beyond the dressing station they saw that "a steady stream of Ford ambulances from the First Aid stations delivered their broken and sometimes lifeless burdens and then immediately drove off for another load. The drivers had not slept for nights, but unshaven, dirty, hollow-eyed, they drove back and forth over the shell-swept roads with their precious burdens of wounded men."[68]

For eight days, the drivers worked in 24-hour shifts. The Company's big GMC ambulances were used to ferry the wounded about 18 kilometers (11 miles) from the Farsoy Farm dressing station back to the 102nd Field Hospital's triage station at Bézu-le-Guéry and from there another 5 to 10 kilometers (3 to 6 miles) to the divisional hospitals in the rear. The Company's ambulance #71138 carried 698 wounded during those eight days.[69] "The ambulances stopped only when necessary to fill gas and oil tanks," wrote Driver Earle Radikin in the Sanitary Train history.[70] During the three weeks they spent in the sector, the 150 men of the combined 101st and 104th Field Hospitals cared for 4,395 casualties, while the 103rd Field Hospital had six operating teams and 35 nurses working 18–20 hours a day.[71]

"First aid men and all others are working until they can not stand up longer and they then try to sleep on the ground and sometimes find their pillow is a dead horse covered with straw," wrote Barlow.[72] On July 23, he recorded: "1300 have been through this station in the last 48 hours. Some have died and we are to[o] busy to bury the dead. There were fifty planes over this farm at once. Small planes were circling around the big bombing planes, evidently on the way toward Metz."[73]

"The stench of the dead bodies seems almost unbearable," wrote Barlow that day. But he also recognized the exhaustion of the Division after two weeks in the sector and a week on the advance. "Here and there is a rifle with bayonet stuck in the ground to mark the spot in the wheat fields where some mothers boy went 'West.' Most all men in this scene of carnage are praying to be wounded so as to be relieved, every one seems to be discouraged with life and gamble at night rather than rest and remark 'The shell marked for me will get me.' Fatalists all."[74]

On July 22 and 23 the Division attacked through Trugny, about five kilometers (three miles) northeast of Farsoy Farm, trying to seize Épieds, where the Germans had stabilized their line. The Germans pulled back from Épieds on July 24, with the pursuit being delayed as elements of the 28th Division relieved part of the 26th. Early on July 25, the 42nd Division moved up to replace the 26th, completing the relief that evening. The Division's artillery and engineers would continue in support of the 42nd Division until early August.[75]

Although the infantry was relieved, the dressing station moved forward on July 25. "We advanced to the town of Épieds as the enemy is retreating but still the fighting continues," wrote Barlow. "The enemy was in this town only a few hours ago, the 101st Artillery is so close to the road they shoot over the Ambulances as they pass, several French Tanks are rolling along evidently to relieve some put out of action yesterday."[76]

At Épieds, "we took time to bury a seven foot German officer found dead in a courtyard," added Barlow. "Many signs around the town marked 'Steensden Verboten' Passing forbidden, but evidently our doughboys could not read 'English,' or possibly did not believe in signs."[77]

It had been a long, debilitating week. But in retrospect, litter-bearer George W. Watt told his sister: "Some people give the Bosche credit for being a good soldier. From what I have seen of them, a company of our Boy Scouts would scare a good number of them.

"Your brother has not won any medals so far, but I am still alive and doing my best. I took part in the big push and what I saw in that drive will make grand telling. The New England boys again covered themselves with glory and the grand old 102nd Infantry once more proved its Yankee mettle that you should be proud to have been born in New England and especially in Connecticut because we have done more than any other American troops being the very first here. In another month we will be wearing our second service stripe.

"I am not driving an ambulance any longer. I was a little too husky for that job. I was more fit to go over the top. Therefore, I am now a full fledged trench veteran."[78]

8

Off the Line

August 1918

As the fighting pushed forward, the 42nd Division took over for the 26th Division on July 26. The next day, "we were moved back from Épieds to a farm just north of Château Thierry, all the 101st Sanitary Train seem to be billeted nearby and all wish the infantry and other units of this division might be relieved for they surely have had more than their share of this 'guerre,'" commented Barlow.[1]

From there, "we were moved from the farm near Château Thierry to Luzancy a quiet little town and well out of the danger zone." Barlow recorded that the "Company were billeted in barns and there are a large number of cases of dysentery due to drinking water in the many towns."[2]

Now completely familiar to the ambulance drivers who had made so many deliveries to the field hospitals there, Luzancy was located on the south side in a loop of the Marne just above La Ferté-sous-Jouarre. The fixed bridge at Luzancy had been destroyed in the fighting of 1914, but the French had installed a temporary suspension bridge to connect with Saâcy-sur-Marne to the east. While the Company rested there, "Richard Gellrich dove from the bridge at Luzancy into the river below when fully clad, on a dare, and was christened Annette Kellerman," after the celebrity diver and swimmer of the period.[3]

The 101st and 104th Field Hospitals had been operating here since July 9, but this region was not perfectly safe. Though now out of German artillery range, the towns along the Marne were still in danger of German aircraft. "Germans make two direct hits with bombs dropped from airplanes over La Ferté and almost wiped the station off the map," noted Barlow on August 2.[4]

On July 16, Lieutenant Sprague's Thresh-Foden vehicles set up as ordered, one at Montreuil-aux-Lions, not far from Bézu-le-Guéry, and the other along the Marne near Luzancy.[5] "Delousing machines are kept busy issuing underwear that has been deloused by a steaming process during the time the men were taking a bath," remarked Barlow on July 30.[6] The two vehicles set up together as a divisional delousing plant at Saâsy-sur-Marne, around the upstream bend of the Marne from Luzancy. At this well-watered, central location, temporary showers were constructed alongside the Thresh-Foden vehicles. The Division's regiments would march their companies to the plant to leave their clothing for delousing, pass through the showers and cresol application, and then collect their freshly steamed and disinfested

On the bank of the Marne at Saâcy on August 10, 1918, one of the Division's Thresh-Foden units "cooks" cooties. The crew has put heavy planks under the front wheels to keep it from bogging down in the riverbank. At right is a stack of compressed coal briquettes, which were found to be the most efficient fuel. It took the crew about an hour to get up sufficient steam to operate the Thresh units. Signal Corps photo by Corporal F.G. Carnochan (National Archives, photo no. 111-SC-19111).

uniforms, or obtain new clothing from the supply truck. Except for the artillery, which was still engaged in the fight, most of the Division's men got "deloused" during the two weeks spent along the Marne.[7]

But this would be the end of the Division's disinfesting unit. With a limited number of Thresh-Foden vehicles in the AEF, and an increasing number of divisions to disinfest, the AEF staff decided to consolidate the disinfesting units into sector rather than division organizations. While the Company's enlisted operators probably remained with their vehicles, they would now be combined with others and assigned to a sector. Relieved of his duties with the disinfesting unit, Lieutenant Sprague was rewarded for his consistent service with a promotion to captain and command of the 103rd Ambulance Company.[8]

Lieutenant Cobey also received a new assignment. The use of the Sanitary Train's vehicles as a provisional truck company had been so successful under Lieutenant Durham that the organization was made permanent on August 3. Cobey was placed in command of the new Provisional Truck Company, which included about 70 men and 28 5-ton trucks, a baggage truck, a repair truck, a tank truck, a car, a motorcycle, and a rolling kitchen. Each of the Train's eight units was assigned two trucks, and Cobey had authority to allocate the rest of the vehicles to the different units upon request. The new structure would make the movement of the Sanitary

Viewed from the rear, the Thresh-Foden unit is unloaded at Saâcy on August 10. Soldiers in various states of undress await their uniforms. There appears to be a pile of bundled blankets prepared for loading by the rear wheel. The unit's crew members wear heavy gauntlets to handle the basket and clothing, which have been heated to 238 F degrees. One of the men wears an overall fatigue suit and a battered campaign hat, and the man on the ladder wears fatigue trousers rather than woolen breeches. Signal Corps photo by Corporal F.G. Carnochan (National Archives, photo no. 111-SC-19099).

Train by truck more efficient, and would permit the rapid augmentation of the Train's 48 ambulances with trucks during heavy fighting.[9]

Barlow assured the women of the Bridgeport Comfort Club, "we haven't even been in a town for six weeks where beer could be purchased, and here's the best of all, not a man on the duty roster of this Company has a venereal disease."[10] But away from the front, discipline became an issue for the Company again. On July 31, "one of our men somewhat under the influence passed the automobile of General Edwards and did not salute and the General in trying to remonstrate with him was told in quite plain language just how to run this here AEF," noted Barlow. Most officers might have taken this as a serious infraction and imposed strict punishment, but Edwards demonstrated why his men were so loyal to him. "The individual was placed under arrest but his most severe punishment was being put on kitchen police (K.P.) for about a month as the General asked charges not be pressed against him."[11]

The next day, those who were minding their behavior witnessed "a fine entertainment" that was "given by men in this division down in a grove near this town and was enjoyed by a large audience from all over the world." However, "the two bands were not heard by the six men just being brought back from La Ferté where they had been A.W.O.L. for a few days but they swore 'Never Again' when set at work digging holes."[12] Then, on August 4, "G. Geer was placed under arrest for being A.W.O.L. for two days."[13]

To keep the Company poised for more open-field action, on August 3, "we were sent on old style maneuvers in the rain." This meant finding a designated position and establishing a dressing station there, then sending litter bearers to evacuate simulated patients from simulated aid stations marked by red-cross guidons. But it didn't go as planned.[14] "Vanlendingham and Chapman lost their way acting as scouts on our maneuvers and entire Company had to do the maneuvers over in the rain."[15] To avoid such mistakes in the future, "Ferris, Harvey, Carleton and Doreski were appointed to act as liason men in our next battle (real)."[16]

After his successful command of the Division's Thresh-Foden disinfesting units, Lieutenant Charles H. Sprague was promoted to captain in September 1918 and would take command of the 103rd Ambulance Company on October 14. Taken in 1919, this photograph shows him in his captain's uniform with three service chevrons for 18 months spent in the zone of advance and a discharge stripe under his YD shoulder patch. He submitted this photograph with his Connecticut Soldiers' Questionnaire in 1920 (courtesy Connecticut State Archives).

To keep up morale and fitness, the Division encouraged sporting events. The Company reconstituted its baseball team, with Private William Ballard and driver Ralph Merrill pitching, driver Leland Gilbert catching, driver Herbert Beers at first base, Private Robert MacDonald at second base, driver George Wills at short stop, driver Albert Ahern at third base, cook Frank Doreski in left field, Sergeant Charles Brendel or Corporal George Widinghoff in center field, and Sergeant William Cowie or Private Marshall in right field. The team won one of its games and lost the other. The Sanitary Train's track and field team also scored well in a divisional meet. Barlow joked, "no other athletic events of late, save Al Sorensen and Hub Beers having a harvesting contest out in one of the wheat fields, Newtown [Beers] won."[17]

The Division also held a variety show that featured the talents of so many. "One fellow sang 'Just a Baby's Prayer at Twilight Hour,'" wrote Barlow, "and all your boys have been whistling it ever since, and as I watch those big husky khaki clad, seemingly war hardened boys of yours loving those two cute, curly haired, French youngsters, down near our kitchen, I know that under those trench mirrors beats a heart as large as an ox and a soul that yearns for those at home."[18]

Behind the lines, the men also saw more and more evidence of America's expanding role in the war. "Secretary Hoover and staff passed through this town but did not stop," noted Barlow on August 5. Herbert Hoover, who had led the Committee for the Relief of Belgium, was now head of the U.S. Food Administration, where he promoted conservation at home to support the efforts overseas. Though a Republican, Hoover was trusted by President Wilson and sometimes served him on European missions.[19]

And they found a few American comforts. "A train with a real American locomotive passes this town each day and almost makes one home-sick," remarked Barlow on August 1.[20] Not quite as often, "a U.S. Commissary wagon comes through these towns every few days and has almost everything to sell and line soon forms and all are clamoring for sweet stuff."[21]

The men could actually afford to purchase their fill of candy since Lieutenant Sprague had turned over to the Company 1,100 Francs that the Bridgeport Comfort Club had raised and sent over.[22] As secretary and treasurer of the Comfort Club in France, Barlow had handled the check, which "was so large we had to get the signature of a Major or a Captain" in order to cash it. "Well Captain Stevens came to our rescue with his John Hancock, and a Y.M.C.A. man gave us the francage," wrote Barlow. "Golly, their paper money is so large here, we thought first we would paper a couple of rooms, but later decided to give each fellow six francs."[23] To be scrupulously fair, "no distinction was made whether they were original or replacement men," reported Barlow.[24] But he also made the effort to track down as many of the original Bridgeport men who had been transferred and distribute the money to them as well.[25]

The original men of the Company had several money questions, in addition to their irregular pay. "We were told when we drilled at the Armory that we would receive a certain amount for each drill, if we had over 90% of the men at the drill," wrote Barlow in August. "Men from Massachusetts and Rhode Island have received their checks since coming to this country, even their members who were not at the border."[26]

On August 13 the Company began its move toward its next assignment. "We hiked from Luzancy this morning, crossed a long swinging bridge that had a French soldier guarding some explosives that were fastened to the bridge and ready to be blown up should the enemy break through," wrote Barlow. "We were put aboard trucks at Saâcy and traveled about 45 kilometers through many small towns. Pitched tents at a farm in the triangle of the road."[27]

Along the road the next day, they passed some soldiers with French uniforms but "a flat four-pointed hat, and they were smiling away at us shouting in fine English, 'Hello, Yanks.' Well, they knew us, but who the deuce are they?" asked Barlow. "What do you know, they were American Polish Regiments and their khaki uniforms haven't arrived yet. As we whizzed past, we shouted out, 'Anybody from Bridgeport?' One lad yelled, 'Nope, Union City and Scoville's Shop.' So I guess this isn't such a large old world after all."[28] That day, "we were taken by trucks over 94 miles of very dusty roads and after 12 hours trying to stand up and eat cement dust, were unloaded at Laignes," recorded Barlow. "Those not on details went scouting about the town for something to eat."[29]

Well south of the Marne, and about 60 kilometers (37 miles) southwest of AEF Headquarters at Chaumont, Laignes had not been occupied or destroyed during the war. It lay within the French 12th Training Area, and the Division would rest here, with headquarters to the east of Laignes at Châtillon-sur-Seine. At Laignes, "we were billeted in some Church property that has a gymnasium attached. Some sleep indoors, but many put up their pup tents in the fields," noted Barlow. "There seems to be a fine class of people in this town, some quite good stores and plenty of wine. The natives can not believe we are part of that noble 26th Division, they have now heard so much about and which was just at Château Thierry, because the men appear so young."[30] "One French lady had a dozen of us at her home recently, played the piano for us and sang in English all the late American songs," remarked Barlow. "Oh Gee, oh Golly, all you had to do was close your eyes and let your mind wander a bit and you were over home in the front parlor down to the girl's house."[31]

Twenty-four-year-old Charles H. Cockerton of Bridgeport was a clerk when he enlisted in the Company on March 21, 1917. He had already been promoted to sergeant when he was sent to Fort Oglethorpe for training during the summer of 1917. He was a steady, popular sergeant throughout the Company's service. Here he shows off his sergeant's whistle chain, his YD shoulder patch, and three chevrons for 18 months in the zone of advance (courtesy Le petit musée du Doughboy).

"Of course, we had to drill five or six hours each day at litter drills, squads up and two's west and all that important stuff," Barlow told the Bridgeport Comfort Club. "Let me say here that these or any fellows who have carried a few thousand litters in actual duty, without ever giving an order, it is mighty hard to make them put any interest in litter drills, and no matter what officers or non coms are put with them, they can never be made to do that street soldier stuff like we did when rookies."[32] Because of that apparent insubordination, tensions arose again between Captain Johnston and some of the noncommissioned officers. In the soldier's way, the enlisted men made light of it in a sarcastic manner. "The stretcher bearermen of our Company are known as the colored battalion, due to a feeling against some of their non-commissioned officers by the officer in charge of the Company," Barlow remarked on August 13.[33]

"Colored battalion" was an allusion to the second-class treatment of black soldiers, like the "separate company" they had camped next to at Niantic. This kind of humor both mocked superiors in a subtle way and forged some cohesion in the ranks. The soldiers used similar humor in deriding the enemy as "Fritz," "Heinie," the "Boche," or "the Hun." The French soldiers, who were fond of their new American allies, referred to them as "Sammies," from Uncle Sam.

Americans were known for contracting formal names in informal situations, and in bestowing nicknames, so many of the men of the Company had one identity on paper and another in conversation. These nicknames were important enough to the men that Barlow would record them when he compiled a company roster. Some names were simply contractions, like Bill Adams, Artie Best, Stan Glover, Lee Hull, Hughey Lawler, Monie Monahan, Rip Morgan, Oppy Oppenheimer, Scotty Scott, or Rad Radikin. Some men were called by shortened versions of their middle names, like John "Andy" Holzheimer, Thomas "Jerry" Bale, Charles "Dud" Mills, and Frank "Ted" Wall. Rocco D. Francolini was simply "Rocco D," while Daniel F. Clare was called "Daniel E." Others likely had nicknames brought from civilian life, like George Herbert "Hub" Beers—which became especially appropriate for his duty as an ambulance driver—or Frank "Buddy" Crump, or Jesse Lodrick "Chunky" James. Charles "Pop" Brendel's nickname probably mocked his youthfulness in a position of experience, while Albert "Pop" Honeck was both fatherly, at age 44, and experienced, like his fellow mechanic, Harry "Old Man" Edes, age 36. Fred "Bloomfield" Pinney of Bloomfield, Connecticut, and Orlo "Esbon" Chandler of Esbon, Oklahoma, were nicknamed for their hometowns. Other nicknames referred to physical characteristics, like Granville "Blondy" Wilcox, George "Wire Whiskers" Cormier, Robert "Beauty" Marston, William "Big Bill" Murphy, Robert "Big Boy" Stewart, George "Slim" Watt (who was not slim), George "Slim" Woolery, Harry "Red" Worley, and Rollia "Daddy Long Legs" Willis. Howard "Parson" Davis was a divinity student before enlisting, while Edwin "Old Reliable" Hough, William "Silent Mac" McElroy, and Charles "Sunny Jim" Palmer were nicknamed for their traits. James "Irish" O'Connell's nickname was obvious. Michael "Barber" Kwasniski had served as a barber for the Company, while Harvey "Farmer" Teter was a Kansas farmer. Because of his bridge dive at Luzancy, Richard Gellrich was given the name of the noted female swimmer and movie star, Annette Kellerman. The ambulance drivers had some of the most distinctive nicknames: Albert "Dragfoot" Ahern; Curtis "Barney Oldfield" Banks, named for the noted racecar driver; Edward "Rubber Knees" Bergeron; William "Bugs" Goodnow; Gus "Mickie" Hannon; George "Blub Blub" Wills; and Benjamin "Dynamite" Wyrtzen. Some nicknames were just whimsical word games, or references to some incident, like Phillip "Fill Up" Brodsky, Frank "Dutch" Deutsch, Antony "Butts" Catullo, Anthony "Nabisco" Diorio, Frederick "Hand Grenade Mike" Keller, Arthur "Peasoup" Lambeau, Arthur "Lumbago" Lieberum, Charles "Spike" Morgan, Martin "Hayshaker" Mortenson, John "Calamity" Murphy, Victor "Lightning" Schaeffer, Alfred "Rip van Winkle" Sorensen, George "Mook" Vennart, George "Piano Legs" Widinghoff, or George "Duck Egg" Wright. Among the men, former captain Stevens was known respectfully as "Skipper," and Lieutenant Sprague as "Doc." Captain Johnston became known disrespectfully as "Dugout" for the safe place where he could be found in action. Barlow recorded his own nickname as "Commissary Dick," while the strangest one of all was for fall-1918 assignee Albert Zahradnik, who was called "the boy with the microscopic eye for dealing out oleo."[34]

With the promotion and departure of Lieutenant Sprague, the Company received two new officers. Lieutenant Thomas McRossie, 46, had been born in Canada but obtained his M.D. at New York University in 1897 and was practicing in Brooklyn when he entered the service. Barlow called him "a dandy, old style Scotch Irish physician, and a regular daddy to us, goes eight miles out of his way to do anything he can for us."[35] Lieutenant Moses Katz had been born in New York City and obtained his M.D. from Illinois Medical College in 1899. He had offices in Westchester County, New York, before coming to France in June 1918 as part of Camp Greenleaf Replacement Draft Company 10. Though fresh from home, with no field experience, they "are well liked by the men," Barlow commented on August 17, "and both are of the few that have come over here for the good they can do and not how much they can learn of surgery or how high they can rise."[36] But Lieutenant Katz would only be with them for about two weeks, for at the end of August he and Lieutenant Lowery were transferred to other units.[37]

There were comings and goings among the enlisted men as well. At the beginning of August, Supply Sergeant Thomas Avallone was sent to a supply truck company.[38] Then Sergeant Grant, who had recovered from his broken hand, was transferred to the 102nd Field Hospital.[39] On August 3, "Phillips was sent to hospital to have his eyes treated."[40] A week later, "Carroll, Ahern and Wyrtzen all sent to some hospital with an undetermined fever (F.U.O.)." This may have been the beginning of the second round of influenza among the troops in France.[41] A week after that, "Jim Carter and Bob Marsten were sent to hospital, making 12 per cent of this Company, now in hospitals," recorded Barlow on August 18. "The men are just showing a reaction from their long service in action."[42]

"But some were coming back as well. On August 1, Dud Mills, Glover, Drury, Sorensen and Williams are back from various hospitals," recorded Barlow.[43] "Caler who was quite severely shell shocked at Château Thierry has returned from the hospital," Barlow noted on August 19. Also returning were ambulance driver Granville Wilcox, who had been wounded in April, and Benjamin Clay, "the latter having been severely burned by gas." Barlow commented, "Clay is a short stocky type from away out West and keeps saying 'Hell Yes.'" A native of Norman, Oklahoma, Benjamin Clay had been sent to France as part of a Fort Riley Medical Casual Detachment in April 1918.[44]

As the Company settled in for a few days, "Edes and some of the other boys have rigged up a shower-bath by placing a steel barrel in a tree and Edes is quite famous for his Yankee ingenuity."[45] The next day, "after instructions were read to us about watching out for spies many not on duty watched farmers using old style treadmills, driven by stallions as most all good horses have been drafted into the service and stallions can not be trusted under fire," remarked Barlow. "The weather is very hot and most all farming is being done by old men, young boys or women."[46] During their time at Laignes, "we have an occasional band concert and are certainly enjoying the fine weather and our stay in this town, the men even marched to church in a body," reported Barlow.[47]

The Company had received two new GMC ambulances at the end of July.[48] While the Company was on the move, the ambulances were given a special assignment. The Division had set up field hospitals at Villotte, near Châtillon-sur-Seine to accommodate the many suffering from diarrhea and general exhaustion from the recent campaign. The Company's ambulances were sent to Villotte to make repeated runs to Base Hospital 15 at Chaumont, 65 kilometers (40 miles) south.[49]

Herbert Beers and his orderly Lodrick James were among those assigned to the special duty. "Our company moved, and then for a day or two we were busy moving sick patients," wrote Beers. With their sanitary duty accomplished they became, in effect, a limousine driver and attendant. "Then one night at about 11 o'clock another fellow [James] and I had orders to be ready to move at 4.30 the next morning. The next morning we got up at said time, reaching said objective at 6.15." From there—probably near AEF Headquarters at Chaumont—"we were to take some officers away for tank instruction," probably to the 302nd Tank Center in Langres, about 20 miles to the southeast. "They hadn't had any breakfast, so when we reached a good town, one of them gave us 50 francs and told us to eat. We did. That day we reached our destination, covering 260 kilos [160 miles] in seven hours. They were all young fellows and certainly used us fine. They always give us plenty of money. In one town we went to a French moving picture show. It was sort of dry, but the French seemed to think it was great."

They passed through Liffol-le-Grand at suppertime. "They are a great bunch of French," Beers continued. "Where we had supper is where some of us had our New Year's party. The lady took us right into her best room and used her best dishes. The whole town soon knew we were there and after supper there was a bunch around asking for some certain ones they knew in the company.

"The trip took three days and the lieutenants said when they went out again, they wanted us to take them. We are seeing all kinds of country, driving all over. Believe me, when I get home I can say that I have toured France. I've been to lots of the big cities that people see and to all kinds of villages and towns which most people do not see. Where we are now they have the most wonderful roads I ever rode on. The country is great and I have enjoyed it all very much.

"Yesterday, I had a trip to the town where Bert Peck is in—Chaumont—a round trip of 80 miles. He is working hard.... From what I hear, the girls are all getting married off,—guess I will have to be an old bachelor or else make up to an old maid with a big roll."[50]

9

Luggin' Litters on the Edge of the Woëvre

September–October 1918

By July 4, 1,019,000 American soldiers had arrived in France and U.S. plans were months ahead of schedule.[1] Between March and July, American divisions had been deployed with the French and even the British during the German advance, but General Pershing was eager to form a unified American army with its own objective. During a meeting on July 24, the Allied commanders agreed on a mission for the AEF. In the east, near the Toul Sector where several of the divisions had gained experience in the trenches, the lines formed an angle or salient near St. Mihiel. German presence here, near the Meuse, would potentially threaten the supply lines for the major assault all along the German lines that was being planned for late September. General Pershing obtained approval to drive the Germans out of this salient.

By August, fifteen American divisions—the 1st, 2nd, 3rd, 4th, 5th, 26th, 28th, 35th, 42nd, 78th, 80th, 82nd, 89th, 90th, and 91st—were trained to fight. The next step was to establish the First Army and bring its component divisions together. The First Army was created on August 10, and by the end of the month its divisions were in motion toward St. Mihiel.[2]

Lieutenant Cobey's Provisional Truck Company returned to duty on August 29. "We were routed out at 4 A.M., packed up all equipment and loaded into trucks and ready to move at 7 A.M," recorded Sergeant Barlow, noting that it was "some contrast to the two or three days it took us to get under way at Niantic" eleven months earlier. "We went through Bar Sur Aube, Soulaines and pitched tents at Sandrupt in some woods eight kilos from Bar le Duc."[3]

Now that the Division was nearing the lines, it took pains to avoid observation by German aircraft. "We are keeping under cover all the time and moving at night and are now up in some other woods nearer Bar le Duc and it is still raining," wrote Barlow on the last day of August. "Some of [the] men went into Bar le Duc to see what could be bought with part of that money sent by the Comfort Club but found very little and that very costly."[4]

The next day, "a priest held communion while standing on the tail board of a truck over in the woods and in a pouring rain," noted Barlow. Having broken regulations by going into town the previous day, "Men were given severe warning and put on their honor not to go over into the town of Bar le Duc." That evening, "we moved at 7 P.M. through Bar le Duc to Chaumont-sur-Aire and were billeted in some more barns."[5]

Captain Johnston had not regained the confidence of the men, including Barlow, and they continued to skirt the edge of disrespect as he sought ways to control them. "The Skipper (Commanding Officer) is telling the sergeants that if the men refuse to work to tell them passes are to be issued tomorrow but he fooled no one but himself," Barlow wrote that day.[6]

While they were camped at Chaumont-sur-Aire, the ambulances that had been doing evacuation work returned to the Company. "Bill Adams broke his wrist again trying to start one of them," remarked Barlow. "Men are enjoying the moving pictures over at the Foyer [du] Soldat, which is really a place provided for the recreation of the French soldiers. We did not mind the most wicked lightning during the thunder shower as many termed it 'Old Stuff.'"[7]

"Well, this Army game is a great game," Lodrick James told his father. "It's travel all the time in all sorts of weather and under all conditions, but it isn't as tough as it sounds and one rather likes it after you get used to it. The only time that it gets monotonous is when you stay in one place too long. Of course, if a fellow could find some particular attraction in one place he wouldn't mind staying, but the only attraction I see in the different towns is the newness of them and as soon as this wears off the attraction is gone and I am ready to move to another place."[8]

To recognize and encourage heroic action, and to maintain morale, soldiers were increasingly cited in orders for bravery or exceptional acts. After their extended service and heroic actions under fire in the fields above Château-Thierry, the Sanitary Train held a ceremony to recognize its heroes on September 5 at Chaumont-sur-Aire. "We were told we had to attend church this morning, every company of the Sanitary train including all ambulance companies, Field hospital etc.," wrote Ted Wall. "Into the Catholic church we marched, those who had been cited were put in the front rows. There were about 20 of us. After mass, a captain of the American Red Cross stepped forward with several papers in his hand, made a speech, after which he read a letter from our commanding general to the boys of the Sanitary Train. There were about 1,000 men present. After reading the citation he called off the names and asked us to step up to the altar. Calling each name and rank he presented us with our citation which I am sending to you. He shook hands as he gave it to us, congratulating us. Guess who was one of the bunch! Bill [Louis]. He went with the infantry as far as it went and as for me I told you in my last letter. It was very impressive. Just like getting a prize at school only different."[9]

Wall had bonded so closely with his fellow Englishman George Wright that they were known in the Company as "the twins." After the citation ceremony, Wall wrote: "George and I have a dugout together and he is now laying on his bunk singing and laughing and acting bughouse. We have a good dugout, but water is scarce although there is plenty of rain, the rainy season having started again and that means three months of good old mud. We have a new idea of getting water with which to wash ourselves. Put two canvass buckets down where the water drips and lo, we can wash ourselves. This morning I washed in the bucket, then got a cup of water cleaned my teeth first and then [shaved] in the same water. One good thing mother, we have good food and we had a wonderful dinner today, consisting of roast beef, mashed potatoes, three slices of bread and butter, plenty of gravy and more after that was finished, yum, yum."[10]

Already they knew, in Ted Wall's words, "we're going to give the boche another 'Lick.'"[11] Barlow agreed: "Some one is going to do some shooting or all these Ambulances and Ammunition Trains would not be moving up."[12]

"After the special church service held for men recently cited in orders, we sneaked up nearer the lines and [stopped] in woods," reported Barlow. "It is still raining and men are threatening dire things if they capture the originator of the expression 'Sunny France.'"[13]

Lodrick James remarked on the rain as well. "It has been raining for the past few days and from all appearances I should judge that the rainy season is on. If it is I don't look forward to the next six weeks with any great amount of pleasure, for it is about the most disagreeable season that one has to contend with in this country. When I remember Allison P. Smith on a rainy day saying that 'Nature was weeping on us this morning,' it seems to me that old Mother Nature must go through a lot of hardship and misery over here."[14]

As Barlow remarked, "sneaked is the right word to use in describing our recent movements for they are all at night and blankets have been placed over the Ambulances to cover the Red Cross."[15] The next day, "the officers are billeted in a beautiful castle," complained Barlow. "We had to knock down our pup tents at midnight after just getting them set up, and are ready to move again."[16]

James Peck told his mother: "You may think we are moving about all the time, and it is quite right. To-day we are camouflaged in some fine large woods and will move again tonight. This will make our fourth front and it sort of makes us feel like old timers. Charles Harang knows this country we're in now, for I remember his telling me that he had hunted and trapped in the woods around here. There are some of the most wonderful forests I've ever seen and would like nothing better than to hunt here next month."[17]

"We moved up again in the rain," wrote Barlow the next day. "This time we moved near the lines at Rupt and Noyon. We were billeted in a large dugout in some woods. The dugout is about 1000 feet long and in the side of a bank and has 14 entrances. In some parts it is reached by going down 40 steps into the bowels of the earth, where water is constantly dripping.

"Duck-boards have been left by the French who made this dugout to make the walking more safe."[18] This complex of concrete dugouts had been constructed by the French, possibly as part of the defensive line constructed between Verdun and Toul after the 1871 Franco-Prussian War. The dugouts "had bunks so close we imagined we were on the *Corsican*," joked Barlow. In honor of the principal places the men were trained, "one dugout was named Niantic and the other Framingham, the latter having a Fort Riley annex."[19]

The Company dressing station would be located in these dugouts at Noyon, while the 101st Ambulance Company established its dressing station in a church at Mouilly. About four kilometers (two and a half miles) back at Genicourt-sur-Meuse, the 101st Field Hospital would operate a triage or sorting station, and the 104th

The Company spent about three days at this French-built dugout near Noyon. "The dugout is about 1,000 feet long and in the side of a bank and has 14 entrances," noted Sergeant Barlow. "In some parts it is reached by going down 40 steps into the bowels of the earth, where water is constantly dripping." The dressing station was probably entered through the door with the red cross above. The men were billeted in the Niantic dugout, the Framingham dugout, and the Fort Riley annex, reflecting the places they were trained. Several men carry litters away from the GMC ambulance. The ambulance flies the required red-cross guidon, and below the U.S. and YD insignia on the side is the small silver eagle that identifies the Company's ambulances (National Archives and Records Administration, U.S. Signal Corps films, "The St. Mihiel Offensive, September 10–25, 1918, 26th Division," 111.H.1325, https://www.youtube.com/watch?v=K8eILOcKWdY).

Field Hospital would treat gas cases. The sick or slightly wounded would be sent to the 102nd Field Hospital at Château-le-Petit Monthirous along the Meuse north of Genicourt.[20]

"Men are kept busy trying to camouflage this dugout," reported Barlow. "Water has to be hauled three miles. Roads are jammed. Hundreds of all caliber guns are being put in place almost hub to hub through these woods and miles of ammunition trains are milling around in the dark."[21]

On September 9, Corporal Merrill posted a notice on the Company bulletin board. After reading it, Barlow told the Bridgeport Comfort Club, "us fellows have finally got our orphans," 11-year-old Marie Louise Decollas and 6-year-old Paul Maillard. The Company appointed Howard "Parson" Davis to act as their "Godfather." According to Barlow, they were two of 500 orphans adopted by soldiers in the AEF.[22]

September 12 was the date for the assault on the salient. With French divisions on both flanks, the 1st, 42nd, and 89th divisions would attack north from the area around Seicheprey, the 2nd, 5th, 90th, and 82nd divisions on their left would pivot to the right to drive in the salient, and the 26th, part of the 4th Division, and the

French 15th Colonial Division would attack east and south to cut off the extremity of the German salient at St. Mihiel. In the 26th Division, the 101st Infantry would attack on the right and the 103rd and 104th on the left. The infantry was ordered to go over the top at 8:00 a.m. after a seven-hour artillery bombardment.[23]

On September 11, Barlow led a detail of litter bearers forward. "Twenty-six of our stretcher bearers were sent up in the pitch dark of midnight to LaCloche and had to put one hand on the shoulder of the man in front and dare not speak above a whisper and to make matters worse, every once in a while a piece of artillery hidden in the woods opens up and after the flash you are blinded."[24]

Barlow captured the litter bearers' experience: "The Worlds greatest battle started at 12.54. Men are looking over the nearest hole to dive into when the enemy starts to reply. We will not have many wounded for a few hours because the doughboys do not go over the top until after this barrage has been on for a few hours. Ten thousand flashes light the sky. Your blood tingles. You grate your teeth and pray, as the enemy shells drop all around, that God will give you the old stuff that will make your mothers proud and you are almost sure, you might be willing to call it off, if it was not for the example of these human devils around you."[25]

Then, at 8:00 a.m., they went over the top. This was a new experience, attacking well-prepared trenches. "Our artillery proved that the steel and cement dugouts of the Hindenburg Line were but chaff in a storm, as the steel girders were twisted, torn and thrown about in all angles," recorded Barlow. "Trenches are blown in, our combat troops are racing after the Bosch as they retreat from the supposedly bomb proof Hindenburg Line. Barb wire, shell holes and tree stumps in all directions."[26]

Barlow continued: "Wounded are brought by stretcher bearers through muddy winding trenches and must come up in the open where trenches are blown up and meet the constant ping, ping, of rifle and machine guns. A wounded man is mighty heavy after he has been carried a mile on a stretcher."[27] The litter bearers seem to have been wearing their packs and their rain slickers while they worked. In addition to that weight, the litter alone weighted about 25 pounds. If the wounded soldier retained his pack and rifle, the loaded litter might weigh more than 200 pounds. Usually two men carried a litter, using shoulder straps as well as the handles, but four might be used for rough or long carries.

Ambulance driver Earle Radikin gave the litter bearers special consideration when he wrote up the history of the Sanitary Train. "The litter bearers at the front had difficulties," he wrote, "for their carry was always long, through unfamiliar territory, and in most cases barbed wire had to be contended with. Since the condition of the roads precluded the possibility of advancing dressing stations and hospitals, the long carry was necessary."[28]

Barlow appreciated some unexpected assistance with his litter squad. "Forty infantry men who had been wounded and sent to the hospital in previous battles had just been returned to the lines in time for this action and were assigned to act with us as stretcher bearers and all were serious minded, well disciplined and very quiet and we love them for Heaven knows it takes a man with guts to go up into that hell after once being brought out on a stretcher."[29]

It may have been during this action that a couple of litter bearers showed real

Litter bearers carry the first casualty of the 103rd Infantry through a trench from the dressing station to the ambulance head in the Bois d'Éparges, on September 12, 1918. Notice that they wear their rain slickers, with gas masks at the ready, and use the over-the-shoulder litter straps to distribute the weight. The lead man has his medical belt over his slicker. Signal Corps photo by Lieutenant E.H. Cooper (National Archives, photo no. 111-SC-23856).

ingenuity. As Barlow described it, "a soldier wounded in such a manner that he could not lie down, was brought in sitting up on a stretcher as the stretcher bearers had found a chair, knocked the legs off and fastened the bottom and back to the stretcher so the wounded man was in a sitting position."[30]

German aircraft were active in support of the German infantry. "During the day the 102nd Ambulance Company dressing station was bombed by an enemy aviator," recorded Radikin in his history. "Three bombs dropping within fifty yards of the station, thirteen men were slightly wounded and were immediately attended."[31]

By coincidence, the Germans had begun to retire from the salient to consolidate their lines even as the American assault began. While some still held the forward trenches, most of the Germans were falling back to the partially finished second line, which was protected by a tangle of barbed wire. The third, Michel Stellung, on the Woëvre plain east of the Heights of the Meuse, was part of the main Hindenburg Line. As the Germans moved through the rough ground along the roads, many were overtaken by the Americans. "Our troops are taking many prisoners," remarked Barlow. "We make use of them by making them carry the wounded with them toward the rear of our lines. Their peculiar old carts and wagons are put into use as stretcher wagons. We are not finding as many of our own wounded as we had expected, due to the enemy retreating. The 26th Division goes ahead."[32]

"The infantry advanced so fast that by the time one dressing station was cleaned up of all wounded, they were perhaps a mile or more ahead," added Barlow. "As we were going from one station to an advanced one something inwardly told H.P. Davis to take a different route than others of his detail, which he did and while on his way, heard a groan and upon investigating he found a doughboy so badly wounded that he could not pull himself out of the shell hole where he had fallen and would most assuredly have died, had not private Davis passed that way."[33]

The regiments on the left stalled among the ravines and barbed wire in front of the second German line, but late in the afternoon of September 12, the 102nd Infantry was pushed ahead and marched along the Grande Tranchée de Calonne, a straight, paved road that led southeast to the town of Vignuelles. Ordered not to stop until it secured Vignuelles, the regiment passed scattered German troops in the woods as it marched, but it kept on and reached Vignuelles about 2:00 a.m. on the thirteenth. When lead elements of the 1st Division arrived there shortly after, the salient had been cut off and eliminated.[34]

The next day, "this Company moved ahead to Dommartin a small town just vacated by the enemy, and we all washed up over at the brook for our first wash in several days," explained Barlow. "Eggs left by the enemy have the date on them but no one takes a chance in eating them but men do eat the bread left by them and no one poisoned as yet."[35]

"This was the best one yet as there were so few wounded," commented James Peck. "We had an interesting time chasing Fritz and eating the food he left behind. It is a wrong impression if you at home think that the German Army is starving. By what they left behind it would seem as if they were fed as good or even better than a lot of the Allies. But we will lick them anyway, if we keep up the good work and I know we will."[36]

The Division then moved forward to the edge of the heights overlooking the Woëvre plain and took over the advance positions on the plains from the French. As most of the First Army withdrew to take position below the Argonne Forest, on September 15 the 26th Division was attached to the French II Colonial Corps in this sector, now called the Troyon Sector.[37] With the Division's front moved to the right, the Ambulance Section established headquarters at Dommartin-la-Montage in one of the shallow ravines above the Woëvre. The 101st and 102nd Ambulance Companies settled there, with a dressing station maintained at Les Éparges on the left. The triage hospital was back at Vaux, with the "sick hospital" at Ambly, along the Meuse.

In this sector, "the artillery fire was at all times most intense and ambulances seemed to be special targets for the enemy's big guns," remembered Earle Radikin.[38]

Barlow remarked: "We set up a dressing station at Dommartin in a stone building that had been wrecked by our own shell fire, there are German wooden field pieces left in the woods that had evidently been used in trying to fool our observers, German carts, bicycles etc. and all billets are alive with German Lice and they are actually different from our now familiar cooties. While we were burying a young American Boy in the Church yard cemetery a French soldier broke his leg near our dressing station."[39]

Living in a former German dugout, they found plenty of German items lying around. "All have some souvenirs to send home, have eaten Boche black bread, each

A member of the Company, with his pack under his poncho, works on a captured German stretcher cart on September 15, 1918, in the Ravine des Feuilles near Saint-Remy-la-Calonne, between Les Éparges and Dommartin-la-Montagne and three kilometers (about two miles) behind the new front line. German litters are stacked in the dugout. The other two men wear rain slickers, with their gas masks in the ready position. The near man wears his overseas cap under his helmet. None of the men can be identified. Signal Corps photo by Sergeant Eikelberry (National Archives, photo no. 111-SC-22443).

loaf dated, drank their soda water, used their paper bandage, postcards, etc.," Barlow told the Comfort Club.[40] There, they also found some new sounds for their faithful Victrola. "By the way we had a picture taken of the Victrola the other day, while it was playing some of the new German music and we had it dolled up with its two service stripes," continued Barlow.[41]

As both sides settled into the new lines, routine sniping and artillery fighting continued, and the dressing station remained busy. "[Charles] Palmer tried to wake up a soldier on a stretcher and found he was dead," remarked Barlow. "The Artillery is pounding away just over the hills and the enemy drops one into this town every few hours just to let us know he still has the range."[42] The Germans also shelled the Company's ambulances at the ambulance head behind the line at Hannonville-sous-les-Côtes, down on the Woëvre plain.[43]

As in other sectors, the Y.M.C.A. moved up to the front as soon as possible. About September 18, Barlow reported: "A Y.M.C.A. truck was stuck in the mud and Lieut Durham bought their entire load and detailed a man to sell the supplies (mostly eatable) but although he had heavy sales he lost money for there was no one around who could know the value of the money now carried around by the troops."[44] As Barlow told the Bridgeport Comfort Club, "men from all the companies horned in, and the doughboys, thinking that it was a regular Y. M., bawled them all out for further orders for not havin' nothin' any good, and Esbon got all mixed up with the change, for you see there's troops from all lands here and each has a little money from his own country."[45]

James Peck remarked: "The barracks that we are living in now were built for Fritz and are very comfortable, but full of fleas. Had kept the cooties down very well lately, but now we have a new fad, chasing fleas. They are hard to get, too, for they jump about 10 feet at a hop. How they can bite, though. Suppose that Fritz had to leave us something to remember him by. The barracks, however, are warm and dry and as we won't be here very long, there is no kick."[46]

Since the St. Mihiel advance, General Pershing's First Army had been on the move, in a complicated shift of 600,000 men, artillery, and equipment 60 miles into position to replace the 220,000-man French Second Army west of Verdun.[47] While the First Army was on the move, the 102nd Ambulance Company remained at Dommartin. "We have had three more days of rain but were paid and gave three cheers for we had beaucoup mail," noted Sergeant Barlow. "That is a fine combination to have both mail and money but does not happen often." He also puzzled at the fact that the "entire AEF seems to have developed a craze of using walking sticks or canes and calling them trench sticks."[48]

With the Division now engaged in offensive operations rather than defending a line of trenches, coordination and communication had become essential. The ambulance companies and field hospitals had mastered their individual duties and had refined their practices to meet field conditions, but they had largely worked independently until July. In preparation for the next campaign, Division Surgeon Porter emphasized efficiency and communication in a circular to the Sanitary Train units on September 23. He specified that ambulance company litter bearers should not be sent forward of infantry battalion aid stations to assist regimental litter bearers as their duty was to evacuate the wounded from the aid stations to the rear, and there were too few of them to serve efficiently in both places.

He charged ambulance company commanders—or the commander of the ambulance section if the companies were working together—with setting up relay stations for litter bearers to maintain an efficient flow of wounded. Since wheeled litters, which were used by both the Germans and the French, had proved to save labor and provide a more comfortable ride for the wounded, the commanders were to have wheeled litters placed where they were most suited for use.

To ensure that the ambulance dressing stations did not become backed up with wounded, he specified that they only control hemorrhage, readjust or reapply dressings and splints, treat severe shock, and administer and record A.T.S. (anti-tetanus serum) if it had not been given at the battalion aid station. Further treatment would be administered at the field hospitals once the wounded passed through the sorting or triage hospital.

The ambulances themselves were only to stay at the dressing station for as long as it took to transfer wounded from light (Ford) to heavy (GMC) ambulances, if both were in use, and to "make ambulance loads uniform or complete if time permits." All of the Sanitary Train's ambulances and trucks were required to fly a red cross guidon in a "uniform position" on the vehicle at all times (despite some feeling that the red cross symbol made them more of a target).

The ambulance section commander was to station himself at the triage hospital and maintain the flow of communication from the battalion aid stations to the ambulance company dressing stations to the section commander, and on to the commander of the Sanitary Train and the division surgeon.[49]

It did not take long to put these orders into operation. The Allied assault on the German lines across the whole Western Front was scheduled to begin on September 26. General Pershing's next element of U.S. participation in the war was a full assault on the German lines from the Argonne Forest east to the Meuse. There, 14 divisions were to attack on a front 20 miles wide. The objective, about 30 miles north, was the German railroad and supply center at Sedan.[50] As a diversion, to keep the Germans guessing about the focus of the attack, the plans called for a sacrificial feint assault by the 26th Division on the German line between Marchéville and Riaville on the Woëvre, to coordinate with the main attack around the Argonne Forest, 40 miles to the west.

In the Troyon Sector, the Division's line was on the edge of the Woëvre plain, just forward of Saulx-lès-Champlon and Fresnes. A battalion of the 102nd Infantry, supported by engineers and machine gunners, would advance about two miles, cross a small river, and attack Marchéville from the southwest. A battalion of the 103rd Infantry, similarly supported, would advance eastward and seize Riaville, about a mile north of Marchéville. Both columns were ordered to hold the towns for about twelve hours, then retire.[51]

Unaware of what was about to begin, ambulance driver Herbert Beers was in a contemplative mood on September 25. "It is just a year ago to-day that the 102d Amb. Co., left for France," he told his mother. "I've spent weeks that have gone like years, and months that have gone like a week. It's the war. To tell the truth it doesn't seem like a year. When the sun shines everything goes along fine, but the rain puts a crimp in the wheel." But a good breakfast, possibly concocted in preparation for action, engaged the men. "This morning for breakfast we had French toast,—it is bread dipped in batter and fried,—bacon, bread and coffee," continued Beers. "They cook the coffee on a little fire outside. A bunch of us stood around the fire and talked over old times and what we were doing a year ago to-day. Believe me, old Camp Niantic and the town we are in to-day are two different places. The town is a bunch of ruined buildings; they were all knocked to pieces four years ago."[52]

Later that day, in preparation for the assault, the Company moved down from Dommartin to Hannonville, just behind the line on the plain of the Woëvre. Four ambulances were stationed there, and four were sent about two miles north to Saulx-lès-Champlon, where the command post was located. This time, the 101st Ambulance Company would support the 102nd Infantry assault. The 102nd Company's litter bearers would go forward with the 103rd Infantry and carry wounded back to Saulx or, if ambulances could get closer to the front, to the closest ambulance head.[53]

That night, while much of the Division pulled back up to the heights, "Holzheimer and Barlow took 40 stretcher bearers to the fake attack at Marcheville and had with them Lieut Upshaw a fine man but who had not seen the lines," wrote Barlow. "They had orders to follow the 3rd battalion of the 103rd Infantry into action and to evacuate all wounded. All wended their way through trenches and some open plains after ten at night and through quite a heavy barrage from the enemy and waited out on the plains until the zero hour of 5 A.M."[54] Lying in the field, the men could do little but watch the fireworks. "During that time our artillery was putting over a barrage. The big shells were going over high in the air from both directions and in the moonlight seemed as though there must be many 'Head On' collisions."[55] The firing was "fine and thick, but compared with what we could see and hear on the northwestern horizon, seemed small," recalled newspaper correspondent Frank Sibley.[56]

Morning brought a heavy fog, which aided the advancing units as they set off behind artillery barrages at 5:30. On the right, the 102nd Infantry battalion moved up the roadside trenches and fought its way into Marchéville by 9:00 and set up defensive positions. It would hold the town for twelve hours, as ordered. While evacuating the battalion's wounded back to Saulx, the 101st Ambulance Company would lose its litter bearer commander, Sergeant Andrew Connell, to shellfire that afternoon.[57]

On the left, the 103rd Infantry battalion, followed by the litter bearers, also worked its way up the roadside trenches before a final dash to the trench on the edge of the town. But machine gun fire pinned them behind trees and bushes before they could enter Riaville.[58] At 10:45 Major Hanson of the 103rd Infantry reported back: "There is much artillery and machine guns in concrete emplacements in Riaville. Our artillery apparently does not destroy them or put them out of action. We have many wounded." Shortly after, he had to retire to the trenches along the road to await the artillery support, but the shelling failed to destroy the defensive emplacements. Stalled outside the town, the infantrymen tried flanking attacks before beginning to pull back about 6:30.[59] The French forces on both flanks did not press their attack so the German defenders focused their fire on the Americans.

Working with the litter bearers, Barlow witnessed the desperate ingenuity of the medical officers in their efforts to save the wounded. "At the fake attack on [Riaville] a shell blew a doughboy's leg away, just below the knee," He recalled. "The medical officer with the 103rd Infantry saw this man as soon as he was brought in by our stretcher bearers and although he had no tools to work with, found a rusty pair of pliers hanging from a beam, gripped the artery with the pliers, tied adhesive tape around the handles so they could not open and then strapped the pliers to the stump of the leg and sent the man to the rear on a stretcher."[60]

The 103rd Infantry battalion counted its casualties as one officer and nine men killed, and two officers and 51 men wounded. "All wounded were carried back and only one dead body was left behind," recorded the regiment's historian.[61] Barlow was not fully satisfied with the performance of his litter bearers. "Fourteen of the 40 men did exceptionally meritorious service in dressing wounded in action and taking them on stretchers back almost two miles through heavy shell fire, across the plains to a cross roads where Ambulances were waiting to rush them to the rear," he wrote.[62] If seven litters did most of the lugging back to the ambulance head, that was more than eight trips apiece. The other 26 men, most of them probably assigned only recently to the Company, were too ignorant or too frightened to be of great assistance.[63]

As the flow of wounded from Marchéville and Riaville increased, the Company's four ambulances at Hannonville were sent to the central dressing station in the ruins of Saulx.[64] "This was the worst day we have had to date in regard to horribly wounded," wrote Barlow. "One part of the Company was lugging stretchers while others were transporting wounded by Ambulances and the remainder as usual were dressing wounds in the dressing station. Our Ambulances kept returning to the front for wounded while other Ambulance Companies took the wounded from our dressing stations to places of safety out of the fighting zone."[65]

Martin N. "Hayshaker" Mortenson was a 19-year-old draftsman when he enlisted on June 30, 1917. He was cited for bravery while working as an ambulance orderly, carrying wounded to the dressing station at Saulx-lès-Champlon on September 25–26, 1918. Mortenson would be promoted to corporal on December 18, 1918. In this photograph he has his red discharge chevron on his left sleeve, a YD pin on his overseas cap, and a service ribbon on his chest (courtesy Le petit musée du Doughboy).

In his Sanitary Train history, ambulance driver Earle Radikin reported: "The dressing station at Saulx was operated continually, under so severe a bombardment that it was nearly demolished. It being in full observation of the enemy, affording a wonderful target for their many direct hits. The personnel, however, were so enthusiastically engaged and devoted to their duties that they did not realize their dangerous position."[66] Although the station was ordered to retire about 6:00 p.m., "realizing that the forward areas had not been cleared, the officers and the men under them volunteered to operate the station at all costs until they knew that every man was cared for," noted Radikin.[67]

After a very long day of "'luggin' litters' in the face of machine gun fire," as Earle Radikin phrased it, Barlow concluded, "the 40 stretcher bearers returned at midnight as they had followed the 103rd when they were relieved and took roll call to see if all were saved."[68] The infantrymen and their supports knew they had fought well and bravely, but their contribution to the great offensive was not immediately clear. However, German military correspondence would confirm that the assault so far from the lines west of Verdun unbalanced their defense for a day.[69] The historian of the 103rd Infantry could only justify it as "the sort of sacrifice attack that has to be made and is made oftentimes, as was this, at considerable cost, for it is not an easy thing to go forward on a mission such as was theirs, to hold for a day, and then withdraw."[70]

On September 29, Division Surgeon Ralph S. Porter reported to General Edwards, commending the 101st and 102nd Ambulance Companies' "exceptionally daring conduct," which "reflects the highest credit on the Commanding Officer, Ambulance Section, (Captain Herbert W. Taylor, M.C.) and on the intrepid and gallant officers and men in those two companies."[71] General Edwards then congratulated Captain Taylor, telling him: "From an observation post I had personally observed the gallant work of the litter bearers under terrific enemy shell-fire, machine gun fire and rifle fire. From previous experience I knew that the wounded of my division would be well cared for under all conditions. My confidence in my sanitary personnel during all our engagements has left my mind free for other matters." He then continued, "but from my point of vantage my view was only superficial. It was not until later that I learned that you had established your dressing station in a daringly advanced position under direct shell fire and that your officers and men continued their operations until the station caved in after many direct hits. Your litter bearers worked unceasingly under this terrific fire for over twenty-four hours, continuously searching for and carrying the wounded. [Division Surgeon] Colonel Porter states that your service was the most remarkable that he has ever known in the United States Army."[72]

Proud of his Division's performance, General Edwards solicited information on acts of extreme bravery that would qualify for the award of a Distinguished Service Cross. About 170 men across the Division were nominated. As he was in temporary command during Johnston's illness, Lieutenant Durham proposed the Company's Sergeant Granville Wilcox; ambulance drivers Curtis Banks, Herbert Beers, Edward Bergeron, James Cooper, Theodore Gilliland, William Goodnow, and Leroy MacKinnon, and orderlies Albert Ahern, Robert MacDonald, William McElroy, Charles

Morgan, and Martin Mortenson. While Wilcox had managed the enlisted men at the dressing station at Saulx, the ambulance men "operated their ambulances from 1:00 o'clock the 26th of September until 4:00 o'clock the 27th under extremely heavy shell fire," read the nomination. "They showed great bravery and showed absolute fearlessness in the face of tremendous shelling that they were subjected to but drove ambulances calmly and cooly into the shell ridden area and collected the wounded from the Dressing Station in Saulx and carried them back to safety."[73] They may have shown "great bravery" and "absolute fearlessness," but those qualities were now expected in the AEF. General Pershing's Adjutant General would reply that "the acts recited in these cases are judged not to meet the standard set for the award of the Distinguished Service Cross."[74]

Barlow resented that no litter bearers were included among the men recommended for citations or medals. "None of these 14 men were cited in orders although their names were turned in to the commanding officer but all the Ambulance drivers who rushed them to the rear were cited in orders," he complained. "The Ambulances were of course under heavy fire as the enemy was shelling all roads but the more the shells came the faster the Ambulances were driven. The Commanding Officer was not up to the plains to see what the stretcher bearers were doing but did of course see the Ambulances when they arrived at Dommartin possibly five kilometers (three miles) from the lines.[75] It only made it worse to see that, in the 101st Ambulance Company, whose litter bearers had worked just to the right, two men—ultimately eight—were awarded Distinguished Service Crosses and three received the Croix de Guerre."[76]

Although he was born in North Carolina, 20-year-old Leroy A. "Roy" MacKinnon was a long-time Connecticut resident and was a clerk at the Union Metallic Cartridge Company when he enlisted in the Company on April 3, 1917. Assigned as a cook at the end of the summer, he was promoted to private 1st class in December and to wagoner in April 1918. He was gassed on the Chemin des Dames on March 17, at Seicheprey on April 20, and at Saulx on September 25, for which he was cited for bravery in action. This photograph was probably taken at the training camp in Niantic in the summer of 1917 (courtesy Le petit musée du Doughboy).

"It is still raining and we moved our dressing station back into the church in the center of the town" of Dommartin reported Barlow the next day.[77] "We are still living in Boche billets and the fleas are thriving," wrote James Peck. "I was lucky enough to get a complete change of clothes tonight and now feel like a new man. It's the first chance I've had to bathe in over a month. I went out and got a few blackberries the other day and they were almost like home."[78]

The Company now had an unusual vehicle on its ambulance line. In his letter to the Comfort Club, Barlow wrote that Lieutenant Charles Comfort, the 102nd Infantry surgeon, had "turned that captured Boche ambulance over to our company and Goodnow is running it and Corp. Davis was reduced to a private at his own request, just to be an orderly on it."[79]

Even in the rugged country around Dommartin, the French had built one of their narrow-gauge railroads with small gasoline-powered locomotives to deliver supplies and artillery ammunition. At the beginning of October, Earle Radikin, with his orderly Frank Crump, "hit a French dinky engine when passing with his G.M.C. Ambulance, but no serious damage done and no one injured," recorded Barlow, explaining, he "hooked it right off the track with his front fender."[80]

At the beginning of October, Barlow reported, "some person in this outfit has found another dog for a mascot and this time it is a brown shaggy mongrel and known as 'Mickey the Mope.' Heaven knows where the bull dog ever went to."[81] In his letter home to the Bridgeport Comfort Club, Barlow joked about Mickey the Mope, "sure it is just a plain yeller dog, but we love him all the same, for there's not a drop of Deutschhound in him, though he has been more asleep than ever, since his best friend, Harry Monahan, went to get his broken wrist fixed up. No one knows just what breed Mickey is but Rip Morgan claims him to be a cross between a window shutter and the Gulf of Mexico."[82]

"All the men when not busy at anything else sit down at the nearest point and remove their shirts to read the seams for cooties," wrote Barlow at the beginning of October.[83] But they did not have to wait long for a visit by the sector's Thresh-Foden units. "While at Dommartin the steam delousing machines came into the town and the enemy observers in balloons thinking the Allies were bringing up heavy artillery, ordered their artillery to send over a few Krupp Calling Cards and the men who were bathing had to run over the hill a la September Morn," wrote Barlow, making a joking reference to the popular 1911 painting "September Morn" by Paul Emile Chabas, showing a nude woman covering herself with her hands at the water's edge.[84]

Following the raids on Marchéville and Riaville, and several trench raids, the Germans increased their gas bombardments.[85] Down in the infantry lines, mustard gas shells rained down. "Many gas patients are coming through and our records show there has been 1200 through this station since we came to this town of Dommartin," noted Barlow at the beginning of October.[86] "They have put up another stove to heat water for the gassed men to have a bath in the church used as a dressing station and the building looks like a foundry as there is smoke coming out of it in all directions," he added.[87]

Under the continued scattering of German artillery fire, Barlow joked about Joseph Wynkoop and Edwin Hough: "there were two men working under their truck, when the first shell came over. Mr. Hough, he beats it. Joe yells, 'Hey, Ned, come back here.' Second shell goes whango. (Nothing said) third shell lands nearer. Oh boy, that Wynkoop fellow had passed Ned and was kicking two rabbits along that had started up his path and so he says between breaths, 'Gee Whiz, Bunnie, if you can't run, get out of the way, and let someone that can."[88]

Under the continuing shell fire on October 4, "we moved our kitchen up on the hill further where it will not be in quite so much danger," noted Barlow.[89] Duty with the rolling kitchens or stationary field kitchen ranges, smoking away in the open, could be dangerous. On September 25 Herbert Beers had written: "Yesterday a shell landed in a kitchen, killing five and wounding seven. It also put 1400 doughnuts, already cooked, out of business. It wasn't our kitchen."[90] Barlow reported on October 4, "Murray of L Company of the 102nd Infantry who was injured by shell fire when at work with his rolling kitchen, died in one of our Ambulances on the way to the dressing station."[91]

Born in Paterson, New Jersey, Joseph Wynkoop was a 22-year-old employee of the *Bridgeport Post* newspaper when he enlisted in the Company in June 1917. Promoted to private 1st class, he was assigned as a wagoner and usually drove one of the Company's trucks rather than an ambulance. He would receive a citation for bravery in action. *Bridgeport Post* photograph (courtesy the Bridgeport History Center, Bridgeport Public Library).

The Company's John Caler was more fortunate. Barlow claimed he had "his clothes torn by shell fire but did not even scratch his body."[92] George "Mook" Vennart and 18-year-old Bert Keane were assigned two of the Sanitary Train's motorcycles and served as messengers.[93] Keane was wounded that day as well. He wrote home to report that that he was wounded in action "while traveling over what he termed an unhealthy road … he connected with a goodly portion of an 88. Although weakened he wended his way to a dressing station where he was given aid." His former employer, the *Bridgeport Telegram*, remarked: "It was then that the youngster displayed what he was made of. After being treated by the Lieutenant in charge he was told that he would have to lie down and wait for an ambulance to take him to the rear. After arguing with the officer in charge regarding an important message for headquarters and assuring his superior that he could drive his machine with one hand he was allowed to make the trip."[94]

Earlier, Barlow had remarked that the Company seemed to train litter bearers, only to have them reassigned. Early in October, another eight of the Company's reliable bearers were detailed to work as regimental litter bearers in the 102nd and 103rd Infantry. In their place, seven men "fresh from the draft" were sent to the Company to learn their duties under fire.[95]

At the same time, Barlow observed, "there are quite a number of 79th Division men around this section and are evidently coming in to relieve us."[96] The 79th Division—mostly draftees from Maryland and Pennsylvania—had arrived in France in July and had been on the right of the Fifth Corps assault on the center of the Meuse-Argonne line on September 26. After taking more than 3,500 casualties in four days of fighting there, it was relieved on October 1 and sent to the Troyon Sector to replace the 26th Division in this quieter section of the lines.[97] Quieter perhaps, but the 26th Division had taken 1,300 casualties, including 249 deaths, during its time there and was happy to be relieved.[98]

Ready to ride, Bert Keane shows off a motorcycle orderly's garb, with turned-down rubber half-hip boots, gauntlets, a rain slicker with the collar buttoned up, and motorcycle helmet and goggles. Only 17 when he left the *Bridgeport Post* to enlist in May 1917, he was the youngest man in the Company. He received a Croix de Guerre for bravery for refusing to let a shrapnel wound deter him from delivering a message on his motorcycle on October 4, 1918 (courtesy Le petit musée du Doughboy).

10

A Bloody Business on the Heights of the Meuse

October–November 1918

With the 79th Division moving in to take over the line on the Woëvre plain, the 26th Division began its move northwest to the area of Verdun to prepare for its next assignment. For the Sanitary Train, the first destination was Ambly-sur-Meuse, about 15 kilometers (9 miles) back along the river.

On October 7, the movement began, with the ambulance companies ordered to travel after dark.[1] "We were all packed up to move but our trucks became stuck in the mud where they had stood and we had much trouble in having them hauled out," reported Sergeant Barlow. Some of the litter-bearer contingent rode in the trucks, "but many had to hike through a hail storm" to reach Ambly.[2]

Back in proximity to the AEF supply train, the Company decided to spend 351 francs of the Comfort Club money on food at the nearby U.S. commissary. But before they could prepare it, they packed up to travel another 15 kilometers (9 miles) north and "left by trucks again in the night and went into a four story brick building one mile from Verdun."[3] Their new home was part of Caserne Bevaux, a group of large French military barracks just south of Verdun. "We could have but two meals per day on account of fires being seen by the enemy," commented Barlow. Although it was temporarily off the line, the Company still had to detail 16 men for guard duty each day.[4]

"This building is alive with soldiers," Barlow continued. "All roll up in a blanket on the cement floor to sleep. The building has many holes through it from shell fire. Blankets have been placed over all places where light might come through, so the airplanes will not see our lights at night and drop a bomb or two on the place."[5] He added, "the mud is deep about the barracks and roads, and so many of the men have colds that the barracks at night sounds like a sanitarium."[6] During the move up and into Caserne Bevaux, four more men had been sent off to the hospital with fevers and other ailments. Barlow remarked, "It surely takes a tough man to stand this life."[7]

The Company had received a $100 check from the Comfort Club at the beginning of October. As treasurer, Barlow made sure the money was distributed fairly. "When we divide our money which the Comfort Club has sent us, we shall pay the recently transferred men," reported Barlow, "as they were with us when we received the next to the last check, and we haven't cashed that as yet."[8] Then, on October 11, "we were paid thirty francs each from the Pershing Fund money that you good people raised last Fourth of July," wrote Barlow to the Comfort Club. "Someone must have had the back gears thrown in on that money, till it began to look like one of those deferred payment policies, but any way we have it and we want to thank you that had any part in it."[9] As he noted, "each Connecticut man received 20 francs (a franc is worth about 20 cents) from the Pershing fund. This money was sent last July but it has been a difficult problem to pick out the Connecticut men in each outfit."[10]

With all that money in hand, "the men spend most of their time off duty by gambling," noted Barlow the next day. "There are crap games in every nook and corner, with some high stakes."[11] But Sergeant Brendel let many of them down that day. "Pop Brendel lost a purse that contained 700 francs," wrote Barlow. "He had the funds of many of the men who had made some money in gambling and of others who were afraid of being bumped off when on duty."[12]

The members of the Comfort Club were eager to send clothing for the Company's orphans. "The best way to do would be to send small amounts of money at different times and let the mothers do as they think best," wrote Barlow. "Little Marie, whom I saw, is rather small for eleven, and rather frail, while not sickly or serious, still her little sad face does not bespeak the best of health. You know the money the Red Cross gives the children, that was raised by different companies in the AEF, is not lumped, but dished out either weekly or monthly, and this does not allow for very much misuse. Marie Louise's Mother is a very rugged woman, I should say about thirty-five, and has one younger child who is a little cross-eyed, but very strong, more like the mother. Mrs. Decollas seemed to wonder what she should do after the boys went home or our year was up, so I shall try and remember and no doubt our gang will be glad to remember our kids, when the right time comes."[13]

None of the Company had been captured—and theoretically they were neutral noncombatants—but the Bridgeport Comfort Club wished to do something for Connecticut prisoners of war. When the Club consulted Barlow, he replied, "I find that the Red Cross are to send each one a package for Xmas. 6x9x11, I believe the law allows them, and also their friends can send them one package a month. So what we have talked of is to send the Home Office of the Red Cross at Paris, say 200 francs, to help them pay for the things they send the boys in prison camps, and as soon as I get back to the company, I shall try to have the boys let me do this."[14]

On October 8—the day the First Army reached its objectives for September 26, having advanced about ten miles—General Pershing opened a new front east of the Meuse River. The 29th and 33rd Divisions had been added to the French XVII Corps to broaden the fighting front and to eliminate the German artillery flanking the American advance from the heights east of the Meuse. The 29th "Blue and Gray" Division attacked north from Samogneux into the hills and woods between Haumont and Brabant that day, while the 33rd Division on the left crossed downstream near Consenvoye.[15] This area of rolling hills and steep ravines, with only a few shattered trees on what were once wooded hillsides, had been fought over since the Battle of Verdun in 1916. Here the German line formed an angle that might be considered the pivot of the whole southern German defense line. The Germans had a very strong trench line screened by barbed wire and studded with concrete pill boxes for machine guns. Behind the front, a heavy concentration of German artillery ensured that it would be extremely difficult to pierce the lines here. But by continuing to feed in assaulting troops to threaten the position, the AEF and French divisions could immobilize the Germans while the advance continued west of the Meuse.

Now in the Neptune Sector, the 26th Division, as part of the First Army reserve, was placed under command of the French Seventeenth Corps. On October 13, the Division's infantry regiments began to move up, with the 104th Infantry taking a position before the Bois d'Haumont to the right of the 29th Division.[16] That day Barlow noted hopefully, "we are all packed ready to move and rumors are that Germany has accepted our peace terms."[17] In his history of the Sanitary Train, Earle Radikin confirmed, "the daily communiques were received with ever increasing optimism, the end of the war was clearly a matter of days. And so when orders came to go in once more, it appeared to be little more than an invitation to be there at the finish."[18]

On October 17, the 104th Ambulance Company was sent forward to establish a tent dressing station along the road near the destroyed village of Samogneux, in the valley along the Meuse and Meuse Canal. Ambulances from the other companies were assigned there as well, to make the three-mile drive up the broad valley northeast of Samogneux. Part way up the road forked, the righthand route leading to the aid station and ambulance head at the destroyed village of Haumont. The left fork led up a narrow valley—almost a ravine—nicknamed "Death Valley," nearer to the battalion aid stations behind the Division's new front. From Samogneux, the ambulances could evacuate the wounded to the 104th Field Hospital at Bras (which would have to relocate to avoid shell fire), or the 101st Field Hospital at Vacherauville, both less than ten kilometers (six miles) back toward Verdun. From there, the wounded would be carried beyond Verdun to the Division's other two field hospitals, which had remained at Caserne Bevaux.[19]

The next day the 102nd Ambulance Company moved forward too. "We moved up nearer the front in the mud and rain this morning at 3(?) A.M.," recorded Barlow. "There is a vast amount of artillery and roads are camouflaged overhead as much as possible by cloth and leaves fastened to wire. We set up a dressing station in a large dugout on the bend of a road."[20] This was the "Chalk Cliff dressing station" occupied by the 113th Ambulance Company of the 29th Division about October 8. It seems to have been constructed by the Germans during the Verdun Campaign and evacuated, with plenty of explosives left, as the 29th Division moved in.[21] It would quickly replace the exposed dressing station of the 104th Ambulance Company, while the 101st Ambulance Company set up a similar dressing station a few kilometers back at Vacherauville.[22] As Barlow put it, "the balance of the Company not driving Ambulances or acting as stretcher bearers are operating the dressing station in the bank at Samogneux, a place that was once a small town but now only a sand bank, a canal and a cross roads."[23]

"There is room for but 40 men below this dugout and the balance of the Company sleep in the Ambulances or have pitched pup tents on the side of the hill," continued Barlow. "During the day they are putting more bags of sand over the dugout used by the officers and which adjoins the dugout used as a dressing station. There are several ten inch guns operated by the French on a cross roads just below us,

On October 18, 1918, the Company took over the "Chalk Cliff" dressing station established by the 113th Ambulance Company near the ruins of Samogneux ten days earlier. The Company would remain here for two weeks, until November 1. Here, in front of spare and blood-stained litters and a draping of camouflage, wounded who have been dressed await an ambulance ride to the field hospital. The soldier on the litter, who has a Thomas splint on his left leg, holds a cup of hot chocolate. Notice the pile of blankets for keeping wounded soldiers warm to prevent shock. The officer at center, looking over his shoulder at the camera, may be Captain Clyde C. "Dugout" Johnston, as the Company's lieutenants would be in the dressing station dugout tending to the wounded. The other Ambulance Company men have not been identified. Signal Corps photo by Lieutenant H.S. Drucker, October 23, 1918 (National Archives, photo no. 111-SC-28368).

which shake the earth when fired. The gas alarm is given often and there are many wounded as we are now near the Argonne Forest and are relieving the 29th Division in this sector."[24]

That day, Barlow recorded that ambulance drivers James Cooper and William Goodnow "were sent to the hospital. Both had to be ordered to go. They did not wish to give up. Goodnow has run away from the Field Hospital on two or three occasions and sneaked back to the Company, when he was supposed to be going to the rear for treatment."[25] But the next day, "Goodnow arrived back and would not allow himself to be sent further back than Verdun and told them he wanted action," exclaimed Barlow. "Now how is Heinie ever going to win the war from birds like that?"[26]

The Division finished relieving the 29th Division and took control of the line in the morning of October 18.[27] Even as the Company entered a zone of intense warfare, experienced men were pulled from it to serve as litter bearers in short-handed infantry regiments and untried, drafted men arrived to join the Company. "Four of our men were transferred to other units and six men from the draft were assigned to

Some of the first wounded to arrive at the Company's Samogneux dressing station on October 23, 1918. The dressing station is heavily protected with sandbags, and the entrance is sealed with a blanket that serves as a gas barrier. The soldier at left—possibly a machine gunner—has a pistol on his belt and a diagnosis tag attached to a button on his blouse. Behind him stands one of the Ambulance Company men wearing half-hip rubber boots and holding a dressing. Above his left hand is a medical belt with hatchet attached. Another wounded man reclines next to a lieutenant with a wounded left forearm. The iodine mark on his forehead indicates he has received anti-tetanus serum. Next to him, a soldier with a Thomas-splinted and bandaged left arm has a diagnosis tag on his chest. All of the soldiers' boots are caked with mud. The Ambulance Company man with moustache and sweater vest has not been identified. Signal Corps photo by Lieutenant H.S. Drucker, October 23, 1918 (National Archives, photo no. 111-SC-28369).

work with this Company," remarked Barlow, who would be responsible for the new men as most of them would be detailed as litter bearers.[28]

As he described: "Our Ambulances are busy bringing wounded from Haumont and Death Valley and there is fierce shelling on both sides. Many combat troops are coming through with tags marked 'Exhaustion.' That is they have gone to the limit of human endurance. Our stretcher bearers are working with the 3rd Battalion of the 103rd Infantry in the woods, north of Haumont, a small town that is absolutely flat from the shelling by the enemy but where there is a good supply of water and the enemy drops a shell into town every few minutes."[29]

"The enemy keeps putting over gas shells and the roads are never free from it," wrote Barlow. "The Infantry carry drums of food from their 'Kitchens' up into the trenches, by stringing them over long poles and holding them on their shoulders.

They do this work mostly at night and keep quite a distance apart as the enemy was in these towns recently and remembers these paths by shelling them at intervals. Food is sometimes left at cross roads in the hope it will reach some who need it but it is generally gassed so that it gases any who eats it."[30]

On October 22, Barlow was up near Haumont with the litter bearers. "Varey lights, gas, shrapnel and high explosive shells are coming over thick and fast and you must dig in if you can," he warned. "The enemy put over some liquid fire in the valley to the rear of Haumont and near the path where the dough boys had been carrying up rations but no one was near it and it rolled off down the valley like so much yellow fumes and did not come up high enough to hurt the stretcher bearers who had dug themselves into some holes in the crest of a sand bank while waiting for more wounded to litter back to Haumont where there was a dressing station in an old cellar."[31]

To maintain a steady evacuation from the ambulance head at Haumont, at least one ambulance was stationed there despite the shelling, to be replaced whenever it made a run to the Samogneux dressing station. "Two men from the 103rd Ambulance Company were killed at Haumont," remarked Barlow on October 21. "Both were on the same Ambulance and one shell is said to have killed both men."[32]

The next day, "shells exploded near the Ambulance driven by Gus Hannon and filled it with a thousand small holes but no one was hurt," commented Barlow. "Many large size shells keep dropping into this section and explode near the roads and dressing stations and some go as far back as Verdun (probably 12 kilometers). Many of the shells that have landed down in the valley where all the artillery horses and mules are kept have proved to be shells that have not exploded and known as 'Duds.'"[33]

Barlow later remembered that Hannon's ambulance "was left by the side of the road, with four flat tires, broken hose connections etc. but when Edes was sent up to bring it back for repairs, he gave the engine a quarter turn and to his astonishment the engine started and he ran the Ambulance back to the rear on four flat tires. Several hundred small pieces of shrapnel were later picked from various parts of this Ambulance but no one had been injured."[34]

Leland Gilbert and his orderly Benjamin Clay had ambulance #73598 up at the Haumont ambulance head on the evening of October 22 as rations were being unloaded for the 102nd Infantry. When heavy shells began falling around 7:00 p.m., all the men crowded into the ambulance head dugout. Ten minutes later an infantryman rushed up to report that a man had been wounded in the field nearby. Clay ran out, trying to get the infantryman to go with him to locate the wounded man, while Gilbert ran to the ambulance to get a litter. Everyone refused to leave the dugout, so Gilbert and Clay searched for several minutes and finally found the man lying in a shell hole with a severe wound. They called for help in carrying the litter the 400 yards to the 102nd Infantry aid station, where he could have his wound dressed. All the men in the dugout refused to help, so they carried him to the dugout to give him first aid themselves, but no one would let them in. Finally, they loaded him into the ambulance and drove over to the aid station. The sergeant there told them the man was dead, but Gilbert felt a weak pulse and saw his eyes roll when he lifted his lids, so they drove about three kilometers (less than two miles) to the 101st Infantry aid station. The doctor there dressed his wound and told them to hurry him down Death Valley to the Company's dressing station, where he "was found to be living but very weak," in the words of Captain Johnston, who almost immediately nominated Gilbert and Clay for Distinguished Service Crosses.[35]

"While at Samogneax wagoners Ahern and Wyrtzen were bringing through the section known as Death Valley an Ambulance loaded with sitting wounded and as they were driving along a shell burst directly in front of them and they of course 'Ducked,'" remembered Barlow. "A piece of shrapnel killed an already wounded soldier who had been sitting directly behind Ahern."[36]

Barlow described the trip from Haumont to Samogneux for the Bridgeport Comfort Club: "Well, cut that old float loose, there, Goodnow, all are ready. Away she goes down the road, two litter patients and six or eight sitting; every once in a while Heinie drops one over on the road and you may get another wound on the way in, for they love a Red Cross flag like a bull loves a red flag. Well you hang on for dear life, for the car is going over shell holes galore, with once in a while the legs or neck of a dead horse or mule thrown in. Then when you have made the ambulance company dressing station you can get your wound redressed if it needs it, leave your pack, rifle, and all equipment, except the toilet articles you need at the hospital and all the money you have." Finally, "they give you a cigarette or cup of cocoa, and record you in their books, put you in another ambulance, for the car that fetched you has already gone back for another load."[37]

But no one was free of the gas and high-explosive shells. "This is the most terrific bombardment we have ever seen or hope to see, the earth seems to be aquiver, the Ambulance men are working night and day and always under shell fire as is every one else in this vicinity. Trucks are overturned, the dressing station is a mass of blood," wrote Barlow on October 23.[38]

When off duty, the ambulance drivers and their orderlies slept either in their ambulances at the dressing station or in small dugouts in the hillside there. Once, recalled Barlow, "a shell burst at night, went through an Ambulance directly under an upper litter where William McElroy was sleeping and above a litter where another soldier was sleeping and out through the rear of the Ambulance and into a second Ambulance where Ralph Merrill was sleeping, on out of the second Ambulance and into the tail board of a truck where Ripple Morgan was sleeping, but the shell injured no one."[39]

Back home, the Mother's Comfort Club was meeting, even as the men in France were more endangered than ever. There, the mothers shared letters from their sons and listened to a reading of the latest two letters from Sergeant and Secretary Barlow. They also sold off unclaimed packages to raise a Christmas fund for the ambulance men. "It is planned to send each boy in the corps $5, officers included, and the surplus will be sent to the boys to use for their Christmas enjoyment as they see fit," reported the *Bridgeport Post*. "As the boys have adopted several little French children it is thought they may use the money for trees for the youngsters or to make their Christmas happy in some way."[40]

They could never imagine that, up at the front, Barlow was working to break in

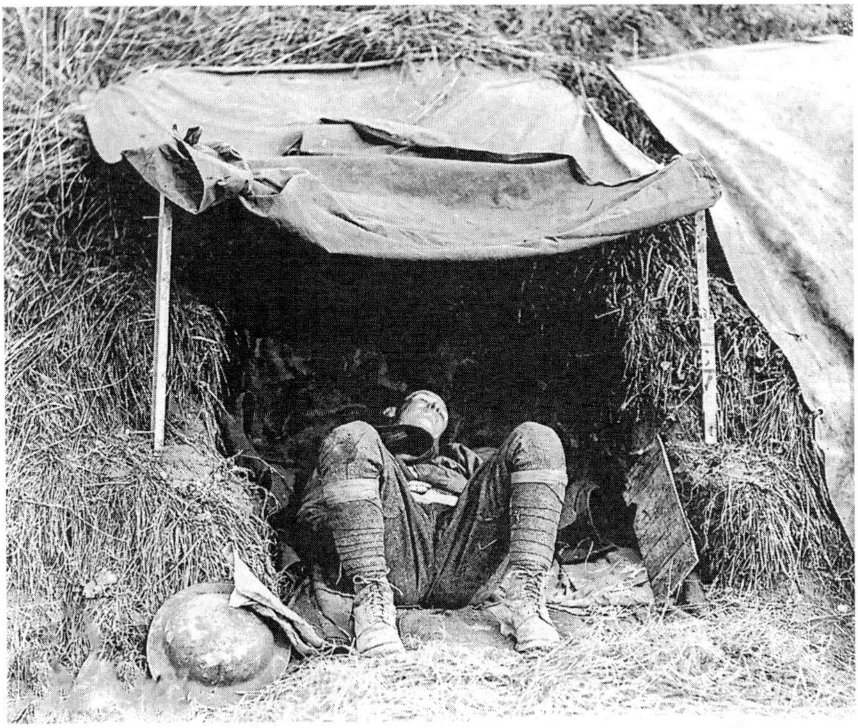

After 14 hours on the road, one of the Company's exhausted wagoners sleeps in a shallow dugout next to the Samogneux dressing station. The tarpaulin or shelter tent half rigged above him will keep out rain and shrapnel splinters. His helmet and gauntlets for driving rest nearby. He has not been identified. Signal Corps photo by Lieutenant George E. Stone, October 27, 1918 (National Archives, photo no. 111-SC-28344).

To the left of the dressing station, a number of the men dug shallow dugouts for sleeping. The Red Cross guidon identifies the dressing station, and the sign directs "wounded able to walk." The photograph makes clear the open, rolling terrain on the Heights of the Meuse. Signal Corps photo by Lieutenant George E. Stone, October 27, 1918 (National Archives, photo no. 111-SC-28343).

the new litter bearers. That was a challenge. On October 23, James Dickens, who had just been assigned to the Company, "moving with the stretcher bearers at night followed the wrong combat troops and led the six men behind him almost into the German trenches. It was a moonlight night and the enemy machine gunners were rat a tat tatting from over in the trees and were covering every point where men were likely to show themselves above the trenches."[41]

The next day, Barlow reported: "Dickens has a high fever and had to be relieved as a stretcher bearer and the man sent to relieve was a new man who had not evidently learned to roll his pack and looked like a furniture van coming up over the hill in Haumont and passing the troops dug in the fox holes was the cause of much laughter."[42]

Barlow continued on October 24: "War certainly is Hell for events preceding these last few days have been nothing more than picnics in comparison. The barrage was so heavy all afternoon that wounded had to be kept under cover until night fall before being removed for it meant almost sure death to move in the open. One man is sent back by the stretcher bearers in the woods north of Haumont to the company headquarters for rations each day and brings them up over the hill in a burlap bag over his shoulder. Nuss was injured in the leg with shrapnel and had to [be] sent to the rear. The dressing station here is simply a hole in the ground down a few steps and where there is hardly room for the wounded to be turned around and this station is in the center of an area that is shelled every afternoon and is denoted only by a small Red Cross flag stuck in the ground nearby."[43]

As Barlow described the processing of the wounded, "the nearest first aid man will fix you up, and the litter bearers will carry you back, but if you are able 'beat it' yourself for the nearest dressing station… Here they will fix you up, put a tag on you, and as soon as the shelling lets up the litter-bearers will carry you down to the road where an ambulance is waiting, or if you can walk, you surely must do so, for here is where every man must show the most stuff he has in him."[44]

Barlow's litter bearers were constantly exposed. "Men waiting to litter wounded to the rear dig themselves in and lie face down and when the shells strike the earth the vibrations of the earth are so great that often when you look up you are surprised and agreeably so at the distance away the last shell landed but you soon duck again for they keep coming over thick and fast," Barlow wrote from experience.[45]

Barlow was probably referring to 19-year-old Moe Cohen of Harrisburg, Pennsylvania, who had been sent over from Camp Greenleaf and joined the Company in October, when he remarked: "A young Jewish boy sent to this Company at the same station, was sent from there up to join the litter bearers over in the woods beyond Haumont. He wandered around the town of Haumont for a time and then returned to the Company and was again sent up to aid the litter bearers and when they were relieved that night and came out of the woods they found this fellow still at Haumont and he was ordered to return with them to the Company. He had evidently been to[o] scared to look for the litter bearers and it was decided he would be much more efficient digging graves near the dressing station than trying to aid the wounded."[46]

On October 26, "the stretcher bearers came back to the Company and were set

Alongside two of the Company's GMC ambulances, some of the men look over the pile of clothing, helmets, and boots removed from wounded at the Samogneux dressing station, which handled 4,000 cases during the Company's two weeks there. Signal Corps photo by Sergeant Carlson, November 1, 1918 (National Archives, photo no. 111-SC-35003).

Across the road from the Samogneux dressing station, the Company established a burying ground for casualties, with rude crosses, each with one of the soldier's dog tags nailed to it. At left is the grave of Private Albert C. Larsen of the 111th Machine Gun Battalion of the 29th Division, who died on October 24, 1918. At right is the grave of Captain Paul Kittredge of Company F of the 101st Infantry, who died on October 23, 1918. Most of the men buried here would be reinterred in the Meuse-Argonne American Cemetery after the war. One of the Company's well-marked GMC ambulances sits in the background. Signal Corps photo by Sergeant Carlson, November 1, 1918 (National Archives, photo no. 111-SC-35000).

to work burying the dead that were lying around the dressing station. These dead were buried just across the road from the dressing station and were near a great heap of clothing and bandages removed from the dead and dying and made a most sickening surrounding."[47]

"The men in the dressing station are working in blood with their sleeves rolled up and still our Ambulances are rolling in from Death Valley and there seems no end to the wounded," wrote Barlow. "There are no billets here and men dug in a crest of a sand bank and about 20 feet above the level of the road."[48]

The officers at the dressing station were nearly as exhausted as the litter bearers. "A replacement officer, past middle life and sent to the Company at Samogneux, could not seem to apply himself to the work and his trying to work on wounded when wearing a gas mask, so disgusted Serg't Brendel that he chased him outside the dressing station," recorded Barlow.[49]

It didn't help morale there that "our Commanding Officer, Clyde C. Johnston is sick again and rumors are that he stuck a thermometer in a cup of hot coffee instead of in his mouth and then handed the thermometer to the nearest medical officer and was ordered to the rear and if reports are true he has been sick during every major engagement to date," recorded Barlow on October 25.[50]

Herbert Beers spoke for the ambulance drivers when he remarked: "Seems to

With their gas masks on their left hips and their mess kits in hand, members of the Company line up at the stationary kitchen between the dressing station and the entrance to the mess crew's dugout (left). At least six men make up the mess crew. The man at left probably ladles hot coffee out of the large can and into the men's cups. Signal Corps photo by Sergeant Carlson, November 1, 1918 (National Archives, photo no. 111-SC-35001).

me that every front we go to things get hotter. When shells explode so close to you that they blow your cigarette out—well, I call that close."[51] He continued, "we had an ambulance post on a corner, and it seemed as if every time we went there the Bosche shelled it for all they were worth. I was up there once and had just finished loading the patients when they began to send the shells over. I was cranking the old boat for all I was worth and she would not go. Jimmie [Peck] had retarded the spark for some unknown reason. I guess he was a bit excited. Any way I saw what the trouble was, made a leap and pulled it down and started in cranking again. Well one landed about 20 feet away, and believe me, I thought my time had come. But I found myself still churning and got the engine started. All the way out the ground was growing new holes."[52]

Twenty-three-year-old Sergeant Charles W. "Pop" Brendel, whose National Guard ambulance service extended back to 1913, was often the Company's 1st sergeant. At Samogneux, he managed the dressing station, evicting a doctor who could not operate with his gas mask on (courtesy Dave Brendel).

"Another time I had a lieutenant out in the ambulance and he had been gassed," remarked Beers. "We got into a shell hole. He kept coughing and crying, 'We'll all be killed. Can't you get me out of here, boys?' I said, 'Keep still. We will soon be out.' Shells were landing all around. Jimmie Peck was with me and we jacked the wheel up, filled the hole with stone and drove on. A piece of shell had punctured one front shoe. Really it was laughable. It must have been funny, too, to have seen Jim and I jumping around. I had to find a pick and believe me I was glad I knew how to use one. One shell landed at the door of the dugout and blew the tin roof off the entrance."[53]

In retrospect, Beers remarked: "The Frenchmen say you are not a soldier until you have been at the front. Now I know it is so. Say, but that was some place! 'Beaucoup' shells and gas! Every time we went up with the car, we didn't expect to come back. Pieces of shell bouncing off the fenders; and some of the fellows coming back wounded and gassed. That is the way it was. Well I've been through it all, but never expect to have to again. [Lodrick] James was at the hospital and missed it all. I'm glad he did." Beers finished, "after you have gone all through it and when it is all over, is the time you think of what could have happened."[54]

On October 27, Barlow recorded: "The Ambulances are still rushing and fifteen or twenty wounded pile into the Ambulance at a small dressing station in the point of an old road at Death Valley and off to the west of Haumont. The enemy are constantly shelling this area and the wounded are so anxious to get out of the area that even the most horribly wounded will set up to make room for a buddy for only a few at a time may be removed if they have to lie on a stretcher."[55] But many were not able to sit, and Barlow noted that with the arrangement of upper and lower stretchers in the ambulances, men "often bleed so freely even after their wounds had been dressed temporarily that the blood runs down on the man on the stretcher below and when removed by the men at the dressing station they do not know who is wounded the most seriously."[56]

After a day or two of rest, the litter bearers were sent back up on October 27. Barlow reported: "More of our stretcher bearers were sent up and this time they are to remove the wounded of the 101st Infantry who are south west of Death Valley. They were caught in a barrage at Death Valley and although they were in charge of Captain Thomas D. McRossie a man whom we all loved and who had been borrowed from another company, all the men had to shift for themselves as both gas and high explosive shells were dropping on all sides and to make it more interesting a few Whiz Bangs (Austrian 88's) were thrown in for good measure."[57] To the Bridgeport Comfort Club, Barlow could joke about the shells from the high-velocity 88-millimeter gun the Allies called the Austrian 88. "Now an Austrian '88' sneaks up behind a fellow without saying a word, then whizz bang! It's away down in the seat of your breeches before it says a word and when you get up off your stomach if there isn't a first aid man working on you, why it missed you. Go ahead and try to make the next dug-out."[58] Under such barrages, many litter bearers and ambulance drivers had assumed the fatalistic logic expressed by Earle Radikin: "You never hear the one that gets you."[59]

Up beyond Death Valley, the litter bearers normally dug themselves little fox holes for protection until they were called out, usually after dark, to retrieve the wounded. But that day, according to Barlow, "several of our men were so exhausted they could not dig a hole for themselves and slept on a pile of trap rock."[60]

Sergeant Barlow was describing his own experience that evening when he wrote: "The sergeant in charge of these stretcher bearers was given an order to deliver to the major of the battalion in action and after going through a barrage for one half mile alone found the dressing station in the woods just back of where the 101st Infantry were in action."

"He delivered the message after going down about 30 steps into a dugout and was told to return with his men to the station at Death Valley and to wait until daylight and to see if the shelling let up. The serg't did not say the men were out side for heaven only knows where they were but he returned toward the rear through another barrage and routed up as many of the men as he could before morning who had been sent up with him, rolled some dead men off the stretchers where they had died, as stretchers were at a premium and were then ready with these stretchers to go ahead at daylight."[61]

Barlow was among those gassed that night. But he was also worried that litter bearers Michael Kwasniski and Dewey Houston had disappeared. "They could not be located and possibly have been gassed for there are so many kinds of gas coming over and being sent over that no one knows how to treat it, as different gases are treated in different manner. When it is all mixed no one knows just what to do." Kwasniski and Houston would eventually turn up unhurt.[62]

As on other fronts, the dedicated Y.M.C.A. sometimes found their way forward and took a hand at evacuating the wounded. "A middle aged Y.M.C.A. man was seen to be acting as a stretcher bearer in this area," remarked Barlow. "He was afraid of nothing and apparently conducted himself as though he were at home. He was finally wounded and had to be sent to the rear."[63]

On October 28, "the stretcher bearers went ahead to where the 101st Infantry wounded men were," Barlow continued. "After all these wounded had been taken back to a point where they could be picked up by the Ambulances it was found that every one of the 16 stretcher bearers had been either killed, wounded or so badly gassed that they had to be sent to hospitals (including Captain Thomas D. McRossie)."[64]

Among the 16 litter bearers was 30-year-old Gaston Derolland, a New York hatmaker who had been born in France. Drafted in June 1918 and trained at Camp Greenleaf, he had returned to his homeland as an American soldier and joined the Company in September. His litter-mate was 32-year-old Nebraska farmer John Walls, who had been trained at Fort Riley, Kansas, and also joined the Company in September. Barlow explained: "Derolland [and] Walls were killed after offering their services with two other men of this detail to bring back a wounded sergeant of the Infantry who had just had his wounds dressed by Hugh Lawler who was at an advanced dressing station. Derolland [and] Walls had almost reached the dressing station at Death Valley when a one pound shell burst at their feet and killed Derolland instantly, wounded Walls so that he died in the dressing station and the wounded sergeant died of his wounds." Barlow remarked: "Derolland seemed to know he was to meet his death and would hardly speak for several weeks prior to this date. This also applies to Slootmaker who seemed to have a glassy stare in his eyes and not to care about his conduct for several weeks before he was killed." Originally a member of the Company, Adrian Slootmaker was serving as a litter bearer for the 101st Infantry when he was killed that day.[65]

After more than a week of nonstop work under such lethal conditions, the Company was on the verge of physical and emotional exhaustion. "Our Ambulance and dressing station men are still plugging away but all are dead tired, muddy, unshaven and depressed," wrote Barlow. "Many have reached the point where they do not care if they are killed or not for no human being can stand this life. All now in this area are hoping they will be wounded so they may be relieved from this hell. The horses and mules are dropping dead from exhaustion on all sides and it appears these human devils can stand more abuse than an animal."[66] "It is little short of miraculous that any of the men who worked so heroically and faithfully in this Hell Hole of all the fronts escaped alive and whole," proposed Earle Radikin in the Sanitary Train history.[67]

Adrian Slootmaker was an 18-year-old newspaper employee when he enlisted in the Company at the end of March 1917. He was transferred to the 101st Infantry as a litter bearer about the end of September or early October 1918. He was killed on October 28, and Sergeant Barlow felt that his "glassy stare" and indifference indicated that he expected to die. Here he wears his campaign hat and has a Connecticut National Guard collar disk on his uniform. His family submitted this photograph with his Connecticut Soldiers' Questionnaire in 1920 (courtesy Connecticut State Archives).

Their mood was not improved by rumors reaching the front that their beloved General Clarence Edwards had been relieved of command of the Division, or "railroaded home," as Barlow phrased it.[68] Presented as a routine transfer home to take command of a training area, Edwards had received his orders on October 22, just as the Division was going into action on the Heights of the Meuse. After the attack of October 23, he had congratulated the units involved, including the ambulance companies at the front. "The attack as planned was difficult of execution, and only to be attempted by trained troops," Edwards wrote. "You carried it out like the veterans you are, and with a dash and valor worthy of the best traditions of the Twenty-sixth Division."[69] His replacement, Brigadier General Frank E. Bamford, who had commanded a brigade in the 1st Division, arrived to take over the Division on October 24. In the midst of the fighting, many did not know of the transfer until later, and many, like Barlow, felt the transfer was an unfair repudiation of Edwards and of National Guard troops.[70]

The 79th Division came up to relieve the 29th Division and the left brigade (101st and 102nd Infantry) of the 26th Division on October 30. On November 1 it took control of the position and, once again, an ambulance company of the 304th Sanitary Train took over the Company's dressing station.[71]

On November 2 the men celebrated. "HURRAY, the old Yankee Division is going to be relieved for our company has been shifted over to the right of Verdun and billeted in a tremendous steel and cement dugout, that is large enough for the

Under the supervision of the supply sergeant (left), members of the Company line up to obtain fresh clothing on November 1, 1918. The man in the overcoat has a new pair of boots. Behind him, a tall wagoner waits, wearing his driving gauntlets, a leather jerkin (vest), and his gas mask on his left hip. The individuals have not been identified. Signal Corps photo by Sergeant Carlson (National Archives, photo no. 111-SC-35002).

entire Company," recorded Barlow. "We are in luck as there is not much to do. All are resting up, that is, all but the Ambulance men. They are still busy as the enemy are retreating and the work is not dangerous."[72] With the Company withdrawn from duty at the dressing station, the ambulance men were now evacuating the wounded to the hospitals in the rear. "Last night there was a nice sunset and Jimmie and I were carrying patients to the hospital," wrote Herbert Beers to his mother on November 3. "We drove through some woods and the leaves on the ground sure did make us both think of evenings at home after a day of hunting. I'll have to stop and watch the planes I guess."[73]

But even the drivers and their orderlies got to enjoy the underground quarters, "which is known as G.H.2 and which was built by the enemy," remarked Barlow. "We certainly have enjoyed our stay in this billet as it is equipped with running water, has electric lights and even a small fountain."[74] Herbert Beers was there on November 7 when he told his mother: "Just at present I am in a nice dry dugout with about ——— (censored) feet of cement on top and electric lights. When we wake up in the morning, 'presto!' and the lights are on, the same at night and they are out. Kind of a tough war, but o---h M---a!" He explained: "There are three of us in the 'apartment' I am in,—Bob [Stewart], Spencer Wills and myself. Spencer takes care of the lights and [Stewart] and I sweep the floor. All Spencer has to do is turn the button. To-day I was in the city and by a little graft bought ten boxes of chocolates and some sardines and cigars. Lee Hull, who is with the Red Cross, furnished me with some cakes and we expect to hold a luncheon 'cette soir.'"[75]

The men also began to talk about the future. Beers wrote: "I suppose Pop has all the corn picked and everything O.K. Gus Hannon, Radikin and Spence Wills are arguing over kisses. Believe me, the girls will find out that the boys are an ardent bunch when we hit the U.S.A., and just at the present moment it looks as if the war will end soon." While eager to return to civilian life, many of them wanted to maintain the close friendships they had formed during the war. "We are thinking of forming a club and have the 'Comfort Club' get it started for us or something to that effect,—a place where we can all meet and always know some one of the bunch will be there," continued Beers. "I think it would be fine. It would be sure to grow into something larger after a while. Well let's hope the war is over by Christmas."[76]

"The enemy is said to be retreating all along the line and there are even rumors of peace," wrote Barlow about November 6. But he lamented, "this old Yankee Division is certainly shattered, torn and bled to death," estimating that a quarter of the Company was then hospitalized for illness or wounds. Referring to the roster, he could list among the absent, Captain Johnston, sergeants Cockerton, Foley, Neill, and Northrop; Corporal Widinghoff; wagoners Ahern, Carter, Cooper, Gilliland, Goodnow, Hannon, and Monahan; orderlies Clay, Davis, James, and Peck; and privates Carleton, Dickens, Ferris, Gariepy, Lilley, MacDonald, Marston, Nuss, O'Connell, Quinn, Thompson, Walker, and Worley.[77]

On November 1, the 101st and 102nd Infantry had moved to the right of the 103rd and 104th, relieving French troops in front of Beaumont, northeast of Verdun. The Division had simply held the line for four days while the divisions on the other side of the Meuse increased the pace of their advance. Then, on November 8, it was ordered to advance.[78]

"It looks as though they were planning to send the Yankee Division into action again," remarked Barlow, "but it seems there surely must be others who are ready now to step in and do their share. This Division has been 208 days in the trenches and has been living on its nervous system for the past few months, the men's bodies have wasted away and it seems as though the sight of many more legless, armless and sightless souls will snap that set of grey cords now worn to a thread so that none of us will go home human." He concluded: "We can readily see now that Lieut Nagle was right when he told us in training last winter that we were to be a sacrifice division. We were, but New England may well be proud of her sons."[79]

The Division pushed its attack on November 9 and 10, gaining a little ground. At 9:30 on the morning of November 11, another attack began, despite expectations that the war was nearly finished. Barlow recorded: "Rumors were rife in regard to a cessation of hostilities and at eleven o'clock the orders came through that the War was over." He imagined, "the World breathed a sigh of relief and tears came to the eyes of two million boys of the American Expeditionary Forces, as they breathed a silent prayer for their comrades in arms and for the loved ones at home." He concluded: "The Armistice is signed and the Chimes of Verdun are ringing for the first time since 1914. It seems useless to try to describe what the men were doing on Armistice Day, as each soldier was doing some thing different but many seemed to be in a daze and did very little but THINK and seemed to be enjoying themselves immensely."[80]

Despite the exhilaration, the soldiers continued their duties. "Moving pictures were being taken as though there were still fighting and the stretcher bearers went through their work before the camera," noted Barlow. But like many, he was pre-occupied with his own feelings: "The depression of this life has been so great that it seemed some invisible weight was pushing your body down and down actually into the mud so that your shoulders had become stooped and your body little more than a carcass but now the Armistice has sealed the gates of Hell, your body seems to come out of the mud, the chest expands and you seem to breath[e] more easily than you have in many months." In the end, "the sunlight seems to penetrate your very soul and you actually want to live to go home and surely the gates of Heaven have been opened and you are communing direct with him above. MAY GOD PREVENT ALL FUTURE WARS."[81]

After sundown on November 11, "all the automobiles lighted their lamps and went glowing down the rough roads among the shining of thousands of little bon-fires," wrote newspaper correspondent Frank Sibley.

"'Put out those lights!' the doughboys would yell at the passing motors.

"'Put out those fires!' was the appropriate response. And then the delighted soldiers would yell in chorus, 'Hoo-oo!'"[82]

Herbert Beers was one who could now drive with his lights on. That night he wrote to his mother, "There are so many places I would like to be to-night. All said and done, I am glad I am at the front. We started things and we are in at the finish. So far I've been through it all without a scratch and I can truly say I've been in some tight places.

"I have just come in from standing on a high hill. All around the sky is illuminated with flares of all colors and faint cheers can be heard. All the Newtown boys as far as I know are O.K. I was up at the front this morning and saw the last shots fired. That is, it was last fired by those guns. Now everything seems so terribly still it seems unnatural. But you can just bet we are not going to be long getting used to it." He asked to have his father "get the fatted calf ready" for his return, concluding, "Gosh! But everybody is uneasy and still if we get the opportunity we sure will celebrate."[83]

11

Ready to Go Home

November 1918–April 1919

The day after the Armistice, Sergeant Robert H. Stewart wrote to his mother: "Well last night was a beautiful night and how the French celebrated. The sky was lit up most of the time and of course the Americans were the men of the hour. Had to go down to a small town and everybody there was happy. It gives one a funny feeling to sit around and not to hear a gun go off. It seemed as if we were dreaming, but one thing that our boys are proud of is that we were among the first in the lines and were still there when hostilities ceased. Just think of it mother, can you blame us for feeling proud?"[1]

When Sergeant Barlow tallied up all the runs the Company's ambulances had made between February 7 and November 11, he concluded they had carried 20,290 wounded men during the Division's 193 days on the line. He believed that was more than were carried by any other ambulance company in the AEF.[2]

Division Surgeon Ralph Porter wasted little time in commending his ambulance companies. On November 16, he wrote: "At the close of active operations, the writer feels under an agreeable obligation to express to you in the most sincere language he is capable of using, which is absolutely inadequate to the occasion, his congratulations in the superb service you have rendered.

"The duties of the Ambulance Section are the back bone of the divisional medical service, and if it had failed no amount of effort or sacrifice on the part of the Division could have compensated.

"You have been on the job and delivered the goods under all conditions and in spite of all handicaps. Your work has been a decisive factor in the success of the Division. There can be and is to my mind, no finer organization in the AEF than the Ambulance Section of the 101st Sanitary Train. You are absolutely the corp d'elite of the Division and I feel there is nothing I can do or say for you individually and collectively that half expresses my deep feeling on the subject."

Porter himself was hoping to be relieved, so his conclusion was almost a farewell. "You can have the proud consciousness of having performed the tip-top of efficiency your important share of the campaign that has led America's victory. May you succeed as well at home in the pursuits of peace."[3]

While Surgeon Porter commended the ambulance companies, Sergeant James Morrell sent a heartfelt thanks to the Bridgeport Comfort Club for all of its support.

"In the eyes of the 102nd Ambulance Company, the Comfort Club has more than gone over [the top] for the 102nd Ambulance company, the purely made in Bridgeport Organization," he wrote. "Our ten months at the front has not been peaches and cream, as the boys would say, but we knew that a certain organization, away across the big pond, made up of the Mothers, Wives, sisters and Sweethearts of the 102nd Ambulance Company boys, were back of us 'tous jours' and we knew that we had to make good with such wonderful support in the good old U.S.A."[4]

The Armistice of November 11 had called for a cessation of hostilities, but also specified the occupation of German territory west of the Rhine River until a formal treaty of peace was signed. The army of occupation was created as the Third Army on November 14. Being near the border, the 26th Division was initially slated for the occupation, but because of its poor health, greatly reduced numbers, and somewhat demoralized demeanor as a result of its hard service and the replacement of its trusted officers, the Division was sent to the rear. For the occupation, General Pershing assigned the 1st, 2nd, 3rd, and 4th Divisions of the Regular Army; the 32nd and 42nd Divisions of the Army National Guard; and the 89th and 90th Divisions of the National Army; and later the 5th and 33rd Divisions. The occupation would last until 1923.

As the new Third Army moved east, the other AEF divisions in France moved to their reserve camps to recuperate and resupply. The soldiers believed their work was done, and those in the Yankee Division felt they should be among the first to return home, having been the first to arrive.[5]

On November 14, the 6th Division relieved the 26th, and that Division began its march south to a billeting area beyond the Neufchâteau area they had occupied the previous winter. On November 14, the Sanitary Train moved to Courcelles-sur-Aire, 23 miles southwest of Verdun, and then to Longchamps-sur-Aire to begin its march on November 17. While the Ambulance Company men marched in column, the ambulances followed to pick up sick and injured men and deliver them to whichever field hospital was serving as the day's triage or forwarding hospital. The column arrived near Montigny-le-Roi on November 22, and the ambulance companies were sent a few miles further to Sarrey.[6]

"This Company left the wonderful dugout at G.H.2 and went on a [150-kilometer (90 mile)] hike (full pack) toward the rear and went through many small towns, including Domrémy the birth place of Joan D'Arc but finally stopped at Sarrey a very small town and where we were billeted in wooden [Adrian] barracks," wrote Barlow.[7] Sarrey was about 45 kilometers (30 miles) south of their old quarters at Liffol-le-Grand. "We have two or three wooden barracks on a main road but down a bank and near a stream that keeps over flowing," noted Barlow. He added, "we all wash up over in the brook and some mornings it is mighty cold."[8]

During the move to Sarrey, a change had occurred at the head of the Division. General Frank Bamford, who had replaced General Edwards in late October, was himself replaced on November 18. The Division's new commander was Major General Harry C. Hale, a West Point-trained Regular Army officer who had commanded a training camp in the U.S. and the 84th Division in France. That division was broken up before it saw action at the front, but Hale certainly had administrative experience and an energetic, kindly nature. He would oversee the Division's return to physical and emotional health.[9]

Looking at his litter bearers, Barlow recognized that they had not recovered from the strain of combat. "The men are thin, haggard and worried to threads but look at the problem in a logical way and agree those in authority are right in keeping us over here until we can recuperate rather than sending us home to have our dear ones worry over our condition," he remarked. Some of them spent their free time writing home, "but many seem to get more relief for their nervous system by gambling and smoking constantly and are at their wits end when trying to be quiet."[10]

Finally, after several revoked promises in the spring and summer, leaves were granted for a few men at a time. On December 16, Barlow told the Bridgeport Comfort Club: "Pop Brendel, Harry Edes, Hub Beers, Ralph Carleton and Sergeant Lieberum are away on permission, look for heavy casualties in the French papers especially among the madamoiselles, for that combination will sure knock 'em dead."[11]

With the Division spread around the area, the ambulance companies resumed their duties of the previous winter, making daily calls at the regimental infirmaries and making deliveries to the 101st or 103rd Field Hospitals at Montigny-le-Roi.[12] But here, the 102nd Ambulance Company had reduced duty, operating just two ambulances. Curtis Banks and his orderly William McElroy operated one and Fred Pinney drove the other with Charles Dudley Mills as orderly.[13] When influenza swept through the Division after it settled in, Camp Hospital No. 8, next to the field hospitals, served as the destination for contagious cases. From the hospitals at Montigny-le-Roi, evacuations might be made to Langres, or to the familiar hospitals at Chaumont or Bazoilles-sur-Meuse.[14]

The litter bearers, however, had to be kept busy. "We are sent down into the lots each day to drill and it seems to rain most of the time," remarked Barlow. "Then during the day a few candles are issued so we may find our way in the barracks after dark and possibly write a letter." He complained, "candles are so scarce that your name is checked when you receive one and you do not receive another until your name comes up again in rotation."[15] Barlow told the Comfort Club, "we have no lights in the barracks so buy candles with the money you have sent us, also matches, cigarettes, scrubbing brushes, a meat cutter for the kitchen, extra cans of milk."[16]

Barlow continued, "All the men seem to have a craving for sweet foods and candies but there is but little chocolate for sale so they spend their money in buying excellent hand made knives from several old men skilled in that work and who do the work in their homes about the town."[17] In their free time, "many are hiking [a few miles east] to Montigny-le-Roi a larger town near here and where those who have money may buy small articles of food," continued Barlow. "More of those checks from the Comfort Club came in and can be put to good use."[18] To control the wanderings of the men, "one of our sergeants is allowed a detail each day and goes with them to Montigny and buys whatever the other men need," reported Barlow, possibly describing his own commissary activity. They would then carry "the merchandise back in bags over their shoulders and distribute to those who have ordered. In this manner only a few men are taken away from the Company each day while the others are at drill, guard duty or on detail work."[19]

As Christmas approached, "we sent 25 francs to each of our orphans for Christmas," and on the day itself they "had an excellent dinner for Christmas, paid for in part by money from our mess fund and the balance from money sent by the Comfort Club," noted Barlow.[20]

On December 13, President Woodrow Wilson had arrived in France to participate in the peace talks that would conclude the war. After a few days in Paris, Wilson, accompanied by his wife, went to Chaumont to confer with General Pershing and to give thanks to the troops. Because it was nearby, and was the first full division to arrive in France, Pershing and Wilson chose the 26th Division for a visit. Wilson wished to see the quarters in which the men were billeted and to have Christmas dinner with enlisted men. Many of the units prepared for at least a drive-by inspection, and a list of representative enlisted men was drawn up, but in the end the Wilsons simply reviewed a battalion made up of the best-drilled infantry companies at Langres, stopped to inspect a billet in Sarrey, then had dinner at Montigney-le-Roi with a table of officers before heading off to England.[21]

Most members of the Division had no contact with the president, but the Company was present at Sarrey. "On Christmas Day, President and Mrs. Woodrow Wilson came to visit us," wrote Barlow, "and Mrs. Wilson pleased us when she said we were some of the Boys she had been praying for."[22] As he told the Bridgeport Comfort Club, "Bob Stewart had showed them our billet and explained everything to

On Christmas Day 1918, President and Mrs. Wilson stopped briefly in Sarrey, where Sergeant Robert Stewart showed them one of the Company's billets. Sergeant Abbott, a Signal Corps photographer, captured President Wilson in top hat as he walked away from the billet with the 26th Division commander, Major General Harry C. Hale, at left, and soldiers in overcoats—probably from the 102nd Ambulance Company—standing at attention at right (National Archives, photo no. 111-SC-36813).

them except a couple of places where we had camouflaged some dirty clothes, and Mrs. Wilson had made a hit with us by saying that we were some of the boys she had been praying for and we had promised that gentleman with the most radiant smile we had ever seen, that we would sure pay back the visit."[23] Division Commander Harry C. Hale would tell the Division the next day, that Wilson "expressed himself as much impressed and greatly pleased with the military appearance of the personnel of your command and the cleanliness and neatness of the surroundings, especially of the billet which he examined."[24]

Sergeant Robert H. "Big Boy" Stewart was a 23-year-old paymaster at the Crane Company pipe and valve factory when he enlisted in the Ambulance Company at the beginning of April 1917. Promoted to sergeant in June, he was a competent and popular noncommissioned officer. He was given the duty of showing one of the Company's billets at Sarrey to President and Mrs. Wilson on Christmas Day, 1918. This photograph was probably taken at Sarrey. Gassed during his service, "Big Boy" Stewart would die of the effects in 1920 (courtesy Le petit musée du Doughboy).

By the end of December, they had begun to send some of their prized possessions home. "When a new man used to appear before the Armistice there was always some one to shout 'What kep you'? meaning of course why had he not come over here before," remarked Barlow, "but now that has been changed and they are singing 'We wana go Home—We wana go Home' and then go out and send a few more souvenirs home to 'Gods Country.'"[25] Barlow added: "We still have our Graphophone but it needs repairing and we have such high hopes of being sent home that Martin Clarke crated up the Graphophone along with about 50 German records found at Chateau Thierry—marked the crate for Bridgeport, Connecticut, and routed it via the American Express at Paris." Sadly, "it did not reach its destination," and the thing from home that had provided them so much comfort overseas was gone.[26]

Just before Christmas, the Sanitary Train established a triage hospital at Bannes. At first the 103rd Ambulance Company was placed there, but early in January the 102nd moved over as well. "We changed our billet and this time the orders were to hike to Bannes a small town about twelve kilometers [south] from Sarrey (pronounced Sorry) but still in the County of Meuse and found it to be a very dirty town of all stone houses and barns and many were on details in trying to clean up the filth," recorded Barlow.[27] He continued: "The 103rd Ambulance Company had been billeted in several old houses and one of them took fire and burned to the ground and on the same day one of their members struck Lieut McRossie who as officer of the day had interfered in a fracas at a café, of which there are eleven in this town of less than a thousand persons. Our Company was billeted in various barns but those who have money are finding rooms at the home of natives and as long as they report for all drills are not reprimanded. Green cord wood is issued to the mess sergeant but he has to watch it very close or it disappears into the various billets where the men are enjoying the fire places."[28]

General Hale had told the Division, "I am here to get the Division into condition to go home, or into condition for any duty demanded of it. And that I mean to do."[29] That meant a strict attention to military appearance and formality, even if the men were focused on their return to civilian life. "On the 4th of January we had an inspection down in a field and the inspecting officers were so long in reviewing outfits in other towns that we stood in the mud and rain for four hours before they arrived," complained Barlow.[30]

The ambulance companies also participated in guard duty. "It requires 25 men each day to maintain the guard system in vogue at Bannes and the various companies take turns in furnishing the men but those not on guard duty have to go on long hikes each morning and afternoon to put us into better physical condition," wrote Barlow, who noted that, "at these hikes we spend some time playing the game known as O'Grady." This seems to have been the Irish children's game O'Grady Says, where the group of players try to sneak up while "O'Grady" turns away, then turns back to catch anyone in motion. Despite all that they had been through, the men could still return to their childhood games among the friends with whom they had experienced the worst of war, and making a game of a required activity was another way to resist regulations.[31]

Athletic competitions had also returned as part of the fitness regimen. Back at Sarrey in December, Barlow had reported, "we had a football game or two down in the lots and the field was so muddy most of the men wore boots," meaning tall rubber boots.[32] The Company's football roster included Edward Bergeron, Daniel Clare, Robert Marston, Robert MacDonald, Ralph Merrill, Charles Morgan, Robert Stewart, Harry Waite, Guy Whitlinger, Granville Wilcox, and Harry Worley. In their first match, the 104th Ambulance Company defeated them 6–0.[33] At Bannes, "the men had a few football games down in a field at the edge of town and also an athletic meet at which our Company won the most points (most of the Sanitary Train seems to be billeted in this town)."[34] At the January 11 track meet, the Company won by four points over the 103rd Ambulance Company. "Pop Brendel was as usual our top individual star," wrote Barlow, "while Caler and Rice, two of our new men, showed up well in the races."[35]

"The storekeepers in Bannes have little to sell and usually greet you with 'Fini' 'Beaucoup Demain,'" remarked Barlow, "but at Langres there are several large stores, military schools of various kinds, an observatory and the entire City is surrounded by a high wall and entrance to City is through walled gates."[36] He continued: "Those not on details are hiking to Langres the nearest large City which is a city set upon a hill about eight kilometers from this town and which has a mountain climbing rail road leading from the railroad station up into the city."[37]

Across the Marne southwest of Bannes, Langres had been a Celtic hilltop town even before the Romans expanded it after Julius Caesar subjugated Gaul. Langres was fortified with the walls Barlow mentioned, beginning in the 1300s. As a secure transportation center not far from army headquarters at Chaumont, General Pershing had selected Langres as the center for AEF training schools in January 1918. From tank training and machine-gun tactics to signaling and engineering, these schools accommodated 5,000 officers and noncommissioned men at a time, and they required an army infrastructure that included a commissary where both officers and enlisted men could purchase food and personal items.

"The U.S. Commissary at Langres is a very large one and there is always several lines of soldiers at the various windows," noted Barlow, before complaining, "the enlisted men have very little chance of spending their money as an officer is given or at least takes the liberty of stepping in front of an enlisted man no matter how long you have been in line but if you were fortunate they sold some excellent chocolate candy in tins that you and your buddy would spend your last franc to secure."[38] Barlow implied that he had an especially strong taste for chocolate. "There was an inspection by Major Jones and there was much talk about an issue of government chocolates but all we received were eight chocolates."[39]

In victory, everyone in the AEF, and especially in the 26th Division, felt a strengthened camaraderie. "Every one seems to be greeted with the expression 'What Outfit Buddy'?" wrote Barlow. "The men are singing many variations of 'Hinkie Dinkie Parley Vous' 'Home Boys Home—Its Home we ought to be' and 'Just a Baby's Prayer at Twilight.'"[40] He added, "the men still believe we are soon to be sent home and are securing the addresses of their buddies so they may correspond when they arrive in the good old U.S.A."[41] In preparation for their return home, "Howard (Parson) Davis has written a play to be used at Bridgeport when we arrive home and those who are to take part have rehearsals in Wall's billet at night," wrote Barlow late in January.[42]

The French had welcomed the "Sammies" into their towns and fed and accommodated them—even as the Americans had cleaned their towns and provided food when needed. This fond and mutually beneficial relationship began to have a financial aspect as the AEF began to move on. "The French people we find are collecting from the U.S. Government for the use of their homes and barns where we have been billeted," reported Barlow shortly before the Sanitary Train left Bannes. "They do not forget to make additional charges for any damage we may have done and the claim is made that one man charged us for digging up his hen yard."[43]

Orders arrived from AEF Headquarters on January 8, informing General Hale that the Division would be sent home and should be moved to the area around Le Mans in northwest France around the twentieth of January to be processed.[44] Just before the move, a new complement of 10 ambulances was delivered to the Company.[45] "We were paid on the 20th and on the 21st we hiked full pack to Bize," a small town about twenty miles west of Bannes by roundabout roads, "but the officer in charge lost the way and we hiked several miles off our course and the men were so fatigued many fell out and had to be picked up by the Ambulances but most of the Ambulances had gone on to Le Mans," wrote Barlow. At Bize, "we were billeted in a barn and on the 22nd hiked 14 kilometers into the town of Vitrey but the train had not arrived and there were no billets so the entire Company slept out doors with the sky for a blanket."[46]

Located east of Bize along the Amance River, Vitrey-sur-Mance was known for the thatch baskets made by the "peasants," according to Barlow. "Won three box cars for our company, thirty men to a car. One was a Boche car that had just been turned over to France and was a pip—heavy well made car, better than the usual French cars."[47] "We entrained at six o'clock in the morning and were assigned some German box cars recently taken from the enemy and a six o'clock at night we detrained at Écommoy and hiked five kilometers to Marigné another small town and were billeted in farms in all corners of the town and some 20 or more men were billeted in a building formerly used as a theatre."[48]

Herbert Beers had a more pleasant trip driving his ambulance. "I left Bannes, which is near Langres, on the 21st of January, with the ambulances, going through St. Florentin, Orleans, Le Mans to Écommoy and from there to Marigné," he wrote his mother. "The first night of the trip we all slept in a hay mow, and had a good sleep. The next night we hit a town outside of Orleans and decided to sleep in a bed if possible. Orleans is a large town and has a trolley car service, so we rode all over town for a few cents. There were ten of us in the party and we had a supper in the best hotel there. It cost us 100 francs. Then we started out looking for a bed. The hotel people wouldn't let us sleep in the place unless we had green tickets from the American Provost Marshal. After about one hour's walking, and another half hour praying with the M.P., we got ten bed tickets. It was worth it for we had the most wonderful beds and rooms—all steam heated. The next night we landed in Écommoy at 9 o'clock. MacDonald and I decided to sleep in a bed again if possible and I started out and the first place I went into the lady let me have a bed. You know the French have about a foot of feathers under you and another foot on top, including the blankets. The next morning we had hot chocolate and toast with 'beaucoup' butter. Also the daughter of the house honored us with her presence at the breakfast table."[49]

Barlow called Marigné "the best town in the divisional area and the cleanest town we have been billeted in."[50] He explained, "Wilcox has his ambulance men in one end of town, while Foley and his bunch have a farm away out the other way, still others in in an ex-cabaret, hall or theatre billet as it is called in the center of town."[51] Since the men were billeted all over Marigné, Barlow explained "all men have to come from their billets at the call of the bugle and must answer all calls in front of a church in the center of the town and many mornings it is so dark the sergeant who calls the roll is unable to see the men at the end of the line."[52]

Herbert Beers told his mother: "Marigné is a very good place, but our billets are sort of—well, I guess you would call it open-air work. I have been to church the last two Sundays and feel very churchy.

"Now the bed is a hard floor, blankets and overcoats.

In late January 1919, the Company arrived at Marigné, south of Le Mans, and spent two months there. Most of the men found this the best town they had occupied. Billeted all over town, "all men have to come from their billets at the call of the bugle and must answer all calls in front of a church in the center of the town and many mornings it is so dark the sergeant who calls the roll is unable to see the men at the end of the line," commented Sergeant Barlow. When off duty, the men developed their musical skills and gave several concerts and dances at the town theater where some of them were billeted. Detail of French postcard, ca. 1914 (author's collection).

"It snowed a little this morning and for the last week has been very cold. The people we live over are very good and we get wood from the kitchen to burn in their fireplace. We burn more in an hour than they would in a week. When the French cut a tree down, they save every twig for the fire. The women set around the room with a pan of coals under their feet and they keep renewing the coals by shoveling them out of the fireplace. The old women go shuffling along the street, carrying their stove with them."[53]

As he told his mother, Beers was living very well. "After having finished a dinner of fresh ham, French fried potatoes and French bread, I feel fit for most anything. I had a whole slice ham and a piece of beef's liver. In the last week I have eaten in the company mess twice. This place is the last stop before leaving for some port of embarkation and may be here for four or more weeks."[54]

"Mail has started to come in and men have found quite good stores at Écommoy and the entire Yankee Division is now in this area," remarked Barlow. "We find that mail does not take so long now to come from the United States and many have purchased pairs of wooden shoes and are sending them home as souvenirs and in several of the homes the shoes are made by hand."[55]

Discipline was also relieved slightly. Barlow recorded, "an order was posted so that the men do not now have to answer retreat on Saturday afternoon and are giving much credit to Lieut Durham who is now in charge." And although they still attended battalion drills and inspections, "Serg't (Pop) Brendel has been placed in charge of a battalion canteen."[56] Soon after, Barlow himself had set up a small commissary to serve the Company. As he described it, "Barlow has a counter near the mess line almost every night and retails at cost price small articles of sweets bought at Écommoy during the day and from money furnished by the Comfort Club and he then uses the same money over the next day."[57]

Sergeant Charles W. "Pop" Brendel, probably at Sarrey or Marigné (courtesy Dave Brendel).

In previous sectors, the Y.M.C.A. and Salvation Army had kept them supplied with coffee, hot chocolate, doughnuts, and candy. In March 1918, the Knights of Columbus had begun to send secretaries to operate similar support facilities, but the Division had not yet encountered them. Here, Barlow reported, "the Knights of Columbus are active in this area and have given us several issues of chocolate and cigarettes."[58]

In this area, the men had plenty of access to alcohol. "Military Police

(M.P's) are doing guard duty at all saloons in this area—a man of enormous size has a still at the edge of town," remarked Barlow. But the authorities tried to maintain control. "Two of the saloons in town were closed by the police for selling to U.S. Troops after hours," Barlow continued.[59]

Back in December, at least ten men had come back from the hospital, including Sergeant Charles Cockerton; ambulance drivers Albert Ahern, James Cooper, Theodore Gilliland, and Gus Hannon; and privates Warren Clark, Clarence Gariepy, Jesse Lodrick James, James Quinn, and Lawrence Woodbury.[60] These drivers may have gotten back to slow start at Sarrey, but here in Marigné they would have plenty of work. Curtis Banks was driving when "some driver left his disabled truck in the road without lights and Silent Mac [McElroy] had to go in with his jaw fractured in two places," as Barlow described it.[61] After this, Barlow reported that the Company received four horses because they had few ambulances left.[62]

Then, at the beginning of February, the Company received a new lot of ambulances. "We now have 14 G.M.C. Ambulances as there are so many sick in the area we had to have two more Ambulances assigned to us for we are again doing the evacuation work for the entire Division," as they had done the previous winter. Here, the sick and injured would be collected from the regiments and carried to the 102nd Field Hospital triage at Écommoy, which was twelve miles southeast of Le Mans and about five kilometers (three miles) northwest of Marigné. They might then be carried about 20 kilometers (12 miles) south from Écommoy to Camp Hospital No. 72 at Château-du-Loir on the Loire River.[63] In March, the Company received orders to send out two ambulances from Marigné each morning at 9:00, each following a different route to pick up the sick and deliver them to the 102nd Field Hospital. At the same time, four ambulance posts were set up around the region, with the 101st Infantry, 101st Engineers, 101st Infantry, and 101st Field Artillery, for direct runs from those and nearby units to either Field Hospital 102 or to Camp Hospital No. 72, or to Camp Hospital No. 52 at Le Mans. Reserve ambulances would be ready at both Ambulance Section headquarters in Marigné and at Field Hospital 102.[64]

"Although many of the men have apparently improved in their physical conditions the reaction of the War is now being felt by many others and they have to be sent to hospitals and oh it is a sad, sad thing to have to be sent away from the old outfit that you love and have hopes of going home with," commented Barlow.[65] In March, Bert Coyle, Bud Crump, and Frank Doreski were carried off to the hospital at Le Mans. None of them would return to the Company, although Crump and Doreski would recover. Coyle, however, had a severe case of pneumonia and died very quickly. He was buried at Le Mans, with Howard "Parson" Davis conducting the ceremony. "Those few of us who were able to be at this our Buddies last resting place were greatly touched," remarked Barlow.[66]

Other familiar faces disappeared as well. Barlow noted that Vinal Brenizer, John Caler, Moe Cohen, John Durden, Enoch Lewis, Bailey MacMillan, and Clyde Weber, "who had not been over here quite as long as some of the rest of us were transferred to Base Hospital #72 and may not be able to go home with the Division."[67] Among those who were abruptly transferred out the next month were Warren Clark, Robert Denson, James Dickens, William Hayden, Milas Kennedy, Guy or John Lawrence, David Morris, and Cleveland Washburn. Barlow speculated that they "will no doubt have to stay in France to aid in the work of cleaning up as they had not been in France as long as many others."[68]

The reassignment of these more recent arrivals was also part of the effort to return men to their original units now that there was no need to feed men indiscriminately into depleted units in action.[69] In March, another group of the Company's original men returned, either from the hospital or from units to which they had been reassigned. They included Arthur Best, Frank Davis, Howard Etheridge, and George Oppenheimer, as well as trench fever volunteers Frederick Pill and David Turner.[70]

Frank H. "Buddy" Crump, a native of Chicago, was 21 when he enlisted in the Company at the end of March 1917. He was wounded during the action at Seicheprey on April 20, 1918, but was back with the Company by July. In March 1919 he was taken sick and was sent to the hospital in Le Mans, missing the return to the U.S. with his comrades and not being discharged until July 1919. In this pensive view he wears a French identification bracelet (courtesy Le petit musée du Doughboy).

Leaves for the men continued. By this time, if men agreed to pay their costs, they could qualify for a one-, three-, or fourteen-day pass to any French city except Paris. The other option was a seven-day, fully paid pass to one of the AEF leave areas. Men from the Company, including Martin Clarke, James Cooper, Stan Glover, William Larson, James O'Connell, Earle Radikin, and Walter Scott, accepted the seven-day pass and visited the port of St. Malo, about 160 kilometers (100 miles) northwest on the coast of Brittany.[71] Barlow himself took a leave in the opposite direction, arriving after many train connections in Canterets, high up in the Pyrennes, not far from the Spanish border. Comfortable hotel quarters, abundant food, hiking in the hills, soaking in the hot springs, and communing with the Y.M.C.A. representatives kept the trip both exotic and familiar. For Barlow, the highlight was a visit to Lourdes, where religious miracle and French culture came together for him.[72]

Besides leaves, special army schools also called away officers and men from the Company. Barlow reported that Captain Durham, George Ferris, Lewis Hough, Charles Kenney, and Basil Osborne were sent off "for a few months special course in this country."[73]

Among the provisions of the AEF was an educational program for soldiers. Because the war ended more quickly than expected, planning for the program was not completed until February. AEF Headquarters then announced several educational opportunities, with scholarships for attendance. Vocational "post schools" would offer anyone practical training in agriculture or a variety of mechanical skills. About 150,000 men took advantage of this training. For those who had attended American colleges, whether or not they had graduated, French universities would enroll about 7,500 men to study letters, science, law, or medicine, while another 2,000 would be welcomed at English universities. For those who had not attended college, the AEF established the University of Beaune at the former hospital complex there. Once it opened on March 1, it would offer to as many as 15,000 men a full range of courses equivalent to what they would get as freshmen or sophomores at an American college. It would be run as a military school, with the students organized into regiments, awakened by réveille, and put through regular drills before classes.[74] This probably sounded like an ideal chance to learn during a time when Barlow reported, "seventy-six men are required for detail work each day and those not on detail must drill at least three hours per day."[75] At least six men from the Company decided to take advantage of the program. But they would return at the end of March. Privates George Ferris, Clarence or William Harris, Edwin or Lewis Hough, Milas Kennedy, Basil Osborne, and Arnold Watkins "came back from schools in France as these schools did not come up to their expectations and they decided to go with the Division," wrote Barlow.[76] Barlow probably captured their feelings when he remarked: "All the sergeants seem to know is Hip-Hip-Hip-Hip and we wished they would shout DIS*MISSED. Still and all we love the old outfit and there never was a man who left who did not wish he was back in it again and this includes its officers."[77]

General Pershing planned to review the Division in the middle of February. All of the units would form on the rifle range at Saint-Biez-en-Belin, just west of Écommoy.[78] Barlow wrote, "it seems to rain most of the time and was raining when we had a practice review of the entire Sanitary Train and we are told there is soon to be a Divisional parade and review by General Pershing."[79] For the review, the men were expected to turn out with full packs, medical belts, and overcoats, with their brassards on the overcoat sleeve. Because of the rainy weather, they also wore their slickers. Cooked lunches were provided. When the day came, because the Company had so many men on ambulance duty, a squad of 25 men from the field hospitals filled out its ranks.[80]

Barlow described the event: "On the 19th we were up at 4 o'clock and hiked eight miles to an enormous rifle range and after waiting almost all day in the rain had a most wonderful Divisional review and the sight of 30,000 war hardened troops with glistening bayonets, marching over the fields and executing military maneuvers just as they are written in the book will never be forgotten by the men who took part and I doubt if other parades will be quite as thrilling. These hardened troops who for several months had hoped not to have to drill any more, showed very plainly they could drill if they had to and the honor of the Division had to be upheld. After the parade we hiked home in the rain remarking about the dash and vim of our commanding General and of the excellent steed he rode."[81]

In the fall, each division of the AEF had been ordered to create a distinctive symbol to wear on the left shoulder of their uniforms. The 26th Division was already marking its equipment with YD for Yankee Division, and in October its men were ordered to sew a YD symbol, cut from the blue fabric of French uniforms and stitched onto an American khaki diamond, on their shoulder by November 20.[82] They met the deadline for the most part, but—especially if they acquired a new blouse—they continued to sew on the correct symbols. In February, Barlow noted, "when the men are off duty they are busy sewing or having sewed to their uniforms their chevrons, service stripes and a grand old YD up there on the left shoulder."[83] Helmets were also to be painted with the divisional insignia. However, in the Yankee Division each regiment, machine gun battalion, and train devised its own symbol. That of the Sanitary Train was a two-inch red cross with "101 ST" in white. Early in March, General Hale approved the symbols and ordered that they be painted on "at once."[84] Soon after, Barlow wrote that, in response to orders, "Martin Clarke and Bill Larson are busy painting official train insignia on all steel helmets."[85]

Despite the frustration of waiting and waiting, without any definite word on a departure, the Company retained its composure. In retrospect, Barlow would suggest: "This was a well balanced Company and there were not a half dozen fist fights among the 200 men all during the time they were away and to any student of Camp Life this seems most incredible."[86] He also pointed out some of the personalities. "In every Company were a few men who could always see the bright side of Life and kept the spirits of the men up by their witty sayings." Ray Pomeroy, Daniel Clare, Howard Davis, and Jerry Mackey were "Company comedians."[87] He specified, "Jerry Mackey used to entertain the Company by his witty sayings and by singing 'I'm an Irish American and Proud of it.'"[88] While he respected the contributions of the Company's original officers and Lieutenant Dunham and Lieutenant McRossie, he credited Sergeant Charles Brendel, Howard "Parson" Davis, and, by implication, himself as the three "who had all been with the Company from the time it was organized to date of demobilizing, [and] have done more to keep up its morale, than from any other source."[89] But they also acknowledged the Bridgeport Comfort Club for all the aid and comfort it supplied. Barlow remarked, "not one of us forgets it and no one ever will."[90]

But in the Company, a continued aversion to their captain, who had returned to command, was also a bond. "Poetry is being circulated in the Company and is not at all complimentary to Captain Johnston," Barlow wrote in late February.[91] A few weeks later, the feeling that Johnston had never respected the work of the litter bearers was expressed when, according to Barlow, "some one posted on a post near the mess shack a drawing of an empty picture frame and under it was marked 'The above is a life sized photograph of all the 102nd Ambulance Company stretcher bearers cited in orders.'"[92]

In December 1918, General Hale had ordered that each organization in the Division compile a history of its activities during the war.[93] Earle Radikin's writing skills had become known beyond the Company, and in February, Barlow noted, "Radikin has been detailed to write the history of the 101st Sanitary Train."[94] After reviewing the records and probably speaking with officers of the different units, he wrote a lively account that emphasized the enlisted perspective. Division Surgeon Ralph Porter and his adjutant, Captain Bernard Lovely—formerly a lieutenant in the Company—signed off on it and it was submitted on March 20 as "101st Sanitary Train, 26th Division AEF *History*." Radikin was not named in the typescript.[95]

Radikin also found time to write a poem in honor of the Bridgeport Comfort Club.

Through the long and dreary days
At Liffol
And the days of Parlez-vous—
Chemin des Dames
Seicheprey, Xivray, Apremont
Northwest of Toul.
The Red, Red days of Hell
On the Marne
At Saint Mihiel and the Woivre
To the finish "On les aura!"
At Verdun.
Just to know someone was with us
Was "for" us all the time
Helped a lot!
Not one of us forgets it
And no one ever will.
And so—
We thank you most sincerely
Comfort Club![96]

The Company had encouraged its performers at Liffol-le-Grand the previous winter, and during the transition to peace this winter a greater array of talent turned out. Thomas Avallone, Edwin Davis, Howard Davis, Anthony Diorio, Charles Kenney, George Widinghoff, and Harry Worley combined to form the Company orchestra, while Thomas Avallone, Frank Deutsch, Gus Hannon, James Morrell, Robert Stewart, David Swartz, Frank Wall, and George Wright made up the double quartet.[97] "Our Company gave an excellent entertainment for the Towns people in the theatre used as a billet, this was the first entertainment in this village in four years and was thoroughly enjoyed by them" reported Barlow in late February. "Benches used as seats were removed after the entertainment and our newly organized orchestra played for dancing and the French girls in their wooden shoes were not long in learning the American dances but the young men of the town did not quite like the idea of them dancing so much with us."[98]

A week or two later, Barlow commented, "we had another entertainment in the theatre billet in which the double quartet and eight piece orchestra was the center of interest. The entertainment committee had made an agreement with the young men of the town that they would allow them to have their own music for every other dance but when their accordion player played several verses of the same tune they did not wish to stop. As long as they kept throwing up small coins to him he did not seem inclined to stop and finally had to be lead out of the building and had without doubt been in league with his comrades to prevent the young ladies of the town having too many dances with the U.S. soldiers."[99]

As they looked back on their service while waiting to be sent home, the men met to establish a veterans' association to maintain a sense of unity after their discharge. They elected Howard Davis as president, Sergeant Charles Brendel as vice president, Wagoner Joseph Wyncoop as secretary, Sergeant William Foley as treasurer, and apparently Walter H. Butler as chaplain.[100]

One day in March, "Rob Stewart ran a G.M.C. truck into the ditch over on one of the side roads but Edes came to the rescue and little was said of the affair as no one was thought to have been injured." Barlow commented, "one of the peculiar reactions from the War is noted in the fact that more Ambulances have been in smash ups since the war than there were during the War and we can only surmise the men are coming back into life."[101]

As rainy March weather continued, the Company held one more evening dance in the theater. During the day, there were delousing treatments and subsequent "cootie" inspections, as well as inspections of the various billets. If everyone was neat enough and clean enough, their division could go home. Near the end of the month Barlow wrote, "we are all ready to move and orders are that no more mail will be forwarded, all automobiles have been turned back to the government and we are also without horses or mules."[102]

Just before the Sanitary Train's marching orders arrived, two more men returned to the Company. Elmer Troland had been transferred from driving an ambulance to working in a laboratory, but now he was back. Litter-bearer Clarence Harris returned from the hospital. "Harris wears but four wound stripes although he is entitled to eight and he holds the record for this Company," exclaimed Barlow.[103]

The first components of the 26th Division were carried to the seaport of Brest, went through a final delousing and processing, and departed for home on March 26. The other regiments and trains would follow.[104] Barlow described the Company's departure: "We left Marigné on the 28th and hiked to Écommoy and entrained in box cars at 7 P.M. Train rations of corned beef and hardtack had of course been issued and we arrived in Brest at midnight and hiked four miles mostly uphill to Camp Pontanezen, another of those so called rest camps and where railroad ties had been thrown down for walks to keep the troops out of the mud and where it seemed to be foggy all the time and raw damp weather penetrated to the very marrow of your bones."[105] He continued, "there are thousands upon thousands of wooden barracks in this camp and strict orders are given that no one must smoke in any barracks and inspectors come through the billets at various hours to see that this order is obeyed."[106]

To keep the men occupied until they could board their ships, "details from each Company had to do detail work and men from this Company had to load ties, coal and sand along with German prisoners down at the shipyards," noted Barlow. At the shipyards, "there were several boats being repaired that had holes in them caused by torpedoes from the submarines."[107] When they had time, "all troops are having money changed into American money and are pleased to use our own coins and paper money for no one seemed to care about the French money and spent it apparently in an effort to rid themselves of it and the paper money was so large and tore so easily it was thrown into games of chance as though it were ordinary paper."[108]

Around Camp Pontanezen, "all the various organizations are doing all within their power to make the men as comfortable as possible and any one is equally as welcome in the Jewish Welfare, Knights of Columbus, Red Cross or Y.M.C.A. and writing material, cigarettes etc. are either given away or sold for very reasonable prices but we are told the government is taking over the Y.M.C.A. canteens," remarked Barlow. "The Salvation Army Huts are crowded at all times and besides moving pictures and other entertainments, cruelers are made by the thousands and the men linger in a home sick mood to see the girls working with sleeves rolled up and in all our experience in France we have not heard a word against the character of any girl or woman working in the interest of the Salvation Army."[109] Beside the chance to interact with American women, there was another good reason to queue up. "Long lines form at all commissary and canteens for the men are stocking up for the trip home as they remember how little there was to be purchased on the trip coming to France," Barlow noted.[110]

About March 30, the Company paid its last visit to a delousing plant.[111] Then, "we were ordered to turn in all emergency rations, had several inspections to see how quickly we could roll packs," and "song books were issued," reported Barlow. "There was no joking on All Fools Day for there [were] so many threats made that if we do this, that or the other thing we will not be allowed to go home with the Division, that all men are serious and hardly dare say their souls are their own."[112] Barlow complained: "All sorts of orders and warning are given in regard to talking to anyone in regard to where we are going or where we have been, until the men are muttering under their breath about the fine treatment and appreciation shown for offering their lives to their Country but still show their love of Country by walking in a dazed like manner and taking all sorts of orders from persons who fought all the war at some seaport. The manner in which we are whispering would make one feel we had done something to be ashamed of."[113]

Finally, "on the 6th we hiked full pack to Brest and went aboard the lighters 'Cuba' and 'Tudor' that took us out into the harbor of Brest."[114] Anchored there was the 20-year-old steamship *Winifredian.* With an overall length of 570 feet and a 59-foot beam, the ship was powered by a triple-expansion engine, with a single screw that could drive the vessel at a top speed of 14 knots. Originally built at Belfast, Ireland, for transatlantic service between Liverpool and Boston, it had been used as a troopship during the Boer War and again since 1914. On this passage, the ship would carry the Division's Sanitary Train, Ammunition Train, and Supply Train. "We soon found that there were more troops aboard than there were hammocks for sleeping purposes but no one seemed to mind it and caused no comment about sleeping on the deck as long as the boat would keep going toward the U.S.A.," commented Barlow.[115]

"On the 8th we had our last glimpse of France," Barlow reported, "and it was not long before there were many crap games started by those not on detail work. The boat is a slow one and makes about 12 knots per hour and although the water was not rough there were many sea-sick."[116] A few days later, "we enjoyed Palm Sunday at sea and on the 14th Eddie McLaughlin of our Company boxed a stoker who was a member of this crew and who are mostly all English fellows but this stoker who posed as

The 570-foot steamship *Winifredian* was 20 years old when the Sanitary Train boarded it for the 13-day passage from Brest to Boston. Boston photographer Leslie Jones captured the *Winifredian* entering Boston on its next passage, in June, again with troops lining the rails and balancing on the booms, eager to set foot back in the United States (courtesy of the Boston Public Library, Leslie Jones Collection).

the 'Pride of Liverpool' was soon led out of the ring a sad but wiser stoker," Barlow remarked. In addition, "A Y.D. flag was raised aboard the ship and our orchestra had many invitations to play for the officers."[117]

Barlow and the Comfort Club officers on board had a wireless message sent to the Comfort Club in Bridgeport, reporting their expected arrival date, but they did not take into account the ship's slow speed and miscalculated by several days.[118] Nevertheless, "all were happy on Good Friday the 18th for although the sea was rough and the air was cold our hearts were warm and now there are many gulls following the ship and surely we must see land soon and sure enough Hoop-la and a couple of Hurrays for there is Gods Country the good old U.S.A.," exclaimed Barlow. "We are to land at Boston and many small boats are coming to meet us in the outer harbor and upon one of them was our General Clarence R. Edwards who made a speech from the bridge of a tugboat amid deafening cheers and the tears in the eyes of the men showed plainly they dearly loved this man."[119] Among the vessels waiting to escort the *Winifredian* was the *Admiral II*, chartered by the City of Bridgeport, with the mayor, city officials, the Comfort Club, and other supporters on board

Born in Antwerp, Belgium, 38-year-old Arthur J. "Peasoup" Lambeau was not yet naturalized when he enlisted in the Company on June 5, 1917. He seems to have served mostly as an officers' orderly and waiter, as he did during the return passage on the SS *Winifredian*. With his private-purchase boots and breeches, and his prominent mustache, he was stylish enough for that duty. The AEF discouraged facial hair as an impediment to safe use of gas masks, but members of the 26th Division had a predilection for mustaches (courtesy Le petit musée du Doughboy).

to welcome home "all the Bridgeport boys."[120] Barlow continued, "after the ship was examined at Quarantine we sailed into Commonwealth Pier and the factory whistles were blowing all over the City and we were so happy we trembled all over."[121]

For those who noticed, the joyous arrival was marred by just one symbol. "Captain Johnston came off the boat at Boston, wearing a wound chevron and there was much comment among the men as to just where he had earned the right to wear a wound chevron."[122]

The arrival was joyous but awkward. "After we disembarked the Red Cross served us cake and coffee at the pier and there were many never to be forgotten reunions and many sad eyed parents whose boy was not coming home to them," remarked Barlow. "There was so much cheering at the Pier that one could not act natural as the many friends and relations looked each soldier over in an effort to find their own loved ones but surely this is the happiest day of our lives."[123]

At Commonwealth Pier, continued Barlow, "we went aboard a real American train and were taken to Camp Devens which is a large military camp but a few miles from Boston and where there are many wooden barracks but we were not to occupy any of them until we had a hot bath, new underwear issued and had body inspection and this work was not finished until 2 o'clock the next morning but then away went the boys, no one could ever hold them now and they care nothing for Army orders. They are 'HOME.' Some took express trains, other freight trains before daylight and bound for their home town (and this included officers)."[124] Wherever they went in New England, Barlow and the other men discovered that "the people can not seem to do enough for us, will not let us pay for anything and give greatly of their time and money in our behalf."[125]

After their 72 hours at home, the men returned to Camp Devens to be processed out of the Army. Barlow reported that some had a disappointing surprise when they returned to camp. "We had been 13 days on the sea coming from France and the men were so anxious to get home they left all their belongings in camp even their treasured souvenirs and many found them stolen when they returned a few days hence and in one case even their squad tent had burned down as the few men left in camp who lived too far from the seacoast to attempt going home before being discharged could not look after the property of so many others."[126]

The final days were a blur of activity. "We had two or three practice divisional reviews and there are many thousands of visitors in camp," remarked Barlow. "We made out employment blanks and had the Company photographed."[127] They were also filmed by a cameraman sent up by the *Bridgeport Post* newspaper to document the activities of Bridgeport soldiers. With the title *Bridgeport's Fighting Yanks*, the film was shown in local theaters even before the men were discharged.[128]

Compared with conditions in France, Camp Devens was comfortable, but not entirely welcoming. "There were good cots in the tents and barracks but no one is able to sleep as the men walk around all night and all they want is that piece of paper (Army Discharge) and to go home," remarked Barlow. "Some of the men tried to have their teeth attended to but they seemed willing to work on officers only and made it plain they cared nought for us and were no doubt aware we would not be there long and did not wish to do any work they could avoid. All we seemed to do was sign slips and have physical examinations where practically every man was so anxious to go home that no matter how badly he had been wounded or needed medical care he swore he was the healthiest man in the United States of America."[129]

On April 22, the New England governors and an estimated 50,000 spectators watched the Yankee Division form and pass in review at Camp Devens. Between a million and two and a half million New Englanders turned out for the grand parade of the Division through Boston on April 25. Marching by brigades, the Division began on Beacon Street, circled the Boston Common, marched up and back on Commonwealth Avenue, crossed over and marched out Boylston Street to Massachusetts Avenue, then on to Columbus Avenue and back toward the Common to disband in Park Square.[130]

The parade was quite a logistical accomplishment. The men were ordered to march with helmets, gas mask bags, belts with canteen, and packs with rolled blankets. The Y.M.C.A. prepared for each man a lunch box with a ham or tongue sandwich, raisin cake, an apple, lemon drops, and a pack of cigarettes. The infantry units marching in the front of the parade were quartered in Boston armories the night before the parade. The rear units, including the Sanitary Train, were brought in by train in the morning. With the first unit stepping off at 1:00 p.m., the Sanitary Train did not begin its march until 3:00 or later.[131] Barlow remarked that it was a very windy day, and "the streets were lined with thousands of persons interested in the Division and who were cheering madly and although the men smiled they were not much interested in parades but did enjoy seeing the Old Man (General Clarence R. Edwards) up there at the head of the parade." Marching so late, they were billeted in the city armories overnight.[132]

"After the parade at Boston we returned to Camp Devens and all government property was turned in except the equipment we were allowed to take home, such as gas-masks, helmets and the clothing we wore," reported Barlow. "Then on the 28th more Ambulance men were cited in orders for bravery in action in France and there was so much comment in regard to the wound stripes worn by the officer who was in command of this Company when in the zones of advance." Even to the end they retained their resentment for Captain Clyde Johnston.[133]

On April 29 Barlow wrote, "it is cold and windy but we do not care for we have turned in our mess-kits, blankets, ticks etc.—were paid a bonus of $60.00, given our railroad fare and DEMOBILIZED. LA GUERRE EST FINIE."[134]

Some of the men headed to their homes elsewhere in Connecticut or New England, but most had a happy train ride home to Bridgeport. There, the Bridgeport Comfort Club was planning a welcome-home celebration for the Company with a parade and a banquet.

Back in uniform on May 5, the men gathered at Captain and Mrs. Sprague's house on Hanover Street around 7:15 in the evening. At 8:00 they stepped off and marched about 10 blocks to the large, elegant Stratfield Hotel on Main Street, with a band playing and Company G of the Connecticut State Guard in the lead. After an informal reception, Mrs. Sprague and Major Adams led the procession into the dining room, where 600 soldiers and family members took their seats and Mrs. Sprague acted as toastmaster. She expressed the joy the Comfort Club found in acting as a support group for the men in France, and the Company's original captain, Frank Stevens, returned the compliment to the Comfort Club. Major Herbert of the Sanitary Train complimented the Company for having transported more wounded than any of the other ambulance companies in the Division, and Major Adams—who was likely prejudiced by his role in raising the Company—called it "the best outfit of its kind in the world." Captain Sprague demonstrated why he was such a popular officer when he praised the privates, calling them "the men who really stood up under hardships." With a bit of levity, he added that "the smokes provided by the Comfort Club, without a doubt helped win the war." As the Company's correspondent with the Comfort Club, Barlow also spoke to express his appreciation. "Time after time, three rousing whoops were given for the Comfort Club, its officers and individual members," noted the newspaper reporter. With dinner followed by dancing in the ballroom, it was a fitting celebration of the men and a happy return to their community.[135]

Colonel Paul Waterman summarized the contributions of the ambulance companies, and especially the 102nd, in a postwar letter documented by Sergeant Barlow. In a fitting summation of and tribute to all of their work, he wrote: "I shall always believe that the 101st Sanitary Train was the best organization of its kind in the AEF, but the Ambulance Section was my special pride, not solely because it was my first command in France, but for the spirit it had and the way it did its work, which permitted a Division Staff Officer to call it 'the corps d'elite of the 26th Division'" and which led General Edwards to issue his inspiring commendation to its commanding officer.

"The 102nd Ambulance Company had my interest from the first, as a

Connecticut unit, but it soon fairly won my admiration and gratitude by its work. It never failed at a single task and I gave it many a hard one. It took one tour of active combat duty after another without a grumble, and, if I recall correctly, it had more than its share. From the Chemin-des-Dames to the Argonne it made an enviable record of gallant and faithful service,—I might better say from Liffol-le-Grand, for those early days were hard too.

"It was at the very front at Château Thierry and its gallantry at [Riaville] was wonderful. It established and maintained the rule of the 26th Division that the Red Cross brassard did not leave the field until every wounded man was cared for and removed and until every other soldier had left, a rule that became a tradition and that meant much to the morale of the Division. I wish its story might be written by someone who knew, but even half the tale would be left untold, to live solely in the memories of the men that saw and did its inspiring deeds."[136]

Postscript

Some of the men who survived the war did not long survive the transition to peace. Ambulance driver Russell Drury had received a Croix de Guerre and Silver Star for his action at Dead Man's Curve in April 1918. Severely gassed, he was honorably discharged on January 21, 1919, and died at home on February 5, while the Company was still in France.

Frank "Buddy" Crump, who had gone to the hospital in 1919 and returned in July, also died soon after, as did John F. Falvo, who had been wounded on October 31 and was discharged in February 1919 with a disability.

Robert "Big Boy" Stewart returned with the Company, but the effects of his gassing overwhelmed him, and he died in Waterbury in October 1920. William Larson also came home with the company, only to die an untimely death.

Back home, the members of the Company dispersed to their homes and to the task of becoming civilians again. Work, courtship, and marriage weakened some of the bonds of the previous two years. No evidence of postwar gatherings of the Company's veterans' association has been found.

Major Frederic Adams, who had raised the Company and eventually commanded the 101st Ambulance Train, returned to his practice in Bridgeport. He died in 1927.

Max H. Landman—or Mordechai Yitzhak b Zishe—one of the three enlistees on the first day of recruiting, returned to New York after the war and married a Russian-born woman. By 1925 they were living in the Bronx with two children, and he worked as a salesman. Max Landman died at age 38 in 1934 and was buried in Montefiore Cemetery at St. Albans, Queens, New York.

Dr. Frank "Skipper" Stevens, the Company's original captain, was mustered out as a major and returned to his medical practice and membership on many medical boards. He died of cancer in 1935 at age 61.[1]

Leland F. Gilbert, the jitney driver who received a Croix de Guerre for his heroics in saving a wounded man at Haumont on October 22, returned to his wife Ethel, whom he had married a month before departing for France. He remained behind the wheel. In 1930 he was working as a chauffeur, owned his home, and had two sons. He died at age 40 in 1936, and was buried at Ridgefield, Connecticut, under a military stone denoting his service.

The Company's oldest enlisted man, Albert "Pop" Honeck, the Company's blacksmith and mechanic, moved into the National Home for Disabled Volunteer

Soldiers in Dayton, Ohio, in 1929. He was living in the Army Y.M.C.A. in El Paso, Texas, when he died in 1938.

Charles Dudley "Dud" Mills, who had enlisted on the first day, returned to his wife and to his job at the Adams Express Company. He remarried about 1925, and he and his second wife had a daughter in the 1930s. By 1940 he was out of work and possibly terminally ill. He died in 1942, at age 58, and was buried under a military headstone.

Sergeant Leslie R. "Dick" Barlow compiled his letters to the Bridgeport Comfort Club and published them in a booklet in 1919. Working as a toolmaker in Bridgeport, he married in his hometown of Watertown in 1920 and settled back in Bridgeport. In 1924 he published a portion of his brief diary entries in the *Bridgeport Post*, then typed up an expanded form of the Company diary, probably with the intention of having it published. But in 1927 he wrote to the Connecticut State Librarian George Godard, "not having the necessary means to have the History published I am doing what I consider most advisable, to place one copy in the Bridgeport Library and one copy in the State Library." He did so with a dedication to his mother, Addie L. Barlow, confirming his role as the Company's historian.[2] In the 1920s Barlow worked for the Humane Society before the Great Depression sent him back to work as a machinist making auto parts. Leslie Richard Barlow died at age 60 in 1946.

Earle E. "Rad" Radikin came home restless: "find civilian life lacking in thrill," he wrote in the Connecticut Military Questionnaire.[3] After working in a Bridgeport office, he would move west to pursue his writing. He settled in Santa Barbara, California, and between 1928 and 1932 he wrote 40 short stories about the war that were published in such pulp magazines as *War Stories* and *War Novels*. He married a nurse in 1946 and died at age 53 in 1947.

As Barlow had speculated when he first met him, Captain Clyde C. Johnston enjoyed the pomp and routines of military service. He returned to his medical practice in Springfield, Massachusetts, in 1919, then was commissioned as a captain in the Medical Corps in 1920. He attended the Army Medical School and the Graduate School of Aviation Medicine in the 1920s. Johnston was promoted to major in 1929, lieutenant colonel in 1937, and colonel in 1943. After deployments at several Army air bases, he was at Fort Sam Houston in San Antonio, Texas, when he died at age 64 in 1948.[4]

Harry D. "Old Man" Edes, the Company's faithful mechanic who kept the ambulances running, settled in Bridgeport upon his return and found work as a mechanic in one of the city's factories. He never married. When he died at age 79 in 1960, he was buried in Arlington National Cemetery, grave number 1297 in Section 38.

John A. "Andy" Holzheimer brought his Croix de Guerre home and returned to his job as an assembler for the Underwood Typewriter Company. In the 1920s he married and moved in with his wife's family in Manchester, Connecticut. By 1940 he was a widower, with his mother, his daughter, and his sister-in-law in his home, and he worked as a typewriter aligner. He died in 1962 at age 69, and his stone in South Windsor memorializes him as a sergeant of the 102nd Ambulance Company.

William D. "Bugs" Goodnow, who kept escaping from the hospital to drive his ambulance, returned to Bridgeport, where he found work as a tinner in a furnace factory. In the early 1920s he married a widow five years older than he was and adopted her son. By 1950 he was self-employed, doing odd jobs. He died in 1964 at age 69.

Granville M. "Blondy" Wilcox also came home with a Croix de Guerre. In 1920 he was living with his remarried mother and working as a laborer in a Rhode Island fabric-dying mill. He then moved west and married in Reno, Nevada, in 1927 before settling in Minneapolis and working as a ventilating salesman. By 1950 he had returned to Providence, Rhode Island, and was managing an apartment house. He died in 1966 and was buried in the Rhode Island Veterans Memorial Cemetery.

Charles W. "Pop" Brendel, the Company's noncommissioned father figure and best athlete, returned to the family hardware business in Rockville, Connecticut. He married in 1922 and by 1930 had two daughters and a son. After a long and successful hardware career, he died in 1967 at age 73, and his gravestone in Rockville commemorates him as a sergeant of the 102nd Ambulance Company. In 2015, his grandson donated his uniform to the National World War I Museum and Memorial in Kansas City, Missouri.

Howard P. "Parson" Davis would live up to his nickname. By 1940 he was a clergyman and lecturer at the Bolton Federated Church in Bolton, Massachusetts. He died at age 73 in 1968, and his grave has two markers. A bronze veteran one denotes his service in the 102nd Ambulance Company, and a granite family one proclaims, "he gently ministered to men."

Dr. Charles H. "Doc" Sprague and his wife Emma returned to the routines of a busy private practice in Bridgeport. In 1929, he was the Foreign Legion's Connecticut delegate for the dedication of the church in Belleau, France, which had been rebuilt as a memorial to the Yankee Division. During the trip, he showed his wife some of the areas where he had served.[5] Their son Charles, who was just three when his father departed for France, would graduate from West Point in 1937 and join the Army Air Force. He was a major when he was shot down over Bali, Indonesia, in February 1942. His death was not confirmed until 1949. Dr. Sprague died in 1972 at age 92. Emma Sprague, the mother of the Bridgeport Comfort Club, lived until age 96, dying in 1976.

Harry A. "Red" Worley, another of the first-day enlistees and one of the Company's musicians, would reply to the Connecticut Military Questionnaire, "well, I can't say I enjoyed the war, but you'd go some to buy my experiences." Asked about his state of mind, he wrote, "I think I am still normal but one can never tell."[6] Shortly after his return, he married and in 1930 was working as a newspaper printer—later a linotype operator—in New Milford, Connecticut. He died at the Veterans' Hospital in West Haven, Connecticut, at age 78 in 1973.

George Herbert "Hub" Beers would return to the family farm in Newtown, but he ended up "an old bachelor" as he never found the "old maid with a big roll" that he remarked upon in September 1918.[7] By 1950 he was a rural mail carrier for the U.S. Post Office. He died in 1973, at age 79, and was buried in Newtown under a stone engraved "YANKEE DIV. W.W.I."

Leroy A. MacKinnon, who was gassed three times, concluded that the war had made him "inclined to be restless."[8] In 1922 he married Mattie Barber, who was three years older, and by 1930 they had two children and were living in Winchester, Connecticut, where he worked as an accountant for an ice company. By 1950 they had moved to Winsted and he was working as a government auditor. He would outlive Mattie by 19 years. When he died at age 77 in 1974, "102 AMB. CO. 26 DIV. WWI" was the top line on his gravestone.

Benjamin B. "Dynamite" Wyrtzen returned home from France at age 20 and got a time-clerk position at the Union Metallic Cartridge plant. In the early 1920s he married and attended New York University. By 1940 the Wyrtzens had two daughters and he was the office manager of a box company, moving on to salesman for the company by 1950. He died in 1975, at age 76, and was buried in Fairfield under a military stone reading "PFC US ARMY WORLD WAR I."

Italian-born John T. Elliano, who came to Bridgeport at age seven and enlisted in the Company in March 1917, became a trench fever volunteer just after being transferred to the 104th Ambulance Company. He eventually recovered and was honorably discharged in March 1919. Back in Bridgeport, he reenlisted in 1924 and served as an Army recruiter. After his second discharge, he became a city surveyor and by 1949 was assistant director of the Federal Housing Authority in Bridgeport. He commanded the Bridgeport post of the Veterans of Foreign Wars and the Bridgeport Veterans' Council, and also rose to colonel of the Connecticut State Guard-Retired. He died at the Veterans Hospital in West Haven, in 1977 and was buried in Stratford.[9]

The Company's youngest recruit, Bertrand Keane, was 17 when he enlisted. After driving ambulances and motorcycles in the Company, he came home with a Croix de Guerre. Adventurous and creative, he went to sea as a steward in 1920. He then returned to New York City and rose to be an editor for Hillman magazine and comic book publishers, marrying a writer in 1941. By 1950 he was running a film studio in New Rochelle. He was 80 when he died in 1978 at Garrison, New York.

Ray E. "Pinaud" Pomeroy, one of the Company's comedians, married in 1922 and by 1930 was working as a mail clerk in Stratford, Connecticut. In 1950 he was a janitor in the Stratford veterans' club. He died at Bridgeport in 1981 at age 87.

Gerald C. Northrop, who timed the German artillery fire to schedule the ambulance departures from the Company's dressing station at Mandres, returned home to New Milford, Connecticut. At age 30 he married a widow eight years older than he was and adopted her daughter. He made a good living as a real estate agent. In later years he remarried, and he died in retirement at Southbury, Connecticut, in 1984, at age 86.

Possibly the last-surviving member of the 102nd Ambulance Company was Anthony W. "Nabisco" Diorio, who was 18 when he enlisted in April 1917. He was gassed twice, at Seicheprey and Haumont, and claimed a rupture from all the heavy lifting, but he returned to a full life. He married in 1922 and by 1930 was working as an accountant. Anthony Diorio died at age 90 in 1989.

Appendix

102nd Ambulance Company Roster

(+ indicates service in the 1st Connecticut Ambulance Company, 1913–1916)

(* indicates original members of the 102nd Ambulance Company, who enlisted between March 14 and September 30, 1917)

(a number listed in an entry is the individual's service ID)

Majors

Frederic J. Adams
Born Saline, MI
Age 48
M.D., New York University, 1895
Physician in Bridgeport
National Guard medical duty since 1904
Chief Surgeon, Connecticut National Guard, October 1916
Drafted into federal service, August 7, 1917
Commanded Ambulance Train
Honorably discharged, April 30, 1919

Paul G. Waterman
Born Westfield, MA
Age 40
M.D., Cornell, 1902
Physician and psychiatrist in Hartford
Private, 5th Connecticut Militia Cavalry, November 1911
Service on Mexican border as surgeon, 1st Connecticut Infantry, July–October 26, 1916
Drafted into federal service as major, August 5, 1917
Surgeon, 101st Field Artillery, August 1917
Assistant division surgeon, September 1917
Director of ambulance companies, September 6, 1917–March 28, 1918
Commanding officer, 101st Sanitary Train, March 28–October 1, 1918
Division surgeon, 4th Division, October 1, 1918
Lieutenant colonel, November 11, 1918
Colonel, May 3, 1919
Relieved of duty with 4th Division, August 3, 1919
Honorably discharged, August 26, 1919

Captains

*Frank W. Stevens ("Skipper")
Born Vineland, NJ
Age 44
M.D., Yale, 1900
Gynecologist in Bridgeport
Private, Hospital Corps, Connecticut Infantry, June 1905–September 1911
Lieutenant and captain, Connecticut Medical Corps, 1908–November 15, 1915
Service on Mexican border, July–October 1916
Drafted into federal service as captain, August 5, 1917
Transferred to 104th Field Hospital, January 9, 1918
School, Langres, January 9–February 24, 1918
Promoted to major, March 10, 1919
Honorably discharged, April 29, 1919

Clyde C. Johnston ("Dugout")
Born Nebraska
Age 32
M.D., University of Maryland, 1909
Physician in Springfield, MA
Lieutenant of medical department, Massachusetts National Guard, June 1916

Commissioned lieutenant in medical detachment of the 104th Infantry, August 1917
Assigned to Company, January 14, 1918
Promoted to captain
Honorably discharged, April 29, 1919

Lieutenants

*Charles H. Sprague ("Doc")
Born Greenwich, NY
Age 37
M.D., Columbia, 1904
Physician in Bridgeport
Private, Connecticut National Guard, 1905–08
Special training at Fort Oglethorpe, GA, June 25–August 25, 1917
Drafted into federal service as 1st lieutenant, August 5, 1917
1st Corps School, Gondrecourt, November 27–December 30, 1917
Transferred to headquarters, 26th Division, March 10, 1918
#26-1779
Special duty commanding delousing machines, March–August 1918
Cited for meritorious service under fire at Raulecourt, June 8, 1918
Promoted to captain, September 16, 1918
Transferred to 103rd Ambulance Company, October 14, 1918
Honorably discharged, April 29, 1919

*Daniel H. Lawler
Born Windsor Locks, CT
Age 30
M.D., University of Maryland, Baltimore, 1912
Physician in Bridgeport
Mustered as lieutenant
Special training at Fort Oglethorpe, GA, June 25–September 1, 1917
Transferred to 102nd Infantry, November 9, 1917
Gassed, March 17, 1918
Transferred to Base Hospital 69
Promoted to captain, November 15, 1918
Honorably discharged, April 29, 1919
Awarded Silver Star

*John Thomas Halliburton Powers ("Nellie")
Born New Glasgow, Nova Scotia, Canada
Age 29
M.D., College of Physicians and Surgeons, Baltimore, 1910
Physician in Bridgeport
Connecticut National Guard Medical Corps, Fall 1917
Drafted into federal service as 1st lieutenant, August 5, 1917
Honorably discharged May 7, 1919

*William T. Nagle
Born Southington, CT
Age 25
M.D., Medico-Chirguical College, Philadelphia, 1914
Physician in Fairfield, CT
Drafted into service as 1st lieutenant, August 5, 1917
Transferred to hospital duty, March 29, 1918
Honorably discharged, July 26, 1918

Frederick L. Gregory
Born Fairfield, ME
Age 32
M.D., McGill University, Montréal, 1912
Physician in Caribou, ME
Called up as 1st lieutenant, Medical Corps, August 10, 1917
Transferred to 101st Field Hospital, December 1, 1917
Transferred to Company, December 1917
Transferred to 102nd Infantry, February 15, 1918
Wounded at Seicheprey, April 20, 1918
Promoted to captain, November 25, 1918
Transferred to 104th Ambulance Company, December 6, 1918
Honorably discharged, April 29, 1919

Thomas V. Daley
Born Kingston, Ontario, Canada
Age 29
M.D., Faculty of Medicine of Queen's University, Kingston, Ontario, 1908
Physician
1st lieutenant, 4th National Guard Ambulance Company (104th Ambulance Company)
Assigned to Company, January 9, 1918
Transferred to 104th Ambulance Company
Promoted to captain
Honorably discharged, April 29, 1919

James F. Cobey
Born New Haven, CT
Age 25
M.D., Yale, 1916
Intern, St. Francis Hospital, Hartford

Drafted into federal service as 1st lieutenant, October 3, 1917
Served with 103rd Field Hospital
Transferred to Company, January 9, 1918
Assigned to command of 101st Sanitary Train Provisional Truck Company, August 3, 1918
Promoted to captain, September 16, 1918
Transferred to headquarters, 101st Sanitary Train
Honorably discharged, May 27, 1919

Robert B. Durham ("Bull")
Born Columbia, SC
Age 25
M.D., University of Georgia, 1913
Surgeon
Assigned to Company, April 1918
Liaison and Transportation Officer, 101st Sanitary Train Ambulance Section, July 1918
In acting command of company, October 1918
In command of company, February 1919
Promoted to captain
Returned to U.S., July 1919

Thomas D. McRossie
Born Napanee, Ontario, Canada
M.D., New York University, 1897
Age 46
Physician, Brooklyn, NY
Drafted into service as lieutenant, April 4, 1918
Training at Fort Oglethorpe, GA
Assigned to 104th Ambulance Company
Assigned to Company, August 1918
Wounded, October 28, 1918,
Promoted to captain, December 1918
Captain, 104th Ambulance Company
Honorably discharged, September 11, 1919

Moses Katz
Born New York City
M.D., Illinois Medical College, 1899
Physician in Yonkers and Mount Vernon, NY
1st lieutenant
Camp Greenleaf Replacement Draft Company 10
Departed for France on SS *Aquitania*, June 8, 1918
Assigned to Company, August 1918
Transferred, August 1918

Joseph H. Cutchin, Jr. ("Get 'em rollin")
Born Whitakers, NC
Age 27
M.D., University College of Medicine, Richmond, Virginia, 1911
Entered service, September 4, 1917
First Lieutenant, 2nd Ambulance Company (103rd Ambulance Company)
Transferred to Company
Promoted to captain, February 2, 1918
Honorably discharged, April 26, 1919

Harry L. Upshaw ("Hawk Eye")
Born Conyers, GA
Age 25
M.D., Atlanta Medical College, 1915
Physician
Enlisted, August 15, 1917
First lieutenant
July 1918 Medical Replacement Draft
Departed for France on the SS *Caronia*, July 14, 1918
Assigned to Company, September 1918
Honorably discharged, April 24, 1918

Everett R. Thomas
Born Bridgeport, OH
1st lieutenant
Sailed for France, December 1917
Served with Base Hospital 31

Dean A. Nesbit
Born Butler, PA
M.D., Jefferson Medical College, Philadelphia, 1914
Physician in Youngstown, OH
1st lieutenant
Sailed for France, December 1917
Served with Base Hospital 31

Bernard H. Lovely
Born New Hampshire
4th Field Hospital
Sailed for France, September 1917
Wounded in action
Assigned to Company
Promoted to captain
Transferred to headquarters, 101st Sanitary Train

Rankin R. Lowery
Born Atmore, AL
Camp Greenleaf Replacement Draft Company Number 7
Departed for France, June 8, 1918
Promoted to captain
Departed France, August 19, 1919

Clarence D. Barrett
Born Youngstown, OH
Age 28
M.D., Ohio State University Medical College, 1914
Departed for France, December 15, 1917
Service in Base Hospital 31, 41st Division
Promoted to captain
Departed France, April 5, 1919

Sergeants

*Charles H. Cockerton
Born Bridgeport
Age 24
Clerk
Enlisted in National Guard, Bridgeport, March 21, 1917
Private 1st Class, May 2, 1917
Sergeant, May 23, 1917
Special training at Fort Oglethorpe, GA, June 25–September 1, 1917
#3298
Honorably discharged, April 19, 1919

*Arthur B. Lieberum ("Lumbago")
Born Bridgeport
Age 36
Undertaker
Enlisted in National Guard, Bridgeport, March 30, 1917
Acting supply sergeant, March 30, 1917
Private 1st Class, May 2, 1917
Sergeant, May 23, 1917
Special training at Fort Oglethorpe, GA, June 25–September 1, 1917
At foot school, January 1918
#3299
Honorably discharged, April 29, 1919

*Paul E. Crocker ("Mrs.")
Born East Templeton, MA
Age 25
Advertising agent
Enlisted in National Guard, Bridgeport, April 3, 1917
Private 1st Class, June 16, 1917
Promoted to sergeant, June 21, 1917
Honorably discharged, November 20, 1918, to accept commission as 2nd lieutenant

*Robert H. Stewart ("Big Boy")
Born Waterbury, CT
Age 23
Assistant paymaster at Crane Company
Enlisted in National Guard, Bridgeport, April 3, 1917
Private 1st Class, May 2, 1917
Sergeant, June 21, 1917
#3309
Cited for bravery in action
Gassed
Honorably discharged, April 29, 1919
Died October 1920 due to effects of gas

*John R. Carter
Born Bridgeport
Appointed mess sergeant, July 18, 1917
#3303
Wounded in action
Honorably discharged, April 29, 1919

*Gerald C. Northrop
Born New Milford, CT
Age 19
Enlisted in National Guard, Bridgeport, March 15, 1917
Private 1st Class, May 2, 1917
Corporal, June 21, 1917
Company recruiting officer, May–July 1917
Sergeant, July 24, 1917
#3308
Wounded in action
Cited in orders for bravery in action on April 20, 1917,
Awarded Croix de Guerre, June 12, 1918
Beau Desert Casual Company from Bordeaux to Camp Merritt, NJ, 1919

+Charles W. Brendel ("Pop")
Born Rockville, CT
Age 23
Hardware salesman
Enlisted in National Guard, Hartford, November 10, 1913
Served in 1st Connecticut National Guard Ambulance Company, 1913–1916
Service on Mexican border, July–October 1916
Assigned to Company, August 5, 1917
Sergeant, September 2, 1917
#3302
Promoted to 1st sergeant
Honorably discharged, April 29, 1919

+William F. Foley
Born Hartford, CT
Age 22

Enlisted in National Guard, Hartford, April 25, 1914
Served with 1st Connecticut Ambulance Company
Service on Mexican border, July–October 1916
Enlisted in National Guard, January 25, 1917
Promoted to sergeant, September 2, 1917
#3305
Served through July 1918
Discharged Camp Devens, November 21, 1918

+John A. Holzheimer ("Andy")
Born Rossville, NY
Age 23
Assembler at Underwood Typewriter Company
Enlisted in National Guard, Hartford, July 8, 1913
Discharged, September 1915
Reenlisted, June 20, 1916
Service on Mexican border as sergeant, July–October 1916
Assigned to Company, August 5, 1917
Supply sergeant, September 2, 1917
#3306
Wounded in action
Cited in orders April 20 and December 28 for bravery in action at Seicheprey
Awarded Croix de Guerre, May 29, 1918
Transferred to intelligence department, 103rd Infantry
Awarded Silver Star for gallantry in directing ambulances at Seicheprey
In Base Hospital 76, November 13, 1918–March 28, 1919
Honorably discharged, April 29, 1919

*Leslie R. Barlow ("Commissary Dick")
Born Watertown, CT
Age 30
Employed at Union Metallic Cartridge Company
Previous service in 2nd Regiment Connecticut National Guard, 1909–1912
2nd Division, Naval Reserve, Connecticut National Guard, 1913–1916
Enlisted in National Guard, Bridgeport, May 23, 1917
Mustered as corporal
Appointed sergeant, December 19, 1917
#3301
Wounded in action (gassed), October 27, 1918
At Base Hospital 28, Limoges, November 1–15, 1918
Honorably discharged, April 29, 1919

Harcourt C. Grant
Born Paris, TN
Age 24
Enlisted in National Guard, Burlington, VT, November 22, 1915
Served in 4th/102nd Field Hospital
Transferred to 104th Field Hospital, December 12, 1917
Transferred to Company as 1st sergeant, January 21, 1918
Hand crushed by ambulance, February 2, 1918
#302869
Transferred to 102nd Field Hospital, August 6, 1918
Honorably discharged, April 29, 1919

*Thomas Avallone
Born New York City
Age 23
Employed at Columbia Graphophone Company
Enlisted in National Guard, Bridgeport, April 3, 1917
Private 1st Class, June 16, 1917
Supply sergeant, February 5, 1918
#3300
Transferred to Supply Truck Company, August 4, 1918
Provisional Truck Company, 101st Sanitary Train October 1, 1918
Returned to Company, January 12, 1919
Honorably discharged, April 29, 1919

*Granville M. Wilcox ("Blondy")
Born Providence, RI
Age 22
Employee of Remington Arms Company
Enlisted in National Guard, Bridgeport, March 23, 1917
Private 1st Class, May 2, 1917
Special training at Fort Oglethorpe, GA, June 25–September 1, 1917
Promoted sergeant, February 5, 1918
#3310
Wounded in action, April 21, 1918
Cited in orders April 20 and October 15 for bravery in action
Awarded Croix de Guerre, June 12, 1918
Awarded Silver Star
Honorably discharged, April 29, 1919

*Arthur Levasseur
Born Messina, NY
Age 25
Clerk and salesman
Enlisted in National Guard, Bridgeport, March 28, 1917
Private 1st Class, May 2, 1917
Cook, August 15, 1917
#3307
Transferred to Medical Detachment, 101st Field Hospital, March 27, 1918
Sergeant, June 21, 1918
Honorably discharged, April 29, 1919

*John A. Forsyth, Jr.
Born Fairfield, CT
Age 21
Enlisted in National Guard, Bridgeport, March 28, 1917
Private 1st Class, April 11, 1917
Special training at Fort Oglethorpe, GA, June 25–September 1, 1917
Transferred to 103rd Field Hospital, February 7, 1918
#3882
Promoted to Sergeant, June 28, 1918
Returned to Company, February 13, 1918
Honorably discharged, April 29, 1919

*James W. Morrell
Born Bridgeport
Age 20
Clerk
Enlisted in National Guard, Bridgeport, April 10, 1917
Private 1st Class, December 26, 1917
#3368
Corporal, April 22, 1918
Sergeant, October 10, 1918
Examined for officer's commission, November 1918
Honorably discharged, April 29, 1919

*Frank J. Deutsch ("Dutch")
Born New York City
Age 23
Clerk at Columbia Graphophone Company
Enlisted in National Guard, Bridgeport, May 9, 1917
Promoted to corporal, December 18, 1917
#3314
Promoted to sergeant, October 20, 1918
Cited in orders December 28 for bravery near Haumont, October 22–27, 1918
Honorably discharged, April 29, 1919

James E. Neill
Born Trenton, NJ
Age 23
Salesman for Remington Typewriter Company
Sergeant in Base Hospital 66
Departed for France on SS *Orduna*, December 18, 1917
#13032
Transferred to Camp Infirmary Section, 101st Sanitary Train
Transferred to Company
Honorably discharged, April 29, 1919

Russell E. Rolfe ("Rookie")
Born Penacook, NH
Age 22
Grocery clerk
Sergeant of New Hampshire National Guard Sanitary Train 1915–1917
Sergeant in Medical Detachment, 26th Division Headquarters Troop
Departed for France on SS *Baltic*, September 10, 1917
#3145
Cited in orders December 28, 1918, for bravery in action
Transferred to Company
Honorably discharged, April 29, 1919

Corporals

George W. Widinghoff ("Piano Legs")
Born Devon, CT
Age 22
Student
Enlisted in National Guard, July 25, 1917
#3390
Wounded in action
Cited for bravery in action
To hospital, October 10, 1918
Honorably discharged, April 29, 1919

Martin N. Mortenson ("Hayshaker")
Born Fairfield, CT
Age 19
Draftsman at Bilton Machine Tool Company
Enlisted in National Guard, Bridgeport, June 30, 1917
Sick in Field Hospital 104, November 1–December 20, 1917
Private 1st Class, January 14, 1918
Returned to Company, January 21, 1918

#3420
Promoted to corporal, December 18, 1918
Cited in orders October 15 and December 28 for bravery in action at Saulx, September 25–26, 1918, and near Haumont, October 22–27, 1918
Awarded Silver Star
Honorably discharged, April 29, 1919

*Edward H. Ashley
Born Waterbury, VT
Age 25
Enlisted in National Guard, Bridgeport, April 10, 1917
Private 1st Class, June 16, 1917
Corporal, December 18, 1917
Injured in accident, December 31, 1917
#3312
Transferred to 101st Field Hospital, May 21, 1918
Honorably discharged, April 29, 1919

*Ray E. Pomeroy ("Pinaud")
Born Danbury, CT
Age 22
Salesman for General Motors
Enlisted in National Guard, Bridgeport, March 17, 1917
Private 1st Class, May 2, 1917
Corporal, May 23, 1917
Special training at Fort Oglethorpe, GA, June 25–September 1, 1917
Served in gun crew on SS *Corsican*, October 1917
#3316
Gassed at Seicheprey, April 20, 1918
In 101st Field Hospital, April 21–30, 1918
Honorably discharged, April 29, 1919

Wagoners (Ambulance and Truck Drivers)

*William P. Adams ("Bill")
Born Boston, MA
Age 31
Circus employee
Enlisted in National Guard, Bridgeport, April 2, 1917
Private 1st Class, May 2, 1917
Special training at Fort Oglethorpe, GA, June 25–September 1, 1917
Promoted to corporal, January 18, 1918
#3311
Reduced to private, April 3, 1918
Private 1st Class, June 14, 1918
Wagoner, August 7, 1918
Honorably discharged, April 29, 1919

Albert J. Ahern ("Dragfoot")
Born Bridgeport
Age 24
Enlisted in National Guard, Bridgeport, March 28, 1917
Private 1st Class, May 2, 1917
#3320
Wagoner, April 11, 1918
Cited in orders October 15 for bravery in action
Wounded in action, October 26, 1918
Honorably discharged, April 29, 1919, 5 percent disabled

Curtis F. Banks ("Barney Oldfield")
Born Westboro, MA
Age 20
Chauffeur student
Enlisted in National Guard, Bridgeport, May 23, 1917
At Base Hospital 15, Chaumont, November 1917–January 1918 for operation
#3398
Wagoner, April 16, 1918
Gassed, April 20, 1918, and October 17, 1918
At Camp Hospital 58, Chatillon-sur-Seine, July 1918, influenza
Cited in orders August 31, October 15, and December 28 for bravery in action at Torcy, July 18–26, Saulx, September 26–27, 1918, and near Haumont, October 22–27, 1918
Treated for gas wound, Base Hospital 83, Revigny, November 1918
Honorably discharged, April 29, 1919

*George Herbert Beers ("Hub")
Born Newtown, CT
Age 23
Enlisted in National Guard, Bridgeport, May 18, 1917
Wagoner, November 1917
Private 1st Class, December 26, 1917
Hospitalized for mumps, February 22–March 14, 1918
#3325
Cited in orders October 15 and December 28 for bravery in action, Saulx, September 25–26, 1918, and near Haumont, October 22–27, 1918
Awarded Silver Star
Honorably discharged, April 29, 1919

*Edward J. Bergeron ("Rubber Knees")
Born Greenfield, MA
Age 24
Filer at Marlin-Rockwell Corporation
Enlisted in National Guard, Bridgeport, July 2, 1917
Private 1st Class, December 26, 1917
#3326
Wagoner, May (August) 1, 1918
Cited in orders October 15 and December 28 for gallantry in action, Saulx, September 25–26, 1918, and near Haumont, October 22–27, 1918
Honorably discharged, April 29, 1919

*Earl R. Carter
Born Bridgeport
Age 23
Enlisted in National Guard, Bridgeport, May 4, 1917
Appointed cook, August 27, 1917
#3317
Wagoner, August 8, 1918
Private 1st Class, November 8, 1918
Cited in orders December 28 for bravery in action near Haumont, October 22–27, 1918
Honorably discharged, April 29, 1919

*James W. Cooper ("Sonny")
Born Wallingford, CT
Age 26
Enlisted in National Guard, Niantic, August 27, 1917
#3395
Wagoner, April 15, 1918
Private 1st Class, August 7, 1918
Wounded in action
Cited in orders October 15 and December 28 for gallantry in action
Honorably discharged, April 29, 1919

Russell E. Drury
Born South Framingham, MA
Age 24
Enlisted in National Guard, Springfield, MA, June 19, 1916
Private 1st Class, July 1, 1916
Medical Detachment 104th Infantry
Transferred to Company, February 24, 1918
#3342
Wagoner, April 15, 1918
Gassed and wounded in action severely, April 20, 1918
Cited in orders April 20 for bravery in action at Dead Man's Curve
Awarded Croix de Guerre
Awarded Silver Star
Honorably discharged, January 21, 1919
Died at Wellesley, MA, February 5, 1919

*Leland F. Gilbert
Born East Norwalk, CT
Age 22
Jitney driver
Enlisted in National Guard, Bridgeport, May 31, 1917
Private 1st Class, December 26, 1917
#3343
Wagoner, April 15, 1918
Wounded in action
Cited in orders December 28 for bravery in action
Awarded Croix de Guerre
Honorably discharged, April 29, 1919

Theodore J. Gilliland
Born Hartford, CT
Age 18
Enlisted in National Guard, Hartford, June 21, 1917
Private 1st Class, December 26, 1917
#3344
Wagoner
Wounded slightly, October 21, 1918
Cited in orders October 15 and December 28 for bravery in action
Honorably discharged, April 29, 1919

*William D. Goodnow ("Bugs")
Born Corinth, NY
Age 19
Enlisted in National Guard, Bridgeport, May 25, 1917
Private 1st Class, December 26, 1917
Transferred to 101st Hospital, December 31, 1917
Returned to Company, March 4, 1918
#3346
Wagoner, June 17, 1918
Wounded in action severely, October 28, 1918
Cited in orders October 15 and December 28 for gallantry in action
Private 1st Class, March 12, 1919
Honorably discharged, April 29, 1919

*Gus F. Hannon ("Mickie")
Born Bridgeport
Age 19
Enlisted in National Guard, Bridgeport, April 4, 1917

#3349
Private 1st Class, December 26, 1917
Wagoner, April 18, 1918
Private, June 17, 1918
Wagoner, September 17, 1918
Cited in orders December 28 for bravery in action
Honorably discharged, April 29, 1918

*Leland J. Hull ("Lee")
Born Bridgeport
Age 22
Enlisted in National Guard, Bridgeport, June 4, 1917
Cook, August 13, 1917
Private, November 14, 1917
#3353
Wagoner, April 15, 1918
Wounded in action
Working with Red Cross, October 1918
Honorably discharged, June 7, 1919

*Bertrand Keane ("Bert")
Born New York City
Age 18 (actually 17)
Employed as reporter by Bridgeport Post Publishing Company
Enlisted in National Guard, Bridgeport, May 16, 1917
Private 1st Class, December 28, 1917
#3356
Company motorcycle orderly
Wounded, October 4, 1918
Wagoner, December 7, 1918
Cited for bravery in action
Awarded Croix de Guerre
Transferred to Headquarters Company, 101st Sanitary Train
Honorably discharged, April 29, 1919

+Martin G. Klingel
Born Freehold, NY
Age 22
Clerk in Hartford
Enlisted in National Guard, Hartford, 1916
Served with 1st Connecticut Ambulance Company
Service on Mexican border, July–October 1916
Assigned to Company, August 5, 1917
#2758
Returned in Saint Aignan Casual Co. 995 on USS *Mount Vernon*, March 1919

*Leroy A. MacKinnon ("Roy")
Born Pinehurst, NC
Age 20
Clerk at Union Metallic Cartridge Company
Enlisted in National Guard, Bridgeport, April 3, 1917
Private 1st Class, June 16, 1917
Cook, August 27, 1917
Private 1st Class, December 22, 1917
#3361
Gassed at Chemin des Dames, March 17, 1918
Wagoner, April 15, 1918
Gassed at Seicheprey, April 20, 1918
At Base Hospital 66
Gassed at Saulx, September 25, 1918
Cited in orders October 15 for bravery in action at Saulx
Honorably discharged, April 29, 1919

*Ralph S. Merrill
Born Nashville, TN
Age 23
Automobile assembler at Locomobile Company
Enlisted in National Guard, Bridgeport, July 25, 1917
#3439
Wagoner, September 14, 1918
Private 1st Class, December 26, 1918
Wounded in action
Cited in orders December 28 for bravery in action near Haumont, October 22–27, 1918
Honorably discharged, April 29, 1919

*Harry B. Monahan ("Monie")
Born Bridgeport
Age 20
Lathe hand at Singer Manufacturing Company
Enlisted in National Guard, Bridgeport, March 31, 1917
Private 1st Class, December 26, 1917
#3367
Wagoner, April 1, 1918
Wounded in action, late September 1918
At Base Hospital 32, Contraxville, October 1–5, 1918
At Base Hospitals 86, 44, 67, 72, 108, Mesves-Bulcy, October 7, 1918–February 5, 1919
Cited for bravery in action
Honorably discharged, April 29, 1919

*Ripple G. Morgan ("Rip")
Born Norwich, CT
Age 25

Enlisted in National Guard, Bridgeport, May 31, 1917
Private 1st Class, December 26, 1917
#3366
Wagoner, April 15, 1918
Wounded in action
Cited for bravery in action
Honorably discharged, April 29, 1919

+Fred E. Pinney ("Bloomfield")
Born Bloomfield, CT
Age 19
Enlisted National Guard, Hartford, June 22, 1916
Served with 1st Connecticut Ambulance Company
Service on Mexican border, July–October 1916
Private 1st Class, December 16, 1917
#3375
Private, June 17, 1918
Wagoner, November 8, 1918
Private 1st Class, March 12, 1919
Wounded in action
Cited for bravery in action
Honorably discharged, April 29, 1919

*Earle E. Radikin ("Rad")
Born Pawtucket, RI
Age 23
Sales clerk in Howland's Department Store, Bridgeport
Enlisted in National Guard, Bridgeport, May 16, 1917
Private 1st Class, December 26, 1917
Wagoner, 1918
#3377
Gassed, Chemin-des-Dames, March 17, 1918
Cited in orders August 31 for bravery in action at Épieds, July 1918
At Base Hospital 42, Bazoilles, October 13–November 1, 1918
Detailed to write 101st Sanitary Train history, February 1919
Honorably discharged, April 29, 1919

+Walter L. Scott ("Scotty")
Born Hartford, CT
Age 22
Enlisted in National Guard, Hartford, June 23, 1916
Served with 1st Connecticut Ambulance Company
Service on Mexican border, July–October 1916
Private 1st Class, December 26, 1917
#3379
Wagoner
Wounded in action
Cited in orders December 28 for bravery in action
Honorably discharged, April 29, 1919

*Elmer F. Troland
Born Bridgeport
Age 19
Assistant auto repairman
Enlisted in National Guard, Bridgeport, May 16, 1917
#3427
Transferred to 101st Field Hospital, March 28, 1918
Wagoner, May 4, 1918
Private, July 18, 1918
Transferred to F Lab 26th Division, September 18, 1918
Returned to Company, March 21, 1919
Honorably discharged, April 29, 1919

*George W. Watt ("Slim")
Born Bridgeport
Age 20
Clerk at Union Metallic Cartridge Company
Enlisted in National Guard, Bridgeport, April 10, 1917
Private 1st Class, June 14, 1917
Private, August 27, 1917
Transferred to 104th Field Hospital, December 11, 1917
Returned to Company, January 21, 1918
#3433
Wagoner
Reassigned as litter bearer, July 1918
Transferred to Medical Detachment 102nd Infantry, October 8, 1918
Cited for bravery in action
Honorably discharged, April 29, 1919

*George S. Wills ("Blub Blub")
Born Bridgeport
Age 20
Enlisted in National Guard, Bridgeport, April 9, 1917
Private 1st Class, December 26, 1917
Wagoner
#3392
Cited in orders December 28 for bravery in action
Honorably discharged, April 29, 1919

*Joseph Wynkoop
Born Paterson, NJ
Age 22
Employed by Bridgeport Post Publishing Company
Enlisted in National Guard, Bridgeport, June 11, 1917
Private 1st Class, December 26, 1917
#3397
Wagoner, April 15, 1918
Cited for bravery in action
Honorably discharged, April 29, 1919

*Benjamin B. Wyrtzen ("Dynamite")
Born Fairfield, CT
Age 18
Clerk
Enlisted in National Guard, Bridgeport, April 3, 1917
Transferred to 104th Field Hospital, December 11, 1917
Returned to Company, January 21, 1918
#3435
Wagoner
Wounded in action
Cited for bravery in action
Honorably discharged, April 29, 1919

Mechanics

*Albert Honeck ("Pop")
Born Herman, MO
Age 44
Previous duty as U.S. Army Quartermaster Department blacksmith in Oklahoma
Enlisted in National Guard, Bridgeport, April 5, 1917
Private 1st Class, May 2, 1917
Mechanic, July 19, 1917
Transferred to 104th Ambulance Company, December 1, 1917
#3604
Horseshoer, May 27, 1918
Honorably discharged, April 29, 1919, 10 percent disabled

Harry D. Edes ("Old Man")
Born Greenfield, MA
Age 36
Machinist
#3335
Mechanic
Honorably discharged, April 29, 1919

Horseshoer

*Martin C. Norup
Born Kolding, Denmark
Age 23
Horseshoer and blacksmith
Enlisted in National Guard, Bridgeport, April 5, 1917
Private 1st Class, May 2, 1917
Transferred to 104th Ambulance Company, December 1, 1917
#3601
Honorably discharged, April 29, 1919

Cooks

*Frank Doreski
Born New York City
Age 21
Enlisted in National Guard, Bridgeport, May 24, 1917
Private 1st Class, January 14, 1918
#3405
Wounded in action severely, April 20, 1918
Cook, September 30, 1918
Sent to hospital, Le Mans, March 1919
Honorably discharged, June 13, 1919, 50 percent disability

Edward J. McLaughlin
Born Boston, MA
Age 22
Shoe cutter
#3365
Cook
Honorably discharged, April 29, 1919

*Frank B. Phillips ("Ma")
Born Sag Harbor, NY
Age 23
Enlisted in National Guard, Bridgeport, May 24, 1917
Private 1st Class, December 26, 1917
Cook, February 12, 1918
#3318
Wounded in action, October 28, 1918
Private 1st Class
Honorably discharged, April 29, 1919

*John J. Safko
Born Yonkers, NY
Age 22
Salesman for Reliance Tobacco Company
Enlisted in National Guard, Bridgeport, June 4, 1917

Private 1st Class, December 26, 1917
Cook, January 3, 1918
Private 1st Class, January 22, 1918
#3378
At Base Hospital 47, Beaune, for flu, September 17–October 7, 1918
Honorably discharged, April 29, 1919

*Joseph A. Safko
Born Yonkers, NY
Age 20
Enlisted in National Guard, Bridgeport, June 4, 1917
#3319
Cook, December 22, 1917
Honorably discharged, April 29, 1919

Bugler

William A. Flynn ("Mickey")
Born Worcester, MA
#3338
Wounded in action
Private 1st Class

Privates

Thomas J. Bale ("Jerry")
Born Danbury, CT
Age 22
Enlisted in National Guard, Bridgeport, June 8, 1917
Detailed at Liverpool to manage Company baggage, October 17, 1917
Rejoined Company, November 26, 1917
Transferred to 101st Field Hospital, December 2, 1917
#3202
Transferred to 101st Ambulance Company, June 28, 1918
Honorably discharged, April 29, 1919

William E. Ballard
Born Bridgeport
Age 20
Worked at Union Metallic Cartridge Company
Enlisted in National Guard, Bridgeport, May 16, 1917
Private 1st Class, December 26, 1917
#3332
Honorably discharged, April 29, 1919

*Frederick C. Beach
Born Stratford, CT
Age 18
Enlisted in National Guard, Bridgeport, May 28, 1917
Transferred to Medical Detachment, 104th Infantry. December 3, 1917
#2965
Transferred to Medical Detachment, Base Hospital 202, September 18, 1918
Transferred to U.S. Debarkation Hospital 1, October 21, 1918
Transferred to U.S. General Hospital 30, October 28, 1918
Transferred to Company A 2nd Battalion Convalescence Group, Camp Upton, New York, December 14, 1918
Honorably discharged, January 4, 1919

*Clayton M. Bell
Born New York City
Age 22
Assistant superintendent, Eastern Malleable Iron Works
Enlisted in National Guard, Bridgeport, May 25, 1917
Transferred to 104th Field Hospital, December 3, 1917
Transferred to 104th Ambulance Company, January 21, 1918
#3632
Gassed and shell-shocked, Seicheprey, April 20, 1918
In hospitals, April 21–November 1, 1918
Evacuated, November 1918
Honorably discharged, March 20, 1919

*Arthur T. Best ("Artie")
Born Bridgeport
Age 21
Enlisted in National Guard, Bridgeport, April 2, 1917
Private 1st Class, December 26, 1917
#3327
Transferred to 101st Ambulance Company, April 25, 1918
Returned to Company, March 12, 1919
Honorably discharged, April 29, 1919

George A. Blackman
Born New Haven, CT
Age 28
Clerk at Wheeler & Company
Enlisted National Guard, Bridgeport, June 4, 1917
Transferred to 104th Ambulance Company January 15, 1918

#3633
Gassed in eyes, Seicheprey, April 20, 1918
Cited for litter-bearer duty at Torcy and beyond, July 18–25, 1918
Honorably discharged, April 29, 1919

Vinal H. Brenizer
Born Queen City, MO
Age 20
Sent to France in Overseas Casuals Detachment, Medical Department, January 12, 1918
#13346
Assigned to Company
Transferred to Base Hospital 72, February 1919
Promoted to corporal, Camp Hospital 114
Departed France on SS *Pocahontas*, June 20, 1919

Herman C. Brey
Born Chicago, IL
Age 25
Post Office clerk
Drafted
#935841
Sent to France in Fort Riley Medical Casual Detachment on SS *Aquitania*, April 2, 1918
Assigned to Company

*Phillip Brodsky ("Fill Up")
Born Rogaton, Russia
Age 21
Mechanic
Enlisted in National Guard, Bridgeport, June 2, 1917
#3399
Transferred to Medical Detachment, 103rd Infantry, October 6, 1918
Wounded slightly, November 5, 1918
At Base Hospital 3, November 7–31, 1918
Honorably discharged, April 29, 1919

*Herbert W. Browning
Born Halesowen, England
Age 18
Enlisted in National Guard, Bridgeport, June 5, 1917
Transferred to 104th Field Hospital, December 11, 1917
Transferred to 104th Ambulance Company, January 21, 1918
#3639
Transferred to 101st Field Hospital, March 28, 1918
Private 1st Class, May 15, 1918
Transferred to 104th Ambulance Company, June 28, 1918
Honorably discharged, April 29, 1919

Walter H. Butler ("Judge")
Born Rockland, ME
Age 30
Enlisted in Headquarters Company, Maine National Guard Field Artillery, July 17, 1917
Transferred to 4th Field Hospital (104th Field Hospital), August 29, 1917
Transferred to Company, September 20, 1917
Promoted to corporal, January 18, 1918
Transferred to Headquarters, 101st Sanitary Train, April 12, 1918
Promoted to sergeant, May 22, 1918
Honorably discharged, April 29, 1919

John O. Caler
Born New York City
Drafted
#935853
Sent to France in Fort Riley Medical Casual Detachment on SS *Aquitania*, April 2, 1918
Assigned to Company
Shell-shocked, July 1918
Wounded in action
Transferred to Base Hospital 72, February 1919

*Ralph H. Carleton
Born Marlboro, MA
Age 27
Bookkeeper at Columbia Graphophone Company
Enlisted in National Guard, Bridgeport, May 12, 1917
Farrier, September 21, 1917
Private, December 6, 1917
#3400
Cited for attending wounded under fire, Chemin-des-Dames, March 17, 1918
Gassed, Mandres, April 20, 1918
At 102nd Field Hospital, Toul, April 22–May 12, 1918
Private 1st Class, June 14, 1918
Cited for carrying messages under fire, Bois d'Haumont, October 10, 1918
Concussion, Bois d'Haumont, October 22, 1918
At 102nd Field Hospital, Verdun, October 22–29, 1918
Honorably discharged, April 29, 1919

Donaldson R. Carr
Born Manchester, NH
Age 18
#3329
Private 1st Class
Cited in orders for bravery in action, December 28

Joseph Carroll
Born Cambridge, MA
#3402
Wounded in action
Private 1st Class
Cited for bravery in action

James H. Carter
Born Vian, OK
Age 22
Farmer
Drafted
#935221
Sent to France in Fort Riley Medical Casual Detachment on SS *Aquitania*, April 2, 1918
Assigned to Company
Private 1st Class
Cited for bravery in action

*Antony Catullo ("Butts")
Born Bridgeport
Age 19
Enlisted in National Guard, Bridgeport, April 2, 1917
Transferred to 104th Field Hospital, December 2, 1917
Transferred to 104th Ambulance Company, January 21, 1918
#3643
Transferred to 101st Field Hospital, March 28, 1918
Transferred to 104th Ambulance Company, June 28, 1918
Transferred to Sanitary Detachment, 101st Engineers, October 6, 1918
Honorably discharged, April 29, 1918

Orlo G. Chandler ("Esbon")
Born Esbon, KS
Drafted
#935283
Sent to France in Fort Riley Medical Casual Detachment on SS *Aquitania*, April 2, 1918
Private 1st Class
Assigned to Company

Percy M. Chapman
Born Ledyard, CT
Age 24
Nurse at Worcester State Hospital
Enlisted in National Guard, Boston, April 1917
Private 1st Class, 103rd Field Hospital
Transferred to Company, February 10, 1918
#3332
Honorably discharged, April 23, 1919

Daniel F. Clare ("Daniel E.")
Born Laconia, NH
Age 27
Enlisted in New Hampshire National Guard Medical Detachment, 103rd Infantry
#3330
Transferred to Company
Private 1st Class
Honorably discharged, April 29, 1919

Warren Clark
Born Frannie, WY
Age 19
Oil derrick man
Drafted
#3448013
Sent to France in Fort Riley Exceptional Medical August Automatic Replacement Draft Company 61 on SS *Baltic*, September 1, 1918
Assigned to Company
Transferred to Field Hospital 324, 306th Sanitary Train, 81st Division, March 1919
Departed France on SS *Manchuria*, June 9, 1919

*Martin Clarke
Born Westport, County Mayo, Ireland
Age 35
Enlisted in National Guard, Bridgeport, May 23, 1917
#3401
Private 1st Class, August 13, 1918
Honorably discharged, April 29, 1919

Benjamin F. Clay, Jr.
Born Norman, OK
Drafted
#93565
Sent to France in Fort Riley Medical Casual Detachment on SS *Aquitania*, April 2, 1918
Gassed, July 1918
Wounded in action, October 22, 1918
Cited in orders for bravery in action, December 28

+Christopher Cody
Born New Brunswick, NJ
Age 22
Served with 1st Connecticut Ambulance Company
Service on Mexican border, July–October 1916
Assigned to Company, August 5, 1917
Enlisted National Guard, Hartford, April 6, 1915
Transferred to 104th Field Hospital, December 11, 1917
Transferred to 104th Ambulance Company, January 21, 1918
#3647
Wounded, April 20, 1918
Return to Company, April 29, 1918
Private 1st Class, May 5, 1918
Honorably discharged, April 29, 1919

Moe Cohen
Born Harrisburg, PA
Age 19
Drafted, May 1, 1918
#442766
Sent to France as part of Camp Greenleaf August Automatic Replacement Draft, Medical Company #11, on SS *Mauretania,* August 27, 1918
Cited for bravery in action
Transferred to Base Hospital 72, February 1919
Returned to U.S., June 1919
Honorably discharged, July 10, 1919

+George J. Cormier ("Wire Whiskers")
Born East Longmeadow, MA
Age 20
Enlisted in National Guard, Hartford, May 28, 1915
Served with 1st Connecticut Ambulance Company
Service on Mexican border, July–October 1916
Assigned to Company, August 5, 1917
Transferred to Medical Detachment, 104th Field Hospital, December 3, 1917
Transferred to 104th Ambulance Company, January 21, 1918
#3649
Private 1st Class, May 5, 1918
Transferred to Medical Detachment, 101st Infantry, June 6, 1918
Honorably discharged, April 29, 1919

*Newton S. Courtney
Born East Lynn, MA
Age 18
Apparently joined Company at Niantic, Summer 1917
Transferred to 101st Field Hospital
#3522
Honorably discharged, April 29, 1919

Nemire Craft
Born Box Elder, MT
Age 31
164th Field Hospital, 116th Sanitary Train, 41st Division
To France on SS *Tuscania*, December 1917
#5076
Transferred to Sanitary Detachment, 101st Machine Gun Battalion, August 1918
Transferred to Company, September 11, 1918
Transferred to 104th Field Hospital
Honorably discharged, April 29, 1919

*Benjamin M. Crawford
Born Richmond, VA
Age 29
Enlisted in National Guard, Bridgeport, July 24, 1917
#3218
Private 1st Class, May 15, 1918
Honorably discharged, April 29, 1919

*Frank Hastings Crump ("Buddy")
Born Chicago, IL
Age 21
Enlisted in National Guard, Bridgeport, March 24, 1917
#3333
Private 1st Class
Wounded in action, April 20, 1918
Sent to hospital, Le Mans, March 1919
Honorably discharged, July 10, 1919
Died in Bridgeport, 1923

*William J. Cumming
Born South Salem, NY
Age 22
Employed by Meigs & Company Department Store, Bridgeport
Enlisted in National Guard, Bridgeport, April 3, 1917
Private, April 3, 1917
Private 1st Class, July 19, 1917
Died following operation for mastoiditis, meningitis, and measles, January 5, 1918

George H. Curtis
Lewiston, ME

Andrew J. Dannerson
Born St. Louis, MO
Age 25
Drafted
#935880
Sent to France in Fort Riley Medical Casual Detachment on SS *Aquitania*, April 2, 1918
Assigned to Company

Edwin F. Davis
Born Burlington, VT
#3970
Private 1st Class

*Frank H. Davis
Born Bridgeport
Age 18
Enlisted in National Guard, Niantic, August 17, 1917
Transferred to 103rd Ambulance Company, December 1, 1917
#3524
Transferred to 104th Field Hospital, April 18, 1918
Wounded in face by mustard gas
At Base Hospital 18, Bazoilles, May 15–May 30, 1918
Honorably discharged, February 13, 1919, 50 percent disability

*Howard P. Davis ("Parson")
Born Middleboro, MA
Age 22
Inspector at Remington Arms Company
Enlisted in National Guard, Bridgeport, May 28, 1917
#3334
Private 1st Class, December 26, 1917
Promoted to corporal but refused appointment
Wounded in action, October 27, 1918
Cited in orders for bravery in action, December 28, 1918
Honorably discharged, April 29, 1919

Owen M. Davis
Born Wells, ME
Age 19
Enlisted in Regular Army, Fort Slocum, New York, October 28, 1916
#124834
Private 1st Class
Transferred to Company
Honorably discharged, October 15, 1919

*James E. Dennery
Born Thompsonville, CT
Age 19
Enlisted in National Guard, Bridgeport, May 11, 1917
Transferred to 104th Field Hospital, December 11, 1917
Transferred to 104th Ambulance Company, January 26, 1918
#3652
Private 1st Class, May 5, 1918
Transferred to medical detachment, 101st Infantry, June 6, 1918
Private, November 20, 1918
Transferred to Base Hospital 20, January 9, 1919
Transferred to Debarkation Hospital 1, February 10, 1919
Transferred to General Hospital 1, March 26, 1919
Honorably discharged, May 9, 1919
SCD 6-1/4 percent disability

Robert H. Denson
Born Atlanta, GA
Drafted
#2587165
Sent to France as part of Camp Greenleaf August Automatic Replacement Draft, Medical Company #11, on SS *Mauretania*, August 27, 1918
Assigned to Company
Transferred, March 1919

Gaston Derolland
Born Paris, France
Age 30
Hat maker in New York City
Drafted
Inducted, New York City, June 24, 1918
#3201348
Medical Corps training at Camp Greenleaf, July 1918
Sent to France as part of Camp Crane Automatic Replacement Draft, Medical Company 1, on SS *Port Lincoln*, September 4, 1918,
Joined Company, September 1918
Killed in action, October 28, 1918

James D. Dickens
Drafted

Assigned to Company, October 1918
Transferred, March 1919

Frank P. Dillon
Born Brooklyn, NY
#3201098
Drafted
Sent to France as part of Camp Crane Automatic Replacement Draft, Medical Company 1, on SS *Port Lincoln*, September 4, 1918
Assigned to Company

*Anthony W. Diorio ("Nabisco")
Born Bridgeport
Age 18
Conductor, Connecticut Consolidated Railway
Enlisted in National Guard, Bridgeport, April 2, 1917
Transferred to 104th Field Hospital, December 11, 1917
Transferred to 104th Ambulance Company, January 2, 1918
#3654
Gassed, Seicheprey, April 20, 1918
Private 1st Class, May 5, 1918
Gassed near Haumont, October 19, 1918
Honorably discharged, April 29, 1919

*George J. Dubee
Born Bridgeport
Age 22
Machinist at Burns & Bassick, Bridgeport
Enlisted in National Guard, Bridgeport, May 31, 1917
#3406
Honorably discharged, April 29, 1919

John L. Durden
Born Springfield, GA
Age 22
Drafted
Inducted, April 28, 1918
#2654496
Sent to France as part of Camp Crane Automatic Replacement Draft, Medical Company 1, on SS *Port Lincoln*, September 4, 1918
Assigned to Company
Transferred to Base Hospital 72, February 1919
Transferred to Camp Hospital 114
Returned from France on SS *Pocahontas*, June 20, 1919
Honorably discharged, July 10, 1919

*John E. Falvo
Born Danbury, CT
Age 21
Enlisted in National Guard, Bridgeport, July 23, 1917
#3225
Private 1st Class, May 16, 1918
Wounded in action, October 31, 1918
Evacuated on USS *Pastores*, December 25, 1918
Arrived Newport News, VA, January 6, 1919
Honorably discharged, February 8, 1919, 10 percent disability
Died in Danbury, 1923

*George H. Ferris ("Mother")
Born Cohoes, NY
Age 26
Draftsman at the Columbia Graphophone Company
Enlisted in National Guard, Bridgeport, June 1, 1917
Private 1st Class, December 20, 1917
#3336
In 103rd Feld Hospital, Toul, May 18–25, 1918
In Base Hospital 72, Allerry, October 10–18, 1918
Honorably discharged, April 29, 1919

*Clifford R. Fulton ("Doc")
Born Bridgeport
Age 19
Enlisted in National Guard, Bridgeport, April 9, 1917
Private 1st Class, June 16, 1917
#3337
Corporal, October 28, 1918
Wounded in action
Cited for bravery in action
Honorably discharged, April 29, 1919

James B. Gambrell
Born South Glenwood, SC
Drafted
#1861860
Sent to France as part of Camp Greenleaf August Automatic Replacement Draft, Medical Company 11, on SS *Mauretania*, August 27, 1918
Assigned to Company

*Clarence D. Gariepy
Born St. Albans, VT
Age 23
Enlisted in National Guard, Bridgeport, June 1, 1917

Private 1st Class, December 26, 1917
#3339
Honorably discharged, April 29, 1919

+James S. Garvin ("Ezra")
Born Toronto, Canada
Age 22
Graduated from Rutgers, 1914
Employed by U.S. Mortgage and Trust Company, New York
Enlisted in National Guard, Hartford, June 22, 1916
Served with 1st Connecticut Ambulance Company on Mexican border, July–October 1916
Married Katherine Anne Cowles, August 1917
Private 1st Class, December 26, 1917
#3340
Badly injured when a truck collided with his ambulance about May 9, 1918
Died of spinal meningitis at Evacuation Hospital 1, May 16, 1918

Fred J. Geer
Born Rutland, VT
Age 29
Enlisted in 2nd Massachusetts Field Hospital (103rd Field Hospital), July 31, 1917
Private 1st Class, October 18, 1917
Transferred to Company, February 7, 1918
#3341
Reduced to private, August 5, 1918
Wounded in action
Transferred to Medical Detachment, 102nd Infantry, January 6, 1919
Honorably discharged, April 29, 1919

George N. Geer
Born Rutland, VT
Age 27
Salesman in Boston
Enlisted in 2nd Massachusetts Field Hospital (103rd Field Hospital), May 1917
#3437
Transferred to Company
Honorably discharged, April 29, 1919

Richard C. Gellrich ("Annette Kellerman")
Born Manchester, NH
#2312940
Sanitary detachment, 3rd Division
Arrived in France, March 1918
Assigned to Company
Wounded in action
Cited for bravery in action
Private 1st Class
Honorably discharged, April 29, 1919

Stanton Glover ("Stan")
Born Rockland, ME
Age 19
Enlisted in Maine National Guard Heavy Field Artillery, July 17, 1917
Transferred to 101st Sanitary Train, August 24, 1917
Assigned to Company, September 1917
#3345
Wounded in action, April 20, 1918
Private 1st Class
Honorably discharged, April 29, 1919

Clarence Harris
Born Brockton, MA
#3437
Wounded in action eight times, a Company record
Wore four wound stripes

William A. Harris
Born Louisville, KY
Drafted
#1580381
Assigned to Company

Clarence W. Harvey
Born West Somerville, MA
Enlisted in Massachusetts National Guard
Private in 101st Field Hospital
Private 1st Class
#3407
Transferred to Company
Honorably discharged, April 29, 1919

William G. Hayden
Born Atlanta, GA
Drafted
#2587120
Sent to France as part of Camp Greenleaf August Automatic Replacement Draft, Medical Company #11, on SS *Mauretania*, August 27, 1918
Assigned to Company
Transferred, March 1919

*John S. Healy
Born New Haven, CT
Age 19
Clerk
Enlisted in National Guard, New Haven, April 10, 1917
1st Connecticut Field Hospital Company

Transferred to Company
#3541
In Base Hospital 15, Chaumont, April 17–May 30, 1918
Honorably discharged, April 29, 1919

Martin Luther Hollingsworth
Born Mound City, MO
Age 23
Farmer
Enlisted in North Dakota National Guard, July 3, 1917
Transferred to 103rd Field Hospital, April 9, 1918
Transferred to Company, May 9, 1918
Transferred to Medical Detachment, 102nd Infantry, October 6, 1918
Killed in action, November 10, 1918

*Edwin M. Hough ("Old Reliable")
Born Westfield, MA
Age 44
Machinist at Locomobile of America
Previous service in Massachusetts and Rhode Island National Guard Infantry
Enlisted in National Guard, Bridgeport, May 9, 1917
#3348
Private 1st Class, December 26, 1918
Training at Vailly, February 10–March 22, 1918
Honorably discharged, April 29, 1919, 10 percent disabled

*Lewis M. Hough
Born New Haven, CT
Age 22
Employed at Remington Arms Company
Enlisted in National Guard, Bridgeport, April 3, 1917
Private 1st Class, June 6, 1917
Sergeant, June 21, 1917
Transferred to Medical Detachment, 103rd Infantry, March 10, 1918
#3939
Honorably discharged, April 30, 1919

Dewey W. Houston
Born Pittsford, VT
Age 19
Enlisted in Vermont National Guard, January 2, 1917
Sanitary Detachment, 1st Vermont Infantry, April 3, 1917
Transferred to 104th Field Hospital, September 4, 1917
Private 1st Class, November 15, 1917
Transferred to Company, January 21, 1918
#3352
Honorably discharged, April 29, 1919

Ralph G. Hull
Born Chelsea, MA
Age 21
Machinist at Remington Arms Company
Enlisted in National Guard, Bridgeport, May 2, 1917
#3408
Honorably discharged with 5 percent disability, December 31, 1918

*Jesse Lodrick James ("Chunky")
Born Hawleyville, CT
Age 24
Farmer
Enlisted in National Guard, Bridgeport, May 17, 1917
Private 1st Class, December 26, 1917
#3354
Wounded in action
Honorably discharged, April 29, 1919

*David S. Jarvis
Born Awamutu District, Waipa, New Zealand
Age 23
Bookkeeper at Columbia Graphophone Company
Enlisted in National Guard, Bridgeport, May 9, 1917
In British hospitals, Aldershot and Le Havre, October 24, 1917–January 25, 1918
In Base Hospital 66, Neufchâteau, March 1–22, 1918
#240173
Promoted to corporal, May 1918
Transferred to Infantry Candidates School, Valbonne, France, May 3, 1918
Promoted to sergeant, July 4, 1918
Discharged, June 25, 1919

*Charles H. Johnson
Born Stratford, CT
Age 21
Real estate agent
Enlisted in National Guard, Bridgeport, April 3, 1917
Private 1st Class December 26, 1917
#3355
Gassed at Seicheprey, April 20, 1918
In Evacuation Hospital 1, Toul, June 8–16, 1918

In Base Hospital 18, Neufchâteau, June 16–July 6, 1918
In Base Hospital 20, July 8–August 20, 1918
In Base Hospital 8, August 22-evacuation
In Fort McHenry Hospital, Baltimore, September 1918–February 1919
Honorably discharged February 20, 1919, 15 percent disability

*Frederick Johnson
Born Brooklyn, NY
Age 22
Employed by Meigs & Company Department Store, Bridgeport
Enlisted in National Guard, Bridgeport, March 30, 1917
Private 1st Class, June 16, 1917
Corporal, December 18, 1917
#2757
Transferred to Training School for Sanitary Troops, July 18, 1918
Sergeant, September 16, 1918
Transferred to 376th Ambulance Company, November 1, 1918

Charles E. Kean
Born Glendive, MT
164th Field Hospital, 116th Sanitary Train, 41st Division
To France on SS *Tuscania*, December 1917
#4500
Transferred to Company

*Frederick Keller ("Hand Grenade Mike")
Born Bronx, NY
Age 20
Shipping clerk at Standard Coupler Company
Enlisted in National Guard, Bridgeport, May 23, 1917
#3410
Private 1st Class, June 14, 1918
Wounded in action
Cited in orders December 28 for bravery in action near Haumont, October 17–27, 1918
Honorably discharged, April 29, 1919

Milas H. Kennedy
Born Rutherford County, NC
Age 23
Farmer
Drafted
#2586809
Sent to France as part of Camp Greenleaf August Automatic Replacement Draft, Medical Company 11, on SS *Mauretania*, August 27, 1918,
Assigned to Company
Transferred, March 1919

Charles H. Kenney
Born Framingham, MA
#71342

William H. Key
Born Eufaula, AL
Drafted
#2655362
Assigned to Company

*William A. Kinsella
Born Fairfield, CT
Age 20
Enlisted in National Guard, Bridgeport, May 13, 1917
Transferred to 104th Field Hospital, December 11, 1917
Transferred to 104th Ambulance Company, January 21, 1918
#3869
Wounded in action, April 20, 1918
Private 1st Class, May 5, 1918
Wounded in action, October 27, 1918
Honorably discharged, April 29, 1919

*Arthur J. Lambeau ("Peasoup")
Born Antwerp, Belgium
Age 38
Enlisted in National Guard, Bridgeport, June 5, 1917
Private 1st Class, December 26, 1917
#3358
Officers' waiter on SS *Winifredian*, April 1919
Honorably discharged, April 29, 1919

*Max H. Landman (Mordechai Yitzhak b Zishe)
Born Brooklyn, NY
Age 22
Gold-plater at Columbia Graphophone Company
Enlisted in National Guard, Bridgeport, March 14, 1917
Private 1st Class, June 16, 1917
Transferred to 101st Ambulance Company, December 1, 1917
#3188
Gassed
In 101st Field Hospital, April 6–June 28, 1918

Transferred to Sanitary Detachment, 102nd Field Artillery, July 22, 1918
Honorably discharged, April 29, 1919

*William Larson
Born Brooklyn, NY
Age 28
Enlisted in National Guard, Bridgeport, May 28, 1917
Transferred to 104th Field Hospital, December 11, 1917
Returned to 102nd Ambulance Company, January 21, 1918
#3413
Private 1st Class, June 14, 1918
Honorably discharged, April 29, 1919

*Hugh J. Lawler ("Hughey")
Born Bridgeport
Age 24
Employed as laborer in corset factory (1910)
Enlisted in National Guard, Bridgeport, April 3, 1917
Transferred to Medical Detachment 102nd Infantry, November 9, 1917
#2852
Wounded in action
Cited for bravery in action
Honorably discharged, April 29, 1919

Guy Lawrence
Born Columbus, KY
Drafted
Assigned to Company

John O. Lawrence
Born Bardwell, KY
Drafted
Assigned to Company

*William C. Leonard
Born Bridgeport
Age 22
Enlisted in National Guard, Bridgeport, March 15, 1917
Private 1st Class, June 16, 1917
Served in gun crew on SS *Corsican*, October 1917
#3359
Transferred to 101st Field Hospital, March 28, 1918
Honorably discharged, April 29, 1919

Jack Levenson
Born Louisville, KY
#1580383
152nd Field Hospital, 113th Sanitary Train, 38th Division
Departed for France on SS *Zealandia*, October 6, 1918
Assigned to Company
Transferred

John Leventhal
Born Dorchester, MA
Enlisted in Massachusetts National Guard
101st Ambulance Company
#3555
Transferred to Company

Enoch Lewis
Born Charleston, MO
Drafted
#3699548
Sent to France as part of Camp Crane August Automatic Replacement Draft, Medical Company 9, on SS *Princess Juliana*, August 23, 1918
Assigned to Company
Transferred to Base Hospital 72, February 1919
Departed France on SS *Seattle*, June 25, 1919

John R. Lilley
Born Fall River, MA
Age 21
#242290
Assigned to Company
Wounded in action

*William C. Louis
Born Brooklyn, NY
Apparently enlisted in Company at Niantic, Summer 1917
#241691
Cited for bravery in action, July 1918
Transferred to 101st Ambulance Company
Honorably discharged, April 29, 1919

*Robert R. MacDonald
Born South Norwalk, CT
Age 20
Clerk at Yale & Towne Manufacturing Company
Enlisted in National Guard, Bridgeport, June 30, 1917
Private 1st Class, December 26, 1917
#3360
Gassed April 20, 1918, while acting as orderly in SSU 647 ambulance
In 102nd Field Hospital, Ménil-la-Tour, April 20–30, 1918

Cited in orders October 15 for bravery in action
Honorably discharged, April 29, 1919

John H. MacIntyre
Born Somerville, MA
#3754
Promoted to sergeant
Transferred to Headquarters Company, 101st Sanitary Train

Joseph P. Mackey ("Jerry")
Born Jamaica Plain, MA
Age 22
Enlisted in 3rd Field Hospital (102nd Field Hospital), summer 1917
Transferred to Company, September 1917
#3415
Transferred to medical detachment, 101st Infantry
Evacuated on SS *Leviathan*, December 1918
Honorably discharged, December 1918

Bailey MacMillan
Born Scott, KY
Age 23
Farmer
Drafted
Assigned to Company
Transferred to Base Hospital 72, February 1919

George A. Marshall
Born Portland, ME
Age 22
Steward in seminary
Enlisted in Maine National Guard Field Artillery, June 29, 1917
Transferred to 101st Sanitary Train, August 24, 1917
Assigned to Company, September 1917
Private 1st Class, December 26, 1917
#3362
Honorably discharged, April 29, 1919

Thomas H. Marshall
Born Everett, MA
Age 23
Salesman
Private in 2nd Massachusetts Field Hospital (103rd Field Hospital), 1917
Transferred to Company
#3418
Promoted to corporal
Honorably discharged, July 21, 1919

Robert H. Marston, Jr. ("Beauty")
Born Boston, MA
Age 22
Dictaphone assembler in Bridgeport
Served in gun crew on SS *Corsican*, October 1917
#3364
Cited for bravery in action
Private 1st Class
Honorably discharged, April 29, 1919

Harry V. McDermott
Born Dunseith, ND
Age 22
Private 1st Class
163rd Field Hospital, 116th Sanitary Train, 41st Division
Departed for France on SS *Tuscania*, December 11, 1917
#5082
Joined Sanitary Detachment, 101st Machine Gun Battalion, August 1918
Transferred to Company, September 11, 1918
Honorably discharged, April 29, 1919

*William M. McElroy ("Silent Mac")
Born Chapinville, CT
Age 37
Clerk at Locomobile Company of America
Enlisted in National Guard, Bridgeport, May 23, 1917
#3363
Private 1st Class, December 26, 1918
Wounded in action
Cited in orders, August 31, October 15, and December 28, for bravery in action at Battle of the Marne, July 18–26, 1918, and Saulx, September 25–26, 1918
Suffered compound fracture of jaw and sprained right arm and knee near Château du Loire, January 25, 1919
At Camp hospital 72, Château du Loire, January 25–31, 1919
At Base Hospital 121, Tours, February 1–8, 1919
At Base Hospital 20, February 8–March 12, 1919
At General Hospital 10, Boston, April 7–June 12, 1919
At General Hospital 2, Baltimore, June 12–14, 1919
Honorably discharged July 17, 1919

Peter F. McGorty
Born Roslindale, MA

Age 22
Enlisted, July 27, 1917
Discharged, March 27, 1919

Mark S. McKie
Born Webberville, MI
Age 22
Farmer
Drafted
#1581229
Private 1st Class
152nd Ambulance Company, 113th Sanitary Train, 38th Division
Departed for France on SS *Zealandia*, October 6, 1918
Assigned to Company

*Charles D. Mills ("Dud")
Born Bridgeport
Age 33
Clerk for Adams Express Company
Enlisted in National Guard, Bridgeport, March 14, 1917
Private 1st Class, May 23, 1917
Special training at Fort Oglethorpe, GA, June 25–September 1, 1917
Private, December 29, 1917
Private 1st Class, January 14, 1918
#3432
Wounded by shrapnel, June 19, 1918, while serving as orderly for SSU 647 driver Tod Gillett
In Base Hospital 18, Bazoilles, June 19–July 25, 1918
Cited in orders December 28 for bravery in action
Honorably discharged, April 29, 1919

LeRoy V. Mitchell
Born Louisville, KY
Age 22
Railroad employee
Drafted
#1580360
113th Sanitary Train, 38th Division
Private 1st Class
Departed for France on SS *Zealandia*, October 6, 1918
Assigned to Company

Earl L. Moore
Born Shippensburg, PA
Age 23
Clerk at Atlantic Refining Company, Philadelphia
Drafted
#236215
Assigned to Company

*Charles D. Morgan ("Spike")
Born Bridgeport
Age 18
Enlisted in National Guard, Bridgeport, May 2, 1917
#3419
Private 1st Class, October 9, 1918
Wounded in action
Cited in orders, October 15 and December 28, for exceptional gallantry
Honorably discharged, April 29, 1919

David Morris
Born Bloomington, KY
Age 22
Farmer
Drafted
#3096453
Sent to France as part of Camp Crane August Automatic Replacement Draft, Medical Company 9, on SS *Princess Juliana*, August 23, 1918
Assigned to Company
Transferred to Camp Hospital 120, March 1919
Departed France, June 27, 1919

James E. Morrow
Born Alpine, KY
Drafted
#3093220
Sent to France as part of Camp Crane August Automatic Replacement Draft, Medical Company 9, on SS *Princess Juliana*, August 23, 1918
Assigned to Company

*John W. Murphy ("Calamity")
Born Yonkers, NY
Age 30
Enlisted in National Guard, Bridgeport, May 19, 1917
Transferred to 104th Field Hospital, December 11, 1917
Return to Company, January 21, 1918
#3421
Transferred to Medical Detachment, 102nd Infantry, October 6, 1918
Honorably discharged, April 29, 1919

Richard P. Nuss
Born Sutton, NE

Age 25
Lumberyard employee
Drafted
#18297
Sent to France as part of Camp Funston Replacement Draft, January 30, 1918
Medical Detachment, 355th Infantry, 89th Division
Transferred to Company
Wounded in right ankle, October 24, 1918
In Convalescent Detachment 180
Departed France on SS *Henderson*, March 19, 1919

*James D. O'Connell ("Irish")
Born East Hampton, CT
Age 32
Enlisted in National Guard, Bridgeport, June 4, 1917
Saddler, September 21, 1917
Private, December 4, 1917
Private 1st Class, December 26, 1917
#3370
Wounded in action, November 8, 1918
Cited in orders, December 28, for bravery in action
Honorably discharged, April 29, 1919

*George F. Oppenheimer ("Oppy")
Born Paramaribo, Surinam
Age 23
Nurse at Locomobile Company of America
Enlisted in National Guard, Bridgeport, April 3, 1917
Private 1st Class, June 16, 1917
#3391
In Base Hospital 36, Neufchâteau, March 25–28, 1918
Transferred to 161st Ambulance Company, 41st Division, April 1918
Returned to Company, March 1919
Honorably discharged, April 29, 1919

Basil T. Osborne
Born New Brighton, PA
Age 25
Divinity student
#1581235
Assigned to Company
Honorably discharged, April 29, 1919

Charles Palmer ("Sunny Jim")
Born Boston, MA
Transferred from Field Hospital Number 1 (101st Field Hospital)
#3372
Private 1st Class

*James A. Peck
Born Newtown, CT
Age 24
Clerk at Manufacturer's Association of Bridgeport
Enlisted in National Guard, Bridgeport, May 16, 1917
Transferred to 104th Field Hospital, December 2, 1917
Returned to Company, January 21, 1918
#3424
Private 1st Class, June 14, 1918
Served as orderly in ambulance driven by Herbert Beers
Wounded in action
In hospital, late October 1918
Cited in orders, December 28, for bravery in action near Haumont, October 22–27, 1918
Honorably discharged, April 29, 1919

Patrick J. Prendergast
Born Roslindale, MA
Transferred from 1st Field Hospital (101st Field Hospital)
#3376
Private 1st Class
Cited for bravery in action

James J. Quinn
Born Malden, MA
Age 23
Student at Boston College
#3923
Private 1st Class
Wounded in action

James R. Rice
Born Morganfield, KY
Age 23
Roofer
Drafted
#1580363
Private 1st Class
Assigned to Company

*Joseph A. Rich
Born Stamford, CT
Age 19
Clerk and machine hand
Enlisted in National Guard, Bridgeport, April 4, 1917
#3426

Transferred to Medical Detachment, 102nd Infantry, August 15, 1918,
Honorably discharged, April 29, 1919

John Rose
Born Cambridge, MA

Walter L. Rose
Born Cambridge, MA
Sanitary Detachment, Division Headquarters
Sanitary Detachment, 101st Infantry
Transferred to Company
#3425
Wounded in action
Sanitary Detachment, Division Headquarters
Honorably discharged, April 29, 1919

Frank J. Scalley
Born New Haven, CT
Age 22
Trolley conductor
Enlisted in National Guard, New Haven, June 22, 1916
Service on Mexican border, July–October 1916
Private 1st Class, February 9, 1917
Private May 16, 1917
102nd Field Hospital
Transferred to 101st Ambulance Company, February 7, 1918
#3196
Transferred to 101st Field Hospital, April 6, 1918
Transferred to 101st Ambulance Company, June 28, 1918
Transferred to 104th Field Hospital, September 6, 1918
Transferred to Company, November 2, 1918
Honorably discharged, April 29, 1919

*Jerry A. Scott
Born Bridgeport
Age 19
Employed by Meigs & Company Department Store, Bridgeport
Enlisted in National Guard, Bridgeport, April 20, 1917
#3277
Transferred to 101st Ambulance Company
Transferred to Battery M, 101st Field Artillery, May 20, 1918
Wounded in action
Honorably discharged, March 25, 1919

Ernest G. Sherman
Born Wilbur, MI
Private 1st Class
Sent to France as part of Overseas Casual Company 66, March 6, 1918
Assigned to Company
Transferred to Sanitary Detachment, 104th Infantry, July 15, 1918
Killed in action, July 23, 1918

*Stanley J. Shipkowski
Born Vilna, Poland
Age 23
Machinist at Farnum Company, Bridgeport
Enlisted in National Guard, Bridgeport, May 24, 1917
Transferred to 104th Field Hospital, December 11, 1917
#3999
Private 1st Class, May 2, 1918
Wagoner, February 25, 1919
Honorably discharged, April 29, 1919

*Adrian C. Slootmaker
Born South Grand Rapids, MI
Age 18
Employed by Bridgeport Post Publishing Company
Enlisted in National Guard, Bridgeport, March 31, 1917
Private 1st Class, May 2, 1917
Transferred to Medical Detachment, 101st Infantry
#3381
Killed in action, October 28, 1918
Cited in orders for bravery in action, March 15, 1919

Philip B. Slover
Born Bowling Green, KY
#1580387
Field Hospital 152, 113th Sanitary Train, 38th Division
Arrived in France, October 1918
Assigned to Company

John W. Smith
Born Springfield, MA
Transferred to 104th Field Hospital
Transferred to Medical Detachment, 102nd Infantry, October 8, 1918

*Alfred C. Sorensen ("Rip van Winkle")
Born Fairfield, CT
Age 20
Enlisted in National Guard, Bridgeport, April 3, 1917
Transferred to 104th Field Hospital, December 2, 1917

Transferred to Office of Surgeon, 102nd Infantry, January 21, 1918
#3430
Private 1st Class, June 16, 1918
Wounded in action
Cited for bravery in action
Transferred to Medical Detachment, 102nd Infantry, October 8, 1918
Honorably discharged, April 29, 1919

*George A. Stevens
Born New York City
Age 23
Enlisted in National Guard, Bridgeport, May 9, 1917
Private 1st Class, December 26, 1917
#3383
Wounded in action
Cited in orders, August 31, for bravery in action
Honorably discharged, April 29, 1919

David Stuart
Born Roxbury, MA

David Swartz
Born East Boston, MA
Age 23
U.S. Mail pneumatic tube operator
Duty in Massachusetts National Guard Field Hospital, 101st Field Hospital
#3384
Promoted to corporal
Transferred to Company
Honorably discharged, April 29, 1919

Harvey L. Teter ("Farmer")
Born Pittsburg, KS
Drafted
#3404325
Sent to France as part of Fort Riley Exceptional Medical August Replacement Draft, Unit 61, on SS *Belgic*, September 1, 1918
Assigned to Company
Transferred to Camp Hospital, March 25, 1919

Roy C. Thompson
Born Manchester, NH
Age 23
Enlisted, May 21, 1917
#3380
Transferred to Company
Wounded in action
Cited in orders, August 31, for bravery in action
Honorably discharged, April 20, 1919

Clarence E. Thorne
Born Kalamazoo, MI
#641469
Sent to France as part of Provisional Casual Company IV, on SS *Olympic*, March 1918
Assigned to Company

*Albert C. Tiska
Born Port Jefferson, NY
Age 19
Enlisted in National Guard, Bridgeport, April 4, 1917
#3883
Private 1st Class, May 15, 1918
Surgeon's assistant, October 3, 1918
Honorably discharged, March 28, 1919

Patrick Tracy
Born New Jersey

Lewis E. Tremblay
Born Merrimack, NH
Age 21
Shipper for American Hardware Company, New Britain, CT
Duty in New Hampshire National Guard Field Hospital (104th Field Hospital)
#3385
Private 1st Class
Transferred to Company
Honorably discharged, April 29, 1919

Smith B. Vanlendingham
Born Vardaman, MS
#936269
Assigned to Company
Private 1st Class
Honorably discharged, April 29, 1919

Harry Waite
Born Pasadena, CA
Age 25
Duty in Massachusetts National Guard Field Hospital (103rd Field Hospital)
Private 1st Class
#3387
Assigned to Company
Wounded in action
Cited for bravery in action
Honorably discharged, April 29, 1919

Roy E. Walker
Born North Platte, NE
Age 23
Automobile mechanic
Drafted

#980573
Sent to France as part of Fort Riley Exceptional Medical August Replacement Draft, Unit 61, on SS *Belgic*, September 1, 1918
Assigned to Company
Transferred

*Thomas A. Walker
Born Brooklyn, NY
Age 21
Enlisted in National Guard, Niantic, August 21, 1917
Transferred to Medical Section, APO 721, January 21, 1918
#3431
Honorably discharged, July 8, 1919

*Frank E. Wall ("Ted")
Born Sheffield, England
Age 23
Silversmith at Whiting Manufacturing Company, Bridgeport
Enlisted in National Guard, Bridgeport, May 28, 1917
Private 1st Class, December 26, 1917
#3388
Cited in orders, August 31, for bravery in action, July 18–26, 1918
Honorably discharged, April 29, 1919

John E. Walls
Born Nebraska City, NE
Age 32
Farmhand
Drafted
#3445528
Sent to France as part of Fort Riley Exceptional Medical August Replacement Draft, Unit 61, on SS *Belgic*, September 1, 1918
Assigned to Company
Killed in action, October 28, 1918

Patrick Walsh
Born Detroit, MI

Cleveland T. Washburn
Born Turlock, CA
Drafted
#3462948
Sent to France as part of Fort Riley Exceptional Medical August Replacement Draft, Unit 61, on SS *Belgic*, September 1, 1918
Assigned to Company
Transferred to Camp Hospital 120, March 1919

Clyde Weber
Born Nortonville, KS
Age 25
Farmer
Drafted
Assigned to Company
Transferred to Base Hospital 72, February 1919

*Joseph C. Wellwood
Born Bridgewater, CT
Age 19
Worked at Remington Arms Company
Enlisted in National Guard, Bridgeport, April 5, 1917
Transferred to 104th Field Hospital, December 2, 1917
Evacuated to Base Hospital 36, Vittel, December 31, 1917
Operated on for mastoid abscess, January 1, 1918
Died of acute nephritis following scarlet fever, aboard an ambulance while being transferred between hospitals, February 17, 1918

*William E. West
Born Fairfield, CT
Age 20
Enlisted in National Guard, Bridgeport, May 4, 1917
Private 1st Class, December 26, 1917
#3389
Cited for bravery in action
Honorably discharged, April 29, 1919

Guy E. Whitlinger
Born Apollo, PA
Age 22
Drafted
Inducted, May 28, 1918
#2582306
Sent to France as part of Camp Greenleaf August Automatic Replacement Draft, Company 12, on SS *Mauretania*, August 27, 1918
Assigned to Company, September 13, 1918
Gassed, October 30, 1918
Honorably discharged, May 4, 1919

*David M. Wiest
Born Cedar Cliff, NY
Age 26
Assembler at Singer Sewing Machine Company, Bridgeport
Enlisted in National Guard, Bridgeport, July 10, 1917
#3434

Private 1st Class, June 14, 1918
Honorably discharged, April 29, 1919

*Frederick I. Williams
Born Bridgeport
Age 19
Chauffeur
Enlisted in National Guard, Niantic, August 17, 1917
Private 1st Class, December 26, 1917
#3422
Wounded in action
Honorably discharged, April 29, 1919

*Rollia Willis ("Daddy Long Legs")
Born Danbury, CT
Age 29
Inspector at Locomobile Company
Enlisted in National Guard, Bridgeport, April 3, 1917
#2759
Honorably discharged, April 29, 1919

Lawrence H. Woodbury
Born Somerville, MA
Duty in Massachusetts National Guard Field Hospital (103rd Field Hospital)
Private 1st Class
Transferred to Company
#3922
Wounded in action
Honorably discharged, April 29, 1919

*Fred V. Woodin
Born Pawling, NY
Age 21
Mechanic
Enlisted in National Guard, Bridgeport, April 2, 1917
Transferred to 103rd Ambulance Company, December 11, 1917
#3577
Transferred to 101st Field Hospital, March 28, 1918
Honorably discharged, April 29, 1919

Carl O. Woodruff
Born Topeka, KS
Age 22
Iron worker
Drafted
#3448050
Sent to France as part of Fort Riley Exceptional Medical August Replacement Draft, Company 60, on SS *Baltic*, September 1, 1918
Assigned to Company
Transferred

George B. Woolery ("Slim")
Born Aylesworth, OK
Drafted
#3509339
Sent to France as part of Camp Greenleaf August Automatic Replacement Draft, Company 12, on SS *Mauretania*, August 27, 1918
Assigned to Company
Wounded in action
Transferred

*Albert E. Wright
Born Bridgeport
Age 18
Drug store clerk
Enlisted in National Guard, Bridgeport, May 20, 1917
Private 1st Class, June 20, 1917
Bugler
Private 1st Class, December 26, 1917
#3396
Transferred to Sanitary Detachment, 101st Field Artillery, May 1918
Gassed, September 30, 1918
In 101st Field Hospital, Verdun, November 1, 1918–Februay 1, 1919
Cited for bravery in action
Honorably discharged, April 29, 1919

Clarence E. Wright
Born Brighton, MA
Age 20
#3578
Private 1st Class
Transferred to Company
Honorably discharged, April 29, 1919

*George Wright ("Duck Egg")
Born London, England
Age 22
Enlisted in National Guard, Niantic, August 18, 1917
Private 1st Class, December 26, 1917
#3404
Cited in orders, December 28, for bravery in action
Honorably discharged, April 29, 1919

Albert Zahradnik ("The boy with the microscopic eye for dealing out oleo")
Mt. Pleasant, PA
Drafted

#2581019
Sent to France as part of Camp Greenleaf August Automatic Replacement Draft, on SS *Mauretania*, August 27, 1918
Assigned to Company
Transferred

Carl W. Zelliner
Born Louisville, KY
Age 22
Traveling salesman
Drafted
#1580375
Private 1st Class
Assigned to Company
Transferred

Thresh-Foden Delousing Machines Crew

Lieutenant

*Charles H. Sprague
(See details under Lieutenants)

Sergeant

*William H. Cowie
Born New London, CT
Age 19
Employed by Meigs & Company Department Store, Bridgeport
Enlisted in National Guard, Bridgeport, April 4, 1917
Private 1st Class, May 2, 1917
Corporal, June 21, 1917
Sergeant, July 21, 1917
#3304
Special duty on delousing machines
Private, September 14, 1918
Corporal, November 10, 1918
Cited in orders, December 28, for bravery in action
Honorably discharged, April 29, 1919

Corporal

+Rocco D. Francolini ("Rocco D.")
Born Avigliana, Italy
Age 23
Enlisted in National Guard, Hartford, March 2, 1915
Served with 1st Connecticut Ambulance Company
Service on Mexican border, July–October 1916
Joined Company, Niantic, August 24, 1917
Corporal, January 18, 1918
#3315
Special duty on delousing machines
Private, September 12, 1918
Transferred to Medical Detachment, 102nd Infantry, October 8, 1918
Honorably discharged, April 29, 1919

Privates

Lewis K. Bass
Born West Medford, MA
Age 23
Salesman
Previous duty with Connecticut National Guard Hospital Corps
#3323
Special duty on delousing machines
Private 1st Class
Honorably discharged, April 29, 1919

*Walter E. Baxter
Born Wallingford, CT
Age 25
Stenographer in New Haven
Enlisted in National Guard, Bridgeport, July 10, 1917
Private 1st Class, December 26, 1917
#3324
Special duty on delousing machines
Honorably discharged, April 29, 1919

*James W. Clark
Born Oakham, Rutland, England
Age 30
Clerk at Lyon & Chase, printers, Bridgeport
Enlisted in National Guard, Bridgeport, June 20, 1917
Private 1st Class, December 21, 1917
#3331
Special duty on delousing machines
Honorably discharged, April 29, 1919

*Bert E. Coyle
Born Windsor, VT
Age 25
Cagemaker at Ashcroft Manufacturing Company
Enlisted in National Guard, Bridgeport, June 4, 1917
#3403

Special duty on delousing machines
Died of bronchopneumonia in hospital at Le Mans, France, March 18, 1919

+Robert E. Kuhn
Born Hartford, CT
Age 18
Enlisted in National Guard, Hartford, May 8, 1916
Served with 1st Connecticut Ambulance Company
Service on Mexican border, July–October 1917
Assigned to Company, August 5, 1917
#3411
Special duty on delousing machines
Awarded Silver Star
Cited in orders, March 15, 1919
Honorably discharged, April 29, 1919

*Michael Kwasniski ("Barber")
Born Poland
Age 25
Enlisted in National Guard, Bridgeport, June 4, 1917
Bugler
Private 1st Class, December 26, 1917
#3357
Special duty on delousing machines
Cited in orders, August 31, for bravery in action
Honorably discharged, April 29, 1919

*George P. Vennart ("Mook")
Born Hartford, CT
Age 18
Reporter for *Hartford Evening Post*
Enlisted in Company, Niantic, August 24, 1917
Private 1st Class, October 26, 1917
Transferred to divisional headquarters, November 7, 1917
Special duty on delousing machines, February 8, 1918
#2730
Transferred to 103rd Ambulance Company, October 16, 1918
Gassed, Bois d'Haumont, November 1, 1918
In 102nd Field Hospital, Verdun
Honorably discharged, April 29, 1919

Trench Fever Volunteers

*David P. Turner
Born Fort Fairfield, ME
Age 40
Enlisted in National Guard, Bridgeport, June 5, 1917
Cook, August 4, 1917
Transferred to 101st Ambulance Company, December 1, 1917
#3288
Trench Fever Volunteer, February–April 1918
In Number 12 Stationary Hospital, St. Pol, January 29-, 1918
Private, August 27, 1918
Transferred to Company D, 319th Infantry, January 6, 1919
Returned to Company, March 6, 1919
Awarded MCC
Honorably discharged, April 29, 1919

*John T. Elliano
Born Mondragone, Caserta, Italy
Age 18
Automatic screw machine operator, Columbia Graphophone Company
Enlisted in National Guard, Bridgeport, March 27, 1917
Acting corporal, August 1917
Transferred to 104th Ambulance Company, January 1, 1918
#3659
Trench Fever Volunteer, February–April 1918
In British trenches on Somme Sector, March 1–29, 1918
In American Ambulance Hospital, Neuilly, Paris, April–July 1918
At Base Hospital 17, Dijon, July–August 1918
Acting sergeant of Military Police, Base Hospital 17 Annex, Plombières, August–October 1918
On duty at Verdun, October 19–November 14, 1918
In Base Hospital, Nantes, January 1919
Honorably discharged, March 13, 1919

*Howard M. Etheridge
Born Thomaston, CT
Age 21
Machinist at M.H. Anderson, Bridgeport
Enlisted in National Guard, Bridgeport, April 2, 1917
Private 1st Class, June 16, 1917
Transferred to 101st Ambulance Company
#3183
Trench Fever Volunteer, February–April 1918
In Number 12 Stationary Hospital, St. Pol, January 29–March 27, 1918

In American Ambulance Hospital, Neuilly, Paris, March 28–July 5, 1918
In Base Hospital 17, Dijon, July 6–November 8, 1918
Transferred to Company D, 319th Infantry, December 4, 1918
Cited for meritorious service
Returned to Company, March 1919
Honorably discharged, April 29, 1919

John Lambert
Born Houlton, ME
Age 19
Enlisted in National Guard, Bridgeport, April 3, 1917
Transferred to 104th Ambulance Company
#3687
Trench Fever Volunteer, February–April 1918
In Number 12 Stationary Hospital, St. Pol, January 29, 1918
Honorably discharged, April 4, 1919

*Harold A. Lucas
Born Redding Ridge, CT
Age 19
Enlisted in National Guard, Bridgeport, April 3, 1917
#3414
Trench Fever Volunteer, February–April 1918
In Number 12 Stationary Hospital, St. Pol, January 29-, 1918
Transferred to 103rd Field Hospital, April 26, 1918
Transferred to 104th Field Hospital, June 24, 1918
Transferred to MTC, February 25, 1919
Honorably discharged, August 13, 1919

*William J. Murphy ("Big Bill")
Born Ireland
Age 26
Enlisted in National Guard, Bridgeport, May 28, 1917
Transferred to 104th Field Hospital, December 11, 1917
Returned to Company, January 21, 1918
#3319
Trench Fever Volunteer, February–April 1918
In Number 12 Stationary Hospital, St. Pol, January 29-, 1918
Awarded MCC
Honorably discharged, April 29, 1919

*Albert F. Noren
Born Bridgeport
Age 25
Gear specialist at Bullard Machine Tool Company
Enlisted in National Guard, Bridgeport, May 7, 1917
#3369
Trench Fever Volunteer, February–April 1918
In Number 12 Stationary Hospital, St. Pol, January 26–March 1, 1918
In American Ambulance Hospital, Neuilly, Paris, March 3–May 5, 1918
Transferred to 103rd Field Hospital, May 5, 1918
Transferred to Chemical Warfare Service, August 25, 1918
Cited for meritorious service as Trench Fever Volunteer
Awarded MCC
Honorably discharged, January 16, 1919

*Joseph J. O'Connor
Born Brooklyn, NY
Age 18
Enlisted in National Guard, Bridgeport, April 3, 1917
Transferred to Sanitary Detachment, 102nd Infantry
#3263
Trench Fever Volunteer, February–April 1918
In Number 12 Stationary Hospital, St. Pol, January 29-, 1918
Honorably discharged February 7, 1919

*Vernon M. Peck
Born Bridgeport
Age 19
Clerk to father
Enlisted in National Guard, Bridgeport, March 26, 1917
Private 1st Class, May 2, 1917
Corporal, June 1, 1917
Special training at Fort Oglethorpe, GA, June 25–September 1, 1917
Private 1st Class, December 18, 1917
#3373
Trench Fever Volunteer, February–April 1918
In Number 12 Stationary Hospital, St. Pol, January 25–May 1, 1918
Transferred to 103rd Field Hospital, May 10, 1918
Returned to Company, August 15, 1918
Returned to hospital, October 1918
Awarded MCC

Detached to 301st Field Artillery, March 10, 1919
Honorably discharged, May 19, 1919

*Frederick Pill
Born Truro, Cornwall, England
Age 27
Enlisted in National Guard, Bridgeport, June 6, 1917
Private 1st Class, December 26, 1917
#3374
Trench Fever Volunteer, February–April 1918
In Number 12 Stationary Hospital, St. Pol, January 29, 1918
Transferred to Company D, 319th Infantry, November 7, 1918
Transferred to Battery D, 313th Field Artillery, February 1, 1919
Returned to Company, March 1919
Awarded MCC
Honorably discharged, April 29, 1919

*Victor Schaeffer ("Lightning")
Born Meriden, CT
Age 19
Enlisted in National Guard, Bridgeport, April 10, 1917
#3429
Trench Fever Volunteer, February–April 1918
In Number 12 Stationary Hospital, St. Pol, January 29, 1918
Awarded MCC
Honorably discharged, April 29, 1919

*John Vassel
Born Smyrna, Turkey
Age 25
Stock clerk for Bridgeport Electric Company
Enlisted in National Guard, Bridgeport, May 23, 1917
Transferred to Sanitary Detachment, 102nd Infantry
#3290
Trench Fever Volunteer, February–April 1918
In Number 12 Stationary Hospital, St. Pol, January 29, 1918
Transferred to 101st Ambulance Company
Transferred to 103rd Field Hospital, May 2, 1918
Awarded MCC
Honorably discharged, April 29, 1919

*Arnold Watkins
Born Nova Scotia
Age 19
Enlisted in National Guard, Bridgeport, June 13, 1917
#3432
Trench Fever Volunteer, February–April 1918
In Number 12 Stationary Hospital, St. Pol, January 29-, 1918
Awarded MCC
Honorably discharged, April 29, 1919

*Harry A. Worley ("Red")
Born New York City
Age 23
Barrel driller at Remington Arms Company
Enlisted in National Guard, Bridgeport, March 14, 1917
Private 1st Class, May 2, 1917
Trench Fever Volunteer, February–April 1918
#3394
In Number 12 Stationary Hospital, St. Pol, January 29, 1918
Awarded MCC
Honorably discharged, April 29, 1919

Detachment of SSU 647 Assigned to Work with Company, April 15–June 26, 1918

Sergeants

Philip Klein

Jack B. Kendrick
Born Connecticut
Gassed at Mandres, April 20, 1918
Cited in orders for bravery in action, April 20, 1918
Awarded Croix de Guerre, May 29, 1918

Corporal

John B. Carey
Born Washington

Mechanics

Edmund G.E. Anderson
Born Connecticut

Lou R. Risley
Born Kansas
Gassed at Mandres, April 20, 1918

Cook

Lawrence Boatman
Born Iowa

Drivers, Privates First Class

Allen H. Ahlers ("Hap")
Born Minnesota

Eric A. Astlett
Born New York

Lawrence Boatman
Born Iowa

Robert W. Bodfish
Born Massachusetts

Deveraux G. Dunlap
Born Texas
Gassed at Mandres, April 20, 1918

Clarence A. Gaynor ("Speed")
Born New York
Gassed at Mandres, April 20, 1918

Tod F. Gillett
Born Florida
Killed in action near Beaumont, June 19, 1918
Awarded Distinguished Service Cross

R. Donnell Harris
Born New York

Wallace McCrackin
Born Montana
Gassed at Mandres, April 20, 1918

John J. McEnness ("Jack")
Born Rhode Island
Gassed at Mandres, April 20, 1918

Leo F. McGuire
Born Oklahoma
Awarded Distinguished Service Cross for bravery in action, April 19–20, 1918

William A. Putnam
Born New York

Henry L. Signor
Born Massachusetts

Clifford O. Soles
Born Massachusetts

Jack R. Swain
Born Texas
Gassed at Mandres, April 20, 1918
Awarded Distinguished Service Cross for rescuing men from destroyed ambulance, June 19, 1918

John B. Titchener
Born New York

Samuel A. Wilder
Born Massachusetts

Grant R. Willard
Born Minnesota
Gassed at Mandres, April 20, 1918

Privates

Mark E. Kerr
Born California

Irving B. Snader ("Horn")
Born Connecticut

Sources: This is a first attempt at a roster of the 102nd Ambulance Company, with separate listings for the Thresh-Foden disinfesting team, the trench fever volunteers, and the members of SSU 647 who served with the Company from April to June 1917. The principal source is Leslie R. Barlow's roster in the company diary. It has been augmented with reference to Service Records, Connecticut: Men and Women in the Armed Forces of the United States During World War, 1917–1920, *the Connecticut Soldiers Questionnaires at the Connecticut State Archives, military transportation records, and miscellaneous records on Ancestry.com and Fold3.com.*

Chapter Notes

Chapter 1

1. Louis C. Duncan, *The Medical Department of the United States Army in the Civil War* (ca. 1910; reprint, Gaithersburg, MD: Olde Soldier books, 1987), 374.
2. John S. Haller Jr., *Farmcarts to Fords: A History of the Military Ambulance, 1790–1925* (Carbondale: Southern Illinois University Press, 1992), 8.
3. Ryan Corbett Bell, *The Ambulance* (Jefferson, NC: McFarland, 2009), 3–4.
4. Bell, *The Ambulance*, 5–10.
5. Bell, *The Ambulance*, 11–12; Haller, *Farmcarts to Fords*, 10.
6. Duncan, *The Medical Department of the United States Army in the Civil War*, 380–81.
7. Duncan, *The Medical Department of the United States Army in the Civil War*, 378, 381.
8. Haller, *Farmcarts to Fords*, 13–15.
9. Haller, *Farmcarts to Fords*, 15–16.
10. Haller, *Farmcarts to Fords*, 28.
11. Duncan, *The Medical Department of the United States Army in the Civil War*, 98–99.
12. Duncan, *The Medical Department of the United States Army in the Civil War*, 106–10, 314–30.
13. Haller, *Farmcarts to Fords*, 46–47.
14. Haller, *Farmcarts to Fords*, 48–49.
15. Heller, *Farmcarts to Fords*, 43, 92.
16. Haller, *Farmcarts to Fords*, 62–64.
17. Jonathan H. Jaffin, "Medical Support for the American Expeditionary Forces in France During the First World War," Thesis, Master of Military Art and Science, U.S. Army Command and General Staff College, Fort Leavenworth, KS, 1991.9, https://apps.dtic.mil/sti/pdfs/ADA241174.pdf, accessed February 2022.
18. Mary C. Gillett, *The Army Medical Department, 1865–1917* (Washington, DC: United States Army Center of Military History, 1995), 332.
19. Mark C. Walsh, *Free Men Shall Stand: The Story of Connecticut's Organized Militia from 1636...* (Hartford: Connecticut National Guard Officers Association, 1991), 119.
20. Walsh, *Free Men Shall Stand*, 122–23.
21. Bell, *The Ambulance*, 146–49.
22. Bell, *The Ambulance*, 146–47; Haller, *Farmcarts to Fords*, 108.
23. *Drill Regulations and Service Manual for Sanitary Troops, United States Army, 1914* (Washington, DC: Government Printing Office, 1917), 95.
24. *Biennial Report of the Adjutant General, State of Connecticut, to the Governor, for the Two Years Ending September 30, 1912* (Hartford: State of Connecticut, 1912), xi; *Drill Regulations*, 230–31.
25. George Curtis Waldo, ed., *History of Bridgeport and Vicinity, vol. 2, Biographical Sketches* (New York and Chicago: S. J. Clarke, 1917), 360–61; *Biennial Report of the Adjutant General, State of Connecticut, to the Governor, for the Two Years Ending September 30, 1914* (Hartford: State of Connecticut, 1914), 77.
26. "Frank W. Stevens. Obituary Record of Graduates of Yale University Deceased during the Year 1934–1935," *Bulletin of Yale University* 94 (October 15, 1935): 201–02; *Biennial Report of the Adjutant General, State of Connecticut*, 1912, 8.
27. Burr H. Curtis, "Otto G. Wiedman, M.D., 1884–1974," *Connecticut Medicine* 39, number 1 (January 1975): 64–65; *Biennial Report of the Adjutant General, State of Connecticut*, 1912, ciii, 8.
28. *Biennial Report of the Adjutant General, State of Connecticut*, 1912, ciii.
29. Otto G. Wiedman, "In Memorium: Dr. Paul Waterman," *American Journal of Psychiatry* 80, number 4 (1924): 840. Waterman died suddenly in 1923 at age 45.
30. *Biennial Report of the Adjutant General, State of Connecticut*, 1912, xxx–xxxi.
31. *Biennial Report of the Adjutant General, State of Connecticut*, 1912, xviii, 113–14.
32. *Encyclopedia of Connecticut Biography, Genealogical-Memorial; Representative Citizens* vol. 10 (New York: American Historical Society, 1917), 231–33; *Biennial Report of the Adjutant General, State of Connecticut*, 1914, 79.
33. *Biennial Report of the Adjutant General, State of Connecticut*, 1912, ix, xi.
34. Gloria P. Stewart, "August 1912: War Comes to Southwestern Connecticut," *Connecticut History* 39, number 2 (Fall 2000): 197–201; *Biennial Report of the Adjutant General, State of Connecticut*, 1912, 118, 184–86.
35. *Biennial Report of the Adjutant General, State of Connecticut*, 1912, 118, 184–86, xviii–xxvi.

36. Stewart, "August 1912," 199.
37. *Biennial Report of the Adjutant General, State of Connecticut*, 1912, xxvi.
38. *Biennial Report of the Adjutant General, State of Connecticut*, 1912, 184–86.
39. *Biennial Report of the Adjutant General, State of Connecticut*, 1912, xvii.
40. Charles F. Mason, *A Complete Handbook for the Sanitary Troops of the U.S. Army and Navy and National Guard and Naval Militia*, 4th ed. (New York: William Wood and Company, 1917); *Biennial Report of the Adjutant General, State of Connecticut*, 1912, xvii, c.
41. *Biennial Report of the Adjutant General, State of Connecticut*, 1914, 22.
42. *Biennial Report of the Adjutant General, State of Connecticut*, 1914, 79; "Robert Moseley Yergason, 1908," *Trinity College Bulletin* 46, number 3 (May 1949):13. During the war, Yergason would serve as an orthopedic surgeon at Camp Humphreys, Virginia, and Embarkation Hospital 4 in New York, being discharged as a major in August 1919. He died in 1949.
43. *Biennial Report of the Adjutant General, State of Connecticut*, 1914, 29, 6.
44. Jeffrey C. Larrabee, "A Tale of Two Trucks: American Casualty Evacuation in World War I," *Icon* 14 (2008): 125–26.
45. *History of the American Field Service in France, "Friends of France," 1914–1917* (Boston and New York: Houghton Mifflin, 1920).
46. *Bridgeport Post*, February 2, 1917.
47. *History of the American Field Service in France*, 32–33.
48. *History of the American Field Service in France*, 34–35, 52.
49. *History of the American Field Service in France*, 36–37.
50. *Biennial Report of the Adjutant General, State of Connecticut, to the Governor, for the Two Years Ending September 30, 1916* (Hartford: State of Connecticut, 1916), 51.
51. *Biennial Report of the Adjutant General, State of Connecticut*, 1916, 6.
52. Peter Wever, "The U.S. Army Medical Belt for Front Line First Aid: A Well-Considered Design That Failed the Medical Department During the First World War," *Military Medicine* 181 (2016): 1187–94.
53. Julie Irene Prieto, *The Mexican Expedition, 1916–1917* (Washington, DC: U.S. Army Center of Military History, 2016), 57.
54. Prieto, *The Mexican Expedition*, 58.
55. Prieto, *The Mexican Expedition*, 44.
56. Prieto, *The Mexican Expedition*, 59.
57. *Biennial Report of the Adjutant General, State of Connecticut*, 1916, 7.
58. *Biennial Report of the Adjutant General, State of Connecticut*, 1916, 8. The officers included Captain Owens, Lieutenant Yergason, Lieutenant Arthur B. Landry of Hartford, and Lieutenant Herbert Oeischlegel of Torrington. Two additional men would head for the border on July 11, *Biennial Report of the Adjutant General, State of Connecticut*, 1916, 52–53.
59. *Report on Mobilization of the Organized Militia and National Guard of the United States, 1916* (Washington, DC: Government Printing Office, 1916), 153, 156.
60. *Biennial Report of the Adjutant General, State of Connecticut*, 1916, 8.
61. Daniel W. Strickland, *Connecticut Fights: The Story of the 102nd Regiment* (New Haven: Quinipiack Press, 1930), 39; *Report on Mobilization of Organized Militia*, 12.
62. Strickland, *Connecticut Fights*, 39–44.
63. *Report on Mobilization of Organized Militia*, 101, 102.
64. Prieto, *The Mexican Expedition*, 49, 51.
65. Prieto, *The Mexican Expedition*, 50.
66. Larrabee, "A Tale of Two Trucks,"140.
67. Prieto, *The Mexican Expedition*, 63.
68. *Biennial Report of the Adjutant General, State of Connecticut, to the Governor, for the Two Years Ending September 30, 1918* (Hartford: State of Connecticut, 1918), 18.
69. *Biennial Report of the Adjutant General, State of Connecticut*, 1918, 4, 6.
70. *Report on Mobilization of Organized Militia*, 156, 151–53.

Chapter 2

1. Julie Irene Prieto, *The Mexican Expedition, 1916–1917* (Washington, DC: U.S. Army Center of Military History, 2016), 64.
2. Prieto, *The Mexican Expedition*, 65.
3. *Bridgeport Telegram*, July 27, 1918.
4. Mary K. Witkowski, *Bridgeport at Work* (Charleston, SC: Arcadia Publishing, 2002), 72.
5. Witkowski, *Bridgeport at Work*, 16–17.
6. George Curtis Waldo, ed., *History of Bridgeport and Vicinity* (New York and Chicago: S. J. Clarke, 1917), 165–66; Witkowski, *Bridgeport at Work*, 86–87.
7. Waldo, *History of Bridgeport and Vicinity*, 187; Witkowski, *Bridgeport at Work*, 28.
8. Waldo, *History of Bridgeport and Vicinity*, 172; Witkowski, *Bridgeport at Work*, 36–37.
9. Waldo, *History of Bridgeport and Vicinity*, 176; Witkowski, *Bridgeport at Work*, 80–81.
10. Waldo, *History of Bridgeport and Vicinity*, 177–81; "The History of the Best Built Car in America," Locomobile Society of America, https://www.locomobilesociety.com/history.cfm, accessed December 2021; Witkowski, *Bridgeport at Work*, 32–33.
11. Waldo, *History of Bridgeport and Vicinity*, 183–85; Witkowski, *Bridgeport at Work*, 38; Luke Mercaldo, "Remington's Allied Rifle Contracts During World War I," Remington Society of America, 2nd Quarter 2012, 22–25, https://www.remingtonsociety.org/remingtons-allied-rifle-contracts-during-wwi/, accessed December 2021. Bridgeport as "the Essen of America" is mentioned

in the *Bridgeport Post*, and in retrospect in the World War I articles published in April 1938.

12. Waldo, *History of Bridgeport and Vicinity*; Abigail Barnes Nova, "Whiting Manufacturing Company: A History of the Firm and its Japanese-Inspired Silver (1860–1890), Thesis, Cooper-Hewitt, National Design Museum, Smithsonian Institution, and Parsons the New School for Design, 2010. Nova_Thesis_2010_05_03__FINAL.pdf; Bridgeport History Center, "Bridgeport Working: Voices from the 20th Century. Companies." https://www.bridgeporthistory.org/News.aspx, accessed December 2021; Witkowski, *Bridgeport at Work*, 60–62.

13. *Biennial Report of the Adjutant General, State of Connecticut, to the Governor, for the Two Years Ending September 30, 1918* (Hartford: State of Connecticut, 1918), 52.

14. Waldo, *History of Bridgeport and Vicinity*, 360–61; Medical Society of the State of New York, *Medical Directory of New York, New Jersey and Connecticut*, vol. 23 (New York: Federal Printing, 1921), 537–39; *Polk's Medical Register and Directory of the United States and Canada, 1917*, 14th ed. (Detroit, New York, Chicago: R. L. Polk & Company, 1917).

15. *Bridgeport Telegram*, February 13, 17, 1917.

16. Robert Wakeman Hill, 1828–1909, http://www.bronsonlibrary.org/filestorage/1521/1545/HILL_FINAL%5B1%5D.pdf, accessed December 2021.

17. *Bridgeport Telegram*, February 19, 1917.

18. "Frank W. Stevens. Obituary Record of Graduates of Yale University Deceased during the Year 1934–1935," *Bulletin of Yale University* 94 (October 15, 1935): 201–02; *Biennial Report of the Adjutant General, State of Connecticut*, 1912, 8.

19. Connecticut Military Census, 1917, accessed through Ancestry.com.; *Medical Directory of New York, New Jersey and Connecticut*, vol. 23, 539.

20. Waldo, *History of Bridgeport and Vicinity*, 564–65; *Bridgeport Post*, February 8, 1917.

21. Philip R. Devlin, "Windsor Locks physician cited for extraordinary valor," in "Connecticut's Irish in World War I," *Shanachie* 30, number 4 (November-December 2018): 12; *Bridgeport Post*, March 8, 1917.

22. *Bridgeport Post*, March 8, 1917.

23. Leslie R. Barlow, "World War Daily Diary of the 102nd Ambulance Company," typescript, Connecticut State Archives, Preface, 7. Barlow apparently kept a daily or multi-day diary and in the 1920s typed it into its present form. He presented copies to the Connecticut State Archives and the Bridgeport Public Library. Another copy is in the collections of the National World War I Museum and Memorial in Kansas City, Missouri. Barlow listed 31 Bridgeport and local men who were "rejected, mostly as physically unfit," Barlow, "World War Daily Diary of the 102nd Ambulance Company," Men Who Answered the Nation's Call, 6.

24. *Bridgeport Telegram*, March 12, 1917.

25. WW1 Veterans, Connecticut Soldiers Questionnaires, 1919, https://ctstatelibrary.org/-ww-1-veterans/, accessed October 2021.

26. WW1 Veterans, Connecticut Soldiers Questionnaires, 1919, https://ctstatelibrary.org/ww-1-veterans/, accessed October 2021; Connecticut, Military Census, March 1917, accessed through Ancestry.com. A year later, in July 1918, many of the local companies celebrated their employees in military service with a special insert in the *Post* and *Telegram* that listed them by name and included photographs of many of them, *Bridgeport Telegram*, July 27, 1918, *Bridgeport Post*, July 30, 1918.

27. WW1 Veterans, Connecticut Soldiers Questionnaires, 1919, https://ctstatelibrary.org/-ww-1-veterans/, accessed October 2021; for Barlow's watch see https://www.worthpoint.com/worthopedia/ww1-inscribed-102nd-ambulance-co-26th-1862711332, accessed 2018–2021.

28. *Bridgeport Evening Post*, May 7, 1919.

29. *Medical Directory of New York, New Jersey and Connecticut*, vol. 23, 554.

30. Barlow, "World War Daily Diary of the 102nd Ambulance Company," Preface.

31. "101st Sanitary Train. 26th Division A.E.F. History." March 1919, photostat typescript in Records, 1917–1919, 26th Division, United States Army, War Records Department, Connecticut State Archives Record Group No. 012, Part II, Series No. 040, Connecticut State Archives, Hartford, 153/336/602. The page number sequence represents the digital version/typescript/photostat numbers. Although the typescript history produced by the Sanitary Train bears the signature of Division Surgeon Ralph S. Porter, it was actually written by the Company's Earle E. Radikin, who was detailed to compile it in February 1919 (see Barlow, "World War Daily Diary of the 102nd Ambulance Company," February 16 to March 1, 1919, 69), and hereafter Radikin will be mentioned as author in text.

32. "101st Sanitary Train. 26th Division A.E.F. History," 154/337/603.

33. Barlow to Bridgeport Comfort Club, July 18, 1918, in Leslie R. Barlow, *Letters to the Bridgeport Comfort* Club (Bridgeport: author, 1919), 3.

34. *Manual for the Medical Department, United States Army, 1916* (Washington, DC: Government Printing Office, 1918), 207–12.

35. "The Early Days of Motorized Military Vehicles," https://www.military.com/veteran-jobs/career-advice/military-transition/gm-military-history-motorized-vehicles.html, accessed January 2022; *Medical Department of the U.S. Army in the World War*, Vol. 3, *Finance and Supply* (Washington, DC: Government Printing Office, 1928), 351, 354, 337, 342; *The First Century of GMC Truck History*, https://www.gmheritagecenter.com/docs/gm-heritage-archive/-historical-brochures/GMC/100_YR_GMC_HISTORY_MAR09.pdf, accessed December 2021; *GMC Ambulances* (Pontiac, MI: General Motors Truck Co., ca. 1917), 2, 8.

36. "United States Army Ambulance Service," Report of the Surgeon General of the Army, *War Department Annual Reports, 1919*, part 3 (Washington, DC: Government Printing Office, 1920), 3200.

37. *Medical Department of the U.S. Army in the World War*, Vol. 3, 363; the total would be increased to 120 sections, or 2,400 ambulances and 3,000 men. Ninety-five of these units would arrive in France by the fall of 1918, with others sent to Italy.

38. *Medical Department of the U.S. Army in the World War*, Vol. 3, 363–65.

39. Peter Wever, *A U.S. Army Medical Base in World War I France: Life and Care at Bazoilles Hospital Center, 1918–1919* (Jefferson, NC: McFarland & Company, 2019), 7–9.

40. *Bridgeport Post*, June 22, 1937.

41. *Medical Training Camp: Ft. Oglethorpe, Georgia, August 1917: Page on Page of Page's Command* (Chattanooga, TN: R. P. Purse, 1917), 59, 14–21, https://www.worldwar1centennial.org/images/Georgia_images/Ft._Oglethorpe_-_Medical_Training_Camp_August_1917/Medical_Training_Camp_pages_32-37.pdf;
https://www.worldwar1centennial.org/images/Georgia_images/Ft._Oglethorpe_-_Medical_Training_Camp_August_1917/Medical_Training_Camp_pages_56-68.pdf, accessed October 2021. At Fort Oglethorpe, Camp Greenleaf trained medical troops while Camp McLean trained officers and Camp Nathan B. Forrest trained infantry and engineers.

42. William N. Bispham, *The Medical Department of the United States Army in the World War, Vol. 7, Training* (Washington, DC: Government Printing Office, 1927), 17–18, 33–34.

43. *Medical Training Camp: Ft. Oglethorpe, Georgia, August 1917: Page on Page of Page's Command*, 59.

44. Michael E. Shay, *The Yankee Division in the First World War* (College Station: Texas A&M University Press, 2008), 1.

45. Barlow to Bridgeport Comfort Club, July 18, 1918, in Barlow, *Letters to the Bridgeport Comfort Club*, 3.

46. Barlow, "World War Daily Diary of the 102nd Ambulance Company," July 28, 12.

47. Barlow, "World War Daily Diary of the 102nd Ambulance Company," July 28, 12.

48. Barlow, "World War Daily Diary of the 102nd Ambulance Company," August 14, 13.

49. Barlow, "World War Daily Diary of the 102nd Ambulance Company," July 29, 12.

50. Emmett J. Scott, *Scott's Official History of the American Negro in the World War* (Chicago: Homewood Press, 1919), chapter 17.

51. Barlow, "World War Daily Diary of the 102nd Ambulance Company," July 30, 12.

52. Barlow, "World War Daily Diary of the 102nd Ambulance Company," August 1, 12.

53. Barlow, "World War Daily Diary of the 102nd Ambulance Company," August 2, 12.

54. Barlow, "World War Daily Diary of the 102nd Ambulance Company," August 3, 12.

55. "101st Sanitary Train. 26th Division A.E.F. History," 155/338/604.

56. Barlow, "World War Daily Diary of the 102nd Ambulance Company," 12.

57. Barlow, "World War Daily Diary of the 102nd Ambulance Company," 14.

58. Barlow, "World War Daily Diary of the 102nd Ambulance Company," 12.

59. Barlow, "World War Daily Diary of the 102nd Ambulance Company," August 12, 13.

60. Barlow, "World War Daily Diary of the 102nd Ambulance Company," August 4, 13; August 8, 16.

61. Barlow, "World War Daily Diary of the 102nd Ambulance Company," August 22, 14.

62. Barlow, "Daily Diary of the 102nd Ambulance Company," August 5, 12; "101st Sanitary Train. 26th Division A.E.F. History," 154/337/603. Barlow says 20 former members were added, but only 10 have been identified, though Barlow listed 12 Hartford men rejected as physically unfit, Barlow, "World War Daily Diary of the 102nd Ambulance Company," 6.

63. Barlow, "World War Daily Diary of the 102nd Ambulance Company," August 7, 13.

64. Barlow, "World War Daily Diary of the 102nd Ambulance Company," August 9, 13.

65. Barlow, "World War Daily Diary of the 102nd Ambulance Company," August 9, 13.

66. Barlow, "World War Daily Diary of the 102nd Ambulance Company," August 13, 13.

67. Barlow, "World War Daily Diary of the 102nd Ambulance Company," August 10, 13.

68. *Drill Regulations and Service Manual for Sanitary Troops United States Army, Corrected to April 15, 1917* (1914; Washington, DC: Government Printing Office, 1917).

69. Barlow, "World War Daily Diary of the 102nd Ambulance Company," August 11, 13.

70. Barlow, "World War Daily Diary of the 102nd Ambulance Company," August 15, 13.

71. Barlow, "World War Daily Diary of the 102nd Ambulance Company," September 6 & 7, 15.

72. Barlow, "World War Daily Diary of the 102nd Ambulance Company," August 15, 13.

73. Barlow, "World War Daily Diary of the 102nd Ambulance Company," August 24, 14.

74. Barlow, "World War Daily Diary of the 102nd Ambulance Company," September 8 & 9, 15.

75. Barlow, "World War Daily Diary of the 102nd Ambulance Company," August 13, 13; September 13, 16.

76. Barlow, "World War Daily Diary of the 102nd Ambulance Company," September 8 & 9, 15.

77. Barlow, "World War Daily Diary of the 102nd Ambulance Company," August 16, 14.

78. "Biographical Sketch," Clarence Ransom Edwards Collection, Massachusetts Historical Society, https://www.masshist.org/-collection-guides/view/fa0323, accessed January 2022.

79. Mark Ethan Grotelueschen, *The AEF Way of War: The American Army and Combat in World War I* (Cambridge: Cambridge University Press, 2007), 146–47; Taylor, *New England in France*, (Boston: Houghton Mifflin, 1920), 19–20.
80. Shay, *The Yankee Division*, 12.
81. Barlow, "World War Daily Diary of the 102nd Ambulance Company," August 17, 14.
82. Barlow, "World War Daily Diary of the 102nd Ambulance Company," August 20, 14.
83. Barlow, "World War Daily Diary of the 102nd Ambulance Company," August 21, 14.
84. Barlow, "World War Daily Diary of the 102nd Ambulance Company," August 27, 15.
85. "101st Sanitary Train. 26th Division A.E.F. History," 156/339/605.
86. Barlow, "World War Daily Diary of the 102nd Ambulance Company," August 21, 14.
87. Barlow, "World War Daily Diary of the 102nd Ambulance Company," August 28, 29 & 30, 15.
88. Barlow, "World War Daily Diary of the 102nd Ambulance Company," September 6 & 7, 15.
89. Barlow, "World War Daily Diary of the 102nd Ambulance Company," August 28, 29 & 30, 15; September 19 & 20, 16.
90. E. G. Taylor, *New England in France, 1917–1919* 30.
91. Harry A. Benwell, *History of the Yankee Division* (Boston: Cornhill, 1919), 24–29; "101st Sanitary Train. 26th Division A.E.F. History," 158/341/607.
92. Barlow, "World War Daily Diary of the 102nd Ambulance Company," September 1, 2 & 3, 15.
93. Barlow, "World War Daily Diary of the 102nd Ambulance Company," September 4, 15.
94. Barlow, "World War Daily Diary of the 102nd Ambulance Company," September 5, 15.
95. Barlow, "World War Daily Diary of the 102nd Ambulance Company," September 6 & 7, 16.
96. R. Stephen Dorsey & Kenneth L. McPheeters, *The American Military Saddle, 1776–1945* (Eugene, OR: Collectors' Library, 1999), 212–13. A discussion of this bag was also found in January 2021 at http://www.mcpheetersantiquemilitaria.com/04_horse_equip/04_item_013.htm.
97. Barlow, "World War Daily Diary of the 102nd Ambulance Company," September 12, 16.
98. Barlow to Bridgeport Comfort Club, July 18, 1918, in Barlow, *Letters to the Bridgeport Comfort Club*, 3.
99. Barlow, "World War Daily Diary of the 102nd Ambulance Company," August 27, 15; September 11 & 12, 16.
100. Barlow, "World War Daily Diary of the 102nd Ambulance Company," September 16 & 18, 16.
101. Barlow, "World War Daily Diary of the 102nd Ambulance Company," September 19 & 20, 16.
102. Barlow, "World War Daily Diary of the 102nd Ambulance Company," September 22, 23 & 24, 16.
103. Barlow, "World War Daily Diary of the 102nd Ambulance Company," September 25, 16.

Chapter 3

1. March 1919, photostat typescript in Records, 1917–1919, 26th Division, United States Army, War Records Department, Connecticut State Archives Record Group No. 012, Part II, Series No.040, Connecticut State Archives, Hartford, 158/341/607. The page number sequence represents the digital version/typescript/photostat numbers; E. G. Taylor, *New England in France, 1917–1919* (Boston: Houghton Mifflin, 1920), 30.
2. U.S. Army WWI Transport Service, Passenger Lists, Outgoing, SS *Corsican*, https://www.fold3.com/image/603936131, accessed November 2021.
3. "S/S Corsican, Allen Line, Norway-Heritage, Hands Across the Sea, http://www.norwayheritage.com/p_ship.asp?sh=corsi, accessed December 2021.
4. U.S. Army WWI Transport Service, Passenger Lists, Outgoing, SS *Corsican*.
5. Leslie R. Barlow, "World War Daily Diary of the 102nd Ambulance Company," typescript, Connecticut State Archives, September 28 & 29, 16–17; Barlow to Bridgeport Comfort Club, July 18, 1918, in Leslie R. Barlow, *Letters to the Bridgeport Comfort Club* (Bridgeport: author, 1919), 4.
6. Barlow, "World War Daily Diary of the 102nd Ambulance Company," September 30, 17.
7. Barlow, "World War Daily Diary of the 102nd Ambulance Company," October 2, 17.
8. Barlow, "World War Daily Diary of the 102nd Ambulance Company," October 4, 17.
9. Barlow, "World War Daily Diary of the 102nd Ambulance Company," October 5, 17.
10. "101st Sanitary Train. 26th Division A.E.F. History," 158/341/607.
11. U.S. Army WWI Transport Service, Passenger Lists, Outgoing, SS *Corsican*.
12. Barlow, "World War Daily Diary of the 102nd Ambulance Company," October 6, 17; History of the 103rd Machine Gun Battalion, History of Company B, 103rd Machine Gun Battalion, Record Group 12, Connecticut State Library, Department of War Records, Records of the 26th Division, Box 27, 40873–40930.
13. Barlow, "World War Daily Diary of the 102nd Ambulance Company," October 7 & 8, 18.
14. Barlow, "World War Daily Diary of the 102nd Ambulance Company," October 10, 11, & 12, 18.
15. Beers to Mother, October 21, 1917, *Newtown Bee*, December 28, 1917.
16. Barlow, "World War Daily Diary of the 102nd Ambulance Company," October 13, 14 & 15, 18.
17. History of the 103rd Machine Gun

Battalion, History of Company B, 103rd Machine Gun Battalion.

18. Barlow, "World War Daily Diary of the 102nd Ambulance Company," October 13, 14 & 15, 18.

19. Barlow to Bridgeport Comfort Club, July 18, 1918, in Barlow, *Letters to the Bridgeport Comfort Club*, 4.

20. Barlow to Bridgeport Comfort Club, July 18, 1918, in Barlow, *Letters to the Bridgeport Comfort Club*, 5. "Steen" was period slang for "many," perhaps derived from sixteen.

21. Barlow, "World War Daily Diary of the 102nd Ambulance Company," October 13, 14 & 15, 18.

22. Barlow, "World War Daily Diary of the 102nd Ambulance Company," November 26 & 27, 22.

23. Beers to Mother, October 21, 1917, *Newtown Bee*, November 16, 1917.

24. Barlow, "World War Daily Diary of the 102nd Ambulance Company," October 18, 18.

25. "101st Sanitary Train. 26th Division A.E.F. History," 161/344/610.

26. Barlow, "World War Daily Diary of the 102nd Ambulance Company," October 19, 18.

27. Barlow, "World War Daily Diary of the 102nd Ambulance Company," Diary, 18.

28. Beers to Mother, October 21, 1917, *Newtown Bee*, November 16, 1917.

29. "101st Sanitary Train. 26th Division A.E.F. History," 160/343/609.

30. Barlow, "World War Daily Diary of the 102nd Ambulance Company," October 19, 18.

31. Beers to Mother, October 21, 1917, *Newtown Bee*, November 16, 1917.

32. Barlow, "World War Daily Diary of the 102nd Ambulance Company," October 20, 21, 22 & 23, 19.

33. Barlow, "World War Daily Diary of the 102nd Ambulance Company," October 20, 21, 22 & 23, 19.

34. Barlow, "World War Daily Diary of the 102nd Ambulance Company," October 18, 18.

35. Barlow, "World War Daily Diary of the 102nd Ambulance Company," October 20, 21, 22 & 23, 19.

36. Barlow, "World War Daily Diary of the 102nd Ambulance Company," October 20, 21, 22 & 23, 19.

37. Barlow, "World War Daily Diary of the 102nd Ambulance Company," October 24, 19.

Chapter 4

1. Beers to Sister, October 26, 1917, *Newtown Bee*, November 30, 1917.

2. "101st Sanitary Train. 26th Division A.E.F. History," March 1919, photostat typescript in Records, 1917–1919, 26th Division, United States Army, War Records Department, Connecticut State Archives Record Group No. 012, Part II, Series No. 040, Connecticut State Archives, Hartford, 161/344/610. The page number sequence represents the digital version/typescript/photostat numbers. As mentioned previously, Leslie R. Barlow reported that Earle E. Radikin was detailed to produce this history of the Sanitary Train in February 1919. It was an almost universal experience for American soldiers to ride in the small French boxcars marked to accommodate either 40 men or 8 horses. "Corned Willie" was canned corned beef, and "goldfish" was canned salmon.

3. Leslie R. Barlow, "World War Daily Diary of the 102nd Ambulance Company," typescript, Connecticut State Archives, October 25, 19.

4. Beers to Sister, October 26, 1917, *Newtown Bee*, November 30, 1917.

5. *Bridgeport Sunday Post*, June 9, 1918.

6. "101st Sanitary Train. 26th Division A.E.F. History," 161/344/610; Barlow, "World War Daily Diary of the 102nd Ambulance Company," October 26, 19.

7. Mark Ethan Grotelueschen, *The AEF Way of War: The American Army and Combat in World War I* (Cambridge: Cambridge University Press, 2007), 27–28, 147–49.

8. Barlow, "World War Daily Diary of the 102nd Ambulance Company," February 7 & 8, 28–29.

9. "Genêts and the Man Who Saved a Million Lives in WWI," https://www.normandythenandnow.com/genets-and-the-man-who-saved-a-million-lives-in-ww1/, accessed January 2022. Adrian also designed the iconic helmet worn by French soldiers; Barlow, "World War Daily Diary of the 102nd Ambulance Company," November 5 & 6, 20–21.

10. Barlow, "World War Daily Diary of the 102nd Ambulance Company," October 26, 19.

11. Barlow, "World War Daily Diary of the 102nd Ambulance Company," October 26, 19.

12. Beers to Sister, October 26, 1917, *Newtown Bee*, November 30, 1917.

13. Barlow, "World War Daily Diary of the 102nd Ambulance Company," October 27, 20.

14. "101st Sanitary Train. 26th Division A.E.F. History," 160/343/609.

15. "101st Sanitary Train. 26th Division A.E.F. History," 160/343/609. The same process took place in Bazoilles and other small farming communities occupied by the troops, see Michael E. Shay, *A Grateful Heart: The History of a World War I Field Hospital* (Westport, CT: Greenwood Press, 2002), 23.

16. "101st Sanitary Train. 26th Division A.E.F. History," 162/345/611.

17. Barlow, "World War Daily Diary of the 102nd Ambulance Company," November 3 & 4, 20.

18. Emerson Gifford Taylor, *New England in France 1917–1919: A History of the Twenty-Sixth Division U.S.A.* (Boston: Houghton Mifflin, 1920), 41.

19. Barlow, "World War Daily Diary of the 102nd Ambulance Company," November 5 & 6, 20.

20. Barlow, "World War Daily Diary of the 102nd Ambulance Company," November 28, 22.
21. Barlow, "World War Daily Diary of the 102nd Ambulance Company," January 15, 16 & 17, 26.
22. Barlow, "World War Daily Diary of the 102nd Ambulance Company," October 28, 29 & 30, 20.
23. Barlow, "World War Daily Diary of the 102nd Ambulance Company," November 15 & 16, 21.
24. Beers to Sister, no date, *Newtown Bee*, December 28, 1917.
25. Barlow, "World War Daily Diary of the 102nd Ambulance Company," January 15, 16 & 17, 26.
26. Barlow, "World War Daily Diary of the 102nd Ambulance Company," October 27, 20.
27. Barlow, "World War Daily Diary of the 102nd Ambulance Company," November 5 & 6, 20.
28. Barlow, "World War Daily Diary of the 102nd Ambulance Company," November 3 & 4, 20, 22; Jim Bond, "Little Tanks: The Development of the American Field Shoe [Boot] During the World War," Doughboy Center, http://www.worldwar1.com/dbc/l_tanks.htm, accessed January 2022.
29. Barlow, "World War Daily Diary of the 102nd Ambulance Company," November 5 & 6, 20.
30. Barlow, "World War Daily Diary of the 102nd Ambulance Company," November 12, 13 & 14, 20.
31. Benwell, *History of the Yankee Division*, 34.
32. Beers to Sister, no date, *Newtown Bee*, December 28, 1917; the use of so-called arctic overshoes was authorized in the summer of 1917 when the Army considered the winter needs of the troops being sent to France, *Medical Department of the U.S. Army in the World War*, vol. 6, 618.
33. Beers to Sister, no date, *Newtown Bee*, December 28, 1918.
34. Barlow, "World War Daily Diary of the 102nd Ambulance Company," December 19 & 20, 24.
35. Barlow, "World War Daily Diary of the 102nd Ambulance Company," December 21 & 22, 24.
36. Barlow, "World War Daily Diary of the 102nd Ambulance Company," January 11, 12, 13 & 14, 26; Robert L. Atenstaedt, *The Medical Response to the Trench Diseases in World War One* (Newcastle upon Tyne, UK: Cambridge Scholars Publishing, 2011), 123–38, 166–78.
37. Barlow, "World War Daily Diary of the 102nd Ambulance Company," January 11, 12, 13 & 14, 26.
38. Barlow, "World War Daily Diary of the 102nd Ambulance Company," January 24, 27.
39. Barlow, "World War Daily Diary of the 102nd Ambulance Company," February 1, 2 & 3, 28.
40. Barlow, "World War Daily Diary of the 102nd Ambulance Company," January 21, 22 & 23, 27.
41. Dan Shadrake, "WWI: Combat Helmet Technology—The Brodie Steel Helmet," https://eandt.theiet.org/content/articles/2014/06/ww1-combat-helmet-technology-the-brodie-steel-helmet/, accessed January 2022.
42. *Medical Department of the U.S. Army in the World War*, vol. 6, 618. The order was addressed to the commanding generals of the 1st, 2nd, 26th, 41st, and 42nd Divisions.
43. Barlow, "World War Daily Diary of the 102nd Ambulance Company," October 28, 29 & 30, 20.
44. Beers to Sister, October 26, 1917, *Newtown Bee*, November 30, 1917.
45. Barlow to Bridgeport Comfort Club, July 18, 1918, in Leslie R. Barlow, *Letters to the Bridgeport Comfort Club* (Bridgeport: author, 1919), 5. John R. Carter had been appointed mess sergeant in July. Several men, including Leland Hull, Arthur Levasseur, Leroy MacKinnon, the Safko brothers, and David Turner, acted as cooks during the winter of 1917–18.
46. Barlow, "World War Daily Diary of the 102nd Ambulance Company," November 5 & 6, 20.
47. Barlow, "World War Daily Diary of the 102nd Ambulance Company," November 15 & 16, 21.
48. Beers to Mr. Morris, no date, *Newtown Bee*, November 30, 1917.
49. Barlow, "World War Daily Diary of the 102nd Ambulance Company," November 15 & 16, 21.
50. Beers to Sister, November 18, 1917, *Newtown Bee*, December 28, 1917.
51. Barlow, "World War Daily Diary of the 102nd Ambulance Company," November 7, 8, 9 &10, 21.
52. Barlow, "World War Daily Diary of the 102nd Ambulance Company," November 15 & 16, 23.
53. Barlow, "World War Daily Diary of the 102nd Ambulance Company," December 19 & 20, 24.
54. Barlow, "World War Daily Diary of the 102nd Ambulance Company," November 5 & 6, 21.
55. Barlow, "World War Daily Diary of the 102nd Ambulance Company," November 5 & 6, 20.
56. Barlow, "World War Daily Diary of the 102nd Ambulance Company," November 15 & 16, 21; December 5, 6, 7 & 8, 23.
57. Barlow, "World War Daily Diary of the 102nd Ambulance Company," January 25, 26, 27 & 28, 27.
58. Barlow, "World War Daily Diary of the 102nd Ambulance Company," November 29 & 30, 22.
59. Barlow, "World War Daily Diary of the 102nd Ambulance Company," November 7, 8, 9 & 10.
60. Barlow, "World War Daily Diary of the 102nd Ambulance Company," January 9 & 10, 26.
61. Barlow, "World War Daily Diary of the

102nd Ambulance Company," Reminiscences, 96–97.

62. William B. Lusk (1869–1953) was born in Northern Ireland, graduating from Queens College, Belfast, before coming to the U.S. in 1894. After attending the Princeton Theological Seminary, he served first as a Presbyterian minister, but, finding the sect too dogmatic, he became an Episcopal rector and was called to St. Stephen's in 1915. "William B. Lusk: 'Daddy,'" Old Ridgefield, November 6, 2016, http://www.naturegeezer.com/2016/11/william-b.html, accessed January 2022.

63. Beers to Sister, no date, *Newtown Bee*, December 28, 1917.

64. *Bridgeport Sunday Post,* June 9, 1918.

65. *Bridgeport Sunday Post,* June 9, 1918.

66. *Bridgeport Sunday Post,* June 9, 1918.

67. Barlow, "World War Daily Diary of the 102nd Ambulance Company," November 11, 22.

68. Barlow, "World War Daily Diary of the 102nd Ambulance Company," December 17 & 18, 23.

69. Barlow, "World War Daily Diary of the 102nd Ambulance Company," January 18, 19 & 20, 26–27.

70. Bailey to Wife, February 1, 1918, author's collection. Bailey mentioned that one was a married woman from New York and the two unmarried women were from Boston. Their names have not been determined.

71. *Bridgeport Post,* October 23, 1918.

72. Barlow, "World War Daily Diary of the 102nd Ambulance Company," November 22, 23, 24 & 25, 22.

73. Barlow, "World War Daily Diary of the 102nd Ambulance Company," December 5, 6, 7 & 8, 21.

74. U.S. Treasury Department, Bureau of War Risk Insurance, Bulletin No. 3, *Family Allowances, Allotments, Compensation, and Insurance for the Military and Naval Forces of the United States Provided Under Act of Congress Approved October 6, 1917* (Washington, DC: Government Printing Office, 1917); Barlow, "World War Daily Diary of the 102nd Ambulance Company," December 9, 10 & 11, 21.

75. Barlow, "World War Daily Diary of the 102nd Ambulance Company," November 7, 8, 9 & 10, 21.

76. Beers to Mr. Morris, no date, *Newtown Bee*, November 30, 1917.

77. Barlow, "World War Daily Diary of the 102nd Ambulance Company," November 5 & 6, 20.

78. Barlow, "World War Daily Diary of the 102nd Ambulance Company," November 5 & 6, 21.

79. Barlow, "World War Daily Diary of the 102nd Ambulance Company," December 12, 13 & 14, 23.

80. Taylor, *New England in France,* 54.

81. Barlow, "World War Daily Diary of the 102nd Ambulance Company," November 12, 13 & 14, 21; Taylor, *New England in France,* 53.

82. Barlow, "World War Daily Diary of the 102nd Ambulance Company," November 12, 13, & 14, 21.

83. Barlow, "World War Daily Diary of the 102nd Ambulance Company," December 1, 2, 3 & 4, 23.

84. Shay, *A Grateful Heart,* 25.

85. "101st Sanitary Train. 26th Division A.E.F. History," 164/347/613.

86. "101st Sanitary Train. 26th Division A.E.F. History," 162/345/611; Barlow, "World War Daily Diary of the 102nd Ambulance Company," November 11, 22.

87. Barlow, "World War Daily Diary of the 102nd Ambulance Company," December 1, 2, 3 & 4, 23; January 21, 22 &23, 27. The list included Bale, Baxter, Beach, Bell, Browning, Catullo, Cormier, Courtney, Crawford, Curtis, Davis, Doreski, Elliano, Etheridge, Falvo, Forsyth, Healy, Honeck, Keane, Landman, Merrill, Murphy, Norup, O'Connor, Peck, Rich, Schaeffer, Scott, Slootmaker, Smith, Sorensen, Tiska, Turner, Vassel, Walker, Watkins, and Wellwood.

88. "101st Sanitary Train. 26th Division A.E.F. History," 163/346/612.

89. "101st Sanitary Train. 26th Division A.E.F. History," 163/346/612.

90. Barlow, "World War Daily Diary of the 102nd Ambulance Company," November 17, 18 & 19, 22.

91. Beers to Sister, no date, *Newtown Bee*, December 28, 1917.

92. Barlow, "World War Daily Diary of the 102nd Ambulance Company," November 20 & 21, 22.

93. Fairchild to Parents, November 23, 1917, *Newtown Bee*, December 21, 1917.

94. Barlow, "World War Daily Diary of the 102nd Ambulance Company," November 22, 23, 24 & 25, 22.

95. Barlow, "World War Daily Diary of the 102nd Ambulance Company," November 22, 23, 24 & 25, 22.

96. Barlow, "World War Daily Diary of the 102nd Ambulance Company," November 29 & 30, 23.

97. Barlow, "World War Daily Diary of the 102nd Ambulance Company," November 26 & 27, 22.

98. Barlow, "World War Daily Diary of the 102nd Ambulance Company," November 26 & 27, 22.

99. Barlow, "World War Daily Diary of the 102nd Ambulance Company," November 28, 22.

100. Barlow, "World War Daily Diary of the 102nd Ambulance Company," November 29 & 30, 22–23.

101. Bailey to Wife, December 1, 1917, author's collection.

102. Barlow, "World War Daily Diary of the 102nd Ambulance Company," December 1, 2, 3 & 4, 23.

103. Barlow, "World War Daily Diary of the

102nd Ambulance Company," December 9, 10 & 11, 23.

104. Barlow, "World War Daily Diary of the 102nd Ambulance Company," December 12, 13 & 14, 23.

105. Barlow, "World War Daily Diary of the 102nd Ambulance Company," December 17 & 18, 24.

106. Beers to Sister, no date, *Newtown Bee*, December 28, 1918.

107. Beers to Sister, no date, *Newtown Bee*, December 28, 1918.

108. Taylor, *New England in France*, 34.

109. "101st Sanitary Train. 26th Division A.E.F. History," 163/346/612. The 103rd Field Hospital had been sent to Dijon, far outside the area.

110. Beers to Sister, October 26, 1917, *Newtown Bee*, February 22, 1918.

111. Wever, *A U.S. Army Medical Base in World War I France*, 21–23.

112. Barlow, "World War Daily Diary of the 102nd Ambulance Company," February 1, 2 & 3, 28.

113. "101st Sanitary Train. 26th Division A.E.F. History," 163/346/612.

114. Barlow, "World War Daily Diary of the 102nd Ambulance Company," January 29, 30 & 31, 28.

115. Barlow, "World War Daily Diary of the 102nd Ambulance Company," December 31, 25.

116. John Rezelman, "Starting Model T Fords," Crooked Lake Review (February 1994), https://www.crookedlakereview.com/articles/67_100/71feb1994/71rezelman.html, accessed January 2022.

117. Barlow, "World War Daily Diary of the 102nd Ambulance Company," December 31, 25.

118. Barlow, "World War Daily Diary of the 102nd Ambulance Company," January 24, 27; Rezelman, "Starting Model T Fords."

119. Barlow, "World War Daily Diary of the 102nd Ambulance Company," January 21, 22 & 23, 27.

120. Barlow, "World War Daily Diary of the 102nd Ambulance Company," January 18, 19 & 20, 27.

121. Barlow, "World War Daily Diary of the 102nd Ambulance Company," October 27, 20.

122. Barlow, "World War Daily Diary of the 102nd Ambulance Company," October 27, 20.

123. Barlow, "World War Daily Diary of the 102nd Ambulance Company," October 28, 29 & 30, 20.

124. Barlow, "World War Daily Diary of the 102nd Ambulance Company," November 1 & 2, 20.

125. Barlow, "World War Daily Diary of the 102nd Ambulance Company," December 15, 24.

126. Bailey to Wife, December 17, 1917, author's collection.

127. Barlow, "World War Daily Diary of the 102nd Ambulance Company," February 1, 2 & 3, 28.

128. Barlow to Bridgeport Comfort Club, July 18, 1918, in Barlow, *Letters to the Bridgeport Comfort Club*, 5–6.

129. Barlow, "World War Daily Diary of the 102nd Ambulance Company," December 21 & 22, 24.

130. Barlow, "World War Daily Diary of the 102nd Ambulance Company," Reminiscences, 97.

131. Barlow, "World War Daily Diary of the 102nd Ambulance Company," December 15 & 16, 24.

132. Barlow, "World War Daily Diary of the 102nd Ambulance Company," January 7 & 8, 26.

133. Barlow, "World War Daily Diary of the 102nd Ambulance Company," December 17 & 18, 23.

134. Barlow, "World War Daily Diary of the 102nd Ambulance Company," December 17 & 18, 23.

135. Barlow, "World War Daily Diary of the 102nd Ambulance Company," December 25, 26 & 27, 24–25.

136. Beers to Mother, December 24, 1917, *Newtown Bee*, January 25, 1918.

137. Beers to Mother, December 24, 1917, *Newtown Bee*, January 25, 1918.

138. Barlow, "World War Daily Diary of the 102nd Ambulance Company," December 25, 26 & 27, 25.

139. Beers to Mother, December 25, 1917, *Newtown Bee*, January 25, 1918.

140. Barlow, "World War Daily Diary of the 102nd Ambulance Company," December 25, 26 & 27, 25.

141. Beers to Mother, December 25, 1917, *Newtown Bee*, January 25, 1918.

142. Barlow, "World War Daily Diary of the 102nd Ambulance Company," December 25, 26 & 27, 24–25.

143. Grotelueschen, *The AEF Way of War*, 146–47; Taylor, *New England in France*, 53; Daniel W. Strickland, *Connecticut Fights: The Story of the 102nd Regiment* (New Haven: Quinnipiack Press, 1930), 199–200.

144. Taylor, *New England in France*, 46. The author owns Sprague's copy.

145. Barlow, "World War Daily Diary of the 102nd Ambulance Company," November 17, 18 & 19, 22.

146. Barlow, "World War Daily Diary of the 102nd Ambulance Company," November 28, 23.

147. Barlow, "World War Daily Diary of the 102nd Ambulance Company," December 31, 26.

148. Barlow, "World War Daily Diary of the 102nd Ambulance Company," December 9, 10 & 11, 23; January 1, 2, 3 & 4, 25.

149. Barlow, "World War Daily Diary of the 102nd Ambulance Company," January 9 & 10, 26; Ancestry.com. search for James F. Cobey, April 2022, producing U.S. Census listings, Yale University student data, and world War I draft card.

150. Barlow, "World War Daily Diary of the 102nd Ambulance Company," January 7 & 8, January 9 & 10, 26.

151. Barlow to Bridgeport Comfort Club, July 30, 1918, in Barlow, *Letters to the Bridgeport Comfort Club*, 6.

152. Barlow, "World War Daily Diary of the 102nd Ambulance Company," January 11, 12 13 & 14, 26.

153. *Bridgeport Sunday Post,* June 9, 1918. Lusk did add the qualification, "Yet some of the doctors are the finest men I have met."

154. Barlow, "World War Daily Diary of the 102nd Ambulance Company," January 15, 26.

155. Barlow, "World War Daily Diary of the 102nd Ambulance Company," January 21, 22 & 23, 27; February 1, 2 & 3, 28.

156. James to Sister, December 31, 1917, *Newtown Bee,* February 1, 1918. Barlow remarked that Red Worley bought the violin, Barlow, "World War Daily Diary of the 102nd Ambulance Company," January 1, 2, 3 & 4, 26. Jesse Bailey remarked on their New Year's Eve dinner as well: "Tonight the Newtown Club gets together again for a big feed. Hub Beers bought two ducks in a nearby town while on his Ford travels and we are to have them cooked by a madame here in town she is some cook too, so we will need no sympathy on our New Years feed." Bailey to Wife, January 1, 1918, author's collection.

157. Beers to Mother, December 24, 1917, *Newtown Bee,* January 25, 1918

158. Barlow, "World War Daily Diary of the 102nd Ambulance Company," January 5, 25.

159. Barlow, "World War Daily Diary of the 102nd Ambulance Company," January 6, 25; January 15, 16 & 17, 26.

160. Barlow, "World War Daily Diary of the 102nd Ambulance Company," January 7 & 8, 9 & 10, 26.

161. Charles Field Mason, *A Complete Handbook for the Sanitary Troops of the U.S. Army and Navy and National Guard and Naval Militia,* 4th ed. (New York: William Wood and Company, 1917), 365.

162. "Division Surgeon's Reports: Twenty-Sixth Division," Report of the Surgeon General of the Army, *War Department Annual Reports, 1919,* part 3 (Washington, DC: Government Printing Office, 1920), 3294.

163. Barlow, "World War Daily Diary of the 102nd Ambulance Company," February 4, 5 & 6, 28.

164. Barlow, "World War Daily Diary of the 102nd Ambulance Company," January 25, 26, 27 & 28, 27.

165. Mason, *A Complete Handbook for the Sanitary Troops of the U.S. Army and Navy,* 254–57. If diagnosed early enough through a spinal tap, meningitis might be treated with injections of "horse serum," but its mortality rate in the AEF was more than 40 percent, Shay, *A Grateful Heart,* 187–88.

166. Barlow, "World War Daily Diary of the 102nd Ambulance Company," January 7 & 8, 26.

167. Barlow, "World War Daily Diary of the 102nd Ambulance Company," December 1, 2, 3 & 4, 23; February 16, 17 & 18, 30.

168. *Bridgeport Telegram,* July 29, 1918. The author may well have been Earle Radikin, who enjoyed writing and performing.

169. R. L. Atenstaedt, "Trench Fever: The British Medical Response in the Great War," *Journal of the Royal Society of Medicine* 99, number 11 (November 2006): 564–68. https://www.ncbi.nlm.nih.gov/pmc/articles/PMC1633565/

170. Atenstaedt, *The Medical Response to the Trench Diseases in World War One,* 80–81.

171. Atenstaedt, *The Medical Response to the Trench Diseases in World War One,* 78, 81.

172. Atenstaedt, *The Medical Response to the Trench Diseases in World War One,* 83–84. One report places the initial total of men selected at 82, of whom 16 decided not to participate.

173. Barlow, "World War Daily Diary of the 102nd Ambulance Company," January 6, 25.

174. Trench Fever Experiment, No.1275-3, GHQ, AEF, June 10, 1918, https://www.fold3.com/image/76743765. The full list of trench fever volunteers who began in the company is included in the Company roster in the appendix.

175. Frank P. Sibley, *With the Yankee Division in France* (Boston: Little, Brown, 1919), 135.

176. Trench Fever Experiment, No.1275-3, GHQ, AEF, June 10, 1918; Atenstaedt, *The Medical Response to the Trench Diseases in World War One,* 99; "12 Bridgeport Men Submit to Trench Fever," *Bridgeport Post,* April 12, 1918,

177. Atenstaedt, *The Medical Response to the Trench Diseases in World War One,* 84; Weed, *Med Dept,* vol. 6, 379–80.

178. Atenstaedt, *The Medical Response to the Trench Diseases in World War One,* 84–85; Trench Fever Experiment, No.1275-3, GHQ, AEF, June 10, 1918.

179. Weed, *Medical Department of the U.S. Army in the World War,* vol. 6, 379–80; Trench Fever Experiment, No.1275-3, GHQ, AEF, June 10, 1918.

180. Sibley, *With the Yankee Division in France,* 136.

181. Atenstaedt, *The Medical Response to the Trench Diseases in World War One,* 85, 100.

182. "12 Bridgeport Men Submit to Trench Fever," *Bridgeport Post,* April 12, 1918.

183. WW1 Veterans, Connecticut Soldiers Questionnaires, 1919, https://ctstatelibrary.org/-ww-1-veterans/, accessed October 2021.

184. Circular 34, Resume of Symptoms and Treatment of Poisoning by Irritant Gasses, June 12, 1918, *Medical Department of the U.S. Army in the World War,* vol. 14, 833; Terrence J. Finnegan, *"A Delicate Affair" on the Western Front: America Learns How to Fight a Modern War in the Woëvre Trenches* (Stroud, Gloucestershire, UK: History Press, 2015), 72–73.

185. Simon Jones, *World War I Gas Warfare Tactics and Equipment* (Botley, Oxford, England: Osprey Publishing, 1994); Circular 34, Resume of Symptoms and Treatment of Poisoning by Irritant Gasses, June 12, 1918, 833–37; Finnegan, *"A Delicate Affair" on the Western Front,* 75–76.

186. Jones, *World War I Gas Warfare,* 30–31.

187. Jones, *World War I Gas Warfare,* 31–32.

188. Jones, *World War I Gas Warfare,* 47, 49, 63.

189. Barlow, "World War Daily Diary of the 102nd Ambulance Company," December 9, 10 & 11, 23.

190. Barlow, "World War Daily Diary of the 102nd Ambulance Company," January 4, 26.

191. Barlow, "World War Daily Diary of the 102nd Ambulance Company," January 15, 16 & 17, 26.

192. Barlow, "World War Daily Diary of the 102nd Ambulance Company," January 18, 19 & 20, 26.

193. Jones, *World War I Gas Warfare*, 49; Circular 34, Resume of Symptoms and Treatment of Poisoning by Irritant Gasses, June 12, 1918, 836; aid station supplies included quantities of chlorinated lime and sodium bicarbonate, a Vermorel tank and sprayer, rubber coats and gloves, a variety of gas masks, and a gas fan to disperse the residue, report of supplies for the 102nd Infantry Dressing Station, Office of the Surgeon, 102nd U.S. Infantry, "Report of Tour of Duty Soissons Front," ca. April 17, 1918, typescript courtesy Peter Wever.

194. Barlow, "World War Daily Diary of the 102nd Ambulance Company," January 29, 30 & 31, 27.

195. Bailey to Wife, January 30, 1918, author's collection.

196. Barlow, "World War Daily Diary of the 102nd Ambulance Company," January 18, 19 & 20, 27.

197. Barlow, "World War Daily Diary of the 102nd Ambulance Company," February 1, 2 & 3, 28.

198. Barlow, "World War Daily Diary of the 102nd Ambulance Company," February 4, 5 & 6, 28.

199. Barlow, "World War Daily Diary of the 102nd Ambulance Company," February 7 & 8, 28.

Chapter 5

1. Leslie R. Barlow, "World War Daily Diary of the 102nd Ambulance Company," typescript, Connecticut State Archives, February 9 & 10, 29.

2. "101st Sanitary Train. 26th Division A.E.F. History," March 1919, photostat typescript in Records, 1917–1919, 26th Division, United States Army, War Records Department, Connecticut State Archives Record Group No. 012, Part II, Series No. 040, Connecticut State Archives, Hartford, 166/349/615. The page number sequence represents the digital version/typescript/photostat numbers. As mentioned previously, Leslie R. Barlow reported that Earle E. Radikin was detailed to produce this history of the Sanitary Train in February 1919.

3. "101st Sanitary Train. 26th Division A.E.F. History," 166/349/615.

4. Barlow, "World War Daily Diary of the 102nd Ambulance Company," February 9 & 10, 29.

5. Barlow, "World War Daily Diary of the 102nd Ambulance Company," February 27, 31.

6. Beers to Mother, February 18, 1918, *Newtown Bee*, April 5, 1918.

7. Barlow, "World War Daily Diary of the 102nd Ambulance Company," February 13, 14 &15, 30.

8. Barlow, "World War Daily Diary of the 102nd Ambulance Company," March 7, 8, 9 & 10, 32.

9. "101st Sanitary Train. 26th Division A.E.F. History," 169/352/618.

10. Barlow, "World War Daily Diary of the 102nd Ambulance Company," February 9 & 10, 29.

11. Barlow, "World War World War Daily Diary of the 102nd Ambulance Company," February 11 & 12, 29.

12. Barlow, "World War Daily Diary of the 102nd Ambulance Company," March 4, 5 & 6, 32.

13. Beers to Mother, February 18, 1918, *Newtown Bee*, April 5, 1918.

14. "101st Sanitary Train. 26th Division A.E.F. History," 167/350/616.

15. Radikin to Father, March 28, 1918, *Bridgeport Evening Post*, May 22, 1918. Radikin may have exaggerated in his description of what was probably Carrière de Froidmont, beyond Ostel near Braye-en-Laonnais. The other principal caves occupied by the Division were the Rouge-Maison above Vailly, Carrière Saint-Blaise behind the 52nd Brigade, Le Panthéon, and Montparnasse.

16. The variety of litters was called for in the report of supplies for the 102nd Infantry Dressing Station, Office of the Surgeon, 102nd U.S. Infantry, "Report of Tour of Duty Soissons Front," ca. April 17, 1918, typescript courtesy Peter Wever.

17. Barlow, "World War Daily Diary of the 102nd Ambulance Company," March 12, 13, 14 & 15, 33.

18. Barlow, "World War Daily Diary of the 102nd Ambulance Company," February 16, 17 & 18, 29.

19. Barlow, "World War Daily Diary of the 102nd Ambulance Company," February 28, 31; Daniel W. Strickland, *Connecticut Fights: The Story of the 102nd Regiment* (New Haven: Quinnipiack Press, 1930), 101–04.

20. Barlow, "World War Daily Diary of the 102nd Ambulance Company," February 13, 14 & 15, 29–30.

21. Barlow, "World War Daily Diary of the 102nd Ambulance Company," February 16, 17 & 18, 30.

22. Beers to Mother, March 9, 1918, *Newtown Bee*, April 5, 1918.

23. Strickland, *Connecticut Fights*, 94–95.

24. Barlow, "World War Daily Diary of the 102nd Ambulance Company," February 16, 17 & 18, 30. The term "Black Maria," denoting a police van for carrying prisoners to jail, apparently originated in Boston in the early 1800s and referred to a black sailors' boardinghouse keeper named Maria Lee, who assisted the police in subduing lawbreakers. However, Barlow probably refers to the ornate nineteenth-century hearse design known as the Black Mariah. In either case, the passengers would not return.

25. Barlow, "World War Daily Diary of the 102nd Ambulance Company," February 19 & 20, 30.
26. Barlow, "World War Daily Diary of the 102nd Ambulance Company," February 21, 22, 23, 30.
27. Barlow, "World War Daily Diary of the 102nd Ambulance Company," February 27, 31.
28. Barlow, "World War Daily Diary of the 102nd Ambulance Company," March 11, 32.
29. Barlow, "World War Daily Diary of the 102nd Ambulance Company," February 21, 22, 23, 30.
30. Barlow, "World War Daily Diary of the 102nd Ambulance Company," February 28, 31.
31. "101st Sanitary Train. 26th Division A.E.F. History," 170/353/619.
32. Barlow, "World War Daily Diary of the 102nd Ambulance Company," February 28, 31; Michael E. Shay, *A Grateful Heart: The History of a World War I Field Hospital* (Westport, CT: Greenwood Press, 2002), 43–46.
33. Shay, *A Grateful Heart*, 44.
34. Beers to Mother, March 9, 1918, *Newtown Bee*, April 5, 1918.
35. Barlow, "World War Daily Diary of the 102nd Ambulance Company," March 11, 32.
36. Barlow to Bridgeport Comfort Club, July 30, 1918, in Leslie R. Barlow, *Letters to the Bridgeport Comfort Club from the Foreign Chapter in France* (Bridgeport: Author, 1919), 7.
37. Radikin to Father, March 28, 1918, *Bridgeport Evening Post*, May 22, 1918.
38. Barlow, "World War Daily Diary of the 102nd Ambulance Company," March 16, 17 & 18, 33.
39. *Bridgeport Post*, April 16, 1918.
40. Barlow, "World War Daily Diary of the 102nd Ambulance Company," March 16, 17 & 18, 33.
41. Barlow to Bridgeport Comfort Club, July 30, 1918, in Barlow, *Letters to the Bridgeport Comfort Club*, 7–8. Barlow uses the soldier's derogatory slang term for the German soldier.
42. On kitchens and cooking equipment, see *Medical Department of the U.S. Army in the World War*, vol. 6, 710–25.
43. Barlow, "World War Daily Diary of the 102nd Ambulance Company," February 13, 14 & 15, 29. Again, "slum" was a soupy mix of canned vegetables, rice, and whatever the mess sergeant had on hand.
44. Barlow, "World War Daily Diary of the 102nd Ambulance Company," February 28, 31.
45. Barlow, "World War Daily Diary of the 102nd Ambulance Company," February 16, 17 & 18, 29.
46. Barlow, "World War Daily Diary of the 102nd Ambulance Company," February 19 & 20, 30.
47. Barlow, "World War Daily Diary of the 102nd Ambulance Company," February 24, 25 & 26, 31.
48. Barlow, "World War Daily Diary of the 102nd Ambulance Company," February 27, 31.
49. Barlow, "World War Daily Diary of the 102nd Ambulance Company," February 28, 31.
50. Barlow, "World War Daily Diary of the 102nd Ambulance Company," March 1, 2 & 3, 31.
51. Barlow, "World War Daily Diary of the 102nd Ambulance Company," March 19, 20 & 21, 33.
52. Barlow, "World War Daily Diary of the 102nd Ambulance Company," March 19, 20 & 21, 33.
53. Barlow, "World War Daily Diary of the 102nd Ambulance Company," March 4, 5 & 6, 31–32.
54. Terrence J. Finnegan, *"A Delicate Affair" on the Western Front: America Learns How to Fight a Modern War in the Woëvre Trenches* (Stroud, Gloucestershire, UK: History Press, 2015), 74.
55. Barlow, "World War Daily Diary of the 102nd Ambulance Company," February 27, 31.
56. Barlow, "World War Daily Diary of the 102nd Ambulance Company," March 12, 13, 14 & 15, 33.
57. Barlow, "World War Daily Diary of the 102nd Ambulance Company," March 12, 13, 14 & 15, 33.
58. Barlow, "World War Daily Diary of the 102nd Ambulance Company," March 16, 17 & 18, 33.
59. Radikin to Father, March 28, 1918, *Bridgeport Evening Post*, May 22, 1918. "Poilu" was French for a French soldier. Radikin introduced this description by saying, "Just before we quit I had an experience that I never expect to forget for the rest of my natural life."
60. *Bridgeport Post*, July 30, 1918; Philip R. Devlin, "Windsor Locks physician cited for extraordinary valor," in "Connecticut's Irish in World War I," *Shanachie* 30, number 4 (November-December 2018): 12, suggests the effects of his gassing may have contributed to his relatively early death at age 59.
61. Radikin to Father, March 28, 1918, *Bridgeport Evening Post*, May 22, 1918.
62. Barlow, "World War Daily Diary of the 102nd Ambulance Company," March 19, 20 & 21, 33.
63. "Sanitation," Report of the Surgeon General of the Army, *War Department Annual Reports, 1919*, part 3 (Washington, DC: Government Printing Office, 1920), 3028.
64. Barlow, "World War Daily Diary of the 102nd Ambulance Company," February 24, 25 & 26, 31.
65. Barlow, "World War Daily Diary of the 102nd Ambulance Company," March 1, 2 & 3, 31.
66. Beers to Mother, March 9, 1918, *Newtown Bee*, April 5, 1918.
67. Barlow, "World War Daily Diary of the 102nd Ambulance Company," February 13, 14 &15, 30.
68. Beers to Mother, March 9, 1918, *Newtown Bee*, April 5, 1918.

69. Barlow, "World War Daily Diary of the 102nd Ambulance Company," February 11 & 12, 29. The use of parachutes by airmen was still rare, though balloon observers often wore them.

70. Barlow, "World War Daily Diary of the 102nd Ambulance Company," March 11, 32.

71. Beers to Mother, February 18, 1918, *Newtown Bee*, April 5, 1918.

72. Barlow, "World War Daily Diary of the 102nd Ambulance Company," March 7, 8, 9 & 10, 32.

73. *Bridgeport Sunday Post*, June 9, 1918.

74. "Disinfestation of Clothing and Bedding: Disinfestation by Steam," *Medical Department of the United States Army in the World War*, vol. 6 (Washington, DC: Government Printing Office, 19), 1018, 1021; Barlow, Diary, January 6, 25; January 15, 16 & 17, 1926.

75. "Foden." https://tractors.fandom.com/wiki/Foden, accessed November 2021; Tim Gosling, "A Moderate Idea of Speed: Tim Gosling delves into the history of the Foden Steam Wagon." https://www.keymilitary.com/article/moderate-idea-speed, accessed November 2021.

76. "Foden"; Gosling, "A Moderate Idea of Speed."

77. "Foden"; Gosling, "A Moderate Idea of Speed"; "Disinfestation of Clothing and Bedding: Disinfestation by Steam," *Medical Department of the United States Army in the World War*, vol. 6, 1024.

78. "Disinfestation of Clothing and Bedding: Disinfestation by Steam," *Medical Department of the United States Army in the World War*, vol. 6, 1016, 1018. By July, the 1st Division would have 2 Foden and 4 horse-drawn units, the 2nd Division would have 2 Foden units, the 3rd Division would have 2 Foden units, the 4th Division would have 1 Foden unit, the 5th Division would have 2 Foden units, the 26th Division would have 2 Foden and 2 horse-drawn units, the 28th Division would have 1 Foden unit, the 32nd Division would have 2 Foden units, the 35th Division would have 2 Foden units, the 42nd Division would have 1 Foden and 3 horse-drawn units, and the 77th Division would have 1 horse-drawn and 1 French unit, "Disinfestation of Clothing and Bedding: Disinfestation by Steam," *Medical Department of the United States Army in the World War*, vol. 6, 1021.

79. "Disinfestation of Clothing and Bedding: Disinfestation by Steam," *Medical Department of the United States Army in the World War*, vol. 6, 1024, 1017. Generally, the men would line up to hand over their clothing in a loose bundle, then line up in reverse order to receive the same bundle of disinfested clothing at the end.

80. This assumes that the noncommissioned officers would drive the two units, with an assistant and two Thresh operators on each. With one man for the truck, that would equal the nine men in the detachment, see Company roster in Appendix; "Disinfestation of Clothing and Bedding: Disinfestation by Steam," *Medical Department of the United States Army in the World War*, vol. 6, 1008. It is unclear when the units began to operate in the field. A photo of number 502 was taken in front of bare trees, suggesting March, and may show the men in training.

81. Barlow, "World War Daily Diary of the 102nd Ambulance Company," March 22, 33.

82. *Bridgeport Sunday Post*, June 9, 1918.

83. Barlow, "World War Daily Diary of the 102nd Ambulance Company," March 22, 33.

84. Barlow, "World War Daily Diary of the 102nd Ambulance Company," March 22, 33.

85. Barlow, "World War Daily Diary of the 102nd Ambulance Company," March 23, 33–34.

86. Barlow, "World War Daily Diary of the 102nd Ambulance Company," March 24, 34.

87. Barlow, "World War Daily Diary of the 102nd Ambulance Company," March 25, 34.

88. "Division Surgeon's Reports: Twenty-Sixth Division," Report of the Surgeon General of the Army, *War Department Annual Reports, 1919*, part 3 (Washington, DC: Government Printing Office, 1920), 3296.

89. "Division Surgeon's Reports: Twenty-Sixth Division," Report of the Surgeon General of the Army, *War Department Annual Reports, 1919*, part 3, 3296.

90. Barlow, "World War Daily Diary of the 102nd Ambulance Company," March 25, 34.

91. Barlow, "World War Daily Diary of the 102nd Ambulance Company," March 26 & 27, 34.

92. Barlow, "World War Daily Diary of the 102nd Ambulance Company," March 26 & 27, 34.

93. Barlow, "World War Daily Diary of the 102nd Ambulance Company," March 28 & 29, 34.

94. Barlow, "World War Daily Diary of the 102nd Ambulance Company," March 28 & 29, 34.

95. Peck to Mother, September 19, 1918, *Newtown Bee*, October 25, 1918.

96. Barlow, "World War Daily Diary of the 102nd Ambulance Company," March 28 & 29, 34.

97. Radikin to Father, March 28, 1918, *Bridgeport Evening Post*, May 22, 1918. Radikin probably refers to members of the 103rd Field Artillery, some of whom he had known at home in Rhode Island.

Chapter 6

1. Leslie R. Barlow, "World War Daily Diary of the 102nd Ambulance Company," typescript, Connecticut State Archives, March 31, 35.

2. Barlow, "World War Daily Diary of the 102nd Ambulance Company," March 30, 35.

3. Barlow, "World War Daily Diary of the 102nd Ambulance Company," March 30, 34–35.

4. Barlow, "World War Daily Diary of the 102nd Ambulance Company," March 31, 35.

5. Barlow, "World War Daily Diary of the 102nd Ambulance Company," March 31, 35.

6. Barlow, "World War Daily Diary of the 102nd Ambulance Company," March 31, 35.

7. "101st Sanitary Train. 26th Division A.E.F. History," March 1919, pages 152–98, photostat typescript in Records, 1917–1919, 26th Division, United States Army, War Records Department, Connecticut State Archives Record Group No. 012, Part II, Series No. 040, Connecticut State Archives, Hartford, 171/354/620. The page number sequence represents the digital version/typescript/photostat numbers. As mentioned previously, Leslie R. Barlow recorded that Earle E. Radikin was detailed to produce this history of the Sanitary Train in February 1919.

8. Barlow, "World War Daily Diary of the 102nd Ambulance Company," April 1, 2, 3 & 4, 35.

9. Barlow, "World War Daily Diary of the 102nd Ambulance Company," April 1, 2, 3 & 4, 35.

10. "101st Sanitary Train. 26th Division A.E.F. History," 171/354/620.

11. "101st Sanitary Train. 26th Division A.E.F. History," 171/354/620.

12. Barlow, "World War Daily Diary of the 102nd Ambulance Company," April 6, 7 & 8, 36; Reminiscences, 92.

13. Barlow, "World War Daily Diary of the 102nd Ambulance Company," April 5, 35.

14. Barlow, "World War Daily Diary of the 102nd Ambulance Company," April 5, 35.

15. Robert W. Bodfish, *A History of Section 647, United States Army Ambulance Service with the French Army* (Worcester: Stobbs Press, 1919), 29.

16. Barlow, "World War Daily Diary of the 102nd Ambulance Company," April 6, 7 & 8, 36.

17. Clyde Johnston, Nomination for Distinguished Service Cross, December 2, 1918, Records, 1917–1919, 26th Division, United States Army, War Records Department, Record Group No. 012, Part II, Series No. 040, Connecticut State Archives, Hartford.

18. Barlow, "World War Daily Diary of the 102nd Ambulance Company," April 22, 38. The Reverend Lusk would leave the lines and return to Bridgeport at the end of April, "The Rev Mr Lusk of Ridgefield, who has started for home, came around and took our names; also said good-bye. He is going to come to Newtown, I think," Beers to Mother, May 1, 1918, *Newtown Bee*, May 24, 1918.

19. Barlow, "World War Daily Diary of the 102nd Ambulance Company," April 6, 7 & 8, 36.

20. Alexander Gardiner, "The Girl Who Wore O.D," *The American Legion Magazine* (April 1928) http://www.oldmagazinearticles.com/WW1_Salvation_Army_Women_in_France-pdf?fbclid=IwAR0KeqvBHNhiLXXH9Vpn5clRWkFrYaJYB8610uJwhEd3sntTDVMwBZXX4eI, accessed March 2022; *Bridgeport Evening Post*, April 22,1919. McIntyre is perhaps best known for promoting and expanding the Salvation Army's "red kettle" donation program at Christmastime.

21. *Bridgeport Telegram*, November 16, 1918.

22. Barlow, "World War Daily Diary of the 102nd Ambulance Company," June 3, 4, 5 & 6, 41. Signal Corps photographers took several photographs of the women in action on April 8 and 9, and one of the photographs of Stella Young with a basin of doughnuts became an iconic image of the Salvation Army "doughnut Lassies."

23. Barlow, "World War Daily Diary of the 102nd Ambulance Company," June 3, 4, 5 & 6, 41. Although the 26th Division adopted the McIntyre group as its own, presenting them with a citation at the conclusion of the war, and Gladys McIntyre would later marry Lieutenant Russell Harmon of the 104th Infantry, the Division would part ways with them at the end of June, and the McIntyres would go on to serve the 82nd, 77th, 37th, 28th, and 42nd Divisions through 1918, Gardiner, "The Girl Who Wore O.D," *The American Legion Magazine* (April 1928).

24. Barlow, "World War Daily Diary of the 102nd Ambulance Company," April 14, 15 & 16, 36.

25. Bodfish, *A History of Section 647, United States Army Ambulance Service with the French Army*, 11–28.

26. Bodfish, *A History of Section 647, United States Army Ambulance Service with the French Army*, 28.

27. Terrence J. Finnegan, *"A Delicate Affair" on the Western Front: America Learns How to Fight a Modern War in the Woëvre Trenches* (Stroud, Gloucestershire, UK: History Press, 2015), 166–73.

28. "101st Sanitary Train. 26th Division A.E.F. History," 172–73/355–56/621–22.

29. Barlow, "World War Daily Diary of the 102nd Ambulance Company," April 9, 10, 11, 12 & 13; April 14, 15 & 16, 36; *Bridgeport Post*, April 20, 1938.

30. *Bridgeport Telegram*, November 16, 1918. Crump was reported gassed on April 20.

31. Barlow, "World War Daily Diary of the 102nd Ambulance Company," April 17, 18, 19 & 20.

32. Finnegan, *"A Delicate Affair" on the Western Front*, 193–285.

33. "101st Sanitary Train. 26th Division A.E.F. History," 175/358/624.

34. "101st Sanitary Train. 26th Division A.E.F. History," 176/359/625.

35. Beers to Mother, May 1, 1918, *Newtown Bee*, May 24, 1918.

36. Bodfish, *A History of Section 647, United States Army Ambulance Service with the French Army*, 29.

37. *Bridgeport Evening Post*, May 19, 1918; "101st Sanitary Train. 26th Division A.E.F. History," 173/356/622; Strickland, *Connecticut Fights*, 143. Lieutenant Comfort treated the wounded at the aid station for 36 hours straight.

38. Barlow, "World War Daily Diary of the 102nd Ambulance Company," April 17, 18, 19 & 20, 37; "101st Sanitary Train. 26th Division A.E.F. History," 174/357/623. Drury would receive a Croix de Guerre and Silver Star for bravery. Further back, an ambulance from the 101st Ambulance Company was blown off the road and driver John Burwell was mortally wounded, "101st Sanitary Train. 26th Division A.E.F. History," 173–74/356–57/622–23.

39. Finnegan, *"A Delicate Affair" on the Western Front*, 283.

40. Barlow, "World War Daily Diary of the 102nd Ambulance Company," April 17, 18, 19 & 20, 37.

41. Bodfish, *A History of Section 647, United States Army Ambulance Service with the French Army,* 31.

42. "101st Sanitary Train. 26th Division A.E.F. History," 177/360/626.

43. Wright to Parents, *Bridgeport Evening Post,* May 28, 1918.

44. Wall to Father, no date, *Bridgeport Post,* August 4, 1918.

45. Barlow, "World War World War Daily Diary of the 102nd Ambulance Company," April 21, 37.

46. "101st Sanitary Train. 26th Division A.E.F. History," 177/360/626.

47. Barlow, "World War Daily Diary of the 102nd Ambulance Company," April 17, 18, 19 & 20.

48. Wright to Parents, *Bridgeport Evening Post,* May 28, 1918.

49. Barlow, "World War Daily Diary of the 102nd Ambulance Company," April 22, 37.

50. Barlow, "World War Daily Diary of the 102nd Ambulance Company," April 22, 37.

51. Barlow, "World War Daily Diary of the 102nd Ambulance Company," April 22, 38.

52. Barlow, "World War Daily Diary of the 102nd Ambulance Company," Reminiscences, 98.

53. Barlow, "World War Daily Diary of the 102nd Ambulance Company," May 1, 2 & 3, 38.

54. *Bridgeport Post,* June 9, 1918.

55. Barlow, "World War Daily Diary of the 102nd Ambulance Company," May 1, 2 & 3, 38.

56. Barlow, "World War Daily Diary of the 102nd Ambulance Company," Reminiscences, 94.

57. Barlow, "World War Daily Diary of the 102nd Ambulance Company," April 28, 29 & 30, 38.

58. Barlow, "World War Daily Diary of the 102nd Ambulance Company," April 9, 10, 11, 12 & 13, 36.

59. Barlow, "World War Daily Diary of the 102nd Ambulance Company," May 1, 2 & 3, 38.

60. Barlow, "World War Daily Diary of the 102nd Ambulance Company," April 9, 10, 11, 12 & 13, 36.

61. *Bridgeport Telegram,* May 28, 1918.

62. Barlow, "World War Daily Diary of the 102nd Ambulance Company," May 9, 10 & 11, 39; Barlow, "Connecticut Boys Receive Baptism of Fire in France," *Bridgeport Post,* January 20, 1924.

63. Barlow, "World War Daily Diary of the 102nd Ambulance Company," May 7 & 8, 39.

64. Beers to Mother, May 1, 1918, *Newtown Bee,* May 24, 1918.

65. Wright to Parents, *Bridgeport Evening Post,* May 28, 1918.

66. Barlow to Bridgeport Comfort Club, July 30, 1918, in Leslie R. Barlow, *Letters to the Bridgeport Comfort Club from the Foreign Chapter in France* (Bridgeport: Author, 1919), 8.

67. Barlow, "World War Daily Diary of the 102nd Ambulance Company," April 23, 38.

68. Wall to Mother, May 31,1918, *Bridgeport Post,* August 4, 1918. The service stripe and wound stripe were authorized in General Order 26 of February 11, 1918.

69. Wills to Mother, May 12, 1918, *Bridgeport Evening Post,* June 2, 1918.

70. Wall to Mother, May 31,1918, *Bridgeport Post,* August 4, 1918.

71. Barlow, "World War Daily Diary of the 102nd Ambulance Company," May 13, 14, 15 & 16, 39.

72. Barlow, "World War Daily Diary of the 102nd Ambulance Company," May 17, 18 & 19, 39. Garvin's body would be returned to the U.S. after the war and buried in the family plot in North Canaan, Connecticut.

73. Barlow, "World War Daily Diary of the 102nd Ambulance Company," May 22, 23, 24 & 25, 40.

74. Barlow, "World War Daily Diary of the 102nd Ambulance Company," April 14, 15 & 16, 36; May 13, 14, 15 & 16, 39.

75. Barlow, "World War Daily Diary of the 102nd Ambulance Company," May 9, 10 & 11, 39.

76. Barlow, "Connecticut Boys Receive Baptism of Fire in France," *Bridgeport Post,* January 20, 1924.

77. Barlow, "World War Daily Diary of the 102nd Ambulance Company," April 24, 25, 26 & 27, 38.

78. Barlow, "World War Daily Diary of the 102nd Ambulance Company," May 7 & 8, 39.

79. Barlow, "World War Daily Diary of the 102nd Ambulance Company," June 3, 4, 5 & 6, 41.

80. Wills to Mother, May 12, 1918, *Bridgeport Evening Post,* June 2, 1918.

81. Wall to Mother, May 31,1918, *Bridgeport Post,* August 4, 1918.

82. Barlow, "World War Daily Diary of the 102nd Ambulance Company," April 5, 35.

83. *Medical Department of the U.S. Army in the World War,* 6, 1007–08.

84. E. G. Taylor, *New England in France, 1917–1919* (Boston: Houghton Mifflin, 1920), 138; *Medical Department of the U.S. Army in the World War,* 6, 1008; Charles F. Mason, *A Complete Handbook for the Sanitary Troops of the U.S. Army and Navy,* 4th ed. (New York: William Wood & Co., 1917), 298.

85. Barlow, "World War Daily Diary of the 102nd Ambulance Company," April 24, 25, 26 & 27, 38.

86. Barlow, "World War Daily Diary of the 102nd Ambulance Company," May 4, 5 & 6, 39.

87. In addition, "All spoiled clothing was classified and sent either to the corps laundry, which had begun operation at Nancy, or turned over to the Salvage Service, then beginning to operate," *Medical Department of the U.S. Army in the World War,* 6, 1008.

88. Unit 502 was photographed by the Signal Corps at Raulecourt on June 6, Signal Corps photographs 14609 and 14610.

89. Philip S. Wainwright, ed., *History of the 101st Machine Gun Battalion* (Hartford: 101st Machine Gun Battalion Association, 1922), 99; Fred A. McKenna, ed., *Battery A 103rd Field Artillery in France* (Providence?: n.p., 1919), 240.
90. *Medical Depart of the U.S. Army in the World War*, 6, 1008.
91. Narayan Sengupta, *American Eagles: The Illustrated History of American Aviation in World War I* (n.p.: author, 2012), 36–37, 117.
92. Sprague to Wife, May 16, 1918, *Bridgeport Evening Post*, June 12, 1918.
93. Sengupta, *American Eagles*, 124–25.
94. Barlow, "World War Daily Diary of the 102nd Ambulance Company," May 17, 18 & 19, 39.
95. Barlow, "World War Daily Diary of the 102nd Ambulance Company," May 19, 20 & 21, 40. In fact, Lufbery's father was American and lived at times in Wallingford, but his French wife had died when Lufbery was very young, and his father left him to be raised by maternal relatives in France.
96. Sprague to Wife, May 23, 1918, *Bridgeport Evening Post*, June 12, 1918.
97. Barlow, "World War Daily Diary of the 102nd Ambulance Company," June 2, 40.
98. Barlow, "World War Daily Diary of the 102nd Ambulance Company," May 12, 39.
99. Barlow, "World War Daily Diary of the 102nd Ambulance Company," May 13, 14, 15 & 16, 39.
100. Barlow, "World War Daily Diary of the 102nd Ambulance Company," May 19, 20 & 21, 40. For a photograph of the performance, taken by a member of the 102nd Machine Gun Battalion, now in the Norwich University Archives, see https://archives.norwich.edu/digital/collection/p16663coll1/id/3755/.
101. Elsie Janis, *The Big Show: My Six Months with the American Expeditionary Forces* (New York: Cosmopolitan Book Corp., 1919), 60–61, 56–78.
102. Barlow, "World War Daily Diary of the 102nd Ambulance Company," May 22, 23, 24 & 25, 40.
103. Bailey to Wife, May 29, 1918, author's collection.
104. Janis, *The Big Show: My Six Months with the American Expeditionary Forces*, 60–61.
105. Barlow, "World War Daily Diary of the 102nd Ambulance Company," June 3, 4, 5 & 6, 41.
106. Barlow, "World War Daily Diary of the 102nd Ambulance Company," May 30, 40; Barlow, "Connecticut Boys Receive Baptism of Fire in France," *Bridgeport Post*, January 20, 1924.
107. Barlow, "World War Daily Diary of the 102nd Ambulance Company," May 4, 5 & 6, 39.
108. Barlow, "World War Daily Diary of the 102nd Ambulance Company," May 7 & 8, 39.
109. Michael E. Shay, *A Grateful Heart: The History of a World War I Field Hospital* (Westport, CT: Greenwood Press, 2002), 64.
110. Barlow, "World War Daily Diary of the 102nd Ambulance Company," May 4, 5 & 6, 39.
111. Barlow, "World War Daily Diary of the 102nd Ambulance Company," May 9, 10 & 11, 39.
112. Barlow, "World War Daily Diary of the 102nd Ambulance Company," May 13, 14, 15 & 16, 39.
113. Barlow, "World War Daily Diary of the 102nd Ambulance Company," May 26, 27 & 28, 40.
114. Barlow noted the move of the 102nd Field Hospital, "World War Daily Diary of the 102nd Ambulance Company," June 2, 41.
115. Barlow, "World War Daily Diary of the 102nd Ambulance Company," June 2, 41.
116. Barlow, "World War Daily Diary of the 102nd Ambulance Company," June 2, 41.
117. Barlow, "World War Daily Diary of the 102nd Ambulance Company," May 26, 27 & 28, 40.
118. Barlow, "World War Daily Diary of the 102nd Ambulance Company," May 17, 18 & 19, 39.
119. Barlow, "World War Daily Diary of the 102nd Ambulance Company," May 29, 40.
120. Barlow, "World War Daily Diary of the 102nd Ambulance Company," June 1, 41.
121. Barlow, "Connecticut Boys Receive Baptism of Fire in France," *Bridgeport Post*, January 20, 1924.
122. Barlow, "Connecticut Boys Receive Baptism of Fire in France," *Bridgeport Post*, January 20, 1924.
123. Barlow, "World War Daily Diary of the 102nd Ambulance Company," June 3, 4, 5 & 6, 41.
124. Jonathan H. Jaffin, "Medical Support for the American Expeditionary Forces in France During the First World War," Thesis, Master of Military Art and Science, U.S. Army Command and General Staff College, Fort Leavenworth, KS, 1991, 90, https://apps.dtic.mil/sti/pdfs/ADA241174.pdf, accessed February 2022. Later, with the arrival of new divisions, the supply would be 50 percent below the requirements in September and 20 percent below in October.
125. Barlow, "World War Daily Diary of the 102nd Ambulance Company," May 17, 18 & 19, 39; Barlow, "Connecticut Boys Receive Baptism of Fire in France," *Bridgeport Post*, January 20, 1924.
126. Wall to Father, *Bridgeport Post*, August 4, 1918.
127. *GMC Ambulances* (Pontiac, MI: General Motors Truck Co., ca. 1917), 8–11.
128. Barlow, "World War Daily Diary of the 102nd Ambulance Company," May 30, 40.
129. Barlow, "World War Daily Diary of the 102nd Ambulance Company," May 31, 41.
130. Barlow, "World War Daily Diary of the 102nd Ambulance Company," May 31, 41.
131. Bodfish, *Section 647*, 34.
132. *Bridgeport Evening Post*, May 5, 1919; WW1 Veterans, Connecticut Soldiers Questionnaires, 1919, https://ctstatelibrary.org/ww-1-veterans/, accessed October 2021.
133. Barlow, "Connecticut Boys Receive Baptism of Fire in France," *Bridgeport Post*, January 20, 1924.
134. Bodfish, *Section 647*, 34. In the reminiscences

he added to his Company diary, Barlow remarked about the men of SSU 647: "we feel proud of your having been with us. You were soldiers and gentlemen all," Barlow, "World War Daily Diary of the 102nd Ambulance Company," Reminiscences, 96.

135. Bodfish, *Section 647*, 34.

136. Barlow, "World War Daily Diary of the 102nd Ambulance Company," June 21, 22, 23 & 24, 42.

137. Barlow, "World War Daily Diary of the 102nd Ambulance Company," June 25, 26 & 27, 42.

138. Barlow, "World War Daily Diary of the 102nd Ambulance Company," June 28 & 29, 42.

Chapter 7

1. Michael E. Shay, *A Grateful Heart: The History of a World War I Field Hospital* (Westport, CT: Greenwood Press, 2002), 66; Leslie R. Barlow, "World War Daily Diary of the 102nd Ambulance Company," July 1, 43.

2. Shay, *A Grateful Heart*, 66; Barlow, "World War Daily Diary of the 102nd Ambulance Company," typescript, Connecticut State Archives, July 2, 43.

3. Barlow, "World War Daily Diary of the 102nd Ambulance Company," July 2, 43.

4. Barlow to Bridgeport Comfort Club, August 4, 1918, in Leslie R. Barlow, *Letters to the Bridgeport Comfort Club from the Foreign Chapter in France* (Bridgeport: Author, 1919), 9.

5. Barlow, "World War Daily Diary of the 102nd Ambulance Company," July 3, 43; Shay, *A Grateful Heart*, 66. On the 4th of July parade in Paris, see Harvey Cushing, *From a Surgeon's Journal, 1915–1918* (Boston: Little, Brown & Company, 1936), 394–95.

6. Barlow, "World War Daily Diary of the 102nd Ambulance Company," July 3, 43.

7. American Battle Monuments Commission, *26th Division, Summary of Operations in the World War* (Washington, DC: Government Printing Office, 1944), 6–10.

8. Barlow, "World War Daily Diary of the 102nd Ambulance Company," July 4, 43–44.

9. Barlow, "World War Daily Diary of the 102nd Ambulance Company," July 5, 44.

10. Barlow, "World War Daily Diary of the 102nd Ambulance Company," July 6 & 7, July 4, 44.

11. Barlow, "World War Daily Diary of the 102nd Ambulance Company," July 8 & 9, 44; "101st Sanitary Train. 26th Division A.E.F. History," March 1919, photostat typescript in Records, 1917–1919, 26th Division, United States Army, War Records Department, Record Group No. 012, Part II, Series No.040, Connecticut State Archives, Hartford, 185–86/368–69/634–35. The page number sequence represents the digital version/typescript/photostat numbers. According to Leslie R. Barlow, this was actually written by Earle E. Radikin, who was detailed to produce it for the Sanitary Train in February 1919.

12. Barlow, "World War Daily Diary of the 102nd Ambulance Company," Reminiscences, 97.

13. "101st Sanitary Train. 26th Division A.E.F. History," 185–86/368–69/634–35; Shay, *A Grateful Heart*, 81, 85; Cushing, *From a Surgeon's Journal*, 393–94.

14. Barlow, "World War Daily Diary of the 102nd Ambulance Company," July 8 & 9, 44.

15. Barlow, "World War Daily Diary of the 102nd Ambulance Company," July 12, 13 & 14, 45.

16. Barlow, "World War Daily Diary of the 102nd Ambulance Company," July 11, 44.

17. Barlow, "World War Daily Diary of the 102nd Ambulance Company," July 10, 44.

18. Barlow, "World War Daily Diary of the 102nd Ambulance Company," July 10, 44; Reminiscences, 81; Barlow's letters would be published in the *Bridgeport Telegram* and in Barlow, *Letters to the Bridgeport Comfort Club.*

19. *The Stars and Stripes*, March 29, 1918; Elizabeth M. Motich, "Orphans of the Front in World War I, Remembering WWI," https://rememberingwwi.villanova.edu/orphans/, accessed April 2022.

20. Barlow, "World War Daily Diary of the 102nd Ambulance Company," July 12, 13 & 14, 45.

21. Barlow, "World War Daily Diary of the 102nd Ambulance Company," July 12, 13 & 14, 45.

22. Barlow to Bridgeport Comfort Club, August 11, 1918, in Barlow, *Letters to the Bridgeport Comfort Club*, 13.

23. Barlow, "World War Daily Diary of the 102nd Ambulance Company," July 12, 13 & 14, 45.

24. Barlow, "World War Daily Diary of the 102nd Ambulance Company," July 10, 44.

25. Barlow, "World War Daily Diary of the 102nd Ambulance Company," July 11, 44.

26. Barlow, "World War Daily Diary of the 102nd Ambulance Company," July 12, 13 & 14, 45.

27. American Battle Monuments Commission, *26th Division, Summary of Operations in the World War*, 10.

28. Barlow, "World War Daily Diary of the 102nd Ambulance Company," July 15, 16 & 17, 45.

29. Barlow, "World War Daily Diary of the 102nd Ambulance Company," July 15, 16 & 17, 45.

30. Earle E. Radikin, "The Kamerad Kid," *War Stories* 18, number 53 (March 28, 1929): 122.

31. Radikin, "The Kamerad Kid," 123.

32. Circular #98, in addition to AEF Bulletin #46, ca. July 12, 1918, in Barlow, "Daily Diary of the 102nd Ambulance Company," 91. The full list of medical code words was: Ambulance (Dog), litters (Cat), litter squad (Slat), walking wounded (Cog), recumbent wounded (Duck), sitting wounded (Nat), dressings (Pad), gasoline (Log), battalion aid station (Pup), dressing station (Bid), field hospital (Fit), anti-tetanus serum (Min), other Allied troops (Stranger), enemies (Visitors).

33. "101st Sanitary Train. 26th Division A.E.F. History," 185/368/634; American Battle Monuments Commission, *26th Division, Summary of Operations in the World War*, 9–12; Frank P. Sibley,

With the Yankee Division in France (Boston: Little, Brown, 1919), 204.

34. Barlow to Bridgeport Comfort Club, August 4, 1918, in Barlow, *Letters to the Bridgeport Comfort Club*, 10.

35. "101st Sanitary Train. 26th Division A.E.F. History," 185–86/368–69/634–35.

36. "101st Sanitary Train. 26th Division A.E.F. History," 185–86/368–69/634–35.

37. "101st Sanitary Train. 26th Division A.E.F. History," 185–86/368–69/634–35.

38. "101st Sanitary Train. 26th Division A.E.F. History," 187/370/636.

39. Radikin, "The Kamerad Kid," 124.

40. Nomination for DSC, Clyde Johnston, December 2, 1918, photostat in Records, 1917–1919, 26th Division, United States Army, War Records Department, Record Group No. 012, Part II, Series No.040, Connecticut State Archives, Hartford.

41. "101st Sanitary Train. 26th Division A.E.F. History,"187/370/636.

42. Barlow, "World War Daily Diary of the 102nd Ambulance Company," July 18 & 19, 45.

43. Nomination for DSC, Clyde Johnston, December 2, 1918.

44. Bailey to Wife, July 27, 1918, author's collection; Bailey would receive a Distinguished Service Cross for bravery in saving and tending to these men. In December, Captain Johnston would nominate Lieutenant Durham for a DSC for his bravery in retrieving them, Nomination for DSC, Clyde Johnston, December 2, 1918.

45. American Battle Monuments Commission, *26th Division, Summary of Operations in the World War*, 15.

46. Barlow, "World War Daily Diary of the 102nd Ambulance Company," July 20 & 21, 41.

47. Barlow, "World War Daily Diary of the 102nd Ambulance Company," July 22, 45. In his diary, Barlow says "We advanced to Paris Farm, just above the town of Chateau Thierry." However, Paris Farm was at a crossroads between Bezu-le-Guery and La Voie du Chatel, well behind the original battleline, so it is likely he was describing the dressing station at Farsoy Farm, less than two kilometers directly north of Chateau Thierry.

48. Barlow, "World War Daily Diary of the 102nd Ambulance Company," July 22, 46.

49. Barlow, "World War Daily Diary of the 102nd Ambulance Company," July 22, 46.

50. "101st Sanitary Train. 26th Division A.E.F. History," 188/371/637.

51. "101st Sanitary Train. 26th Division A.E.F. History," 188/371/637.

52. Barlow, "World War Daily Diary of the 102nd Ambulance Company," July 20 & 21, 45.

53. Barlow, "World War Daily Diary of the 102nd Ambulance Company," July 23, 47.

54. *History of the 101st United States Engineers, American Expeditionary Forces, 1917–1918–1919* (Cambridge, MA: Committee of the Regiment, 1926), 210.

55. "101st Sanitary Train. 26th Division A.E.F. History," 188/371/637.

56. Barlow, "World War Daily Diary of the 102nd Ambulance Company," July 22, 46.

57. Barlow, "World War Daily Diary of the 102nd Ambulance Company," July 22, 46. On shell shock, see Shay, *A Grateful Heart*, 200–02.

58. Strickland, *Connecticut Fights*, 189.

59. *History of the 101st United States Engineers*, 210. The historian may have mistaken the GMC ambulances for 3-ton army vehicles built by the White Motor Company.

60. Radikin, "The Kamerad Kid," 121–22. Radikin personalized the story to the degree of giving the protagonist his service number, 3377.

61. *Manual for the Medical Department, United States Army, 1916, Corrected to June 15,1918* (Washington, DC: Government Printing Office, 1918), 248, 294; Shay, *A Grateful Heart*, 198; Peter C. Wever, "Prevention of Tetanus During the First World War," *Medical Humanities* 38, issue 2 (December 2012): 78–82.

62. Barlow, "World War Daily Diary of the 102nd Ambulance Company," July 22, 46.

63. Barlow, "World War Daily Diary of the 102nd Ambulance Company," July 23, 46.

64. Barlow, "World War Daily Diary of the 102nd Ambulance Company," July 22, 46.

65. Wall to Mother, September 3, 1918, *Bridgeport Telegram*, November 4, 1918; "101st Sanitary Train. 26th Division A.E.F. History," 188/371/637.

66. Barlow, "World War Daily Diary of the 102nd Ambulance Company," July 22, 46.

67. Barlow, "World War Daily Diary of the 102nd Ambulance Company," July 22, 46.

68. *History of the 101st United States Engineers*, 210.

69. "101st Sanitary Train. 26th Division A.E.F. History," 187/370/636; Barlow, "World War Daily Diary of the 102nd Ambulance Company," Reminiscences, 97.

70. "101st Sanitary Train. 26th Division A.E.F. History," History of the 101st Sanitary Train, 188/371/637.

71. "101st Sanitary Train. 26th Division A.E.F. History," 189/372/638.

72. Barlow, "World War Daily Diary of the 102nd Ambulance Company," July 22, 46.

73. Barlow, "World War Daily Diary of the 102nd Ambulance Company," July 23, 46.

74. Barlow, "World War Daily Diary of the 102nd Ambulance Company," July 23, 46–47.

75. American Battle Monuments Commission, *26th Division, Summary of Operations in the World War*, 17–20.

76. Barlow, "World War Daily Diary of the 102nd Ambulance Company," July 25 & 26, 47.

77. Barlow, "World War Daily Diary of the 102nd Ambulance Company," July 25 & 26, 47.

78. George Watt to Sister, August 10, 1918, *Bridgeport Telegram*, October 1, 1918.

Chapter 8

1. Leslie R. Barlow, "World War Daily Diary of the 102nd Ambulance Company," typescript, Connecticut State Archives, July 27 & 28, 47.

2. Barlow, "World War Daily Diary of the 102nd Ambulance Company," July 29 & 30, 47.

3. Barlow, "World War Daily Diary of the 102nd Ambulance Company," Reminiscences, 97.

4. Barlow, "World War Daily Diary of the 102nd Ambulance Company," August 2 & 3, 48.

5. Orders No. 114, July 14, 1918, Copies of U.S. Army records pertaining to the 26th Division, 1917–19, Connecticut State Archives Record Group No. 012, Part II, Series No.040, Box 12: Nos. 4474–5585, Connecticut State Archives, Hartford.

6. Barlow, "World War Daily Diary of the 102nd Ambulance Company," July 29 & 30, 47.

7. *History of the 101st Engineers, American Expeditionary Forces, 1917–1918–1919* (Boston: Regimental Committee, 1926), 224; Daniel W. Strickland, *Connecticut Fights: The Story of the 102nd Regiment* (New Haven: Quinnipiack Press, 1930), 202.

8. "Sanitation," *U.S. Army Medical Department in the World War*, vol. 6, 1022; Barlow, "World War Daily Diary of the 102nd Ambulance Company," August 1, 47.

9. Michael E. Shay, *A Grateful Heart: The History of a World War I Field Hospital* (Westport, CT: Greenwood Press, 2002), 80.

10. Barlow to Bridgeport Comfort Club, August 4, 1918, in Leslie R. Barlow, *Letters to the Bridgeport Comfort Club from the Foreign Chapter in France* (Bridgeport: Author, 1919), 12.

11. Barlow, "World War Daily Diary of the 102nd Ambulance Company," July 31, 47.

12. Barlow, "World War Daily Diary of the 102nd Ambulance Company," August 1, 48.

13. Barlow, "World War Daily Diary of the 102nd Ambulance Company," August 4 & 5, 48.

14. Barlow, "World War Daily Diary of the 102nd Ambulance Company," August 2 & 3, 48; Shay, *A Grateful Heart*, 87.

15. Barlow, "World War Daily Diary of the 102nd Ambulance Company," August 4 & 5, 48.

16. Barlow, "World War Daily Diary of the 102nd Ambulance Company," August 6, 7, 8 & 9, 48.

17. Barlow to Bridgeport Comfort Club, August 11, 1918, in Barlow, *Letters to the Bridgeport Comfort Club*, 14.

18. Barlow to Bridgeport Comfort Club, August 4, 1918, in Barlow, *Letters to the Bridgeport Comfort Club*, 12. Barlow alludes to the fact that many men kept their polished metal pocket mirror for shaving in their left breast pocket.

19. Barlow, "World War Daily Diary of the 102nd Ambulance Company," August 4 & 5, 48.

20. Barlow, "World War Daily Diary of the 102nd Ambulance Company," August 1, 48.

21. Barlow, "World War Daily Diary of the 102nd Ambulance Company," August 6, 7, 8 & 9, 48.

22. Barlow, "World War Daily Diary of the 102nd Ambulance Company," August 1, 48.

23. Barlow to Bridgeport Comfort Club, August 11, 1918, in Barlow, *Letters to the Bridgeport Comfort Club*, 12–13.

24. Barlow, "World War Daily Diary of the 102nd Ambulance Company," August 4 & 5, 48.

25. Barlow to Bridgeport Comfort Club, August 11, 1918, in Barlow, *Letters to the Bridgeport Comfort Club*, 13.

26. Barlow to Bridgeport Comfort Club, August 22, 1918, in Barlow, *Letters to the Bridgeport Comfort Club*, 18.

27. Barlow, "World War Daily Diary of the 102nd Ambulance Company," August 13, 49.

28. Barlow to Bridgeport Comfort Club, August 22, 1918, in Barlow, *Letters to the Bridgeport Comfort Club*, 16.

29. Barlow, "World War Daily Diary of the 102nd Ambulance Company," August 14, 49.

30. Barlow, "World War Daily Diary of the 102nd Ambulance Company," August 15, 49.

31. Barlow to Bridgeport Comfort Club, August 22, 1918, in Barlow, *Letters to the Bridgeport Comfort Club*, 17.

32. Barlow to Bridgeport Comfort Club, August 22, 1918, in Barlow, *Letters to the Bridgeport Comfort Club*, 20.

33. Barlow, "World War Daily Diary of the 102nd Ambulance Company," August 13, 49.

34. Barlow, "World War Daily Diary of the 102nd Ambulance Company," Nicknames, 88.

35. Barlow to Bridgeport Comfort Club, August 22, 1918, in Barlow, *Letters to the Bridgeport Comfort Club*, 17.

36. Barlow, "World War Daily Diary of the 102nd Ambulance Company," August 17 & 18, 43; Barlow to Bridgeport Comfort Club, August 22, 1918, in Barlow, *Letters to the Bridgeport Comfort Club*, 17.

37. Barlow, "World War Daily Diary of the 102nd Ambulance Company," August 25, 26, 27 & 28, 43.

38. Barlow, "World War Daily Diary of the 102nd Ambulance Company," August 4 & 5, 48. Sergeant Holzheimer replaced him.

39. Barlow, "World War Daily Diary of the 102nd Ambulance Company," August 6, 7, 8 & 9, 48.

40. Barlow, "World War Daily Diary of the 102nd Ambulance Company," August 2 & 3, 48.

41. Barlow, "World War Daily Diary of the 102nd Ambulance Company," August 10, 11 & 12, 48–49.

42. Barlow, "World War Daily Diary of the 102nd Ambulance Company," August 17 & 18, 43.

43. Barlow, "World War Daily Diary of the 102nd Ambulance Company," August 1, 4.

44. Barlow, "World War Daily Diary of the 102nd Ambulance Company," August 19 & 20, 43.

45. Barlow, "World War Daily Diary of the 102nd Ambulance Company," August 19 & 20, 43.

46. Barlow, "World War Daily Diary of the

102nd Ambulance Company," August 21, 22, 23 & 24, 43.

47. Barlow, "World War Daily Diary of the 102nd Ambulance Company," August 25, 26, 27 & 28, 43.

48. Barlow, "World War Daily Diary of the 102nd Ambulance Company," July 31, 47.

49. "101st Sanitary Train. 26th Division A.E.F. History," March 1919, photostat typescript in Records, 1917–1919, 26th Division, United States Army, War Records Department, Connecticut State Archives Record Group No. 012, Part II, Series No.040, Connecticut State Archives, Hartford, 190/373/639. According to Leslie R. Barlow, this was actually written by Earle E. Radikin, who was detailed to produce it for the Sanitary Train in February 1919; "Division Surgeon's Report: Twenty-Sixth Division," Appendix E, Report of the Surgeon General of the Army, *War Department Annual Reports, 1919*, part 3 (Washington, DC: Government Printing Office, 1920), 3301.

50. Beers to Mother, September 5, 1910, *Newtown Bee*, October 4, 1918.

Chapter 9

1. Harvey Cushing, *From a Surgeon's Journal, 1915–1918* (Boston: Little, Brown & Company, 1936), 394.

2. American Battle Monuments Commission, *26th Division, Summary of Operations in the World War* (Washington, DC: Government Printing Office, 1944), 22–23.

3. Leslie R. Barlow, "World War Daily Diary of the 102nd Ambulance Company," typescript, Connecticut State Archives, August 29, 50.

4. Barlow, "World War Daily Diary of the 102nd Ambulance Company," August 31, 50.

5. Barlow, "World War Daily Diary of the 102nd Ambulance Company," September 1, 50.

6. Barlow, "World War Daily Diary of the 102nd Ambulance Company," September 1, 50–51.

7. Barlow, "World War Daily Diary of the 102nd Ambulance Company," September 2, 3 & 4, 51.

8. James to Father, September 10, 1918, *Newtown Bee*, November 1, 1918.

9. Wall to Mother, September 5, 1918, *Bridgeport Telegram*, November 4, 1918; the other men from the Company cited here were ambulance drivers Curtis Banks and Earle Radikin, orderly William McElroy, and Privates Michael Kwasniski, George Stevens, and Roy Thompson, Barlow to Bridgeport Comfort Club, September 18, 1918, in Leslie R. Barlow, *Letters to the Bridgeport Comfort Club from the Foreign Chapter in France* (Bridgeport: Author, 1919), 24.

10. Wall to Mother, September 5, 1918, *Bridgeport Telegram*, November 4, 1918.

11. Wall to Mother, September 5, 1918, *Bridgeport Telegram*, November 4, 1918.

12. Barlow, "World War Daily Diary of the 102nd Ambulance Company," September 5 & 6, 51.

13. Barlow, "World War Daily Diary of the 102nd Ambulance Company," September 5 & 6, 51.

14. James to Father, September 10, 1918, *Newtown Bee*, November 1, 1918.

15. Barlow, "World War Daily Diary of the 102nd Ambulance Company," September 5 & 6, 51.

16. Barlow, "World War Daily Diary of the 102nd Ambulance Company," September 7, 51.

17. Peck to Mother, September 8, 1918, *Newtown Bee*, October 25, 1918.

18. Barlow, "World War Daily Diary of the 102nd Ambulance Company," September 8, 51.

19. Barlow to Bridgeport Comfort Club, September 18, 1918, in Barlow, *Letters to the Bridgeport Comfort Club*, 26; the dugout complex is depicted in National Archives and Records Administration, U.S. Signal Corps films, "The St. Mihiel Offensive, September 10–25, 1918, 26th Division," 111.H.1325, https://www.youtube.com/watch?v=K8eILOcKWdY. The Company's Noyon dressing station and ambulances, plus 104th Ambulance Company horse-drawn ambulances, are shown from 5:49 to 6:32.

20. "101st Sanitary Train. 26th Division A.E.F. History," March 1919, photostat typescript in Records, 1917–1919, 26th Division, United States Army, War Records Department, Connecticut State Archives Record Group No. 012, Part II, Series No. 040, Connecticut State Archives, Hartford, 191/374/640. Leslie R. Barlow recorded that Earle E. Radikin was detailed to produce this history of the Sanitary Train in February 1919.

21. Barlow, "World War Daily Diary of the 102nd Ambulance Company," September 9, 51.

22. Barlow, "World War Daily Diary of the 102nd Ambulance Company," September 9, 51; Barlow to Bridgeport Comfort Club, September 18, 1918, in Barlow, *Letters to the Bridgeport Comfort Club*, 26.

23. American Battle Monuments Commission, *26th Division, Summary of Operations in the World War*, 26–30.

24. Barlow, "World War Daily Diary of the 102nd Ambulance Company," September 11, 52.

25. Barlow, "World War Daily Diary of the 102nd Ambulance Company," September 12, 52.

26. Barlow, "World War Daily Diary of the 102nd Ambulance Company," September 12, 52. Although the front line was well constructed, with deep trenches and concrete dugouts, the actual Hindenburg Line in this sector was far to the rear, see American Battle Monuments Commission, *26th Division, Summary of Operations in the World War*, 23–24.

27. Barlow, "World War Daily Diary of the 102nd Ambulance Company," September 12, 52.

28. "101st Sanitary Train. 26th Division A.E.F. History," 192/375/641.

29. Barlow, "World War Daily Diary of the 102nd Ambulance Company," September 13 & 14, 53.

30. Barlow, "World War Daily Diary of the 102nd Ambulance Company," Reminiscences, 98.
31. "101st Sanitary Train. 26th Division A.E.F. History," 192/375/641.
32. Barlow, "World War Daily Diary of the 102nd Ambulance Company," September 13, 52.
33. Barlow, "World War Daily Diary of the 102nd Ambulance Company," Reminiscences, 93.
34. American Battle Monuments Commission, *26th Division, Summary of Operations in the World War*, 26–30.
35. Barlow, "World War Daily Diary of the 102nd Ambulance Company," September 13 & 14, 53.
36. Peck to Mother, September 19, 1918, *Newtown Bee*, October 25, 1918.
37. American Battle Monuments Commission, *26th Division, Summary of Operations in the World War*,42–43.
38. "101st Sanitary Train. 26th Division A.E.F. History," 192/375/641.
39. Barlow, "World War Daily Diary of the 102nd Ambulance Company," September 15, 53.
40. Barlow to Bridgeport Comfort Club, September 18, 1918, in Barlow, *Letters to the Bridgeport Comfort Club*, 27.
41. Barlow to Bridgeport Comfort Club, September 18, 1918, in Barlow, *Letters to the Bridgeport Comfort Club*, 27.
42. Barlow, "World War Daily Diary of the 102nd Ambulance Company," September 16, 17 & 18, 53.
43. Barlow, "World War Daily Diary of the 102nd Ambulance Company," September 19 & 20, 53.
44. Barlow, "World War Daily Diary of the 102nd Ambulance Company," September 16, 17 & 18, 53.
45. Barlow to Bridgeport Comfort Club, October 1, 1918, in Barlow, *Letters to the Bridgeport Comfort Club*, 31.
46. Peck to Mother, September 19, 1918, *Newtown Bee*, October 25, 1918.
47. Edward G. Lengel, *To Conquer Hell: The Meuse-Argonne, 1918* (New York: Henry Holt, 2008), 69; American Battle Monuments Commission, *26th Division, Summary of Operations in the World War*, 49.
48. Barlow, "World War Daily Diary of the 102nd Ambulance Company," September 21, 22 & 23, 54.
49. Circular Letter 96, Office of Division Surgeon, September 23, 1918, photostat typescript in Records, 1917–1919, 26th Division, United States Army, War Records Department, Connecticut State Archives Record Group No. 012, Part II, Series No. 040, Connecticut State Archives, Hartford.
50. Lengel, *To Conquer Hell: The Meuse-Argonne, 1918*, 69; American Battle Monuments Commission, *26th Division, Summary of Operations in the World War*, 49.
51. American Battle Monuments Commission, *26th Division, Summary of Operations in the World War*, 45.
52. Beers to Mother, September 25, 1918, *Newtown Bee*, November 1, 1918.
53. "101st Sanitary Train. 26th Division A.E.F. History," 192/375/641.
54. American Battle Monuments Commission, *26th Division, Summary of Operations in the World War*, 45; Barlow, "World War Daily Diary of the 102nd Ambulance Company," September 24 & 25, 54.
55. Barlow, "World War Daily Diary of the 102nd Ambulance Company," September 24 & 25, 54.
56. Frank P. Sibley, *With the Yankee Division in France* (Boston: Little, Brown, 1919), 288–89.
57. American Battle Monuments Commission, *26th Division, Summary of Operations in the World War*, 45–46.
58. American Battle Monuments Commission, *26th Division, Summary of Operations in the World War*, 45.
59. Charles R. Cabot, *History of the 103rd Infantry, August, 1917, to November, 1918* (n.p.: 103rd U.S. Infantry, 1919), 25; American Battle Monuments Commission, *26th Division, Summary of Operations in the World War*, 45–46.
60. Barlow, "World War Daily Diary of the 102nd Ambulance Company," Reminiscences, 97.
61. Cabot, *History of the 103rd Infantry*, 25.
62. Barlow, "World War Daily Diary of the 102nd Ambulance Company," September 24 & 25, 54.
63. For instance, Barlow had noted the arrival of eight drafted men trained at Camp Greenleaf on September 20, Barlow, "World War Daily Diary of the 102nd Ambulance Company," September 19 & 20, 53.
64. "101st Sanitary Train. 26th Division A.E.F. History," 192/375/641.
65. Barlow, "World War Daily Diary of the 102nd Ambulance Company," September 26, 54.
66. "101st Sanitary Train. 26th Division A.E.F. History," 193/376/642.
67. "101st Sanitary Train. 26th Division A.E.F. History," 193/376/642.
68. "101st Sanitary Train. 26th Division A.E.F. History," 153/336/602; Barlow, "World War Daily Diary of the 102nd Ambulance Company," September 26, 54.
69. Emerson Gifford Taylor, *New England in France 1917–1919: A History of the Twenty-Sixth Division U.S.A.* (Boston: Houghton Mifflin, 1920), 238.
70. Cabot, *History of the 103rd Infantry*, 25.
71. Barlow, "World War Daily Diary of the 102nd Ambulance Company," 77. Captain Taylor commanded the 103rd Ambulance Company.
72. 330.1 (C.O. Tr) General Edwards to Captain Herbert W. Taylor, commanding Ambulance Section, in Barlow, "World War Daily Diary of the 102nd Ambulance Company," 75.
73. 102nd Ambulance Company, Miscellaneous

Correspondence, photostat typescript in Records, 1917–1919, 26th Division, United States Army, War Records Department, Connecticut State Archives Record Group No. 012, Part II, Series No.040, Box 11: 8412–8422, Connecticut State Archives, Hartford.

74. 102nd Ambulance Company, Miscellaneous Correspondence.

75. Barlow, "World War Daily Diary of the 102nd Ambulance Company," September 24 & 25, 54.

76. Barlow, "World War Daily Diary of the 102nd Ambulance Company," September 24 & 25, 54; *Welcome Home YD* (Boston: Everett Press, 1919).

77. Barlow, "World War Daily Diary of the 102nd Ambulance Company," September 27, 28 & 29, 55.

78. Peck to Mother, September 27, 1918, *Newtown Bee*, October 25, 1918.

79. Barlow to Bridgeport Comfort Club, November 3, 1918, in Barlow, *Letters to the Bridgeport Comfort Club*, 37.

80. Barlow, "World War Daily Diary of the 102nd Ambulance Company," October 1, 2 & 3, 55; Barlow to Bridgeport Comfort Club, November 3, 1918, in Barlow, *Letters to the Bridgeport Comfort Club*, 35.

81. Barlow, "World War Daily Diary of the 102nd Ambulance Company," October 1, 2 & 3, 55.

82. Barlow to Bridgeport Comfort Club, November 3, 1918, in Barlow, *Letters to the Bridgeport Comfort Club*, 34.

83. Barlow, "World War Daily Diary of the 102nd Ambulance Company," October 1, 2 & 3, 55.

84. Barlow, "World War Daily Diary of the 102nd Ambulance Company," Reminiscenses, 98; Barlow to Bridgeport Comfort Club, November 3, 1918, in Barlow, *Letters to the Bridgeport Comfort Club*, 34.

85. Cabot, *History of the 103rd Infantry*, 25.

86. Barlow, "World War Daily Diary of the 102nd Ambulance Company," October 1, 2 & 3, 55.

87. Barlow, "World War Daily Diary of the 102nd Ambulance Company," October 1, 2 & 3, 55.

88. Barlow to Bridgeport Comfort Club, November 3, 1918, in Barlow, *Letters to the Bridgeport Comfort Club*, 34.

89. Barlow, "World War Daily Diary of the 102nd Ambulance Company," October 4 & 5, 55.

90. Beers to Mother, September 25, 1918, *Newtown Bee*, November 1, 1918.

91. Barlow, "World War Daily Diary of the 102nd Ambulance Company," October 4 & 5, 55.

92. Barlow, "World War Daily Diary of the 102nd Ambulance Company," October 4 & 5, 55.

93. Barlow mentioned their motorcycles in Barlow to Bridgeport Comfort Club, November 3, 1918, in Barlow, *Letters to the Bridgeport Comfort Club*, 35; each ambulance company was authorized to have six motorcycles.

94. *Bridgeport Telegram*, Dec. 2, 1918. While Keane's encounter with shrapnel from an "Austrian 88" shell earned him an award, Barlow recorded, "A piece of shrapnel went through the sleeve of Bert Keane but did not even scratch him," Barlow, "World War Daily Diary of the 102nd Ambulance Company," October 4 & 5, 55. Keane would be awarded a Croix de Guerre for this action.

95. Barlow, "World War Daily Diary of the 102nd Ambulance Company," October 4 & 5, 55.

96. Barlow, "World War Daily Diary of the 102nd Ambulance Company," October 4 & 5, 55.

97. Lengel, *To Conquer Hell: The Meuse-Argonne, 1918*, 96–103, 186, 204.

98. American Battle Monuments Commission, *26th Division, Summary of Operations in the World War*, 48.

Chapter 10

1. Michael A. Shay, *A Grateful Heart: The History of a World War I Field Hospital* (Westport, CT: Greenwood Press, 2002), 115.

2. Leslie R. Barlow, "World War Daily Diary of the 102nd Ambulance Company," October 6, 7 & 8, 55, Connecticut State Archives, Hartford.

3. Barlow, "World War Daily Diary of the 102nd Ambulance Company," October 7 & 8, 56.

4. Barlow, "World War Daily Diary of the 102nd Ambulance Company," October 10 & 11, 56.

5. Barlow, "World War Daily Diary of the 102nd Ambulance Company," Columbus Day, 56.

6. Barlow, "World War Daily Diary of the 102nd Ambulance Company," October 13 & 14, 56.

7. Barlow, "World War Daily Diary of the 102nd Ambulance Company," October 7 & 8, 56, October 10 & 11, 56. The sick men were Sergeant James Neil, Corporal George Widinghoff, and Privates George Ferris and Lewis Trembly.

8. Barlow, "World War Daily Diary of the 102nd Ambulance Company," October 4 & 5, 55; Barlow to Bridgeport Comfort Club, November 1918, in Leslie R. Barlow, *Letters to the Bridgeport Comfort Club from the Foreign Chapter in France* (Bridgeport: Author, 1919), 39.

9. Barlow to Bridgeport Comfort Club, November 3, 1918, in Barlow, *Letters to the Bridgeport Comfort Club*, 36.

10. Barlow, "World War Daily Diary of the 102nd Ambulance Company," Columbus Day, 56.

11. Barlow, "World War Daily Diary of the 102nd Ambulance Company," Columbus Day, 56.

12. Barlow, "World War Daily Diary of the 102nd Ambulance Company," Columbus Day, 56.

13. Barlow to Bridgeport Comfort Club, November 1918, in Barlow, *Letters to the Bridgeport Comfort Club*, 38.

14. Barlow to Bridgeport Comfort Club, November 1918, in Barlow, *Letters to the Bridgeport Comfort Club*, 38.

15. Edward G. Lengel, Edward G. *To Conquer Hell: The Meuse-Argonne, 1918* (New York: Henry Holt and Company, 2008), 256, 276–78.

16. American Battle Monuments Commission,

26th Division, Summary of Operations in the World War (Washington, DC: Government Printing Office, 1944), 51.

17. Barlow, "World War Daily Diary of the 102nd Ambulance Company," October 13 & 14, 56.

18. "101st Sanitary Train. 26th Division A.E.F. History," March 1919, photostat typescript in Records, 1917–1919, 26th Division, United States Army, War Records Department, Connecticut State Archives Record Group No. 012, Part II, Series No. 040, Connecticut State Archives, Hartford, 195/378/644. Leslie R. Barlow recorded that Earle E. Radikin was detailed to produce this history of the Sanitary Train in February 1919.

19. "101st Sanitary Train. 26th Division A.E.F. History," 195–96/378–79/644–45.

20. Barlow, "World War Daily Diary of the 102nd Ambulance Company," October 18, 56.

21. Ralph J. Robinson, *Ambulance Company 113, 29th Division* (Baltimore: n.p., 1919), 110–16.

22. "101st Sanitary Train. 26th Division A.E.F. History," 195/378/644.

23. Barlow, "World War Daily Diary of the 102nd Ambulance Company," October 20 & 21, 57.

24. Barlow, "World War Daily Diary of the 102nd Ambulance Company," October 19, 57.

25. Barlow, "World War Daily Diary of the 102nd Ambulance Company," October 19, 57.

26. Barlow, "World War Daily Diary of the 102nd Ambulance Company," October 20 & 21, 57.

27. American Battle Monuments Commission, *26th Division, Summary of Operations in the World War*, 53.

28. Barlow, "World War Daily Diary of the 102nd Ambulance Company," October 20 & 21, 57.

29. Barlow, "World War Daily Diary of the 102nd Ambulance Company," October 20 & 21, 57.

30. Barlow, "World War Daily Diary of the 102nd Ambulance Company," October 20 & 21, 57.

31. Barlow, "World War Daily Diary of the 102nd Ambulance Company," October 22, 58. Varey or Vary lights were colored signal flares fired by a Very pistol.

32. Barlow, "World War Daily Diary of the 102nd Ambulance Company," October 20 & 21, 57–58. The casualties were Wagoner (Driver) Owen Rooney and Orderly Thomas McDonough of the 103rd Ambulance Company, killed on October 17, "101st Sanitary Train. 26th Division A.E.F. History," 196/379/645.

33. Barlow, "World War Daily Diary of the 102nd Ambulance Company," October 22, 58.

34. Barlow, "World War Daily Diary of the 102nd Ambulance Company," Reminiscences, 97.

35. The recommendation was denied, but citations were issued, Lieutenant Clyde Johnston, October 24, 1918, Recommendation for Distinguished Service Cross; Lieutenant Robert Durham, Recommendation for Distinguished Service Cross for Private Benjamin Clay, photostats in Records, 1917–1919, 26th Division, United States Army, War Records Department, Connecticut State Archives Record Group No. 012, Part II, Series No. 040, Connecticut State Archives, Hartford.

36. Barlow, "World War Daily Diary of the 102nd Ambulance Company," Reminiscences, 92.

37. Barlow to Bridgeport Comfort Club, December 16, 1918, in Barlow, *Letters to the Bridgeport Comfort Club*, 41.

38. Barlow, "World War Daily Diary of the 102nd Ambulance Company," October 23, 58.

39. Barlow, "World War Daily Diary of the 102nd Ambulance Company," Reminiscences, 92.

40. *Bridgeport Post*, October 23, 1918.

41. Barlow, "World War Daily Diary of the 102nd Ambulance Company," October 23, 58.

42. Barlow, "World War Daily Diary of the 102nd Ambulance Company," October 24, 58.

43. Barlow, "World War Daily Diary of the 102nd Ambulance Company," October 24, 59.

44. Barlow to Bridgeport Comfort Club, December 16, 1918, in Barlow, *Letters to the Bridgeport Comfort Club*, 41.

45. Barlow, "World War Daily Diary of the 102nd Ambulance Company," October 24, 59.

46. Barlow, "World War Daily Diary of the 102nd Ambulance Company," Reminiscences, 94.

47. Barlow, "World War Daily Diary of the 102nd Ambulance Company," October 26, 59. The scene would be captured by Signal Corps photographers the next day. On October 23 and 27, and November 1, a Signal Corps photographer and filmmaker visited the Company's dressing station at Samogneux. The still images are reproduced here, while the moving picture can be seen at National Archives and Records Administration, U.S. Signal Corps films, Meuse-Argonne Offensive, September 26 to November 11, 1918, 26th Division, 24916, 111.H.1414, https://www.youtube.com/watch?v=WPP3kIRWowU. The 102nd Ambulance Company dressing station at Samogneux is pictured at 1:23–2:15, 6:20–6:34, 6:57–7:07, and 10:12–10:43.

48. Barlow, "World War Daily Diary of the 102nd Ambulance Company," October 26, 59.

49. Barlow, "World War Daily Diary of the 102nd Ambulance Company," Reminiscences, 94. The identity of the officer has not been determined.

50. Barlow, "World War Daily Diary of the 102nd Ambulance Company," October 25, 59.

51. Beers to Mother, Nov. 3, 1918, *Newtown Bee*, November 29, 1918.

52. Beers to Mother, Nov. 3, 1918, *Newtown Bee*, November 29, 1918.

53. Beers to Mother, Nov. 3, 1918, *Newtown Bee*, November 29, 1918.

54. Beers to Mother, November 7, 1918, *Newtown Bee*, December 20, 1918.

55. Barlow, "World War Daily Diary of the 102nd Ambulance Company," October 27, 59–60.

56. Barlow, "World War Daily Diary of the 102nd Ambulance Company," October 27, 60.

57. Barlow, "World War Daily Diary of the 102nd Ambulance Company," October 27, 60.

58. Barlow to Bridgeport Comfort Club, Decem-

ber 16, 1918, in Barlow, *Letters to the Bridgeport Comfort Club*, 40.

59. Earle E. Radikin, "The Kamerad Kid, *War Stories* 18, number 53 (March 28, 1929): 122.

60. Barlow, "World War Daily Diary of the 102nd Ambulance Company," October 27, 60.

61. Barlow, "World War Daily Diary of the 102nd Ambulance Company," October 27, 60.

62. Barlow, "World War Daily Diary of the 102nd Ambulance Company," October 28, 61.

63. Barlow, "World War Daily Diary of the 102nd Ambulance Company," October 28, 61.

64. Barlow, "World War Daily Diary of the 102nd Ambulance Company," October 28, 61. Barlow would comment: "It is safe to estimate that 85% of the enlisted personnel of this Company were wounded or gassed in action, for many had not been credited with being gassed for they had learned from others the small amount of benefit, other than rest, that could be gained in the hospitals for those who were gassed and of the many difficulties and inconveniences in again being able to reach your original Company and decided they would rather claim they were not gassed so that they might stay with the Company," Barlow, "World War Daily Diary of the 102nd Ambulance Company," Reminiscences, 92.

65. Barlow, "World War Daily Diary of the 102nd Ambulance Company," October 28, 60–61. The shell was likely fired by a Maxim one-pound "pom-pom" gun frequently used for antiaircraft fire, which had a range of about two miles.

66. Barlow, "World War Daily Diary of the 102nd Ambulance Company," October 29, 30 & 31, 61.

67. "101st Sanitary Train. 26th Division A.E.F. History," 195/378/644.

68. Barlow, "World War Daily Diary of the 102nd Ambulance Company," October 29, 30 & 31, 61.

69. Frank P. Sibley, *With the Yankee Division in France* (Boston: Little, Brown, 1919), 308–09.

70. Sibley, *With the Yankee Division in France*, 309–11; Emerson G. Taylor, *New England in France, 1917–1919* (Boston: Houghton Mifflin, 1920), 249–51, 262–63.

71. American Battle Monuments Commission, *26th Division, Summary of Operations in the World War*, 57–58.

72. Barlow, "World War Daily Diary of the 102nd Ambulance Company," November 2, 61.

73. Beers to Mother, November 3, 1918, *Newtown Bee*, November 29, 1918.

74. Barlow, "World War Daily Diary of the 102nd Ambulance Company," November 11, 62.

75. Beers to Mother, November 7, 1918, *Newtown Bee*, December 20, 1918.

76. Beers to Mother, November 7, 1918, *Newtown Bee*, December 20, 1918.

77. Barlow, "World War Daily Diary of the 102nd Ambulance Company," November 3, 4, 5 & 6, 62.

78. American Battle Monuments Commission, *26th Division, Summary of Operations in the World War*, 58–59.

79. Barlow, "World War Daily Diary of the 102nd Ambulance Company," November 7, 8, 9 & 10, 62.

80. Barlow, "World War Daily Diary of the 102nd Ambulance Company," November 11, 62–63.

81. Barlow, "World War Daily Diary of the 102nd Ambulance Company," November 11, 62–63.

82. Sibley, *With the Yankee Division in France*, 341.

83. Beers to Mother, November 11, 1918, *Newtown Bee*, December 20, 1918.

Chapter 11

1. Stewart to Mother, November 12, 1918, *Bridgeport Telegram*, November 30, 1918.

2. Leslie R. Barlow, "World War Daily Diary of the 102nd Ambulance Company," Reminiscences, 95, Connecticut State Archives, Hartford.

3. Porter to Officers and Men of the Ambulance Section, November 16, 1918, in Leslie R. Barlow, *Letters to the Bridgeport Comfort Club from the Foreign Chapter in France* (Bridgeport: Author, 1919), 46.

4. Morrell to Bridgeport Comfort Club, in Barlow, *Letters to the Bridgeport Comfort Club*, 45.

5. Michael E. Shay, *A Grateful Heart: The History of a World War I Field Hospital* (Westport, CT: Greenwood Press, 2002), 142–43.

6. Shay, *A Grateful Heart*, 129–31.

7. Barlow, "World War Daily Diary of the 102nd Ambulance Company," November 12 to December 12, 64.

8. Barlow, "World War Daily Diary of the 102nd Ambulance Company," December 13 to January 1, 64.

9. Emerson Gifford Taylor, *New England in France 1917–1919: A History of the Twenty-Sixth Division U.S.A.* (Boston: Houghton Mifflin, 1920), 281–84.

10. Barlow, "World War Daily Diary of the 102nd Ambulance Company," December 13 to January 1, 64.

11. Barlow to Bridgeport Comfort Club, December 16, 1918, in Barlow, *Letters to the Bridgeport Comfort Club*, 44.

12. Shay, *A Grateful Heart*, 134–35.

13. Barlow to Bridgeport Comfort Club, December 16, 1918, in Barlow, *Letters to the Bridgeport Comfort Club*, 44. Truck drivers Edwin Hough, Ripple Morgan, Ray Pomeroy, and Joseph Wynkoop had also turned in their vehicles.

14. Shay, *A Grateful Heart*, 134–35.

15. Barlow, "World War Daily Diary of the 102nd Ambulance Company," December 13 to January 1, 64.

16. Barlow to Bridgeport Comfort Club, December 16, 1918, in Barlow, *Letters to the Bridgeport Comfort Club*, 44.

17. Barlow, "World War Daily Diary of the 102nd Ambulance Company," December 13 to January 1, 65.

18. Barlow, "World War Daily Diary of the 102nd Ambulance Company," December 13 to January 1, 64.

19. Barlow, "World War Daily Diary of the 102nd Ambulance Company," December 13 to January 1, 64–65.

20. Barlow, "World War Daily Diary of the 102nd Ambulance Company," December 13 to January 1, 64.

21. The visit made Wilson the first U.S. president to travel to Europe during his term in office. He wished to contribute to the peace negotiations as well as to promote his plan for the League of Nations, Taylor, *New England in France 1917–1919*, 284–86; Frank P. Sibley, *With the Yankee Division in France* (Boston: Little, Brown, 1919), 347–48.

22. Barlow, "World War Daily Diary of the 102nd Ambulance Company," December 13 to January 1, 64; the Wilsons' visit was captured by Signal Corps cameramen, see National Archives and Records Administration, U.S. Signal Corps films, "President Wilson Visits Chaumont, France, December 25, 1918," 111.H.1231, https://www.youtube.com/watch?v=CJWkHOybn7k. (The Wilsons' billet visits are depicted from 4:20 to 6:38.)

23. Barlow to Bridgeport Comfort Club, March 15, 1919, in Barlow, *Letters to the Bridgeport Comfort Club*, 48.

24. Harry C. Hale to Commanding Officers, December 26, 1918, in Daniel W. Strickland, *Connecticut Fights: The Story of the 102nd Regiment* (New Haven: Quinnipiack Press, 1930), 302.

25. Barlow, "World War Daily Diary of the 102nd Ambulance Company," December 13 to January 1, 65.

26. Barlow, "World War Daily Diary of the 102nd Ambulance Company," December 13 to January 1, 65.

27. Barlow, "World War Daily Diary of the 102nd Ambulance Company," January 1 to January 15, 1919, 65.

28. Barlow, "World War Daily Diary of the 102nd Ambulance Company," December 13 to January 1, 65.

29. Sibley, *With the Yankee Division in France*, 348.

30. Barlow, "World War Daily Diary of the 102nd Ambulance Company," December 13 to January 1, 65.

31. Barlow, "World War Daily Diary of the 102nd Ambulance Company," January 1 to January 15, 1919, 66.

32. Barlow, "World War Daily Diary of the 102nd Ambulance Company," December 13 to January 1, 64.

33. Barlow to Bridgeport Comfort Club, December 16, 1918, in Barlow, *Letters to the Bridgeport Comfort Club*, 44–45.

34. Barlow, "World War Daily Diary of the 102nd Ambulance Company," January 1 to January 15, 1919, 66.

35. Barlow to Bridgeport Comfort Club, March 15, 1919, in Barlow, *Letters to the Bridgeport Comfort Club*, 48.

36. Barlow, "World War Daily Diary of the 102nd Ambulance Company," January 1 to January 15, 1919, 66.

37. Barlow, "World War Daily Diary of the 102nd Ambulance Company," January 1 to January 15, 1919, 66.

38. Barlow, "World War Daily Diary of the 102nd Ambulance Company," January 1 to January 15, 1919, 66.

39. Barlow, "World War Daily Diary of the 102nd Ambulance Company," January 16 to February 1, 67. Major Frederick E. Jones was then in command of the 101st Sanitary Train.

40. Barlow, "World War Daily Diary of the 102nd Ambulance Company," January 1 to January 15, 1919, 66.

41. Barlow, "World War Daily Diary of the 102nd Ambulance Company," January 1 to January 15, 1919, 66.

42. Barlow, "World War Daily Diary of the 102nd Ambulance Company," January 16 to February 1, 66.

43. Barlow, "World War Daily Diary of the 102nd Ambulance Company," January 1 to January 15, 1919, 66.

44. Taylor, *New England in France*, 288.

45. Barlow to Bridgeport Comfort Club, March 15, 1919, in Barlow, *Letters to the Bridgeport Comfort Club*, 48–49.

46. Barlow, "World War Daily Diary of the 102nd Ambulance Company," January 16 to February 1, 67.

47. Barlow to Bridgeport Comfort Club, March 15, 1919, in Barlow, *Letters to the Bridgeport Comfort Club*, 49.

48. Barlow, "World War Daily Diary of the 102nd Ambulance Company," January 16 to February 1, 67. Ecommoy and Marigne-Laille were about 500 kilometers west of Vitrey-sur-Mance.

49. Beers to Mother, January 20, 1919, *Newtown Bee*, February 21, 1919.

50. Barlow to Bridgeport Comfort Club, March 15, 1919, in Barlow, *Letters to the Bridgeport Comfort Club*, 49.

51. Barlow to Bridgeport Comfort Club, March 15, 1919, in Barlow, *Letters to the Bridgeport Comfort Club*, 49.

52. Barlow, "World War Daily Diary of the 102nd Ambulance Company," January 16 to February 1, 67.

53. Beers to Mother, January 20, 1919, *Newtown Bee*, February 21, 1919.

54. Beers to Mother, January 20, 1919, *Newtown Bee*, February 21, 1919.

55. Barlow, "World War Daily Diary of the 102nd Ambulance Company," January 16 to February 1, 67.

56. Barlow, "World War Daily Diary of the

102nd Ambulance Company," February 1 to February 15, 68.

57. Barlow, "World War Daily Diary of the 102nd Ambulance Company," February 16 to March 1, 69.

58. Barlow, "World War Daily Diary of the 102nd Ambulance Company," February 1 to February 15, 68.

59. Barlow, "World War Daily Diary of the 102nd Ambulance Company," February 16 to March 1, 69.

60. Barlow, "World War Daily Diary of the 102nd Ambulance Company," December 13 to January 1, 64.

61. Barlow to Bridgeport Comfort Club, March 15, 1919, in Barlow, *Letters to the Bridgeport Comfort Club*, 49.

62. Barlow, "World War Daily Diary of the 102nd Ambulance Company," January 16 to February 1, 67; Barlow to Bridgeport Comfort Club, March 15, 1919, in Barlow, *Letters to the Bridgeport Comfort Club*, 49, adds that Ted Gilliland and Ray Pomeroy managed the teams, but the horses were passed on to another unit two weeks later.

63. Barlow, "World War Daily Diary of the 102nd Ambulance Company," February 1 to February 15, 67; Shay, *A Grateful Heart*, 153.

64. 26th Division Surgeon, Memorandum to All Medical Officers, March 4, 1919, photostat in Copies of U.S. Army records pertaining to the 26th Division, 1917–19, Connecticut State Archives Record Group No. 012, Part II, Series No. 040, Box 12: Nos. 4474–5585, Connecticut State Archives, Hartford.

65. Barlow, "World War Daily Diary of the 102nd Ambulance Company," February 1 to February 15, 67–68.

66. Barlow, "World War Daily Diary of the 102nd Ambulance Company," March 1 to April 1, 70.

67. Barlow, "World War Daily Diary of the 102nd Ambulance Company," February 1 to 15, 68.

68. Barlow, "World War Daily Diary of the 102nd Ambulance Company," March 1 to April 1, 70.

69. Taylor, *New England in France*, 284.

70. Barlow, "World War Daily Diary of the 102nd Ambulance Company," March 1 to April 1, 69–70.

71. Barlow to Bridgeport Comfort Club, March 15, 1919, in Barlow, *Letters to the Bridgeport Comfort Club*, 51.

72. Barlow to Bridgeport Comfort Club, March 15, 1919, in Barlow, *Letters to the Bridgeport Comfort Club*, 52–54.

73. Barlow to Bridgeport Comfort Club, March 15, 1919, in Barlow, *Letters to the Bridgeport Comfort Club*, 51.

74. *The Stars and Stripes*, February 21, 1919.

75. Barlow, "World War Daily Diary of the 102nd Ambulance Company," February 1 to 15, 68.

76. Barlow, "World War Daily Diary of the 102nd Ambulance Company," April 1 to May 1, 71.

77. Barlow, "World War Daily Diary of the 102nd Ambulance Company," February 1 to 15, 68.

78. Shay, *A Grateful Heart*, 148.

79. Barlow, "World War Daily Diary of the 102nd Ambulance Company," February 16 to March 1, 68–69.

80. Shay, *A Grateful Heart*, 148.

81. Barlow, "World War Daily Diary of the 102nd Ambulance Company," February 16 to March 1, 69.

82. Orders No. 219, 26th Division, November 12, 1918, photostat in Copies of U.S. Army records pertaining to the 26th Division, 1917–19, Connecticut State Archives Record Group No. 012, Part II, Series No.040, Box 12: Nos. 4474–5585, Connecticut State Archives, Hartford.

83. Barlow, "World War Daily Diary of the 102nd Ambulance Company," February 16 to March 1, 69.

84. Shay, *A Grateful Heart*, 148–49. The 26th Division was the only one to have a separate insignia for each regiment and train.

85. Barlow, "World War Daily Diary of the 102nd Ambulance Company," February 16 to March 1, 69.

86. Barlow, "World War Daily Diary of the 102nd Ambulance Company," Reminiscences, 98.

87. Barlow, "World War Daily Diary of the 102nd Ambulance Company," Reminiscences, 98.

88. Barlow, "World War Daily Diary of the 102nd Ambulance Company," Reminiscences, 97.

89. Barlow, "World War Daily Diary of the 102nd Ambulance Company," Reminiscences, 96.

90. Barlow, "World War Daily Diary of the 102nd Ambulance Company," Reminiscences, 96.

91. Barlow, "World War Daily Diary of the 102nd Ambulance Company," February 16 to March 1, 69.

92. Barlow, "World War Daily Diary of the 102nd Ambulance Company," March 1 to April 1, 70.

93. Charles R. Cabot, *History of the 103rd Infantry, August, 1917, to November, 1918* (n.p.: 103rd U.S. Infantry, 1919), 3.

94. Barlow, "World War Daily Diary of the 102nd Ambulance Company," February 16 to March 1, 69.

95. Barlow, "World War Daily Diary of the 102nd Ambulance Company," February 16 to March 1, 69; "101st Sanitary Train, 26th Division A.E.F. *History*," 152/335/601, 197/380/646.

96. Barlow to Bridgeport Comfort Club, March 15, 1919, in Barlow, *Letters to the Bridgeport Comfort Club*, 56.

97. Barlow to Bridgeport Comfort Club, March 15, 1919, in Barlow, *Letters to the Bridgeport Comfort Club*, 49.

98. Barlow, "World War Daily Diary of the 102nd Ambulance Company," February 16 to March 1, 68.

99. Barlow, "World War Daily Diary of the 102nd Ambulance Company," February 16 to March 1, 69.

100. Barlow, "World War Daily Diary of the 102nd Ambulance Company," March 1 to April 1, 70.
101. Barlow, "World War Daily Diary of the 102nd Ambulance Company," March 1 to April 1, 70.
102. Barlow, "World War Daily Diary of the 102nd Ambulance Company," March 1 to April 1, 70.
103. Barlow, "World War Daily Diary of the 102nd Ambulance Company," March 1 to April 1, 70.
104. Taylor, *New England in France*, 301.
105. Barlow, "World War Daily Diary of the 102nd Ambulance Company," March 1 to April 1, 70.
106. Barlow, "World War Daily Diary of the 102nd Ambulance Company," April 1 to May 1, 71.
107. Barlow, "World War Daily Diary of the 102nd Ambulance Company," April 1 to May 1, 71.
108. Barlow, "World War Daily Diary of the 102nd Ambulance Company," March 1 to April 1, 70–71.
109. Barlow, "World War Daily Diary of the 102nd Ambulance Company," April 1 to May 1, 71.
110. Barlow, "World War Daily Diary of the 102nd Ambulance Company," April 1 to May 1, 72.
111. Shay, *A Grateful Heart*, 154.
112. Barlow, "World War Daily Diary of the 102nd Ambulance Company," April 1 to May 1, 71.
113. Barlow, "World War Daily Diary of the 102nd Ambulance Company," April 1 to May 1, 72.
114. Barlow, "World War Daily Diary of the 102nd Ambulance Company," April 1 to May 1, 72.
115. Barlow, "World War Daily Diary of the 102nd Ambulance Company," April 1 to May 1, 72.
116. Barlow, "World War Daily Diary of the 102nd Ambulance Company," April 1 to May 1, 72.
117. Barlow, "World War Daily Diary of the 102nd Ambulance Company," April 1 to May 1, 72.
118. Barlow, "World War Daily Diary of the 102nd Ambulance Company," April 1 to May 1, 72.
119. Barlow, "World War Daily Diary of the 102nd Ambulance Company," April 1 to May 1, 72.
120. *Bridgeport Post*, April 18,1919.
121. Barlow, "World War Daily Diary of the 102nd Ambulance Company," April 1 to May 1, 72.
122. Barlow, "World War Daily Diary of the 102nd Ambulance Company," Reminiscences, 96.
123. Barlow, "World War Daily Diary of the 102nd Ambulance Company," April 1 to May 1, 73.
124. Barlow, "World War Daily Diary of the 102nd Ambulance Company," April 1 to May 1, 73.
125. Barlow, "World War Daily Diary of the 102nd Ambulance Company," April 1 to May 1, 73.
126. Barlow, "World War Daily Diary of the 102nd Ambulance Company," April 1 to May 1, 73.
127. Barlow, "World War Daily Diary of the 102nd Ambulance Company," April 1 to May 1, 73. A copy of this "yard-long" photograph has not been located.
128. *Bridgeport Post*, April 23, 1919.
129. Barlow, "World War Daily Diary of the 102nd Ambulance Company," April 1 to May 1, 73.
130. *Welcome Home YD* (Boston: Everett Press, 1919).
131. *Bridgeport Post*, April 24, 1919.
132. Barlow, "World War Daily Diary of the 102nd Ambulance Company," April 1 to May 1, 74, 73.
133. Barlow, "World War Daily Diary of the 102nd Ambulance Company," April 1 to May 1, 74.
134. Barlow, "World War Daily Diary of the 102nd Ambulance Company," May [April] 29, 1919, 74.
135. *Bridgeport Standard Telegram*, May 6, 1919. Built in 1909, the eight-story, 275-room Stratfield was the premier hotel in Bridgeport.
136. Barlow, "World War Daily Diary of the 102nd Ambulance Company," Reminiscences, 78.

Postscript

1. "Frank W. Stevens. Obituary Record of Graduates of Yale University Deceased during the Year 1934–1935." *Bulletin of Yale University* 94 (October 15, 1935): 201–02. For each of these men, data on marriage, employment, and death were derived from marriage, census, and death and grave records accessed through Ancestry.com.
2. Sergeant L.R. Barlow, "Connecticut Boys Receive Baptism of Fire in France," *Bridgeport Post*, January 20, 1924; Barlow to Godard, May 28, 1927, bound in "World War Daily Diary of the 102nd Ambulance Company," Connecticut State Library.
3. WW1 Veterans, Connecticut Soldiers Questionnaires, 1919, https://ctstatelibrary.org/ww-1-veterans/, accessed October 2021; see also https://www.ancestry.com/discoveryui-content/view/29956:2278.
4. *Army and Air Force Register*, 1948, vol. 1, 935.
5. *Bridgeport Post*, September 26, 1919.
6. WW1 Veterans, Connecticut Soldiers Questionnaires, 1919, https://ctstatelibrary.org/ww-1-veterans/, accessed October 2021; see also https://www.ancestry.com/discoveryui-content/view/29956:2278.
7. Beers to Mother, September 5, 1918, *Newtown Bee*, October 4, 1918.
8. WW1 Veterans, Connecticut Soldiers Questionnaires, 1919, https://ctstatelibrary.org/ww-1-veterans/, accessed October 2021; see also https://www.ancestry.com/discoveryui-content/view/29956:2278.
9. *Bridgeport Post*, January 12, 1949, January 4, 1977.

Bibliography

Manuscripts

Barlow, Leslie R. Diary. Entries reprinted in "Connecticut Boys Receive Baptism of Fire in France." *Bridgeport Post,* January 20, 1924.

______. "World War Daily Diary of the 102nd Ambulance Company," typescript, Connecticut State Archives, Hartford. (Additional typescript copies are at the Bridgeport Public Library and the National World War I Museum and Memorial, Kansas City, MO.)

Beers, G. Herbert. Letters. *Newtown Bee,* 1917–19.

Connecticut, Military Census, March 1917, accessed through Ancestry.com.

Copies of U.S. Army records pertaining to the 26th Division, 1917–19, Record Group No. 012, Part II, Series No. 040, Box 12: Nos. 4474–5585, Connecticut State Archives, Hartford.

James, Jesse Lodrick. Letters. *Newtown Bee,* 1918.

"101st Sanitary Train. 26th Division A.E.F. History." March 1919, photostat typescript in Records, 1917–1919, 26th Division, United States Army, War Records Department, Connecticut State Archives Record Group No. 012, Part II, Series No. 040, Connecticut State Archives, Hartford. According to Leslie R. Barlow, this was written by Earle E. Radikin, who was detailed to produce it for the Sanitary Train in February 1919.

102nd Ambulance Company, Miscellaneous Correspondence, photostats in Records, 1917–1919, 26th Division, United States Army, War Records Department, Connecticut State Archives Record Group No. 012, Part II, Series No.040, Box 11: 8412–8422, Connecticut State Archives, Hartford.

Peck, James. Letters. *Newtown Bee,* 1918.

Radikin, Earle E. Letter, *Bridgeport Evening Post,* May 22, 1918.

Sprague, Charles H. Letter. *Bridgeport Evening Post,* June 12, 1918.

Wall, Frank E. Letters. *Bridgeport Evening Post.*

Wills, G. Spencer. Letter. *Bridgeport Evening Post,* June 2, 1918.

World War I Veterans, Connecticut Soldiers Questionnaires, 1919, https://ctstatelibrary.org/ww-1-veterans/, accessed October 2021.

World War I Veterans, Miscellaneous Articles (Bridgeport Men), NPC 556, Bridgeport History Center, Bridgeport Public Library.

Wright, George. Letter. *Bridgeport Evening Post,* May 28, 1918.

Manuals

Drill Regulations and Service Manual for Sanitary Troops United States Army, Corrected to April 15, 1917. 1914; Washington, D.C.: Government Printing Office, 1917.

Manual of Splints & Appliances for the Medical Department of the United States Army. New York: Oxford University Press, 1917.

Mason, Charles Field. *A Complete Handbook for the Sanitary Troops of the U.S. Army and Navy and National Guard and Naval Militia,* 4th ed. New York: William Wood and Company, 1917.

Medical Department, U.S. Army. *Manual for the Medical Department, United States Army, 1916.* Washington, D.C.: Government Printing Office, 1916.

Books, Articles, and Films

Adams, William P. "I Ain't Dead Yet." *Yankee Doings* 10, number 2 (February 1932): 3.

American Battle Monuments Commission. *26th Division, Summary of Operations in the World War.* Washington, D.C.: Government Printing Office, 1944.

Archer, Gregory. *Private Heller and the Bantam Boys: An American Medic in World War I.* Guilford, CT: Rowman & Littlefield, 2015.

Atenstaedt, Robert L. *The Medical Response to the Trench Diseases in World War One.* Newcastle upon Tyne, UK: Cambridge Scholars Publishing, 2011.

______. "Trench Fever: The British Medical Response in the Great War." *Journal of the Royal Society of Medicine* 99, number 11 (November 2006): 564–68. https://www.ncbi.nlm.nih.gov/pmc/articles/PMC1633565/

Barlow, Leslie R. *Letters to the Bridgeport Comfort Club.* Bridgeport: Author, 1919.

Bell, Ryan Corbett. *The Ambulance: A History*. Jefferson, NC: McFarland, 2012.

Benwell, Harry A. *History of the Yankee Division*. Boston: Cornhill Company, 1919.

Biennial Report of the Adjutant General, State of Connecticut, to the Governor, for the Two Years Ending September 30, 1912. Hartford: State of Connecticut, 1912.

Biennial Report of the Adjutant General, State of Connecticut, to the Governor, for the Two Years Ending September 30, 1914. Hartford: State of Connecticut, 1914.

Biennial Report of the Adjutant General, State of Connecticut, to the Governor, for the Two Years Ending September 30, 1916. Hartford: State of Connecticut, 1916.

Biennial Report of the Adjutant General, State of Connecticut, to the Governor, for the Two Years Ending September 30, 1918. Hartford: State of Connecticut, 1918.

Bispham, William N. *The Medical Department of the United States Army in the World War, vol. VII, Training*. Washington, D.C.: Government Printing Office, 1927.

Bodfish, Robert W. *A History of Section 647, United States Army Ambulance Service with the French Army*. Worcester: Stobbs Press, 1919.

Bond, Jim. "Little Tanks: The Development of the American Field Shoe [Boot] During the World War," Doughboy Center, http://www.worldwar1.com/dbc/l_tanks.htm, accessed January 2022.

Bowerman, Guy Emerson, Jr. *The Compensations of War: The Diary of an Ambulance Driver During the Great War*. Austin: University of Texas Press, 2012. [SSU 585]

Bratten, Jonathan D. *To the Last Man: A National Guard Regiment in the Great War, 1917-1919*. Fort Leavenworth, KS: Combat Studies Institute Press, 2020, https://www.armyupress.army.mil/Portals/7/combat-studies-institute/csi-books/-to-the-last-man.pdf.

Bruckner, Judy A. *Memories of a WW1 Ambulance Driver As Told by Charles C. Leonard, Sr.*, n.p.: author, 2021. [SSU 644]

Cabot, Charles R. *History of the 103rd Infantry, August, 1917, to November, 1918*. n.p.: 103rd U.S. Infantry, 1919.

Catalogue of Official A.E.F. Photographs Taken by the Signal Corps, U.S.A. Washington, D.C.: Government Printing Office, 1919.

Corrigan, David. "The Connecticut National Guard on the Mexican Border." *Connecticut Explored* (Spring 2017).

Curtis, Burr H. "Otto G. Wiedman, M.D., 1884–1974." *Connecticut Medicine* 39, number 1 (January 1975): 64–65.

Cushing, Harvey. *From a Surgeon's Journal, 1915–1918*. Boston: Little, Brown, 1936.

Davis, Delbert M., ed. *307 At Home And In France*. New York?: Harold Breul, 1919. [307th Ambulance Company]

Devlin, Philip R. "Windsor Locks physician cited for extraordinary valor," in "Connecticut's Irish in World War I," *Shanachie* 30, number 4 (November-December 2018): 12.

"Division Surgeon's Reports: Twenty-Sixth Division," Report of the Surgeon General of the Army, *War Department Annual Reports, 1919*, part 3. Washington, D.C.: Government Printing Office, 1920, 3292–3304. https://books.google.com.mx/books?id=EHYsAAAAIAAJ&pg=PA3301&lpg=PA3301&dq=AEF+field+hospital,+Villotte&source=bl&ots=BhlokUJiVn&sig=ACfU3U20e2fjrKD4-UHLmIiWAYa250g6zw&hl=en&sa=X&ved=2ahUKEwi25Pjkga32AhVllmoFHaL0AykQ6AF6BAglEAM#v=onepage&q=AEF%20field%20hospital%2C%20Villotte&f=false

Dorsey, R. Stephen, and Kenneth L. McPheeters. *The American Military Saddle, 1776–1945*. Eugene, OR: Collectors' Library, 1999.

Duncan, Louis C. *The Medical Department of the United States Army in the Civil War*. ca. 1910; reprint, Gaithersburg, MD: Olde Soldier books, 1987.

"The Early Days of Motorized Military Vehicles," https://www.military.com/veteran-jobs/career-advice/military-transition/gm-military-history-motorized-vehicles.html, accessed November 2021.

Encyclopedia of Connecticut Biography, Genealogical-Memorial; Representative Citizens, vol. 10. New York: American Historical Society, 1917.

Finnegan, Terrence J. *"A Delicate Affair" on the Western Front: America Learns How to Fight a Modern War in the Woëvre Trenches*. Stroud, Gloucestershire, UK: History Press, 2015.

"Foden." https://tractors.fandom.com/wiki/Foden, accessed November 2021.

"Frank W. Stevens. Obituary Record of Graduates of Yale University Deceased during the Year 1934–1935." *Bulletin of Yale University* 94 (October 15, 1935): 201–02.

Gabriel, Richard A. *Between Flesh and Steel: A History of Military Medicine from the Middle Ages to the War in Afghanistan*. Lincoln, NE: Potomac Books, 2013.

Gardiner, Alexander. "The Girl Who Wore O.D," *The American Legion Magazine* (April 1928) http://www.oldmagazinearticles.com/WW1_Salvation_Army_Women_in_France-pdf?fbclid=IwAR0KeqvBHNhiLXXH9Vpn5clRWkFrYaJYB861OuJwhEd3sntTDVMwBZXX4eI, accessed March 2022.

Gilchrist, H. L. "Delousing the American Army in France," *The Military Surgeon* 47, number 2 (August 1920): 129–48.

Gillett, Mary C. *The Army Medical Department, 1865–1917*. Washington, D.C.: US Army Center of Military History, 1995.

______. *The Army Medical Department, 1917–1941*. Washington, D.C.: US Army Center of Military History, 2009.

GMC Ambulances. Pontiac, MI: General Motors Truck Co., ca. 1918.

Gosling, Tim. "A Moderate Idea of Speed: Tim

Gosling delves into the history of the Foden Steam Wagon." https://www.keymilitary.com/article/moderate-idea-speed. Accessed November 2021.

Graham, Milton P., ed. *History of Ambulance Company 161, A.E.F., 1917–1919.* Aberdeen, WA: Welsh-Richards Company, 1919.

Grotelueschen, Mark Ethan. *The AEF Way of War: The American Army and Combat in World War I.* Cambridge: Cambridge University Press, 2007.

Haller, John S., Jr. *Farmcarts to Fords: A History of the Military Ambulance, 1790–1925.* Carbondale and Edwardsville: Southern Illinois University Press, 1992.

Harvey, William C. and Eric T., ed. *Letters from Verdun: Frontline Experiences of an American Volunteer in World War I France.* Philadelphia: Casemate, 2009. [SSU 31]

Henry, Mark R. *The US Army of World War I.* Botley, Oxford, UK: Osprey Publishing, 2003.

History of Ambulance Company Number 139. 1919. Reprint; London: Read Books Ltd., 2013.

History of the American Field Service in France, "Friends of France," 1914–1917. Boston and New York: Houghton Mifflin, 1920.

History of the 101st Engineers, American Expeditionary Forces, 1917–1918–1919. Cambridge, MA: Regimental Committee, 1926.

Hoff, Thomas A. *US Doughboy 1916–19.* Botley, Oxford, UK: Osprey Publishing, 2005.

Horton, Charles H. *Stretcher Bearer: Fighting for Life in the Trenches.* Oxford: Lion Books, 2013.

Iodine and Gasoline: A History of the 117th Sanitary Train. N.P: n.p., 1919.

Jaffin, Jonathan H. "Medical Support for the American Expeditionary Forces in France During the First World War," Thesis, Master of Military Art and Science, U.S. Army Command and General Staff College, Fort Leavenworth, KS, 1991.9, https://apps.dtic.mil/sti/pdfs/ADA241174.pdf, accessed February 2022.

Janis, Elsie. *The Big Show: My Six Months with the American Expeditionary Forces.* New York: Cosmopolitan Book Corp., 1919.

Jones, Simon. *World War I Gas Warfare Tactics and Equipment.* Botley, Oxford, UK: Osprey Publishing, 1994.

Keegan, John. *The First World War.* New York: Penguin Random House, 1999.

Larrabee, Jeffrey C. "A Tale of Two Trucks: American Casualty Evacuation in World War I." *Icon* 14 (2008): 123–50.

Lengel, Edward G. *To Conquer Hell: The Meuse-Argonne, 1918.* New York: Henry Holt and Company, 2008.

Mayhew, Emily. *Wounded: A New History of the Western Front in World War I.* Oxford: Oxford University Press, 2014.

McCormack, Robert L. *Remember the Brave: New England's 26th (Yankee) Division with the American Expeditionary Force in World War I France 1917–1919.* N.p.: n.p. n.d.

McKenna, Fred A., ed. *Battery A 103rd Field Artillery in France.* Providence?: n.p., 1919?.

Medical Training Camp: Ft. Oglethorpe, Georgia, August 1917: Page on Page of Page's Command. Chattanooga, TN: R. P. Purse, 1917.

National Archives and Records Administration, US Signal Corps films, "Meuse-Argonne Offensive, September 26 to November 11, 1918, 26th Division," 24916, 111.H.1414, https://www.youtube.com/watch?v=WPP3kIRWowU. (The 102nd Ambulance Company dressing station at Samogneux is pictured at 1:23–2:15, 6:20–6:34, 6:57–7:07, and 10:12–10:43.)

______. "Occupation of Toul-Boucq Sector (Lorraine), April 3-June 28, 1918, 26th Division," 111.H.1034, Reels 1-4, https://www.youtube.com/watch?v=kCGZDszExq0. (General Edwards observing the lines with Montsec in the distance is pictured at 10:45-11:10; a French wheeled litter, carrying a casualty on the narrow-gauge railroad, and applying a Thomas splint are pictured at 17:45-19:50; Drury and Keller's destroyed ambulance at Dead Man's Curve and another ruined ambulance near Beaumont are shown at 20:04-20:33.)

______. "President Wilson Visits Chaumont, France, December 25, 1918," 111.H.1231, https://www.youtube.com/watch?v=CJWkHOybn7k. (The Wilsons' billet visits are depicted from 4:20 to 6:38.)

______. "The St. Mihiel Offensive, September 10–25, 1918, 26th Division," 111.H.1325, https://www.youtube.com/watch?v=K8eILOcKWdY. (The Company's Noyon dressing station and ambulances, 104th Ambulance Company horse-drawn ambulances, ambulance loading, and litter bearers are shown from 5:49 to 6:48.)

Orcutt, Philip Dana. *The White Road of Mystery: The Note-Book of an American Ambulancier.* New York: John Lane Company, 1918. [American Field Service Section 31]

Pease, Shawn A., ed. *Shadowboxing the Apocalypse: The WW1 Correspondence of Dr. Theo Hascall, 103rd Field Artillery, 26th Yankee Division.* Providence: Rhode Island Philatelic Society, 2018.

Polk's Medical Register and Directory of the United States and Canada, 1917, 14th ed. Detroit, New York, Chicago: R. L. Polk & Company, 1917.

Pottle, Frederick A., *Stretchers: The Story of a Hospital Unit on the Western Front.* New Haven: Yale University Press, 1929.

Prieto, Julie Irene. *The Mexican Expedition, 1916–1917.* Washington, D.C.: US Army Center of Military History, 1016. p. 58 https://history.army.mil/html/books/077/77-1/cmhPub_077-1.pdf

Radikin, Earle E. "The Kamerad Kid." *War Stories* 18, number 53 (March 28, 1929): 121–29.

Report on Mobilization of the Organized Militia and National Guard of the United States, 1916. Washington, D.C.: Government Printing Office, 1916.

"Robert Moseley Yergason, 1908." *Trinity College Bulletin* 46, number 3 (May 1949):13

Robinson, Ralph J. *Ambulance Company 113, 29th*

Division. Baltimore, MD: Lord Baltimore Press, 1919.

Sengupta, Narayan. *American Eagles: The Illustrated History of American Aviation in World War I*. n.p.: Author, 2012.

Service Records, Connecticut: Men and Women in the Armed Forces of the United States During World War, 1917–1920. Hartford: Office of the Adjutant General, n.d. https://www.fold3.com/title/778/connecticut-wwi-service-rosters, accessed 2020.

Shay, Michael E. *A Grateful Heart: The History of a World War I Field Hospital*. Westport, CT: Greenwood Press, 2002.

_____. *The Yankee Division in the First World War: In the Highest Tradition*. College Station: Texas A&M University Press, 2008.

Sibley, Frank P. *With the Yankee Division in France*. Boston: Little, Brown, 1919.

Stewart, Gloria P. "August 1912: War Comes to Southwestern Connecticut." *Connecticut History* 39, number 2 (Fall 2000): 197–201.

Strickland, Daniel W. *Connecticut Fights: The Story of the 102nd Regiment*. New Haven: Quinnipiack Press, 1930.

Taylor, Emerson Gifford. *New England in France 1917–1919: A History of the Twenty-Sixth Division U.S.A.* Boston: Houghton Mifflin, 1920.

Wainwright, Philip S., ed. *History of the 101st Machine Gun Battalion*. Hartford: 101st Machine Gun Battalion Association, 1922.

Waldo, George Curtis, ed. *History of Bridgeport and Vicinity, vol. 2, Biographical Sketches*. New York and Chicago: S. J. Clarke, 1917.

Walsh, Mark C. *Free Men Shall Stand: The Story of Connecticut's Organized Militia from 1636*. Hartford: Connecticut National Guard Officers Association, 1991.

Weed, Frank W. *The Medical Department of the United States Army in the World War, Vol. 6, Sanitation*, chapter 12, "Prevention of Louse Infestation." Washington, D.C.: Government Printing Office, 1926.

Welcome Home YD: In Commemoration of the Foreign Service and Home-Coming of the 26th Division, Official Programme. Boston: n.p., 1919.

Wever, Peter. "Prevention of Tetanus During the First World War." *Medical Humanities* 38, issue 2 (December 2012): 78–82.

_____. *A U.S. Army Medical Base in World War I France: Life and Care at Bazoilles Hospital Center, 1918–1919*. Jefferson, NC: McFarland, 2019.

_____. "The U.S. Army Medical Belt for Front Line First Aid: A Well-Considered Design That Failed the Medical Department During the First World War." *Military Medicine* 181 (2016): 1187–94.

Wiedman, Otto G. "In Memorium: Dr. Paul Waterman." *American Journal of Psychiatry* 80, number 4 (1924): 840

Witkowski, Mary. *Bridgeport at Work*. Charleston, SC: Arcadia Publishing, 2002.

Index

Numbers with ***bold italics*** indicates illustration